The Effects of Mental Retardation, Disability, and Illness on Sibling Relationships

This book is printed on recycled paper.

THE EFFECTS OF MENTAL RETARDATION, DISABILITY, AND ILLNESS ON SIBLING RELATIONSHIPS
Research Issues and Challenges

edited by

Zolinda Stoneman, Ph.D.
Director
Georgia University Affiliated Program
for Persons with Developmental Disabilities
University of Georgia
Athens, Georgia

and

Phyllis Waldman Berman, Ph.D.
Health Scientist Administrator
Mental Retardation and
Developmental Disabilities Branch
National Institute of Child Health
and Human Development
Bethesda, Maryland

Baltimore•London•Toronto•Sydney

Paul H. Brookes Publishing Co.
P.O. Box 10624
Baltimore, Maryland 21285-0624

Copyright © 1993 by Paul H. Brookes Publishing Co., Inc.
All rights reserved.

(This work may be reproduced in whole or part for the official use of the United States Government or any authorized agency thereof.)
This book is based on a conference held in April, 1991, sponsored by The National Institute of Child Health and Human Development.

Typeset by The Composing Room of Michigan, Inc., Grand Rapids, Michigan.
Manufactured in the United States of America by
The Maple Press Company, York, Pennsylvania.

Library of Congress Cataloging-in-Publication Data

The Effects of mental retardation, disability, and illness on sibling
  relationships: research issues and challenges / edited by Zolinda
  Stoneman, Phyllis W. Berman.
    p. cm.
  Includes bibliographical references and index.
  ISBN 1-55766-113-8
  1. Chronically ill children—Family relationships—Congresses. 2. Mentally handicapped children—Family relationships—Congresses. 3. Handicapped children—Family relationships—Congresses. 4. Developmentally disabled children—Family relationships—Congresses. 5. Brothers and sisters—Congresses. I. Stoneman, Zolinda, 1947–   II. Berman, Phyllis W.
  [DNLM: 1. Chronic Disease—congresses. 2. Handicapped—congresses. 3. Mental Retardation— congresses. 4. Sibling Relations—congresses. WS105.5.F2 E278]
  RJ380.E34 1993
  155.9′16—dc20
  DLC
  for Library of Congress   92-49879
                                                                         CIP

British Library Cataloguing-in-Publication data are available
from the British Library.

Contents

Contributors... vii
Preface... ix

SECTION I CONCEPTUAL ISSUES IN RESEARCH

CHAPTER 1 Sibling Relations in the Family Context
Zolinda Stoneman and Gene H. Brody................. 3

CHAPTER 2 Contemporary Themes in Research on Sibling Relationships of Nondisabled Children
Wyndol C. Furman............................... 31

CHAPTER 3 Ethnographic and Ecocultural Perspectives on Sibling Relationships
Thomas S. Weisner.............................. 51

CHAPTER 4 Issues and Interventions for Young Siblings of Children with Medical and Developmental Problems
Debra J. Lobato................................ 85

CHAPTER 5 Adult Sibling Relationships of Persons with Mental Retardation
*Marsha Mailick Seltzer
and Marty Wyngaarden Krauss*.................... 99

CHAPTER 6 Siblings and Out-of-Home Placement
Jan Blacher................................... 117

SECTION II RESEARCH PERSPECTIVES

CHAPTER 7 Siblings of Persons with Mental Retardation: A Historical Perspective and Recent Findings
Glenna C. Boyce and W. Steven Barnett............. 145

CHAPTER 8 Siblings of Children with Physical Disabilities and Chronic Illnesses: Studies of Risk and Social Ecology
George W. Howe............................... 185

CHAPTER 9 Siblings of Children with Chronic Illnesses: A Categorical and Noncategorical Look at Selected Literature
Agatha M. Gallo and Kathleen A. Knafl............ 215

CHAPTER 10 Siblings of Children with Learning Disabilities
Lily L. Dyson................................. 235

Chapter 11	Siblings of Children with Dual Diagnosis *Keith A. Crnic and Janice Lyons*........................ 253
SECTION III	**METHODOLOGICAL ISSUES FOR FUTURE CONSIDERATION**
Chapter 12	Parameters for Inclusion in Studies on Sibling Relationships: Some Heuristic Suggestions *Gene H. Brody and Zolinda Stoneman*.............. 275
Chapter 13	Measurement Considerations in the Identification and Assessment of Stressors and Coping Strategies *Wendy C. Gamble and E. Jeanne Woulbroun*.......... 287
Chapter 14	Lifetime Research on Siblings of Persons with Mental Retardation *Louis Rowitz*.................................... 321
Chapter 15	Toward a More General Model for Research on the Well-Being of Siblings of Persons with Disabilities *W. Steven Barnett*............................... 333
Conclusion	Common Themes and Divergent Paths *Zolinda Stoneman*............................... 355

Index... 367

Contributors

W. Steven Barnett, Ph.D.
Department of Education Theory,
 Policy and Administration
Rutgers University Graduate School of
 Education
10 Seminary Place
New Brunswick, New Jersey 08903

Phyllis Waldman Berman, Ph.D.
Mental Retardation and Developmental
 Disabilities Branch
National Institute of Child Health and
 Human Development
6130 Executive Boulevard
Executive Plaza North, Room 631
Bethesda, Maryland 20892

Jan Blacher, Ph.D.
School of Education
University of California, Riverside
3401 Watkins Drive
Riverside, California 92521

Glenna C. Boyce, Ph.D.
Early Intervention Research Institute
Utah State University
Logan, Utah 84322-6580

Gene H. Brody, Ph.D.
Child and Family Development
Dawson Hall
University of Georgia
Athens, Georgia 30602

Keith A. Crnic, Ph.D.
Department of Psychology
Pennsylvania State University
612 Moore Building
University Park, Pennsylvania 16802

Lily L. Dyson, Ph.D.
Department of Psychological
 Foundations in Education
Faculty of Education
University of Victoria
P.O. Box 3010
Victoria, British Columbia V8W 3N4
CANADA

Wyndol C. Furman, Ph.D.
Psychology Department
University of Denver
Denver, Colorado 80208

Agatha M. Gallo, Ph.D., R.N.
University of Illinois at Chicago
College of Nursing
Department of Maternal and Child
 Nursing (M/C 802)
845 South Damen Avenue
Chicago, Illinois 60612

Wendy C. Gamble, Ph.D.
Family Studies FCR-210
School of Family and Consumer
 Resources
University of Arizona
Tucson, Arizona 85721

George W. Howe, Ph.D.
George Washington University
Center for Family Research
Ross Hall, Room 613
2300 Eye Street, NW
Washington, DC 20037

Kathleen A. Knafl, Ph.D.
University of Illinois at Chicago
College of Nursing (M/C 802)
Department of Psychiatric Nursing
845 South Damen Avenue
Chicago, Illinois 60612

Marty Wyngaarden Krauss, Ph.D.
Heller School
P.O. Box 9110
Brandeis University
Waltham, MA 02254-9110

Debra J. Lobato, Ph.D.
Child Development Center
Rhode Island Hospital
593 Eddy Street
Providence, Rhode Island 02903

Janice Lyons, M.S.
Department of Psychology
Pennsylvania State University
612 Moore Building
University Park, Pennsylvania 16802

Louis Rowitz, Ph.D.
University of Illinois at Chicago
School of Public Health (M/C 922)
P.O. Box 6998
Chicago, Illinois 60680

Marsha Mailick Seltzer, Ph.D.
Waisman Center
University of Wisconsin–Madison
1500 Highland Avenue
Madison, Wisconsin 53705

Zolinda Stoneman, Ph.D.
Georgia University Affiliated Program
  for Persons with Developmental
  Disabilities
University of Georgia
Athens, Georgia 30602

Thomas S. Weisner, Ph.D.
Departments of Psychiatry and
  Anthropology
Room C8-881, NPI
University of California, Los Angeles
760 Westwood Plaza
Los Angeles, California 90024-1759

E. Jeanne Woulbroun, M.S.
Family Studies FCR-210
School of Family and Consumer
  Resources
University of Arizona
Tucson, Arizona 85721

PREFACE

Most individuals with mental retardation, disability, or chronic illness have brothers and/or sisters. It is important from both developmental and public policy perspectives to gain a comprehensive understanding of the effects of these family contexts on individual siblings and on the sibling relationship. Although insight can be gained from educational and clinical experiences with siblings, as well as from personal accounts of siblings, in-depth understanding of siblings of individuals with disabilities must come from systematic research. The purpose of this volume is to present cutting-edge research findings concerning siblings and disability and to provide a discussion of conceptual and methodological challenges in this field of study.

The chapters in this volume were developed for an invited conference, "Research on Siblings of Individuals with Mental Retardation, Physical Disabilities, and Chronic Illness," sponsored by the Mental Retardation and Developmental Disabilities Branch of the National Institute of Child Health and Human Development. The conference provided an opportunity for leading researchers from multiple disciplines and perspectives to share findings and insights concerning siblings of individuals with mental retardation, disabilities, and chronic illness.

During the $2^1/_2$ days of the conference, researchers presented state-of-the-art findings, discussed methodological challenges and advances, and focused on unanswered questions in need of further research. Discussion among researchers was lively and animated, reflecting the excitement that accompanies the renewed interest of the research community in siblings. After slumbering in relative obscurity since the early 1960s, when Farber published his classic series of monographs on families of children with mental retardation (Farber 1959, 1960, Farber & Jenne, 1963), research on siblings of individuals with disabilities is undergoing a new, energized awakening that is reflected in the work in this volume.

These chapters focus on the differential effects of various disabilities on siblings and the sibling relationship, as well as on generalized effects across mental retardation, disability, and chronic illness. Researchers address the multiple effects of a child with a disability on typical siblings and on the relationship between siblings.

The information presented in this volume will be of interest to researchers, educators, health specialists, early childhood professionals, therapists, clinicians, students, family members, and all those concerned with understanding and improving sibling relationships. Many of the studies described in the following chapters represent extensive, ongoing programmatic research efforts that are only beginning to yield rich and important findings. The breadth and scope of these research efforts ensure that our knowledge base will expand rapidly over the next few years. The success and innovation of these data-collection efforts also lay the foundation for new researchers to enter the field and for increased vitality among more seasoned investigators who have devoted years to the study of siblings.

Researchers who were invited to submit papers represent a lifespan continuum in their interests, tracing important aspects of the sibling relationship from the preschool years through childhood, adolescence, adulthood, and old age. This perspective across chapters allows an examination of how sibling relationships change over time, as well as how sibling outcomes differ across the lifespan. The importance of understanding siblings in the context of their family, their community, and their culture is emphasized throughout the work presented here. Authors were requested to address the influences of ethnicity wherever possible, since sibling research (and family research in general) has often ignored siblings from minority families.

The authors represented in this volume come from diverse disciplinary backgrounds, including psychology, education, nursing, economics, sociology, family studies, and anthropology, and they use a diverse array of qualitative and quantitative methods to study siblings. Some researchers intensively study a small number of siblings, while others focus on more general processes across larger populations. The volume includes the perspective of researches who study typical siblings, as well as those studying siblings of individuals with disabilities. This melding of viewpoints creates a larger context for understanding issues common to all siblings, as well as issues specific to siblings of persons with disabilities.

The first section of the volume, "Conceptual Issues in Research," includes six chapters that set the stage for understanding the sibling relationship of individuals with mental retardation, disability, and chronic illness. These chapters present broad themes and models that underlie research efforts and guide the design of studies. Stoneman and Brody present a family-context model of sibling relations that includes characteristics of the individual siblings, parenting styles, and the marital relationship as important determining factors. Furman's chapter discusses the relevance of the growing body of research on siblings without disabilities to understanding and studying siblings of children with disabilities.

In his chapter, Weisner argues that the culture in which siblings live is the single most important factor to consider. He describes why ethnographic research methods are an important vehicle for achieving this cultural understanding. Lobato's chapter considers the developmental characteristics of preschool children's thinking, cognitive processing, and emotional characteristics and uses that developmental perspective to explain this unique reaction of young children to disability or illness in a sibling. Seltzer and Krauss's chapter draws upon data from their longitudinal study of families of adults with mental retardation to focus attention on the importance of the sibling relationship to aging persons with disabilities. Blacher takes a lifespan perspective in addressing the impact of out-of-home placement on the brothers and sisters of individuals being placed.

The second section of this volume, "Research Perspectives," provides critical, comprehensive reviews of current research on siblings of individuals with specific disabilities, including mental retardation, physical disabilities, chronic illness, learning disabilities, and dual diagnoses. These authors summarize research findings, discuss theoretical and methodological advances, and identify unanswered questions and important directions for future research. Boyce and Barnett's chapter provides a historical overview of trends in research on siblings of children with mental retardation. Howe presents a discussion of the risk and protective factors that help to explain outcomes for siblings of children with chronic illness and physical disabilities. Gallo and Knafl focus their attention on the contributions of categorical and noncategorical approaches to studying siblings of children with chronic illness. The final two chapters in this section focus on relatively unexplored topics with little existing research to guide our understanding, namely siblings of children with learning disabilities (Dyson) and of children with dual diagnoses (Crnic & Lyons).

Chapters in the third section of this volume, "Methodological Issues for Future Consideration," describe procedural challenges and innovations in studying siblings. Brody and Stoneman discuss the relevance of methodological advances in the general sibling literature to the study of siblings of individuals with disabilities or chronic illnesses. Gamble and Woulbroun focus on challenges in the conceptualization and measurement of sibling stress and coping. In his chapter, Rowitz discusses methodological problems that arise in conducting lifespan research on siblings of persons with disabilities. In the final chapter, Barnett draws on family and economic theories to create an innovative model for the measurement of sibling well-being.

Although there is still much more to learn about siblings of persons with mental retardation, disability, and chronic illness, the research presented in this volume demonstrates that the study of siblings and sibling relationships is thriving. Data currently being collected in large programmatic research efforts should yield rich new findings. This volume summarizes the current state of our knowledge and proposes some challenges for future study.

REFERENCES

Farber, B. (1959). Effects of a severely mentally retarded child on family integration. *Monographs of the Society for Research in Child Development, 24*(2).

Farber, B. (1960). Family organization and crisis: Maintenance of integration in families with a severely mentally retarded child. *Monographs of the Society for Research in Child Development, 25*(1).

Farber, B., & Jenne, W. C. (1963). Family organization and parent–child communication: Parents and siblings of a retarded child. *Monographs of the Society for Research in Child Development, 28*(7).

The Effects of Mental Retardation, Disability, and Illness on Sibling Relationships

SECTION I

CONCEPTUAL ISSUES IN RESEARCH

CHAPTER 1

Sibling Relations in the Family Context

*Zolinda Stoneman
and Gene H. Brody*

Research on families of children with disabilities or chronic illness has focused primarily on the mother–child dyad. Researchers have often ignored the fact that most children, including those with mental retardation, disabilities, or chronic illness, live in families in which other children are also present. Little is known about factors that influence the relationship between individuals with disabilities or illnesses and their nondisabled brothers and sisters. The relationship between siblings is one of the most powerful, longest-lasting human relationships, characterized by a wide range of emotional responses that can quickly change from warm to hostile and back again (Dunn & Kendrick, 1982). Sibling relationships can be characterized by friendship, trust, and sharing of confidences. They can be hostile and conflicted, or distant and disengaged. Understanding more about sibling relationships in which one child has a disability or chronic illness is important from a theoretical as well as a social policy perspective.

Sibling relations do not take place in isolation. Relationships between brothers and sisters develop against a backdrop of complex, interconnected family relationships. A systems approach to the study of the family rests on the assumption that families are composed of different subsystems that mutually influence one another. Thus, the nuclear family with two children could

---

Partial support for preparation of this manuscript was provided by Grant No. 04-DD-000-58 from the Administration on Developmental Disabilities, U.S. Department of Health and Human Services to the Georgia University Affiliated Program for Persons with Developmental Disabilities.

Research reported in this paper was primarily supported by the National Institute of Child Health and Human Development Grant No. HD 16817-01A1 and National Foundation for the March of Dimes Grant No. 12-120. Research on nondisabled siblings was supported by the National Science Foundation (BNS 84-15505) and the National Institute of Mental Health (MH 40704).

be partitioned into a spousal subsystem, mother–child and father–child subsystems, and a sibling subsystem. Triadic family subsystems (i.e., father–mother–younger sibling) would also exist in this hypothetical family. Events in any one subsystem are assumed to have an impact on the other family subsystems. Similarly, changes that accrue to one family member affect the entire family system. The sibling relationship is influenced by a myriad of factors within the family. It is impossible for researchers to understand the sibling relationship without considering the family system in which the siblings are socialized.

Research on the determinants of the quality of sibling relationships is sparse, especially that concerning sibling pairs in which one individual has a disability or chronic illness. In this chapter, the authors present a model developed to explain relationship differences among siblings, with particular emphasis on sibling pairs in which one child has a chronic illness or disability. The primary focus is on differences in the form and quality of the relationship between siblings, rather than on the impact of one sibling on the individual personalities or competence of his or her brothers or sisters. As such, it can be considered a family-process model, rather than a model designed to predict child outcomes.

The authors' model, originally developed to account for variability in the relationships of typical siblings (Brody & Stoneman, 1987), posits that the sibling relationship is directly affected by specific characteristics of the individual siblings, by characteristics of the family in which the children live, and by the childrearing strategies used by the children's parents or primary caregivers. The childrearing strategies used by parents, in turn, are influenced by several factors, including characteristics of the parents and the emotional climate of the family and of the individual siblings. Although factors originating outside the nuclear family (i.e., social support, school) exert undeniably important influences on family functioning, including the relationship between siblings, the discussion in this chapter will focus on intrafamily variables.

The most significant modification of the authors' original model of sibling relations is an expansion of the range of child characteristics included as predictor variables. This expansion was implemented to include in the model characteristics associated with children who have a disability or illness and to track the impact of those characteristics through the multiple interconnected components of the family system. Components of the model representing familial influences on parenting draw heavily on the work of Belsky (1984), who articulated the importance of considering the marital relationship, the characteristics of parents, and the qualitative aspects of the overall family climate when accounting for between-family variations in parenting. The authors will utilize their own research on typical siblings and on siblings of children with mental retardation to illustrate key components of the proposed model. Throughout the paper, however, an attempt will be made to consider the impact of various disabilities and illnesses on sibling relations, rather than restricting the presentation solely to the impact of a child with mental retardation.

Interactions among family members, including those between siblings, can be conceptualized as being affected by both direct and indirect social influences (Bronfenbrenner, 1979). Influences on siblings that result from interacting with a brother or sister constitute direct effects. As children play together, they learn important social and communication skills. For children with disabilities or chronic illness, in-home interactions with siblings may constitute the primary means of learning about social competencies. Nondisabled siblings may learn compassion and helpfulness from daily interactions with a child who is less able, or, unfortunately, these youngsters may learn aggressive, maladaptive social behaviors from these interactions. This social learning feeds back into the sibling relationship, influencing its subsequent quality. In addition, parents exert direct influences on the sibling relationship as they encourage prosocial interaction or punish verbal or physical conflict.

Many important effects that occur within the family context, however, are not the result of direct social influence. These indirect effects are the result of broader, systemic influences, in which, for instance, one family member may create a certain set of family conditions that have an impact on the behavior of the whole family. A child requiring constant supervision and monitoring may drain the energies of parents, thus making them less interactive with their other children, resulting in sibling jealousy and dissension. Conversely, a warm, satisfying marriage between parents may provide mothers and fathers with the positive perspective and support necessary for parents to utilize effective parenting strategies that positively influence the sibling relationship. Both direct and indirect effects are included in the proposed model.

THE SIBLING RELATIONSHIP

There is a long history of concern over possible negative effects of being reared in a home with a child with a disability or chronic illness (Cohen, 1962; Farber, 1959, 1960; Farber & Jenne, 1963; Jordan, 1962; Kaplan, 1969; SanMartino & Newman, 1974; Schild, 1964). This literature has focused on negative mental health outcomes that might accrue to these children, as well as on deleterious effects of illness and disability on the sibling relationship itself. Historically, a pathological model has guided most researchers in this area. Only recently have researchers begun to study possible benefits to siblings raised in this family context and to attempt to identify the factors that contribute to healthy sibling relations.

One of the first tasks in developing a model of sibling relationships is to identify those characteristics of the sibling relationship that constitute important outcome variables. In conceptualizing important qualitative aspects of the sibling relationship, the authors focus their attention on four relationship dimensions: 1) sibling roles and role asymmetry, 2) social engagement, 3) warmth/positivity, and 4) conflict. Each of these is discussed briefly.

Roles and Role Asymmetry

The inclusion of role asymmetry as a key sibling relationship dimension implies how important social roles are in organizing behavior and interpersonal interaction (Sarbin, 1954; Stoneman & Brody, 1982, 1987, 1990). Roles are macro-units of behavior, consisting of predictable, socially defined patterns of response. Role enactments are complimentary; smooth social exchange requires that both interactants accept and competently enact complimentary, mutually consistent roles. Thus, effective social functioning requires behavioral and cognitive competencies that underlie the child's ability to know the expectations of complimentary roles and to coordinate behavior during social exchanges.

Some role enactments emerge spontaneously during sibling interaction (i.e., one child directs the play behavior of another) while other roles are ascribed by parents (i.e., a father asks a sibling to watch a brother or sister while the parent is otherwise occupied). Although enactments of assigned and spontaneous roles can be conceptualized as separate social processes, there are consistencies between the roles ascribed for siblings by parents and the spontaneous interactive roles assumed during sibling interactions (Stoneman, Brody, Davis, Crapps, & Malone, 1991). This suggests that there is a multifaceted process through which these roles are acquired and enacted within the family context.

Role relationships between individuals differ in their degree of symmetry. In general, sibling role relationships during childhood are asymmetrical, with older brothers and sisters assuming more powerful, dominant roles in relation to their younger siblings (Brody, Stoneman, & MacKinnon, 1982; Stoneman, Brody, & MacKinnon, 1984). With age, role relations between nondisabled siblings become increasingly symmetrical (Cicirelli, 1982), approximating the more equalitarian, role-sharing relationships found between peers and friends (Hartup, 1979). When one child has a disability, this normative pattern may not apply. As posited by Farber (1960), the authors' work with older siblings of children with mental retardation (Stoneman, Brody, Davis, & Crapps, 1989) showed that sibling role relations for these children actually become less, rather than more symmetrical through the childhood years. Sibling pairs that include a child with mental retardation may be on a trajectory that points them toward adolescent and adult sibling roles characterized by dominance by the older nondisabled sibling, rather than toward more symmetrical adult or adolescent sibling friendships. These dominant social roles, such as benefactor or advocate, may prove adaptive in assisting the person with a disability to live in a more independent fashion. It is also plausible, however, that this role structure may deny that individual the egalitarian social friendship that makes many relationships between adult siblings mutually satisfying.

Concerning younger siblings of children with mental retardation, sibling roles have been of interest to researchers and theoreticians because of the role reversals that occur when younger nondisabled children equal, and eventually surpass, the cognitive competence of their older siblings with mental retardation. Farber (Farber, 1959, 1960; Farber & Jenne, 1963) described what he termed a "role crossover" that occurs as younger nondisabled siblings became more competent than their older siblings with mental retardation. The authors' research (Brody, Stoneman, Davis, & Crapps, 1991; Stoneman et al., 1991) confirmed the occurrence of this role crossover by using data obtained from observations of the sibling relationship, as well as from maternal reports of the younger sibling's childcare responsibilities for the older sibling with mental retardation. Observed interactions across activities between younger siblings and their older brothers and sisters with mental retardation were characterized by younger sibling dominance, while comparable interactions between comparison siblings were characterized by older sibling dominance (Brody et al., 1991). When ascribed sibling roles were examined (Stoneman et al., 1991), the authors found that parents assign younger siblings frequent caregiving responsibilities for their older siblings with mental retardation. These children assume roles, such as "babysitter," that are normative for older, not younger, siblings.

At present, the generalizability of these role patterns across different types of disabilities and illnesses is unclear. It is tempting to suggest that since most disabilities and chronic illnesses place added caregiving demands on families, similar role patterns would be found across disability and illness groups. It seems equally plausible, however, that the cognitive deficits that are used to define mental retardation may create role asymmetries unique to this disability. These issues are considered later in this chapter as the authors discuss the possible ramifications that specific disability-related child characteristics may have for the sibling relationship.

Sibling Social Engagement

The second component of the sibling relationship of interest for the model is social engagement (e.g., the amount of time that siblings spend engaged in play or other activities with each other, or the frequency of visits or phone contact between adult siblings). During childhood, siblings spend significant portions of the nonschool day playing and interacting together. Siblings differ, however, in the amount of time they spend together and in the activities that form the context for their interactions (Stoneman et al., 1984). Some siblings are seemingly inseparable playmates, choosing to spend large amounts of time together, while other siblings are socially disengaged, seldom playing or interacting with each other except when forced to do so by a given family activity or context.

In the authors' work with siblings of children with mental retardation, it was initially expected that these siblings would spend less time together than comparison siblings because of the limited play and interactive skills of the child with mental retardation. During 2 hours of naturalistic in-home observations of sibling pairs in which the younger child was mentally retarded and similar observations of a matched set of comparison siblings (Stoneman et al., 1987), the authors did not find this expected decrement in sibling engagement. Siblings spent a great deal of time together, being engaged in active interaction with each other approximately 25% of the time, regardless of their gender or the disability status of the younger child. In-home naturalistic observations of sibling pairs in which the older child was mentally retarded yielded similar findings.

Children engaged in a wide variety of activities during these in-home naturalistic observations (Stoneman, Brody, Davis, & Crapps, 1987). Girls accommodated the lesser competencies of younger sisters with mental retardation by engaging in noncompetitive physical activities such as rough-and-tumble play and tickling games. Forty percent of the interactions between girls with mental retardation and their older sisters involved these types of activities, as compared to five percent for comparison sisters. Boys, on the other hand, used toys to engage their younger brothers with mental retardation in play. Many siblings seemed to be quite adept at selecting play materials and activities that could bridge the competency differences between themselves and their siblings with mental retardation and allow for sustained social interaction.

These findings suggest that the level of sibling social engagement does not necessarily differ between pairs of siblings with and without a member with a disability. Variability among siblings in their level of social engagement, however, is substantial. Thus, the challenge becomes one of ascertaining those factors that contribute to high levels of social engagement for some siblings and disengagement for others.

Affective Tone

The final aspect of the sibling relationship of interest for the model is its affective tone. In the authors' work (Brody et al., 1991; Stoneman, 1989; Stoneman et al., 1987), few differences were found between sibling pairs that included a child with mental retardation and comparison sibling pairs in the level of observed sibling positives or negatives. This has held true in observations during semistructured activities scripted by the researchers as well as during naturalistic in-home observations. In one study (Stoneman, Brody,

Davis, & Crapps, 1989), younger siblings with mental retardation were more negative toward their older brothers and sisters than comparison siblings, but the older nondisabled siblings did not reciprocate these negatives. Although sibling pairs that included a child with mental retardation did not differ from nondisabled siblings in their expression of positive and negative affect, there was wide variability within these groups of children. Some siblings in each group experienced high levels of conflict and negativity. Discord between siblings is one of the most common and persistent childrearing problems reported by parents of nondisabled children (Clifford, 1959; Kelly & Main, 1979). The problem is also an issue for families of siblings where one child is disabled or ill. There is little data, however, to explain why some sibling dyads experience high rates of conflict while others do not. Similarly, there are few models to explain why some siblings, but not others, have warm, close relationships characterized by high rates of prosocial behavior. The impact of specific disability- or illness-related factors on sibling affectivity has also received only minimal research attention.

A FAMILY-CONTEXT MODEL

In the following sections, the authors briefly examine the predictors of sibling role asymmetry, engagement, positivity/warmth, and conflict as posited in the family context model (see Figure 1). Although all paths depicted in the model represent sources of influence that flow toward the sibling relationship, most of these paths are actually bidirectional, representing transactional family processes. In addition, there are paths of influence between other components of the model not depicted by arrows (i.e., between child characteristics and family characteristics). For purposes of this chapter, the authors decided only to draw those paths that indicate direct or indirect influences on the sibling relationship. As such, the paths represented can be viewed as being a subset of the reciprocal sources of family influence potentially included in the model. The authors begin the discussion of the model by considering the direct and indirect effects attributable to characteristics of the individual siblings.

Characteristics of the Individual Siblings

Child characteristics directly affect the sibling relationship. These characteristics also exert indirect influence on siblings through their effects on the parenting process. Individual sibling characteristics of interest for the model can be divided into two broad classes: characteristics specific to children with chronic illness or disability, and individual-difference dimensions common to all children. In this chapter, the authors focus on the first of these sets of characteristics, namely, those associated with disability or illness in a sibling. Child characteristics that have been identified in the mainstream developmental

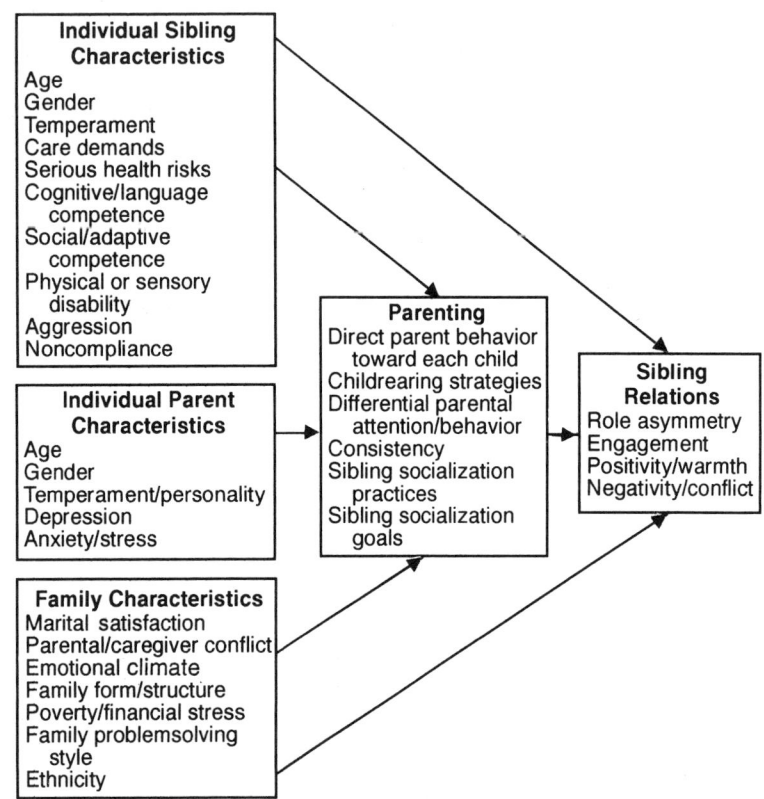

Figure 1. Sibling relations in the family context. (Most paths are bidirectional. Only direct and indirect effects on the sibling relationship are included in the figure.)

literature as being important predictors of the quality of the sibling relationship (i.e., gender, age, temperament) are the focus of another chapter in this volume (Brody & Stoneman, chap. 12) and are not discussed here. Seven illness or disability-related child characteristics affecting the sibling relationship are included in the proposed model: 1) care demands, 2) serious health risks, 3) cognitive/language competence, 4) social/adaptive competence, 5) physical disability, 6) sensory loss, 7) aggression, and 8) noncompliance.

Care Demands Of the set of variables specific to children with an illness or disability, care demands probably have received the most attention from researchers. Nondisabled siblings are often required to assume added childcare and household chores when a sibling is ill or disabled, since that sibling requires more care than would a nondisabled sibling at a comparable age (Farber, 1960; Gath, 1974). Parents are believed to obtain their children's (particularly their daughter's) assistance in caring for the child with an illness or disability, reinforcing a surrogate-parent role for these older girls (Farber, 1960; Farber & Jenne, 1963; Gath, 1974). These added caregiving demands have been thought to create stress and resentment in the nondisabled sibling that can compromise the quality of the sibling relationship (Farber, 1960; Farber & Jenne, 1963; Seligman, 1983).

For older siblings of children with mental retardation (but not for comparison older siblings), the authors found greater childcare demands to be associated with an increase in observed sibling conflict, as well as a decrease in positive sibling interaction (Stoneman, Brody, Davis, & Crapps, 1988). The association between increased demands and sibling conflict seemed to apply only to childcare responsibilities. In fact, increased older sibling responsibility for household chores corresponded to less, rather than more, observed sibling conflict.

As with older siblings, it has been suggested that younger siblings placed in caregiving roles may experience "role tension," characterized by anxiety and conflict (Farber, 1960), as well as resentments arising from role overloads (Holt, 1958; Simeonsson & McHale, 1981; Stoneman et al., 1988). These negative effects might be expected to compromise the sibling relationship. Contrary to these expectations, younger nondisabled siblings who assumed more childcare roles had less conflicted sibling relations than did siblings with fewer responsibilities (Stoneman et al., 1991).

The direction of effect underlying this unexpected association may flow from parents to siblings, or vice versa. Parents may be considering the quality of the sibling relationship when placing the younger sibling in a variety of surrogate-parent roles, assigning these responsibilities only when siblings are able to interact with a minimum of conflict. An alternate explanation would be that younger siblings who assume more childcare responsibilities may inhibit the overt expression of their negative feelings because of guilt or parental sanction. This inhibition was suggested in a literature review by Crnic and Leconte (1986). Of course, it is possible that the expected relationships were not found because these children do not hold negative feelings toward their older brothers and sisters with disabilities.

Another potential effect of increased care demands on siblings is a decrease in time spent socializing with peers. In the authors' work (Stoneman et al., 1988, 1991), no evidence was found that brothers or sisters of children with mental retardation hesitated to have friends visit them at home, as has been suggested in the literature (e.g., Parfit, 1975). When intragroup differences were examined (Stoneman et al., 1988), however, it was found that demands rooted in family responsibilities were directly related to decreased opportunities for spending time with friends and participating in out-of-home activities. These intragroup relationships are particularly interesting in light of the failure to find that older siblings of children with mental retardation, in general, were disadvantaged in their peer relations or out-of-home activities as compared to comparison children.

In general, siblings of children with mental retardation have greater caregiving responsibilities than other children (McHale & Gamble, 1989; Stoneman et al., 1988, 1991), but those caregiving responsibilities do not uniformly result in negative outcomes in the sibling relationship. The effects of caregiving on the sibling relationship seem to be related to the birth order of the siblings and the magnitude of the nondisabled sibling's caregiving responsibilities as compared to those of their peers.

Health Risks In the model, serious health risks refers to children who have chronic health problems that place them in danger of frequent hospitalization, episodes of serious illness, and, for some children, early death. These health problems can occur alone, or in conjunction with another disability (i.e., a child with Down syndrome who also has serious heart problems). Part of the potential effect of a child's health risks can be subsumed under the earlier discussion of the impact on siblings of increased care demands. Accounting for the increased burden of care placed on families of children with special medical needs, however, does not fully capture the potential impact. The authors believe that health risks in one sibling directly influence well siblings' play and social interaction with their less healthy brothers and sisters. For purposes of the model, the authors propose that when one child in the sibling pair has a medical condition that compromises his or her health and stamina, the sibling relationship is directly affected.

Potential sources of influence on the sibling relationship include behavior inhibitions that arise from a fear of harming the sibling, as in refraining from engaging in rough-and-tumble play with a child who has a serious heart condition. Physical weakness in a sibling can preclude sustained, active, competitive play. Cyclic illnesses can make the sibling's capabilities unpredictable over time, forcing the siblings to adapt to changing limitations or risk factors in the ill sibling. Psychological factors also come into play. Emotional reactions of nondisabled siblings to the ever-present possibility of crisis or death of a brother or sister with a life-threatening illness would be expected to affect the roles, warmth and closeness, and level of engagement between siblings.

It is plausible that factors such as the onset and course of an illness may exert direct influences on the siblings relationship, but there is no empirical base documenting these influences. Research on ill siblings has primarily focused on effects that accrue to healthy siblings from living in the same home as an ill brother or sister with a serious illness (see Gallo & Knafl, chap. 9, this volume). Little attention has been paid in the research to the effects of health risks on the quality of the sibling relationship. This is an important area for future research.

Cognitive and Language Competence The third child characteristic included in the model is the cognitive and language competence of the sibling with a disability. Since interactions between children are often verbally mediated, it might be expected that siblings with limited verbal abilities would experience difficulty in maintaining social exchanges with their brothers and sisters. Similarly, deficient cognitive skills might be expected to limit the sibling's ability to engage in more sophisticated types of sustained play. The authors' research (Stoneman et al., 1984, 1988, 1991) supports this contention for children with mental retardation. Joint object play between siblings was diminished when the sibling with mental retardation had fewer language competencies. The limited abilities of the less competent children with mental retardation seemed to make it difficult for them to engage in complex cognitive play with their siblings, which requires symbolic competencies and is often mediated by language (Stoneman et al., 1988). The more severe the skill deficit of the child with mental retardation, the larger were the discrepancies between his or her play levels and those of the older sibling, and the harder these discrepancies appeared to be for the children to overcome. High rates of social interaction between siblings across studies (Brody et al., 1991; Stoneman et al., 1987, 1988) suggest that there is motivation for interaction, but that it is difficult for siblings with substantial language and cognitive deficits to engage in prolonged sequences of joint play with their brothers and sisters.

This conclusion is further reinforced by the diminished level of interaction found in a small study focusing on older siblings of children with severe mental retardation (Stoneman & Brody, 1984). Findings from this observational study suggested that siblings of lower-functioning children had a difficult time bridging the competency differences between themselves and their less competent siblings, which resulted in depressed levels of social engagement (Stoneman & Brody, 1984). Thus, less pronounced cognitive and language delays, as are found in children with mild or moderate levels of mental retardation, seem to alter the context of sibling interactions, but not their frequency. More dramatic deficits in cognitive and language competency, however, seem to result in an overall decrease in the amount of sibling interaction.

Social and Adaptive Competence In addition to cognitive and language competence, the social and adaptive competence of siblings with disabilities are also associated with the ability of siblings to sustain mutually satisfying social interactions. In fact, the authors (Stoneman et al., 1987) found the adaptive skills of younger siblings with mental retardation to be a stronger predictor of observed sibling interactions than were language skills. During naturalistic family observations, children with more advanced adaptive competencies engaged in less solitary activity, spent a greater proportion of their family interactions with their siblings, were playmates with siblings more often, and had more symmetrical sibling role relationships. For children with mental retardation and their younger siblings, the discrepancy in adaptive skills between the two children was strongly related to observed sibling role asymmetry (Brody et al., 1991). Similarly, for children with mental retardation and their younger siblings, observed role asymmetry and frequency of sibling play were predicted by the adaptive competence of the sibling with mental retardation (Stoneman et al., 1989).

Others have suggested that the level of adaptive competencies of children with mental retardation may determine the extent to which nondisabled siblings participate in their care, with families of less competent children requiring more childcare assistance from siblings (Farber, 1959). As expected (Stoneman et al., 1988, 1991), sibling responsibilities for the care of children with mental retardation, such as help with dressing, feeding, and so on, tended to be greater when these children had fewer adaptive skills. Less adaptively competent children seem to place greater demands for caregiving on siblings, regardless of the birth order of the sibling pair.

In addition to sibling childcare, care demands can also be conceptualized as encompassing general household chores and responsibilities. Somewhat surprising findings (Stoneman et al., 1991) suggest that younger siblings of mentally retarded children, as a group, have fewer household chores than comparison children. Within-group differences emerged, however. Younger siblings of less adaptively competent children with mental retardation were called upon to take greater responsibility for their own personal care and more frequently assisted in meal preparation than did nondisabled siblings of more adaptively competent children with mental retardation. Overall, parents may be concerned about the added childcare duties assumed by these younger nondisabled siblings and may try to compensate by relieving them of other household chores. For the least competent children with mental retardation, however, demands on parents may be so great that parental concerns are overcome and younger siblings are enlisted to help.

A set of findings not directly related to sibling relations is nonetheless relevant to a discussion on the social and adaptive skills of children with mental retardation. The authors have consistently found that children with mental retardation experience only limited social opportunities as compared to same-age nondisabled peers (Stoneman et al., 1988, 1991). These children have fewer friends visit them at home, are less likely to visit the homes of friends, and participate in fewer out-of-home activities. The less competent the children with mental retardation, the fewer the social opportunities available to them.

These children seem to be caught in a disadvantageous cycle in which impoverished social experience could prevent them from learning the skills necessary to increase their base of community friendships. It seems that the concerns expressed by researchers and practitioners relating to the amount of time that nondisabled siblings of children with mental retardation spend playing with friends may have obscured a more dramatic difference, namely, the decreased opportunity that children with mental retardation themselves have for peer interactions in contexts other than school. These children appear to be exposed frequently to the friends of their nondisabled siblings, but have limited opportunity to have their own friends over to visit or to go to their friends' homes to play. It would seem plausible that the lack of time spent with friends may contribute in part to the lags in social and play skills that often characterize children with mental retardation. These limited social opportunities may exert an indirect negative influence on the quality of the sibling relationship by depressing the social skills that siblings with mental retardation bring to the sibling relationship.

Physical or Sensory Disability Surprisingly little is known about the effects of physical or sensory disabilities on the sibling relationship. Several important direct effects might be anticipated. Children's play typically revolves around fine and gross motor movement. Running, swinging, playing video games, riding a bike, coloring, and even reading a magazine all involve movements that are impossible for many children with physical disabilities. It would seem likely that the presence of a physical disability in a sibling would restrict the type of activities that the children could engage in together. Because of the verbal language difficulties experienced by many children with disabilities such as cerebral palsy, communication between siblings could be difficult, particularly if no assistive technology is available to compensate for verbal-production problems.

A child's inability to move around the house, the yard, the neighborhood, and the community may place limits on the level of engagement of some siblings. The level of impact might be assumed to be related to the physical accessibility of the environment and the type of adaptive equipment available to the child with a disability. It is the authors' expectation that physical disability in one sibling would primarily affect the activities that act as the context for sibling interactions. The emotional or affective quality of the relationship would not be expected to differ from that of nondisabled siblings, with the exception of the possible impact of increased care demands, discussed earlier.

Almost nothing is known about the effects of sensory disabilities on the sibling relationship. As with physical disability, vision loss might be expected to limit the types of activities that form the context for sibling interactions. Hearing loss, on the other hand, may have its major impact on the communication between siblings, particularly for those children for whom an alternate mode of communication is not yet established. It is plausible that substantial hearing loss in one sibling, particularly a child who relies on signed communication, may cause that child to have closer, more intense sibling relationships because of the social isolation caused by limited access to peers and others who are able to communicate with the child using sign.

Aggression Perhaps the child characteristic that has the greatest potential impact on the sibling relationship is overt physical aggression. In the authors' observational studies, they have been struck by the force with which some children with disabilities attack their siblings, sometimes causing physical harm even when under the direct supervision of an adult. Although these bouts resulted in crying and struggle, in general, nondisabled siblings did not reciprocate this intense level of aggression. This finding is unlike those from Patterson's (1980) study of siblings of children with aggressive conduct-disorders, who reciprocated aggressive attacks, thereby escalating the level of aggression.

Although the authors did not have a large enough sample of such children to conduct separate analyses (most children with mental retardation do not exhibit physically aggressive behavior), anecdotal evidence suggests that children who display high levels of sibling aggression have less engaged, less close relationships with their siblings. More research is needed to understand the impact of aggression on the sibling relationship when the aggressive child has a disability or illness.

Noncompliance When a child with a disability consistently ignores or resists the requests of a sibling, as was the case with many of the children with mental retardation that the authors have studied (Brody et al., 1991, Stoneman et al., 1989), the sibling seems to respond by becoming increasingly directive and by repeating requests. This creates accentuated role asymmetry, as the sibling spends increased time and effort in dominant, managing roles. It is also likely that noncompliance would be associated with conflict, particularly when the form of the noncompliance is active resistance, rather than passive ignoring of the sibling's request.

The authors (Stoneman et al., 1991) found that when children with mental retardation were noncompliant with the requests and commands of their younger nondisabled siblings, parents were less likely to assign babysitting roles to the younger siblings. Assigning the younger sibling caregiving responsibility in the parent's absence is, perhaps, the epitome of an ascribed surrogate-parent role. Thus, high levels of noncompliance on the part of a sibling with a disability appears to directly affect the sibling relationship by altering the role relations between siblings as the nondisabled siblings escalate their managing attempts, creating more accentuated patterns of sibling role asymmetry. In addition, noncompliance may have an indirect effect, as parents are reluctant to assign extensive childcare tasks, such as babysitting, to nondisabled siblings when compliance with sibling requests by the child with a disability is low.

The Effects of Individual Sibling Characteristics on Parenting

In addition to direct effects of individual sibling characteristics on the sibling relationship, the model also includes an indirect pathway through which individual child characteristics affect sibling relations through their influence on parenting. In the past, many researchers assumed that influence flowed only from parent to child. But beginning with the work of Bell (1968), this view has been discredited. It is now accepted that childrearing behavior is influenced by child behaviors and characteristics. Aspects of parenting believed to be affected by child characteristics include the behavior that parents direct to each sibling, parental childrearing strategies and attitudes, differential parental behavior that "favors" one sibling over the other, consistency and predictability of parenting and discipline across time, specific behaviors utilized by parents to socialize the sibling relationship, and goals that parents hold for the sibling relationship.

In the model, the authors posit that the child characteristics that have an influence on parenting include age, gender, temperament, care demands, serious health risks, cognitive/language and social/adaptive competence, physical or sensory disability, aggression, and noncompliance. One frequently studied child variable that influences parenting is temperament. Associations between difficult child temperaments and compromised parenting have been well documented in the literature. Difficult temperament has been associated with increased parent commands, control, power assertion, negativity and hostility, impatience, reduced teaching effort, decreased use of reasoning, parent–child power struggles, and lower parenting self-efficacy (e.g., Buss, 1981; Cutrona & Troutman, 1986; Gordon, 1983; Keller & Bell, 1979; Maccoby, Snow, & Jacklin, 1984; Milliones, 1978).

Ianna, Hallahan, and Bell (1982) observed adult women interacting with child confederates who either did or did not exhibit distractible behavior during a series of tasks. Adults were found to respond to the distractible behavior by changing their interaction styles. When interacting with the distractible confederate, adults made more demands on the child's attention, provided more instruction, and more often asked the child about the task and about his performance.

Child noncompliance and aggression have also been implicated as negative influences on parenting. Brunk and Henggeler (1984), for example, asked confederate children to simulate noncompliant, passive, withdrawn behavior or aggressively noncompliant behavior patterns and then observed a group of mothers interacting with the confederate children. Mothers provided more help and rewards to the children behaving in a passive/withdrawn manner. They engaged in more ignoring, commanding, and discipline with the confederate aggressively noncompliant group. Anderson, Lytton, and Romney (1986) studied mothers of conduct disordered and nondisabled children while interacting with children in both classifications. Their findings indicated that maternal behaviors are strongly driven by the characteristics of the children. When interacting with conduct-disordered children, mothers in both groups were more negative and gave more commands than when these same mothers interacted with children who exhibited less difficult behaviors.

Regarding children with mental retardation, it appears that certain aspects of their behavior, probably those arising from their cognitive deficits and low levels of compliance, predispose caregivers to engage in high levels of managing and structuring of the interaction. The authors' findings (Brody et al., 1991; Stoneman et al., 1987, 1988) concerning the high level of managing roles assumed by older nondisabled siblings of children with mental retardation are reminiscent of the often-reported finding of increased managing by parents of these children (e.g., Cunningham, Reuler, Blackwell, & Deck, 1981; Marshall, Hegrenes, & Goldstein, 1973; Stoneman, Brody, & Abbott, 1983).

Although there is evidence of the effects of some child characteristics on parenting, much has yet to be learned about the effects on parenting of characteristics specific to disability and chronic illness. In addition to having a direct effect on parenting and the parent–child relationship, child characteristics also exert indirect effects. For the current discussion, the authors are primarily interested in the indirect effects of the characteristics of one sibling on the manner in which parents interact with other siblings in the family.

When the authors used naturalistic observational strategies to examine the indirect effects of the presence of a child with mental retardation on a nondisabled sibling's in-home interaction with his or her parents (Stoneman et al., 1987), several unexpected findings emerged. First, no support was found for the contention that maternal attention would be drawn to the sibling with mental retardation at the expense of the nondisabled child. In families with a younger sister with mental retardation, interactions between mothers and older sisters did not differ from those of a matched comparison sample. Older brothers of boys with mental retardation actually interacted with their mothers more than comparison older brothers. Although rates of father–child interaction were low in the study, older comparison sisters interacted with their fathers over eight times as frequently as older sisters whose younger siblings were mentally retarded. This finding suggests a need to more closely examine the indirect effects of disability-related child characteristics on the father–child relationship, particularly for girls.

Younger brothers with mental retardation received much more attention from both mothers and fathers than did same-age male comparison siblings; rates for girls did not differ between sibling groups (Stoneman et al., 1987).

The increased time spent with sons with mental retardation was not associated with a decrease in the time spent with nondisabled sons. This pattern, however, does affect the relative (differential) amount of attention the two children receive. Although nondisabled brothers of children with disabilities and their peers received similar amounts of parent attention, intrafamily comparisons suggest that these boys were disadvantaged in relation to their younger brothers with mental retardation, who received much more parental attention than they did. Thus, absolute parent attention did not differ between the two groups of brothers, but differential parent attention differed quite dramatically.

The above discussion addresses a few examples of the impact that the characteristics of individual children in the family can have on parenting and on the parent–child relationship. Child characteristics can exert a direct influence, in which a child's behavior affects the way that parents treat that child, or an indirect influence, in which the behavior of one child affects the way in which parents interact with other children in the family. In addition, the behavior and characteristics of one or both children can have an impact on the differential behavior that parents direct toward the siblings.

The Effect of Individual Parent Characteristics on Parenting

The effect of parents' personalities and individual difference characteristics on their childrearing behavior is a relatively new area of study. Perhaps the most frequently studied parent characteristic is depression. As with the majority of work related to parenting, information on mothers far exceeds that concerning fathers. In general, the literature suggests that depressed mothers are inconsistent in disciplining children (Susman, Trickett, Iannotti, Hollenbeck, & Zahn-Waxler, 1985; Zelkowitz, 1982), are more verbally and physically punitive (Longfellow, Zelkowitz, & Saunders, 1982; Zelkowitz, 1982), are more likely to induce guilt and anxiety as a means of controlling their children's behavior (Susman et al., 1985), are less tolerant of their children (Zelkowitz, 1982), and are less nurturing, warm, and affectionate (Longfellow et al., 1982).

In a study of both maternal and paternal depression and its relationship to parenting (Stoneman, Brody, & Burke, 1989a), the authors found that depressed mothers and fathers of girls were more likely to endorse the use of authoritarian control as a parenting strategy. Depressed fathers of boys showed the opposite pattern. It is plausible that, as fathers become distressed, they seek to limit interactions with boys, who tend to be more abrasive than girls (Emery, Hetherington, & Dilalla, 1984). Fathers may achieve this limited interaction by taking a less authoritarian stance, thereby avoiding conflict.

In general, findings linking depression and childrearing are consistent with Kuczynski's (1984) conceptualization of automatic parenting, in which parents experiencing distress or depression choose less cognitively demanding, more automatic discipline strategies, rather than more intentional, effortful strategies such as rational guidance. Control through rational guidance has been shown to be an effective strategy for achieving long-term socialization goals (see Kuczynski, 1984), but may make too many cognitive demands on the parent to be effectively implemented during times of personal or marital stress. The authors found that parenting strategies associated with depression (inconsistency, anxiety induction, punitive control techniques) were associated with conflicted, distressed sibling relationships (Brody, Stoneman, & MacKinnon, 1986), suggesting that parent depression has a negative indirect effect on the quality of the sibling relationship, mediated by the compromising effects of depression on parenting.

Depression becomes an especially important factor when considered in light of the work on chronic sorrow in parents of children with disabilities (e.g., Olshansky, 1962). Given the extensive literature suggesting that these parents often experience feelings of hurt, sorrow, and depression, understanding the link between these negative mood states and parenting takes on added importance. Damrosch and Perry (1989) collected data suggesting that fathers' adjustment to a child with Down syndrome is characterized by steady, gradual recovery. Mothers, on the other hand, reported a periodic crisis pattern, characterized by emotional peaks and valleys. Mothers also reported higher frequencies for chronic sorrow, self-blame, and expressions of negative affect. These findings suggest that the relationship between depression and parenting may follow different patterns for mothers and fathers. It would appear that these negative emotional states experienced by parents of children with disabilities may sometimes compromise parenting, which, in turn, may negatively affect the parent's ability to socialize the sibling relationship. Although the effects of anxiety and stress on parenting behavior have not been studied, the authors anticipate that the relationship between these parent characteristics and childrearing would be similar to those documented for depression.

Parent temperament/personality is also included in the authors' model. Although the impact of these parent dimensions on childrearing has not been directly addressed in studies of families of children with disabilities, a "goodness-of-fit" model (i.e., Lerner & Lerner, 1987) would predict that parent temperament and other personality characteristics influence the tolerance and expectations of parents for their children's behavior, thereby influencing their parenting responses.

There is still much to learn about the effect that specific parent characteristics have on childrearing attitudes and behaviors. Future research should be aimed at clarifying the effects of the parent characteristics included in the authors' model. As this new information is collected, it is probable that the number of individual parent characteristics included as predictor variables will expand to include characteristics not currently included in the model.

The Effect of Family Characteristics
on Parenting and on the Sibling Relationship

Most studies examining families of children with disabilities have focused on the possible effects of child illness and disability on the family; few researchers have conceptualized family factors as predictor, rather than outcome, variables. In the authors' proposed model, characteristics of the family exert both direct and indirect influences on the sibling relationship. The indirect effects of family characteristics on the sibling relationship are mediated by parenting. Family characteristics of importance to the model include marital satisfaction, parent or caregiver conflict, emotional climate of the home, family problemsolving style, family form and structure, poverty, financial stress, and ethnicity.

One family characteristic often mentioned in the literature is the marital relationship. Two components of the spousal relationship that have generated much interest in the research on parenting are marital satisfaction (e.g., Belsky, 1981, 1984; Brody, Pellegrini, & Sigel, 1986; Callan & Noller, 1986; Goldberg & Easterbrooks, 1984; Johnson & Lobitz, 1974; Kemper & Reichler, 1976; Oltmanns, Broderick, & O'Leary, 1977) and spousal conflict (e.g., Block, Block, & Morrison, 1981; Dielman, Barton, & Cattell, 1977; Emery et al., 1984; Forehand, Long, Brody, & Fauber, 1986; Kemper & Reichler, 1976, Long, Forehand, Fauber, & Brody, 1987; Porter & O'Leary, 1980).

Emery et al. (1984) suggested that when parents are dissatisfied with their marriages and spousal conflict is high, parenting is often compromised. In their view, spousal disharmony creates inconsistencies in parenting, not only in the sense that mothers and fathers may employ different parenting strategies, but also because individual parents will become inconsistent from one occasion to another. Inconsistency in parenting has been associated with negative child outcomes (e.g., Becker, 1964; Block, Block, & Gjerde, 1986; Block et al., 1981; Emery et al., 1984; Hetherington, Cox, & Cox, 1981; Patterson, 1980). It is plausible that inconsistent parenting would also be associated with negative outcomes in the sibling relationship.

In addition to associations with parenting inconsistency, there are a few studies that suggest that marital discontent and spousal conflict are also associated with other important aspects of parenting, namely, increased punitiveness, decreased use of reasoning as a discipline strategy, and fewer parental rewards (e.g., Dielman et al., 1977; Kemper & Reichler, 1976). Goldberg and Easterbrooks (1984) found that among parents of 20-month-old children, marital satisfaction and spousal harmony were related to more tolerant and supportive parental attitudes, less strict parental beliefs, more sensitive father–child interaction, and fewer feelings of annoyance directed toward the child. In a clinic sample of families of boys with behavior problems, Johnson and Lobitz (1974) found a strong association between marital dissatisfaction and observed parental negativeness toward sons. Brody, Pellegrini, and Sigel (1986), however, studying families of school-age children, obtained somewhat different findings. In their study, mothers who were more dissatisfied with their marriages were more actively involved and responsive during a teaching task with their children. Maritally dissatisfied fathers showed greater intrusiveness and gave their children less positive feedback.

The authors found that mild marital and individual distress reported by fathers strongly predicted both inconsistent fathering and lack of parental agreement concerning discipline strategies (Stoneman, Brody, & Burke, 1989a). Effects found for fathers and their daughters were more significant than those found for any other parent–child gender combination. When fathers experience distress, fathering seems to be differentially disrupted for girls. Individual and marital distress and family conflict were also related to specific parental beliefs about discipline. The strongest relationship was between distress reported by fathers of girls and less endorsement of rational guidance as a control strategy.

For mothers and their daughters, parent depression, family conflict, marital unhappiness, and parenting inconsistency were strongly related to high levels of observed mother–child conflict. Family conflict was associated with increased negativity directed by mothers to their older and younger girls, as well as from older daughters to their mothers. A series of studies by Cummings et al. (Cummings, Iannotti, & Zahn-Waxler, 1985; Cummings, Zahn-Waxler, & Radke-Yarrow, 1981, 1984) demonstrated that even very young children were sensitive to conflict between adults, with the negative effects of repeated exposure being cumulative. The gender-related findings in this study are consistent with a suggestion made by Block (1983) that the salience of the family milieu is greater for girls than for boys because girls are more closely supervised by parents and are assigned chores and responsibilities that keep them at home, proximal to parents, more often than boys.

The literature provides contradictory evidence as to whether the presence in the family of a child with a disability or chronic illness has a negative effect on the marital relationship (Crnic, 1990; Friedrich, 1979; Morgan, 1988). If it is assumed that child disability and chronic illness put stress on at least some marriages, it can be concluded, based on the findings reviewed above, that these stressed marital relationships may have negative ramifications for parenting, and, indirectly, for sibling socialization.

Emery et al. (1984) concluded from an extensive literature review that marital unhappiness and conflict are related to behavior problems in children. A particularly strong relationship has been found between marital problems and undercontrolled behavior in children. Thus, the literature suggests a link between events that transpire in the spousal relationship and behavioral outcomes for individual children. There seems to be a similar link for agonistic and prosocial behavior characterizing the sibling relationship. In a study of the association between family characteristics and qualitative aspects of the sibling interaction, the authors (Brody, Stoneman, & Burke, 1987b) found mothers' marital satisfaction and the level of parental conflict to predict the affective quality of observed sibling interactions. The best predictor of younger siblings' prosocial behavior toward brothers and sisters was low parental conflict in the children's families. For older siblings, prosocial behavior was associated with high levels of marital satisfaction among mothers. Similarly, for younger siblings, low maternal marital satisfaction was related to high sibling agonism. In another study (Brody, Stoneman, McCoy, & Forehand, 1992), the authors found that an open, facilitative family problemsolving style was associated with nonconflicted sibling relationships. These studies form the basis for the direct arrow in the model between family characteristics and sibling relations.

The authors included ethnicity in the model as an important family characteristic. Little is known about the influence of ethnicity on parenting or sibling relations in families where one child has a disability or chronic illness. Data suggest the rates of disability and chronic health problems are elevated in minority populations (Baumeister, Dokecki, & Kupstas, 1988; Bowe, 1983; Stoneman, 1990), probably due to the higher incidence of poverty and poverty-related circumstances (i.e., poor prenatal care, drug use during pregnancy, inadequate nutrition) in these groups. More research is needed on the association between family characteristics and parenting, with particular need for an empirical base on the influences of ethnicity and poverty on parenting.

PARENTING AND THE SIBLING RELATIONSHIP

The importance of understanding the effects of individual sibling, parent, and family characteristics on parenting arises from a premise that is central to the model. This premise is that the quality of the sibling relationship is directly affected by the childrearing strategies used by parents to socialize their individual children and to socialize the sibling relationship. In an earlier manuscript (Brody et al., 1987b), the authors suggested that parents foster positive sibling relationships by not favoring one child over the other, by responding to sibling conflict by either ignoring the conflict or instituting a nonjudgemental consequence such as time-out for both children, and by setting clear rules and expectations for sibling behavior.

In the current model, the authors have expanded their original thinking and included six parenting variables that they believe represent successful strategies for socializing positive sibling relationships:

1. *Direct maternal and paternal behavior* sets the stage for the social development of each individual sibling. Through interactions with parents, children learn important prosocial skills such as sharing, cooperative

play, and altruism. As parents socialize each child in the family, they teach children the skills needed to develop constructive sibling relationships.

2. *Childrearing strategies* are the type of discipline used by parents to socialize each individual child, ranging from less effective strategies, such as the automatic parenting behaviors described by Kuczynski (1984) to more effortful, reasoned responses to child misbehavior.

3. *Differential parental attention/behavior* focuses on intrafamily differences in parenting experienced by siblings, including parent favoritism of one sibling over the other (differential parenting is addressed in more depth in Brody & Stoneman, chap. 12, this volume).

4. *Consistency* of parenting includes individual temporal consistency (each parent responds in a manner that is predictable across time) and across-parent consistency (mothers and fathers respond in a similar manner.)

5. *Sibling socialization practices* refers to parenting practices directly focused on assisting siblings in learning how to interact with each other. Positive socialization practices include setting clear rules and expectations for sibling behavior and responding to sibling conflict and dissension with effective discipline strategies. Sibling socialization practices also include the ascribed roles assigned to siblings by parents, including babysitting, monitoring, and assisting with their physical care.

6. *Sibling socialization goals* refers to parents' desired outcome for the sibling relationship. Not all parents share a common view of the "perfect" sibling relationship. For some parents, warmth and cooperation between siblings is the goal; for others, a competitive sibling relationship is acceptable. In addition, parents differ in the importance they place on socializing the relationship between their children and in their tolerance for sibling conflict or disengagement.

Evidence has been reported that suggests that events transpiring within the parent–child subsystem are related to the quality of the sibling relationship. Patterson (1980) reported that coercive exchanges between parents and children are related to qualitative aspects of sibling interactions. In a study of nondisabled siblings and their mothers, the authors (Brody, Stoneman, & MacKinnon, 1986) found that maternal reports of childrearing practices were consistently associated with the quality of observed sibling interactions without mothers present. Associations between childrearing practices and sibling behavior were found twice as often for the older sibling as for the younger sibling. For older siblings, serving as a socialization agent by directing sibling behavior and sibling helping were positively related to those maternal childrearing practices that encourage curiosity and openness, as well as to the value that the mother placed on a life separate from her children. These same sibling roles were negatively related to maternal inconsistency and the use of anxiety induction as a discipline strategy. Maternal use of nonpunitive control techniques and mother's enjoyment of her maternal role, respectively, were related to less agonistic behavior and more prosocial behavior in the older siblings. The younger sibling's prosocial behavior was related to maternal value placed on a life separate from her children and the avoidance of guilt induction as a discipline strategy.

When parents show clear favoritism to one or the other sibling, the sibling relationship suffers. Differential attention toward the younger child was found to be associated with lower rates of verbalizations and prosocial and agonistic behavior directed by siblings to each other (Brody, Stoneman, & Burke, 1987a). This differential behavior seemed to depress the overall level of sibling interaction, resulting in social disengagement. In a recent study (Brody, Stoneman, & McCoy, 1992), the authors found both direct and differential parent behavior to be associated, both contemporaneously and longitudinally, with variations in the quality of the sibling relationship. Parent positivity toward the children was associated with positive sibling behavior. Conversely, parent negativity and differential parent behavior were associated with negative sibling behavior. Paternal behavior appeared to have particular significance for the sibling relationship, possibly because of the relative scarcity of fathers' attention compared to that of mothers in the children's everyday lives. McHale and Pawletko (1992) suggest that the effects of differential treatment are complex, and differ depending on the behavior domain being studied and the disability status of the siblings.

Although there is much yet to be learned about specific parenting behaviors and their effect on the sibling relationship, there is clear evidence of the importance of parenting in socializing the relationship between siblings. Parenting is influenced and shaped by many factors, both inside and outside the family. The manner in which parents socialize their individual children, as well as the manner in which they socialize the sibling relationship, affects the quality of interactions between siblings, as well as the roles that they assume with each other.

CONCLUDING COMMENTS

For many years, the sibling relationship was studied apart from the family context. It was as if researchers believed that siblings lived alone on an island, divorced from other familial influences. It is only by examining the development and maintenance of sibling relations within the family context that researchers can begin to understand the complexity and richness of the social forces that shape this relationship. For siblings of children with a disability or chronic illness, explanatory models must include recognition of the pervasive impact on the entire family system of child characteristics associated with these conditions. These influences create a complex network of direct and indirect effects that shape and mold the sibling relationship across development. In this chapter, the authors have offered a family process model to explain the socialization of the sibling relationship within the family context. The model is not comprehensive or exhaustive. Other influences, from both within and without the family, affect siblings' feelings and behavior. Some of the specific associations in the model are based on scant empirical data. It is presented in the spirit of encouraging research on siblings within the context of multiple family influences. Further research, including longitudinal studies of the sibling relationship, will be needed to assess the predictive utility of the model.

REFERENCES

Anderson, K.E., Lytton, H., & Romney, D.M. (1986). Mothers' interactions with normal and conduct-disordered boys: Who affects whom? *Developmental Psychology, 22,* 604–609.

Baumeister, A.A., Dokecki, P.R., & Kupstas, F. D., (1988). *Preventing the new morbidity: A guide for state planning for the prevention of mental retardation and related disabilities associated with socioeconomic conditions.* Nashville, TN: Vanderbilt University.

Becker, W.C. (1964). Consequences of different kinds of parental discipline. In M.L. Hoffman & L.W. Hoffman (Eds.), *Review of child development research* (pp. 169–208). New York: Russell Sage.

Bell, R.Q. (1968). A reinterpretation of the direction of effects in studies of socialization. *Psychological Review, 75,* 81–95.

Belsky, J. (1981). Early human experience: A family perspective. *Developmental Psychology, 17,* 3–23.

Belsky, J. (1984). The determinants of parenting: A process model. *Child Development, 55,* 83–96.

Block, J. (1983). Differential premises arising from differential socialization of the sexes: Some conjectures. *Child Development, 54,* 1335–1354.

Block, J.H., Block, J., & Gjerde, P.F. (1986). The personality of children prior to divorce: A prospective study. *Child Development, 57,* 827–840.

Block, J.H., Block, J., & Morrison, A. (1981). Parental agreement–disagreement on child-rearing orientations and gender-related personality correlates in children. *Child Development, 52,* 965–974.

Bowe, F. (1983). *Black adults with disabilities—a statistical report drawn from census bureau data.* Washington, DC: The President's committee on employment of the handicapped.

Brody, G.H., Pellegrini, A.D., & Sigel, I.E. (1986). Marital quality and mother–child and father–child interactions with school-age children. *Developmental Psychology, 22,* 291–297.

Brody, G.H., & Stoneman, Z. (1987). Sibling conflict: Contributions of the siblings themselves, the parent–sibling relationship, and the broader family system. *Journal of Children in Contemporary Society, 19,* 39–53.

Brody, G.H., Stoneman, Z., & Burke, M. (1987a). Child temperaments, maternal differential behavior, and sibling relations. *Developmental Psychology, 23,* 354–362.

Brody, G.H., Stoneman, Z., & Burke, M. (1987b). Family system and individual child correlates of sibling behavior. *American Journal of Orthopsychiatry, 57,* 561–569.
Brody, G.H., Stoneman, Z., Davis, C.H., & Crapps, J.M. (1991). Observations of the role relations and behavior between older children with mental retardation and their younger siblings. *American Journal on Mental Retardation, 95,* 527–536.
Brody, G.H., Stoneman, Z., & MacKinnon, C.E. (1982). Role asymmetries in interactions between school-aged children, their younger siblings, and their friends. *Child Development, 53,* 1364–1370.
Brody, G.H., Stoneman, Z., & MacKinnon, C.E. (1986). Contributions of maternal child-rearing practices and play contexts to sibling interactions. *Journal of Applied Developmental Psychology, 7,* 225–236.
Brody, G.H., Stoneman, Z., & McCoy, J.K. (1992). Associations of maternal and paternal direct and differential behavior with sibling relationships: Contemporaneous and longitudinal analyses. *Child Development, 63,* 82–92.
Brody, G.H., Stoneman, Z., McCoy, K., & Forehand, R. (1992). Contemporaneous and longitudinal associations of sibling conflict with family relationship assessments and family discussions about sibling problems. *Child Development, 63,* 391–400.
Bronfenbrenner, U. (1979). *The ecology of human development: Experiments by nature and design.* Cambridge, MA: Harvard University Press.
Brunk, M.A., & Henggeler, S.W. (1984). Child influences on adult controls: An experimental investigation. *Developmental Psychology, 20,* 1074–1081.
Buss, D.M. (1981). Predicting parent–child interactions from children's activity level. *Developmental Psychology, 17,* 59–65.
Callan, V.J., & Noller, P. (1986). Perceptions of communicative relationships in families with adolescents. *Journal of Marriage and the Family, 48,* 813–820.
Cicirelli, V., (1982). Sibling influences throughout the lifespan. In M.E. Lamb & B. Sutton-Smith (Eds.), *Sibling relationships* (pp. 267–284). Hillsdale, NJ: Lawrence Erlbaum Associates.
Clifford, E. (1959). Discipline in the home: A controlled observational study of parental practices. *Journal of Genetic Psychology, 95,* 45–82.
Cohen, P.C. (1962). The impact of the handicapped child on the family. *Social Casework, 43,* 137–142.
Crnic, K.A. (1990). Families of children with Down syndrome: Ecological contexts and characteristics. In D. Cicchetti & M. Beeghly (Eds.), *Children with Down syndrome: A developmental perspective* (pp. 399–423). Cambridge: Cambridge University Press.
Crnic, K.A., & Leconte, J.M. (1986). Understanding sibling needs and influences. In R.R. Fewell & P.F. Vadasy (Eds.), *Families of handicapped children* (pp. 75–98). Austin: PRO-ED.
Cummings, E.M., Iannotti, R.J., & Zahn-Waxler, C. (1985). Influence of conflict between adults on the emotions and aggression of young children. *Developmental Psychology, 21,* 495–507.
Cummings, E.M., Zahn-Waxler, C., & Radke-Yarrow, M. (1981). Young children's responses to expressions of anger and affection by others in the family. *Child Development, 52,* 1274–1282.
Cummings, E.M., Zahn-Waxler, C., & Radke-Yarrow, M. (1984). Developmental changes in children's reactions to anger in the home. *Journal of Child Psychology and Psychiatry, 25,* 63–73.
Cunningham, C.E., Reuler, E., Blackwell, J., & Deck, J. (1981). Behavioral and linguistic developments in the interactions of normal and retarded children with their mothers. *Child Development, 52,* 62–70.

Cutrona, C.E., & Troutman, B.R. (1986). Social support, infant temperament, and parenting self-efficacy: A mediational model of postpartum depression. *Child Development, 57,* 1507–1518.

Damrosch, S.P., & Perry, L.A. (1989). Self-reported adjustment, chronic sorrow, and coping of parents of children with Down syndrome. *Nursing Research, 38,* 25–30.

Dielman, T.E., Barton, K., & Cattell, R.B. (1977). Relationships among family attitudes and child rearing practices. *The Journal of Genetic Psychology, 130,* 105–112.

Dunn, J., & Kendrick, C. (1982). *Siblings: Love, envy, and understanding.* Cambridge, MA: Harvard University Press.

Emery, R.E., Hetherington, M., & Dilalla, L.F. (1984). Divorce, children, and social policy. In H.W. Stevenson & A.E. Siegel (Eds.), *Child development research and social policy* (pp. 189–266). Chicago: University of Chicago Press.

Farber, B. (1959). Effects of a severely mentally retarded child on family integration. *Monographs of the Society for Research in Child Development, 24*(2).

Farber, B. (1960). Family organization and crisis: Maintenance of integration in families with a severely mentally retarded child. *Monographs of the Society for Research in Child Development, 25*(1).

Farber, B., & Jenne, W.C. (1963). Family organization and parent–child communication: Parents and siblings of a retarded child. *Monographs of the Society for Research in Child Development, 28*(7).

Forehand, R., Long, N., Brody, G.H., & Fauber, R. (1986). Home predictors of young adolescents' school behavior and academic performance. *Child Development, 57,* 1528–1533.

Friedrich, W.N. (1979). Predictors of the coping behavior of mothers of handicapped children. *Journal of Consulting and Clinical Psychology, 47*(6), 1140–1141.

Gath, A. (1974). Sibling reactions to mental handicap: A comparison of the brothers and sisters of mongol children. *Journal of Child Psychology and Psychiatry, 15,* 187–198.

Goldberg, W.A., & Easterbrooks, M.A. (1984). Role of marital quality in toddler development. *Developmental Psychology, 20,* 504–514.

Gordon, B.N. (1983). Maternal perception of child temperament and observed mother–child interaction. *Child Psychiatry and Human Development, 13,* 153–167.

Hartup, W.W. (1979). The social worlds of childhood. *American Psychologist, 34,* 944–950.

Hetherington, E.M., Cox, M., & Cox, R. (1981). Effects of divorce on parents and children. In M. Lamb (Ed.), *Nontraditional families* (pp. 233–288). Hillsdale, NJ: Lawrence Erlbaum Associates.

Holt, K.S. (1958). Home care of severely retarded children. *Pediatrics, 22,* 744–755.

Ianna, S.O., Hallahan, D., & Bell, R.Q. (1982). The effects of distractible child behavior on adults in a problem-solving setting. *Learning Disability Quarterly, 5,* 126–132.

Johnson, S.M., & Lobitz, G.K. (1974). The personal and marital adjustment of parents as related to observed child deviance and parenting behaviors. *Journal of Abnormal Child Psychology, 2,* 193–207.

Jordan, T.E. (1962). Research on the handicapped child and the family. *Merrill-Palmer Quarterly, 8,* 243.

Kaplan, F. (1969). Siblings of the retarded. In S. Sarason & J. Doris (Eds.), *Psychological problems in mental deficiency* (pp. 186–208). New York: Harper and Row.

Keller, B.B., & Bell, R.Q. (1979). Child effects on adult's method of eliciting altruistic behavior. *Child Development, 50,* 1004–1009.

Kelly, F.D., & Main, F.O. (1979). Sibling conflict in a single-parent family: An empirical case study. *American Journal of Family Therapy, 7,* 39–47.

Kemper, T.D., & Reichler, M.L. (1976). Marital satisfaction and conjugal power as determinants of intensity and frequency of rewards and punishments administered by parents. *The Journal of Genetic Psychology, 129,* 221–234.

Kuczynski, L. (1984). Socialization goals and mother–child interaction: Strategies for long-term and short-term compliance. *Developmental Psychology, 20,* 1061–1073.

Lerner, R.M., & Lerner, J.V. (1987). Children in their contexts: A goodness-of-fit model. In J.B. Lancaster, J. Altmann, A.S. Rossi, & L.R. Sherrod (Eds.), *Parenting across the lifespan: Biosocial dimensions* (pp. 377–404). New York: Aldine De Gruyter.

Long, N., Forehand, R., Fauber, R., & Brody, G.H. (1987). Self-perceived and independently observed competence of young adolescents as a function of parental marital conflict and recent divorce. *Journal of Abnormal Child Psychology, 15,* 15–27.

Longfellow, C., Zelkowitz, P., & Saunders, E. (1982). The quality of mother–child relationships. In D. Belle (Ed.), *Lives in stress: Women and depression.* Beverly Hills: Sage Publications, 163–176.

Maccoby, E.E., Snow, M.E., & Jacklin, C.N. (1984). Children's dispositions and mother–child interaction at 12 and 18 months: A short-term longitudinal study. *Developmental Psychology, 20,* 459–472.

Marshall, N.R., Hegrenes, J.R., & Goldstein, S. (1973). Verbal interactions: Mothers and their retarded children vs. mothers and their nonretarded children. *American Journal of Mental Deficiency, 77,* 415–419.

McHale, S.M., & Gamble, W.C. (1989). Sibling relationships of children with disabled and nondisabled brothers and sisters. *Developmental Psychology, 25,* 421–429.

McHale, S.M., & Pawletko, T.M. (1992). Differential treatment of siblings in two family contexts. *Child Development, 63,* 68–81.

Milliones, J. (1978). Relationship between perceived child temperament and maternal behaviors. *Child Development, 49,* 1255–1257.

Morgan, S.B. (1988). The autistic child and family functioning: A developmental–family systems perspective. *Journal of Autism and Developmental Disorders, 18,* 263–280.

Olshansky, S. (1962). Chronic sorrow: A response to having a mentally defective child. *Social Casework, 43,* 190–193.

Oltmanns, T.F., Broderick, J.E., & O'Leary, K.D. (1977). Marital adjustment and the efficacy of behavior therapy with children. *Journal of Consulting and Clinical Psychology, 45,* 724–729.

Parfit, J. (1975). Siblings of handicapped children. *Special Education/Forward Trends, 2,* 19–21.

Patterson, G.R. (1980). Mothers; The unacknowledged victims. *Monographs of the Society for Research in Child Development, 45*(5, Serial No. 186).

Porter, B., & O'Leary, K.D. (1980). Marital discord and childhood behavior problems. *Journal of Abnormal Child Psychology, 8,* 287–295.

SanMartino, M., & Newman, M.B. (1974). Siblings of retarded children: A population at risk. *Child Psychiatry and Human Development, 4,* 168–177.

Sarbin, T.R. (1954). Role theory. In G. Lindzey (Ed.), *Handbook of social psychology* (Vol. 1, pp. 223–258). Reading, MA: Addison-Wesley.

Schild, S. (1964). Counseling with parents of mentally retarded children living at home. *Social Work, 9,* 86–91.

Seligman, M. (1983). Siblings of handicapped persons. In M. Seligman (Ed.), *The family with a handicapped child* (pp. 147–174). New York: Grune and Stratton.

Simeonsson, R.J., & McHale, S.M. (1981). Review: Research on handicapped children: Sibling Relationships. *Child: Care, Health, and Development, 7,* 153–171.

Stoneman, Z. (1990). Conceptual relationships between family research and mental retardation. In N.W. Bray (Ed.), *International review of research in mental retardation* (Vol. 15, pp. 161–202). Orlando, FL: Academic Press.

Stoneman, Z., & Brody, G.H. (1982). Strengths inherent in sibling interactions involving a retarded child: A functional role theory approach. In N. Stinnett, B. Chesser, J. DeFrain, & P. Knaub, (Eds.), *Family strengths: Positive models for family life* (pp. 113–129). Lincoln: University of Nebraska Press.

Stoneman, Z., & Brody, G.H. (1984). Research with families of severely handicapped children: Theoretical and methodological considerations. In J. Blacher (Ed.), *Severely handicapped young children and their families: Research in review* (pp. 179–214). New York: Academic Press.

Stoneman, Z., & Brody, G.H., (1987). Observational research on retarded children, their parents, and their siblings. In S. Landesman & P.M. Vietze (Eds.), *Living environments and mental retardation* (pp. 423–449). Washington, DC: American Association on Mental Retardation.

Stoneman, Z., & Brody, G.H. (1990). Families with a mentally retarded child. In G.H. Brody & I. Sigel (Eds.), *Research methods for studying at-risk families* (pp. 31–58). Hillsdale, NJ: Lawrence Erlbaum Associates.

Stoneman, Z., Brody, G.H., & Abbott, D. (1983). In-home observations of young Down syndrome children with their mothers and fathers. *American Journal of Mental Deficiency, 87*(6), 591–600.

Stoneman, Z., Brody, G.H., & Burke, M. (1989a). Marital quality, depression, and inconsistent parenting: Relationships with observed mother–child conflict. *American Journal of Orthopsychiatry, 59*(1), 105–117.

Stoneman, Z., Brody, G.H., & Burke, M. (1989b). Sibling temperaments and maternal and paternal perceptions of marital, family, and personal functioning. *Journal of Marriage and the Family, 51,* 99–113.

Stoneman, Z., Brody, G.H., Davis, C.H., & Crapps, J.M. (1987). Mentally retarded children and their older siblings: Naturalistic in-home observations. *American Journal on Mental Retardation, 92*(3), 290–298.

Stoneman, Z., Brody, G.H., Davis, C.H., & Crapps, J.M. (1988). Childcare responsibilities, peer relationships, and sibling conflict: Older siblings of mentally retarded children. *American Journal on Mental Retardation, 93*(2), 166–173.

Stoneman, Z., Brody, G.H., Davis, C.H., & Crapps, J.M. (1989). Role relations between mentally retarded children and their older siblings: Observations in three in-home contexts. *Research in Developmental Disabilities, 10,* 61–76.

Stoneman, Z., Brody, G.H., Davis, C.H., Crapps, J.M., & Malone, D.M. (1991). Ascribed role relations between children with mental retardation and their younger siblings. *American Journal on Mental Retardation, 95,* 537–550.

Stoneman, Z., Brody, G.H., & MacKinnon, C. (1984). Naturalistic observations of children's activities and roles while playing with their younger siblings and friends. *Child Development, 55,* 617–627.

Susman, E.J., Trickett, P.K., Iannotti, R.J., Hollenbeck, B.E., & Zahn-Waxler, C. (1985). Child-rearing patterns in depressed, abusive, and normal mothers. *American Journal of Orthopsychiatry, 55,* 237–251.

Zelkowitz, P. (1982). Parenting philosophies and practices. In D. Belle (Ed.), *Lives in stress: Women and depression* (pp. 154–162). Beverly Hills: Sage Publications.

CHAPTER 2

Contemporary Themes in Research on Sibling Relationships of Nondisabled Children

Wyndol C. Furman

This volume has particular promise in that it brings together authors with a diversity of perspectives and interests who may greatly benefit from one another. This particular chapter is written from the perspective of someone interested in sibling relationships between children who do not have disabilities. In particular, the author discusses a number of the most common themes that have emerged in this field. These themes may prove to be useful in research on siblings of children with disabilities, and, conversely, research on atypical relationships could enrich understanding of sibling relationships of children without disabilities. There are four central themes to the chapter: 1) the variation in the quality of sibling relationships, 2) the importance of multiple perspectives on sibling relationships, 3) the role of parenting in sibling relationships, and 4) the role of individual characteristics in sibling relationships. Certainly, these subjects have already appeared in some research on relationships of siblings with disabilities. It is hoped, however, that the delineation of these themes can move researchers and professionals toward the goal of a more integrated field.

QUALITATIVE FEATURES

Sibling relationships are very diverse in nature. Some are asymmetrical ones in which one child serves as a caregiver to the other, whereas others are more egalitarian in nature, more similar to friendships. Their affective tones can also vary considerably. Relationships can be close or distant, harmonious or conflicted, cooperative or competitive.

Contemporary investigators have been interested in studying the diversity of these relationships. Both self-report measures and observational techniques have been used to assess the qualities of sibling relationships. Table 1 presents the list of features that the author and his colleagues have focused on in their work on sibling relationships. These features were the ones that emerged from interviewing fifth and sixth grade children about their sibling relationships (Furman & Buhrmester, 1985). In these interviews, the children provided rich portraits of their relationships, mentioning an average of eight different characteristics.

Based on these interviews, this author developed a 51-item Sibling Relationship Questionnaire to measure 17 relationship qualities. The questionnaire was administered to 198 fifth- and sixth-grade children who were predominately from Caucasian, middle-class families in Denver, Colorado. A principal components analysis with an oblique rotation revealed four factors: Warmth/Closeness, Relative Status/Power, Conflict, and Rivalry. The qualities that loaded on each factor are listed in Table 1.

It would be interesting to determine if these same four factors emerged in studies of relationships between siblings with disabilities. Begun (1989)

Table 1. Factor pattern coefficients of Sibling Relationship Questionnaire scales

	Factors			
Qualities	Warmth/ closeness	Relative status/power	Conflict	Rivalry
Intimacy	70			
Prosocial behavior	83			
Companionship	78			
Similarity	70			
Nurturance by sibling	28	−77		
Nurturance of sibling	26	85		
Admiration by sibling	67	25	−29	
Admiration of sibling	69	−28		
Affection	69		−36	
Dominance by sibling		−65	55	
Dominance over sibling		80	41	
Quarreling			88	
Antagonism			92	
Competition			63	36
Parental partiality				96

From Furman, W. and Buhrmester, D. (1985). Children's perceptions of sibling relationships. *Child Development, 56,* 448–461; reprinted by permission.

Scores are factor loadings on a principal component analysis with a general promax rotation. Factor loading below .25 are not presented. Factors are minimally correlated ($-.20 > r < .20$) except Conflict and Rivalry ($r = .35$).

found some interesting results with this measure in a study of sisters of individuals with developmental disabilities, but she simply assumed that the factors and scales were appropriate. Certainly, many of the descriptors that investigators have used to characterize these relationships fall within the domains assessed by this measure. But asymmetry and instrumental activities are more common in these relationships, suggesting that researchers may want to examine the features of work, responsibility, and guilt more extensively (McHale & Gamble, 1989; Miller, 1974; Stoneman & Brody, 1984; Zetlin, 1986). In this respect these relationships may bear some resemblance to those in other cultures in which strong emphasis is placed on work, sibling caregiving, and prescribed roles (see Zukow, 1989). Finally, even when a feature applies to relationships between siblings both with and without disabilities, the behavioral manifestation of that feature may differ; for example, Miller (1974) found that children expressed anger directly toward nondisabled siblings, but only indirectly toward those with disabilities.

In any case, the study of relationship qualities provides researchers with a different picture than that obtained by examining family-constellation variables (i.e., gender, gender of sibling, relative age, and age spacing between siblings). The characteristics of these relationships are not exclusively, or even primarily, determined by family-constellation variables. In fact, although each of the qualitative factors was to some extent related to constellation variables, only status/power was strongly related to them. Not surprisingly, the older members of the dyads were seen as having more power and status than younger members, but even this finding is unlikely to hold when the older member of the dyad has a disability. Thus, sibling relationships vary considerably within any type of family constellation, as well as between different family constellations. These findings indicate that if one is to understand the influence of siblings on each other, one cannot consider family-constellation variables alone, but must also examine the qualitative features of sibling relationships.

The importance of directly examining the features of these relationships is nicely illustrated by efforts to account for the fact that older sisters of siblings with disabilities seem to have more adjustment problems than other siblings (Farber, 1959; Fowle, 1968; Gath, 1974; Grossman, 1972). The traditional explanation had been that the older sisters suffer the most because of the extra burden of care. Yet, when recent investigators have directly assessed the amount of caregiving, they have found it to be relatively unrelated to adjustment (McHale & Gamble, 1989; Stoneman & Brody, 1984). McHale and Gamble (1987), in fact, suggested that the older sisters may be vulnerable because they are the recipients of more negative behaviors from siblings, regardless of whether the siblings have disabilities or not. No matter which explanation ultimately proves to be correct, it is apparent that researchers need to examine the relational processes and features directly, and not simply infer them from constellation factors. Such studies are particularly important because family-constellation variables may affect parent–child relationships or marital relationships, rather than sibling relationships per se.

MULTIPLE PERSPECTIVES

Although emphasis has been placed on the importance of assessing the qualitative features of a sibling relationship, it must also be recognized that there is not just one perspective on the sibling relationship. Each child will experience the relationship in a different way, particularly if one of them has a disability. Parents have their own view of the relationship, and, as outsiders, researchers and professionals have yet another.

This point seems to have first been made by Olson (1977), who distinguished between insiders' and outsiders' perspectives on a relationship. (Olson also distinguished between subjective data, which are the perceptions or interpretations of a reporter [e.g., a rating scale], and objective data, which are less influenced by personal perceptions or interpretations [e.g., frequency counts].) An insider is a member of the relationship being studied (e.g., a sibling described his or her own sibling relationship). An outsider is someone, such as a social scientist, who is uninvolved in the relationship. In the author's own work (Furman, Jones, Buhrmester, & Adler, 1989), it was proposed that a third type of perspective be added—that of a participant observer, or someone who is indirectly involved in the relationship. In the present case, that could be a parent reporting on his or her children's sibling relationship. It is also important to remember that meaningful differences occur among different reporters who have the "same" perspective; for example, two children are likely to describe a sibling relationship differently because they experience it differently (Rowe & Plomin, 1981).

The author and his colleagues, as well as Olson, argued that multiple perspectives should be incorporated when studying a relationship, because the different perspectives provide different information (Furman, 1984; Furman et al., 1989; Olson, 1977). In part, different information is discovered because of the methodological limitations associated with the different approaches. For example, some evidence suggests that mothers' reports on the adjustment of their children without disabilities may be strongly colored by their own adjustment to their children with disabilities (Gabel, McDowell, & Cerreto, 1982; Simeonsson & McHale, 1981). Even outsiders, such as teachers, may be influenced by knowledge of the disabled status of a sibling (Blackard & Barsh, 1982; Richey, Ysseldyke, Potter, Regan, & Grenner, 1981). Yet, it is important to remember that discrepancies may also occur because of meaningful differences in perspectives.

For example, insiders, participant observers, and outsiders will have been exposed to the relationship in different contexts and for different amounts of time. Second, the three will differ in how well they know the context of a behavior or the meaning of the behavior within that particular relationship. Third, the attitudes, feelings, and personal involvement of insiders and participant observers result in different perspectives than those of outsiders. Fourth, the three differ in how motivated or capable they are of sharing their perspectives. Finally, insiders, participant observers, and outsiders use different reference groups when comparing, interpreting, or evaluating the quality of a sibling relationship (for further detail, see Furman et al., 1989).

Clearly, there is not only one accurate view of a relationship. Accordingly, professionals should not assume that the results obtained from two different perspectives will correspond. In his review of family measures, Olson (1977) found the correlations among different perspectives to be low. Of course, the low relations may in part be the result of methodological problems, but unfortunately there are few guidelines as to what the level would theoretically be if the measures were ideal. In fact, relatively little is known about the factors that may increase or decrease the amount of convergence among the perspectives.

The importance of multiple perspectives seems equally important for studies of relationships that include a sibling with a disability. In fact, the magnitude of the differences in perspectives may be greater in studies of these relationships. For example, McHale and Gamble (1989) found the differences between family ratings and time-use data on sibling relationships were greater in families with children with retardation than in those with nondisabled children.

One perspective that it would be particularly valuable to obtain is that of the child with the disability. This child is likely to have a different experience of the relationship than his or her sibling. In some cases, the problem lies in finding means of obtaining valid reports from children with disabilities. Although this seems to be a thorny problem, it is hoped that efforts will be made to solve it.

An Empirical Example

Over the last few years, the author and his colleagues have conducted a series of studies that examined the level of concordance among different perspectives. In the most recent study (Furman & Giberson, in press), 62 third-through seventh-grade children, their older siblings, their mothers, and most of their fathers completed Sibling Relationship Questionnaires in their homes. The first six rows of Table 2 depict the pattern of factor-score correlations among the family members. There is a moderately high level of agreement on warmth, conflict, and relative status/power (mean $r = .46$). These correlations are quite similar to those obtained in several previous studies (see Furman et al., 1989), although the amount of agreement on relative status/power has varied. When the study has included ratings of siblings who are both older and younger, the agreement has been quite high (mean $r = .78$); when the

Table 2. Correlations among different perspectives' SRQs

	Factors			
Dyad	Warmth/ closeness	Conflict	Relative status/power	Rivalry
Mother–Father	73[a]	72[a]	55[a]	25
Mother–Child	32[b]	44[a]	36[a]	26[b]
Mother–Sibling	47[a]	40[a]	43[a]	45[a]
Father–Child	28[b]	47[a]	44[a]	−09
Father–Sibling	42[a]	49[a]	59[a]	14
Child–Sibling	42[a]	33[a]	42[a]	45[a]
Mother–Observer	33[b]	37[b]	49[a]	−21
Father–Observer	28	31[b]	48[a]	−19
Child–Observer	38[b]	28[b]	57[a]	−02
Sibling–Observer	40[a]	44[a]	69[a]	−23

[a] $p < .01$.
[b] $p < .05$.

study has only included younger siblings, the correlations have been lower ($r = .22$).

The agreement on rivalry is quite variable, and in previous studies has generally been low. Perhaps there really is less agreement about rivalry, but it is also possible that family members, particularly parents, may be unwilling to admit to preferential treatment of certain children. In fact, the variance of these scores is much less than that of other factor scores. Recently, the author and his colleagues have been trying to assess rivalry in a less-threatening manner by asking whether children complain about differential treatment or are concerned about being treated equally, rather than whether, in the respondent's opinion, the children actually are treated differently.

The children and their mothers were also observed in their homes while they participated in a series of structured tasks for 40 minutes. In particular, after a warm-up task the 3 were asked to discuss how a series of 10 common chores were carried out in their family and whether there should be any changes. Next, the triad was asked to discuss three problems that they had identified in the sibling relationship. Then, the three were given a poster board and art material and asked to make something together. Finally, the three discussed a positive experience they had together.

Ten undergraduate raters watched the videotapes and then completed similar questionnaires describing their impressions of the relationships. In effect, the author and his colleagues wanted to determine if outsiders who observed a set of interactions would perceive the same relationship qualities as the parents and children themselves perceived. The level of agreement among these outsiders and the various family members is shown in the bottom four rows of Table 2. In general, the level of agreement among the observers is as great as it is among family members. This finding helps rule out the possibility that the families have simply constructed a set of beliefs about the nature of the sibling relationship that does not reflect the actual patterns of interactions.

PARENTS AND SIBLING RELATIONSHIPS

In an earlier paper (Furman & Buhrmester, 1985), the author proposed a model of some of the major factors that may influence sibling relationships. This model is depicted in Figure 1. Although the list was not intended to be exhaustive, it was suggested that family-constellation variables, parent–child relationships, and the cognitive, social, and personality characteristics of the children may be among the more important determinants of the nature of sibling relationships.

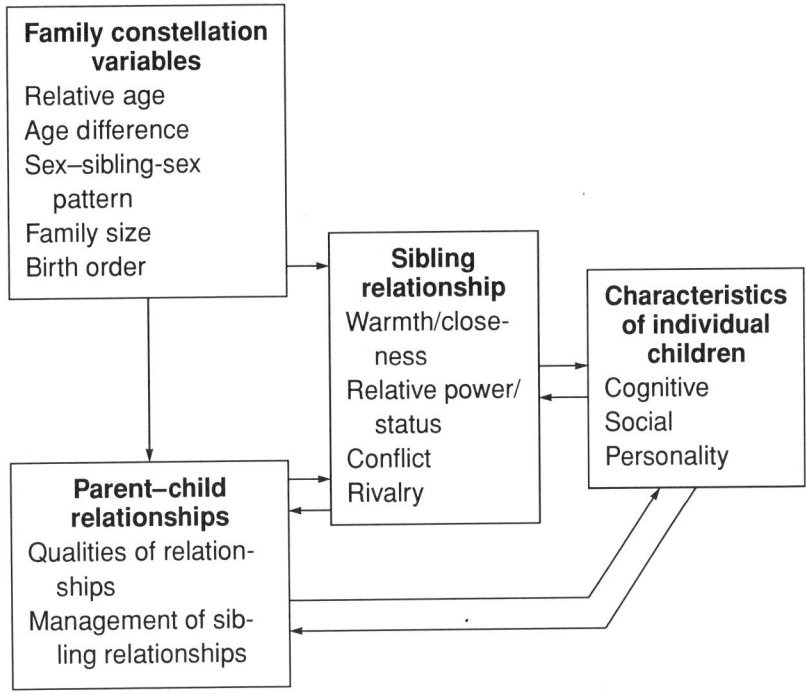

Figure 1. Factors associated with sibling relationship qualities. (From Furman, W., & Buhrmester, D. [1985]. Children's perceptions of the qualities of sibling relationships. *Child Development, 56,* 448–461; reprinted by permission.)

How might parents play a role in shaping sibling relationships? The author believes that there are at least five potential links (Furman & Giberson, in press). In particular, parents may have an impact through: 1) the general characteristics of their relationships with their two children, 2) differences in the two children's relationships with them, 3) their techniques of disciplining the children or responding to specific sibling interactions, 4) anticipatory management strategies or efforts to foster positive sibling interactions and decrease negative ones in the future, and 5) their marital relationship. One should also remember that the sibling relationship may, in turn, affect parents through each of these channels. Examples of such bidirectional links are presented below.

Parent–Child Relationships

The author believes that the general characteristics of parent–child and sibling relationships are associated with one another. For example, warm parent–child interactions are likely to foster warm interactions between siblings. Theorists from many different camps expect this kind of similarity. Attachment theorists proposed that in their early interactions with caregivers, children develop internal working models of relationships, which then serve as the basis for subsequent relationships (Bowlby, 1973). Family systems theorists stress the interdependencies in the functioning of different subsystems (Minuchin, 1974). Social learning theorists expect similarities because of modeling effects. The two could also possibly be linked through either behavioral displacement or contagion mechanisms. For example, after a conflict with a parent, a child may be likely to vent his or her anger toward a sibling, or may be more likely to respond adversely to a sibling's irritating behavior. Of course, it is expected that conflicts between siblings could carry over into interactions with parents as well.

Consistent with these ideas, maternal responsivity to school-age children's needs has been found to be positively correlated with prosocial behavior between siblings and negatively correlated with antisocial behavior between siblings (Bryant & Crockenberg, 1980). Similarly, teenagers' attitudes toward siblings with retardation have been found to parallel those of their parents (Gralicker, Fishler, & Koch, 1962).

Differential Treatment

The relative nature of two siblings' relationships with their parents may also be predictive of the quality of their sibling relationships. Specifically, differences between parents' interactions with two children have been shown to be associated with sibling rivalry and conflict. For example, if a mother responded to one child's needs more than the other's, the children were likely to be disparaging and discomforting toward each other (Bryant & Crockenberg, 1980). Similarly, differences in mothers' positivity toward or amount of communication with siblings have been found to be associated with fewer prosocial behaviors and less communication between siblings (Brody, Stoneman, & Burke, 1987). When mothers were more responsive, affectionate, or attentive to one child, competitive and controlling interactions between siblings were more common (Stocker, Dunn, & Plomin, 1989).

Siblings of children with disabilities reported more differential treatment than did siblings of children without disabilities, but they were not less satisfied (McHale, Gamble, & Pawletko, 1989). Those siblings who were dissatisfied with how parents treated them were more depressed and anxious, however (McHale & Gamble, 1989; McHale et al., 1989). Interestingly, the more satisfied the children were, the less time they spent with their mothers (relative to their younger siblings) (McHale & Pawletko, in press).

These findings point out an interesting issue that has received little attention in the literature to date. How exactly should differential treatment be assessed? Certainly, one should not expect parents to interact identically with siblings of different ages, especially if one of them has a disability. Differential treatment is usually measured in an attempt to index parental favoritism, but it seems difficult to determine when a specific act reflects favoritism and when it does not. Differential treatment may seem legitimate in light of the limitations of a child with a disability (Farber, 1959; Powell & Ogle, 1985). Moreover, it is not clear what effects are caused by those differential acts that do not stem from favoritism. McHale et al. (1989) did not have to address this thorny problem, because they examined satisfaction with differential treatment, but other investigators, particularly those using observational approaches, will need to give careful thought to their conceptualization of differential treatment. In any case, what is striking is how powerful this variable seems to be, even when assessed in a rather simple manner.

Disciplinary Strategies

The two potential links discussed above center on the general nature of parents' relationships with their children. Parenting behavior may, however, be somewhat domain-specific (Costanzo & Woody, 1985), and thus, researchers need to consider how parents respond to specific sibling interactions or to the absence of certain interactions (e.g., when children are not spending time with one another).

The techniques that are used in response to various sibling interactions may influence sibling relationships in several ways. Like parent–child interactions in general, the strategies that parents use might serve as models for how siblings are to behave with one another. Similarly, sibling conflict or rivalry may be particularly likely if the two children are disciplined differently for some episode that occurred in their relationship. Finally, social learning theorists expect reinforcement or punishment techniques to affect the frequencies of different behaviors. In fact, direct teaching methods may foster positive interactions among siblings. For example, the reinforcement of cooperative play and time-out for fights has been shown to decrease rates of sibling conflict (Allison & Allison, 1971; Leitenberg, Burchard, Burchard, Fuller, & Lysaght, 1977; O'Leary, O'Leary, & Becker, 1967). Miller and Cantwell (1976) trained siblings of children with retardation to serve as therapists for their siblings by having them act in positive ways toward them. Children's behavior toward siblings may also be influenced by what they expect their parents to do. For example, siblings of children with retardation commonly believe that their parents would not be tolerant of negative behavior toward the child, and that they would be punished if they did not engage in the prescribed activities with them.

Anticipatory Management

Of course, parents not only respond to their children's sibling behavior, but also do things to either encourage or discourage certain aspects of the sibling relationship before difficulties arise. Such anticipatory-management strategies fall into three categories: 1) establishing rules (e.g., "no fist fighting"), 2) planning or structuring activities (e.g., taking the children on trips together), and 3) having discussions with one or both siblings about problems that might arise in the future. As defined here, anticipatory strategies are initiated by parents, but the impetus for behavior may actually be the children's actions in the past. Thus, the boundaries between anticipatory management and disciplinary strategies are somewhat fuzzy, although the distinction seems to have heuristic value.

Anticipatory-management strategies are expected to foster positive interactions and reduce negative ones for two reasons. First, the strategies that parents use are more likely to reduce problems than exacerbate them. Second, parents who use such anticipatory strategies are likely to be different from those who tend to respond only to the immediate problem at hand, although this hypothesis has not been tested empirically.

Most work on anticipatory management has examined the impact of discussions. For example, Dunn and Kendrick (1981) found that conversations about newborn siblings' needs and intentions promoted subsequent positive interactions among siblings. A number of investigators have found that open communication about a child's disability fosters the adjustment of both the child (Beardslee, 1981; Spinetta & Mahoney, 1978) and the sibling (Gogan & Slavin, 1981; Grossman, 1972; Lavine, 1977). Such communication seems particularly important because siblings of children with disabilities are very curious and often have not been provided with much information (Grossman, 1972; Schreiber & Feely, 1965). Anecdotal evidence also suggests that parents can promote caring attitudes toward children with disabilities by assigning certain roles to the siblings, such as teacher or protector (Bank & Kahn, 1982).

Parents' Marriage

Although its effects may not be as direct as those of the four potential mechanisms already discussed, the quality of the marital relationship may also be linked to sibling relationships. Parents' interactions with one another serve as a model for the children. Their interactions with their partners may also affect their functioning as parents, which in turn may influence the children's sibling relationships in the ways described above. This link has received little attention empirically, but MacKinnon (1989) did find that parents' descriptions of their spouse or ex-spouse in positive terms were associated with positive sibling interactions. This link may be particularly worth examining in families with a child with a disability because of the increased risk of marital conflict and divorce in such families (Fotheringham & Creel, 1974; Price-Bonham & Addison, 1978).

An Empirical Study

This brief review should show that there is clear evidence that parents' behavior and relationships are linked with sibling relationships in a number of ways. At the same time, it should be equally evident that more is known about some links than about others. In part, this reflects the fact that most of the work to date consists of isolated studies on single mechanisms. Thus, it is difficult to integrate the literature into a coherent picture that reveals the relative roles played by the various mechanisms. The author and his colleagues have begun to conduct a series of studies to examine the different links simultaneously (Furman & Giberson, in press; Katz & Furman, 1990).

The first study examined maternal perceptions of sibling relationships, disciplinary techniques, anticipatory management, and mother–child relationships. The participants were 88 predominantly white, middle- to upper–middle-class mothers with two or more children (with one in the fifth or sixth grade).

The mothers completed a battery of questionnaires that included the Sibling Relationship Questionnaire (SRQ) (Furman & Buhrmester, 1985), the Parent–Child Relationship Questionnaire (PCRQ) (Katz & Furman, 1990), and a Parental Management Inventory (PMI) (Katz & Furman, 1990).

The Sibling Relationship Questionnaire is described above. The Parent–Child Relationship Questionnaire was similar in form, and assessed perceptions of the qualities of individual parent–child relationships. It consisted of 23 three-item scales, which fell under five dimensions: Warmth (affection, admiration for, and by, mother), Personal Closeness (companionship, nurturance, prosocial behavior, intimacy, and similarity), Disciplinary Warmth (positive evaluations, democratic process, and provision of rationales), Power Assertion (verbal punishment, dominance, deprivation of privileges, quarreling, rejection, and physical punishment), and Possessiveness (protectiveness, possessiveness).

The Parental Management Inventory was designed to examine those disciplinary techniques and anticipatory management strategies that mothers perceive themselves as using when managing their children's sibling relationships. Disciplinary techniques were assessed by asking mothers how often they used each of 11 specific discipline strategies in response to various positive and negative sibling interactions. These strategies were grouped into five scales: Positive Principled Discipline (verbal praise, physical praise, and rewards), Negative Principled Discipline (inductive techniques such as discussion, expressions of disappointment, and requests for changes in behavior), Punishment (demands or yelling, threats, and deprivation of privileges or punishment), Ignoring Positive Behavior, and Ignoring Negative Behavior. Anticipatory-management strategies were assessed by asking mothers how often they used such techniques to increase positive sibling interactions and decrease negative sibling interactions in the future.

As shown in Table 3, mother–child relationship qualities were strongly associated with sibling-relationship qualities. Ratings of warmth in mother–child relationships were positively associated with warmth in sibling relationships and negatively related to ratings of conflict. High ratings of personal closeness and disciplinary warmth were also related to greater ratings of warmth among siblings. However, when power assertion by mothers was rated high, sibling warmth was seen as low and sibling conflict as high.

To assess the role of differential treatment, differences in the mother's ratings on her interactions with the focal child and with the sibling were derived. Consistent with the hypotheses, differences in perceived warmth, personal closeness, and power assertion were associated with reports of greater sibling rivalry. Differences in perceived warmth were also associated with lower ratings of warmth/closeness between siblings.

Mothers' perceptions of their management techniques were closely linked to their perceptions of their relationships with their children (see Table 4). Ratings of frequent use of positive and negative principled discipline were

Table 3. Correlations of sibling relationship qualities and parent–child relationship qualities

Parent–child relationship quality	Sibling relationship quality			
	Warmth/ closeness	Conflict	Relative status/power	Rivalry
Warmth	.54[a]	−.33[b]	−.01	−.24[b]
Personal closeness	.41[a]	−.01	−.13	−.26[b]
Disciplinary warmth	.33[a]	.02	.08	−.11
Power/assertion	−.37[a]	.44[a]	.11	.13
Possessiveness	.21	−.01	−.15	−.16

From Katz and Furman (1990).
[a] $p < .01$.
[b] $p < .05$.

Table 4. Correlations of parental management techniques and parent–child relationship qualities

Management technique	Parent–child relationship quality				
	Warmth	Personal closeness	Disciplinary warmth	Power assertion	Possessiveness
Positive principled discipline	.30[a]	.47[a]	.23[a]	−.11	.05
Negative principled discipline	.15	.32[a]	.25[b]	.05	.20
Punishment	−.14	−.02	.02	.43[a]	.04
Anticipatory socialization	.23[b]	.54$_a$	−.17	−.03	.30[a]
Ignoring negative behavior	−.26[b]	−.52[a]	−.36[a]	.17	−.14
Ignoring positive behavior	−.24[b]	−.37[a]	−.29[a]	.14	.02

From Katz and Furman (1990).
[a] $p < .01$.
[b] $p < .05$.

associated with high ratings in the three warmth dimensions. Anticipatory socialization was also related to warmth and personal closeness, as well as to possessiveness. Mothers who reported ignoring positive or negative behaviors frequently described their relationships with their children as relatively low in the three warmth dimensions. Finally, reported use of punishment was associated with power assertion.

Contrary to expectations, ratings of maternal management techniques were not closely related to those of sibling-relationship qualities. The few relations that were observed have not been found in subsequent efforts to replicate the findings. Perhaps stronger relations would be found using observational data; after all, mothers may not always do what they say they do. Another methodological problem is that the author, like other investigators, has used measures of absolute level to assess changes in level. For example, the author and his colleagues speculated that anticipatory management techniques should decrease the amount of conflict, not that it should be associated with an initially low level of conflict. Unfortunately conflict was assessed in terms of absolute level. Of course, changes cannot be readily assessed with cross-sectional data. In fact, it is not even clear if snapshots of variables over time actually capture the process of change and influence, particularly when the variables have a long history of interacting with one another (see Furman & Giberson, in press, for further discussion).

It is also possible that the relation between the two is mediated by the parent–child relationship. That is, children may interpret parental interventions as more indicative of "how my parent chooses to interact with me," than of "how I should interact with my sibling." Thus, the parents' discipline may influence the parent–child relationship, which in turn may affect sibling relationships.

It is also possible that management techniques and sibling-relationship qualities are not related. The most common thing that mothers reported doing was nothing. Anecdotally, mothers often said that they did not think there was much they could do to change their children's relationship with one another. Certainly, they could stop a fight or encourage some positive interaction, but they did not feel that they could change the general tenor of the relationship, which had already been established by the children's personalities and interests, for better or worse. The author's impression is that parents of younger children make more efforts to alter their children's relationship with one another. Thus, one might expect management techniques to be more closely related to preschool children's sibling relationships, a topic that the author is currently examining.

Additionally, it seems possible that parents may make greater efforts to shape or alter the relationship if it is dysfunctional. Finally, parents of a child with a disability may also make more efforts to shape their children's relationship with one another because of the special demands involved in that relationship.

Regardless of whether management techniques ultimately prove to be linked to sibling-relationship qualities, this study illustrates how the general characteristics of parent–child relationships and differential treatment may be related to sibling relationship qualities. Of course, the study is limited in scope in that the author and his colleagues simply assessed mothers' perceptions of these variables.

In subsequent studies (Furman & Giberson, in press), however, the author has incorporated observational data, as well as data on the perceptions of fathers and children. In general, the results of this initial study have been replicated using the different methods. Although it is beyond the scope of this chapter to describe all the findings in detail, a few warrant mention.

Like the first study conducted, this study found perceptions of parent–child-relationship qualities to be significantly related to perceptions of sibling-relationship qualities. These patterns of relations were found in the perceptions of both father–child and mother–child relationships. Maternal differential treatment was again found to be related to the quality of the sibling relationship. Such patterns were found both using the mothers' ratings and in the observations of their interactions with their children. Interestingly, differential treatment by fathers was not related to perceptions of sibling relationships. Perhaps these differences are less salient or less important to children than differences in treatment by mothers, who even today have primary responsibility for childrearing in most families. At the same time, one should not discount the role of fathers, because the general characteristics of these relationships were found to be related to sibling-relationship qualities.

In this study, the author and his colleagues also examined links between marital-relationship qualities and sibling-relationship qualities. Both parents completed a Marital Relationship Questionnaire. This measure consisted of 24 three-item scales, which loaded on five factors: Warmth, Conflict, Power, Traditionality, and Exclusivity. As expected, ratings of high conflict and low warmth in marital relationships were associated with ratings of conflict in sibling relationships.

Finally, perceptions of marital relationships were also associated with perceptions of parent–child relationships. Specifically, the ratings of warmth in the two relationships were related, as were the ratings of conflict. Marital conflict was also associated with less warmth among siblings. These findings are consistent with the idea that marital and sibling relationships may also be indirectly linked through the parent–child relationships.

INDIVIDUAL CHARACTERISTICS

The author also proposed that the social, cognitive, and personality characteristics of the children, as well as the parents' behavior, would be important determinants of the qualitative features of the sibling relationship. And, of course, one would expect the children's own experience in the sibling relationship to affect them.

Several investigators have examined how temperamental characteristics may influence sibling relationships. Brody et al. (1987) found that persistence, emotional intensity, and activity level were all related to patterns of sibling interaction, but that the specific relations depended on the sex and relative age of the children. Similarly, Stocker et al. (1989) found shyness, activity level, and sociability to be linked to competitive and cooperative behavior among siblings.

In the literature on the sibling relationships of children with disabilities, some work has examined the impact of the severity of disorder. This research has typically focused on the impact on the nondisabled child (e.g., Farber, 1959; Grossman, 1972; Simeonsson & McHale, 1981; Tew & Laurence, 1973), but some work suggests that higher levels of functioning are associated with greater warmth and competition between siblings (Begun, 1989) and with more symmetrical relationships (Stoneman, Brody, Davis, & Crapps, 1987).

Interestingly, relatively little work has examined how the characteristics of the sibling of the child with a disability may influence the relationship. Similarly, in the research on the relationships between siblings without disabilities, Stocker et al. (1989) were some of the few investigators to collect data on both children simultaneously. Even these investigators, however, did not try to determine how the characteristics of the two are related to one another and how such similarities or differences may influence the pattern of interactions. Social psychologists have long been aware of the influence of similarity (and perhaps complementarity) of characteristics in interpersonal attraction (Berscheid & Walster, 1978), but such models have not yet been applied to sibling relationships.

An Empirical Example

In a recent study (Lanthier & Furman, 1991), the author examined how personality characteristics of the children may be related to the quality of their sibling relationships. Fifty mothers and their two elementary school-age children completed Sibling Relationship Questionnaires and Porter and Cattell's (1975) Child Personality Questionnaire. Both the younger and older siblings' level of anxiety were positively associated with perceptions of conflict, and negatively associated with perceptions of warmth. Younger siblings' emotional toughness and neuroticism were positively related to complaints about rivalry, whereas the younger siblings' extroversion was inversely related to complaints about rivalry. Perhaps the most interesting pattern here was that the younger sibling's characteristics seemed to be a stronger predictor of the relationship qualities than the older sibling's characteristics were. Although not as consistent, some interactions between the pair's characteristics emerged as well. For example, similarity in introversion–extroversion was associated with warmth. That is, when both were introverted or when both were extroverted, the relationship was described as warm, but when one was introverted and the other extroverted, the relationship was usually not as close.

Developmental Status

Before closing this section, one characteristic of the children in particular warrants mentioning—developmental status. Interestingly, past literature has yielded relatively inconsistent findings. For example, Bigner (1974) found that the amount of power attributed to older siblings increased with the age of the subject, but Minnett, Vandell, and Santrock (1983) reported the opposite trend. Some studies, primarily case reports, have found increased warmth and decreased conflict with age (Cicirelli, 1982; Minnett et al., 1983; Ross & Milgram, 1982), but other studies have not found such systematic trends.

In the author's work, he and his colleagues examined third-, sixth-, ninth-, and twelfth-grade children's perceptions of their sibling relationships (Buhrmester & Furman, 1990). Relationships were rated as more egalitarian as the children grew older. Adolescents also reported less companionship, intimacy, and affection with their siblings than younger children did. Interestingly, ratings of conflict with younger siblings were relatively high at all age levels, but ratings of conflict with older siblings decreased with age.

Less is known about developmental changes in sibling relationships of mentally retarded children, although Stoneman et al. (1987) found that these relationships become less symmetrical with age. In any case, one would expect the developmental status of both children to influence their relationship markedly.

CONCLUDING COMMENTS

In this paper, the author outlines a series of themes that have characterized his own and others' research on sibling relationships between nondisabled children. Certainly, these themes are not the exclusive property of that field. The examples in this paper clearly indicate that similar work is being conducted in studies of sibling relationships of children with disabilities. It is hoped, however, that the discussion of these themes will encourage further thinking and research in these directions. Such work would be of mutual benefit to both fields.

For investigators interested in the sibling relationships of nondisabled children, studies of relationships with children with disabilities can provide an important extension of the models that the author and his colleagues have developed. One can determine if the models developed with garden variety sibling relationships are applicable to different populations. Such investigations can help find what sibling relationships are like when the two participants are very different and are treated quite differently. By taking these naturalistic opportunities to study phenomena that are relatively uncommon in sibling relationships between nondisabled children, researchers may discover new facets of sibling relationships. Such studies will help professionals who work with children understand these relationships and the processes underlying them in both typical and atypical populations.

It is hoped that investigators studying the sibling relationships of children with disabilities could also find such work beneficial. The initial studies of special or atypical populations often consist of comparisons between that population and a normal one. Such comparisons are certainly valuable, but other issues are important as well. The common idea underlying all the themes described here is that there is marked variation among sibling relationships. This is just as true of the sibling relationships of children with mental retardation, physical disabilities, and acute and chronic illness as it is of the sibling relationships of nondisabled children. Perhaps the discussion of these themes will trigger some work examining such variation.

Through mutual sharing, researchers can move toward an integrated study of sibling relationships. In a little-known but provocative paper, Donald Campbell (1969) described the scholarly and pragmatic pressures that lead investigators to form themselves into clusters or groups interested in the same topic. Although there is much merit in the collaboration that can occur as a result, he observed that two negative consequences are that some topics or points are left unstudied and that the different clusters have little to do with each other. The analogy he drew was to that of a fish with many scales clumped together in different spots, with little between them. He suggested that science would be more complete and integrated if we were each able to develop our own area of specialization—a fish scale that overlaps with others, but is not identical to them. Perhaps volumes such as this one can help us recognize our similarities and foster the process of dressing the fish.

REFERENCES

Allison, T.S., & Allison, S.L. (1971). Time out from reinforcement: Effect on sibling aggression. *The Psychological Record, 21,* 81–86.

Bank, S., & Kahn, M.D. (1982). *The sibling bond.* New York: Basic Books.

Beardslee, W.R. (1981). Self-understanding and coping with cancer. In G.P. Koocher & J.E. O'Malley (Eds.), *The Damocles syndrome: Psychosocial consequences of surviving childhood cancer* (pp. 144–163). New York: McGraw-Hill.

Begun, A.L. (1989). Sibling relationships involving developmentally disabled people. *American Journal of Mental Retardation, 93,* 566–574.

Berscheid, E., & Walster, E. (1978). *Interpersonal attraction* (2nd ed.). Reading, MA: Addison-Wesley.

Bigner, J.A. (1974). Second-borns' discrimination of sibling role concepts. *Developmental Psychology, 10,* 564–573.

Blackard, M.K., & Barsh, E.T. (1982). Parents' and professionals' perceptions of the handicapped child's impact on the family. *Journal of The Association for the Severely Handicapped, 7,* 62–70.

Bowlby, J. (1973). *Attachment and loss: Vol. 2. Separation.* New York: Basic.

Brody, G., Stoneman, Z., & Burke, M. (1987). Child temperament, maternal differential behavior and sibling relationships. *Developmental Psychology, 23,* 354–362.

Bryant, B.K., & Crockenberg, S.B. (1980). Correlates and dimensions of prosocial behavior: A study of female siblings with their mothers. *Child Development, 51,* 529–544.

Buhrmester, D., & Furman, W. (1990). Age differences in perceptions of sibling relationships during middle childhood and adolescence. *Child Development, 61,* 1387–1398.

Campbell, D.T. (1969). Ethnocentrism of disciplines and the fish-scale model of omniscience. In C.W. Sherif & M. Sherif (Eds.), *Interdisciplinary relationships in the social sciences* (pp. 328–348). Chicago: Aldine.

Cicirelli, V.C. (1982). Sibling influence throughout the lifespan. In M.E. Lamb & B. Sutton-Smith (Eds.), *Sibling relationships: Their nature and significance across the lifespan* (pp. 267–284). Hillsdale, NJ: Lawrence Erlbaum Associates.

Costanzo, P.R., & Woody, E.Z. (1985). Domain-specific parenting styles and their impact on the child's development of particular deviance: The example of obesity proneness. *Journal of Social and Clinical Psychology, 3,* 425–445.

Dunn, J., & Kendrick, S. (1981). Interaction between young siblings: Association with the interaction between mother and first-born. *Developmental Psychology, 17,* 336–343.

Farber, B. (1959). Effects of a severely mentally retarded child on family integration. *Monographs of the Society for Research in Child Development, 24*(2, Serial No. 71).

Fotheringham, J.B., & Creel, D. (1974). Handicapped children and handicapped families. *International Review of Education, 20,* 355–377.

Fowle, C. (1968). The effect of a severely mentally retarded child on his family. *American Journal of Mental Deficiency, 73,* 468–473.

Furman, W. (1984). Some observations on the study of personal relationships. In J.C. Masters & K. Yarkin Levin (Eds.), *Interfaces between developmental and social psychology* (pp. 15–42). New York: Academic Press.

Furman, W., & Buhrmester, D. (1985). Children's perceptions of the qualities of sibling relationships. *Child Development, 56,* 448–461.

Furman, W., & Giberson, R.S. (in press). Identifying the links between parents and their children's sibling relationships. In S. Shmuel (Ed.), *Close relationships in social–emotional development.* Norwood, NJ: Ablex.

Furman, W., Jones, L., Buhrmester, D., & Adler, T. (1989). Children's, parents' and observers' perceptions on sibling relationships. In P.G. Zukow (Ed.), *Sibling interaction across culture: Theoretical and methodological issues* (pp. 165–183). New York: Springer-Verlag.

Gabel, H., McDowell, J., & Cerreto, M.C. (1982). Family adaptation to the handicapped infant. In S.G. Garwood & R.R. Fewell (Eds.), *Educating handicapped infants: Issues in development and intervention* (pp. 455–494). Rockville, MD: Aspen Systems.

Gath, A. (1974). Sibling reactions to mental handicap: A comparison of the brothers and sisters of mongol children. *Journal of Child Psychology and Psychiatry, 15,* 187–198.

Gogan, J.L., & Slavin, L. (1981). Interviews with brothers and sisters. In G.P. Koocher & J.E. O'Malley (Eds.), *The Damocles syndrome: Psychosocial consequences of surviving childhood cancer* (pp. 101–111). New York: McGraw-Hill.

Gralicker, B., Fishler, K., & Koch, R. (1962). Teenage reactions to a mentally retarded sibling. *American Journal of Mental Deficiency, 66,* 838–843.

Grossman, F.K. (1972). *Brothers and sisters of retarded children.* Syracuse, NY: Syracuse University Press.

Katz, T.A., & Furman, W. (1990). *Mothers and sibling relationships.* Unpublished manuscript, University of Denver.

Lanthier, R.P., & Furman, W. (1991). *Stress and personality as predictors of sibling relationship dimensions.* Unpublished manuscript, University of Denver.

Lavine, M.B. (1977). An exploratory study of siblings of blind children. *Journal of Visual Impairment and Blindness, 71,* 102–197.

Leitenberg, H., Burchard, J.D., Burchard, S.M., Fuller, E.J., & Lysaght, T.V. (1977). Using positive reinforcement to suppress behavior: Some experimental comparisons with sibling conflict. *Behavior Therapy, 8,* 168–182.

MacKinnon, C.E. (1989). An observational investigation of sibling interactions in married and divorced families. *Developmental Psychology, 25,* 36–44.

McHale, S.M., & Gamble, W.C. (1987). Sibling relationships and adjustment of children with disabled brothers and sisters. *Journal of Children in Contemporary Society, 19,* 131–158.

McHale, S.M., & Gamble, W.C. (1989). Sibling relationships of children with disabled and nondisabled brothers and sisters. *Developmental Psychology, 25,* 421–429.

McHale, S.M., Gamble, W.C., & Pawletko, T.M. (1989, April). *Sibling relationships and adjustment in children with disabled and nondisabled brothers and sisters.* Paper presented at the meeting of the Society for Research in Child Development, Kansas City, MO.

McHale, S.M., & Pawletko, T.M. (1992). Differential treatment of siblings in two family contexts. *Child Development, 63,* 68–81.

Miller, N., & Cantwell, D.P. (1976). Siblings as therapists: A behavioral approach. *American Journal of Psychiatry, 133,* 447–450.

Miller, S.G. (1974). An exploratory study of sibling relationships in families with retarded children. *Dissertation Abstracts International, 35,* 2994B–2995B. (University Microfilm No. 74–26, 606).

Minnett, A.M., Vandell, D.L., & Santrock, J.W. (1983). The effects of sibling status on sibling interaction: Influence of birth order, age spacing, sex of child, and sex of sibling. *Child Development, 54,* 1064–1072.

Minuchin, S. (1974). *Families and family therapy.* Cambridge, MA: Harvard University Press.

O'Leary, K., O'Leary, D., & Becker, B. (1967). Modification of a deviant sibling interaction pattern in the home. *Behavior Research and Therapy, 5,* 113–126.

Olson, P.H. (1977). Insiders' and outsiders' views of relationships: Research studies. In G. Levinger & H.L. Rausch (Eds.), *Close relationships: Perspectives on the meaning of intimacy* (pp. 115–135). Amherst, MA: University of Massachusetts Press.

Porter, R.B., & Cattell, R.B. (1975). *Children's personality questionnaire handbook.* Champaign, IL: Institute for Personality and Ability Testing.

Powell, T.H., & Ogle, P.A. (1985). *Brothers and sisters: A special part of exceptional families.* Baltimore: Paul H. Brookes Publishing Co.

Price-Bonham, S., & Addison, S. (1978). Families and mentally retarded children: Emphasis on the father. *The Family Coordinator, 3,* 221–230.

Richey, L.S., Ysseldyke, J., Potter, M., Regan, R.R., & Grenner, J. (1981). *Teachers' attitudes and expectations for siblings of learning-disabled children.* (Research Report No. 39). Minneapolis: University of Minnesota Institute of Research on Learning Disabilities. (ERIC Document Reproduction Service No. 203613)

Ross, H.G., & Milgram, J.I. (1982). Important variables in adult sibling relationships. In M.E. Lamb & B. Sutton-Smith (Eds.), *Sibling relationships: Their nature and significance across the lifespan* (pp. 123–152). Hillsdale, NJ: Lawrence Erlbaum Associates.

Rowe, D.C., & Plomin, R. (1981). The importance of nonshared (E_1) environmental influences in behavioral development. *Developmental Psychology, 17,* 517–531.

Schreiber, M., & Feeley, M. (1965). Siblings of the retarded: A guided group experience. *Children, 12,* 221–225.

Simeonsson, R.J., & McHale, S.M. (1981). Review: Research on handicapped children: Sibling relationships. *Child: Care, Health and Development, 7,* 153–171.

Spinetta, J.J., & Mahoney, L.J. (1978). The child with cancer: Patterns of communication and denial. *Journal of Consulting and Clinical Psychology, 46,* 1540–1541.

Stocker, C., Dunn, J., & Plomin, R. (1989). Sibling relationships: Links with child temperament, maternal behavior, and family structure. *Child Development, 60,* 715–727.

Stoneman, Z., & Brody, G.H. (1984). Research with families of severely handicapped children: Theoretical and methodological considerations. In J. Blacher (Ed.), *Severely handicapped young children and their families: Research in review* (pp. 179–214). New York: Academic Press.

Stoneman, Z., Brody, G.H., Davis, C.H., & Crapps, J.M. (1987). Mentally retarded children and their older same-sex siblings: Naturalistic in-home observations. *American Journal of Mental Retardation, 92,* 290–298.

Tew, B., & Laurence, K.M. (1973). Mothers, brothers, and sisters of patients with spina bifida. *Developmental Medicine and Child Neurology, 15,* 69–76.

Zetlin, A.G. (1986). Mentally retarded adults and their siblings. *American Journal of Mental Deficiency, 91,* 217–225.

Zukow, P.G. (Ed.). (1989). *Sibling interaction across culture: Theoretical and methodological issues.* New York: Springer-Verlag.

CHAPTER 3

Ethnographic and Ecocultural Perspectives on Sibling Relationships

Thomas S. Weisner

Imagine a child of age 3, with developmental delays, with two siblings—an older sister and a younger brother. The delay is of uncertain origin and prognosis. The child has delays in speech, an odd gait and other motor problems, and does not seem able to sustain attention for very long. What is the single most important thing to know about this child and his or her siblings in order to understand the course of their lives together?

Of course there are many things that it would be important to know about the child with delays and his or her siblings: their age difference; their family circumstances; their IQs and neurological conditions; their temperaments; their parents' socioeconomic status; what schools they attend; what services they might receive; the nature of the interactional style between mother and child, or between siblings and child; the stimulation provided in the home; the emotional climate of the home, especially with regard to the delay and any stigma attached to the delay; their parents' beliefs about the delay; and many others. Each of these features is important and worthy of study, and every one of them has been identified as a significant influence on sibling relationships and child outcomes. However, the author would not select any one of them as being *the* most important. In the author's view, the single most important fact for a researcher to know is the *cultural place* in which the siblings are growing up.

This research has been supported by grants HD 19124, HD 11944, from 1985 to 1990, and currently by HD 19124-06, from NICHD (Prof. Ronald Gallimore, Principal Investigator).

The Department of Psychiatry and Biobehavioral Sciences at UCLA has also provided important support. I would like to thank Charlene Pease and Dr. Jenni Coots, who provided important assistance in data analysis, as well as Project CHILD field researchers Dr. Lucinda Bernheimer, Dr. Cathy Matheson, Sandra Kaufman, and Lori Stolze.

What if this sibling group grows up in South India, for instance (Nuckolls, in press a), perhaps in a Scheduled ("untouchable") caste, or in a Brahmin farming caste? In such cultural places, there is a possibility of marriage between certain categories of cousins, and siblings are involved in lifelong negotiations and alliances based on dowry and marriage arrangements. Furthermore, siblings' marriages and life chances often depend on the fate of one's brothers' and sisters' marriages (Kolenda, in press). In North India, a key to sibling relations is the obligation of brothers to act as "trustees" of their married sisters: a brother checks on the sister's well-being and her children's well-being, has her to his house for extensive visits, and brings her gifts. In Central India, joint families with large numbers of siblings prefer to have sets of brothers marrying sets of sisters. In South India, the possibility of marriage between the children of brother and sister (between 10% and 30% of marriages in parts of Sri Lanka and South India are between cross-cousins [McGilvray, 1988]) often leads to lifelong solidarity—or enmity. The greater the dowry, the greater the interest brothers have in their sister's household and children, and the more reciprocity there is between the households (deMunck, in press). In North India, brothers expect to remain together in joint households, and if they do not, they feel compelled to produce culturally acceptable accounts to explain why they cannot (Derne, in press).

Perhaps the siblings are growing up among the Maasai, a pastoral society, or among Bantu horticulturalists in East Africa; if so, the paths of boys and girls are going to be very different. The Maasai boys will spend years as warriors, protecting livestock in their natal communities; the girls will likely marry an older man who is senior to the warriors. In a village among the Bantu Abaluyia of Western Kenya, in which horticulture, livestock, migratory wage labor, and trade are the basis of the economy, older siblings will be caring for younger ones, and boys will inherit whatever land or other resources are available. The older siblings will also be expected to assist in the education and bridewealth payments of their younger siblings and their siblings' children (Weisner, 1987; Zukow, 1989).

Or the siblings may be living in Polynesia (Marshall, 1983; Ritchie & Ritchie, 1979), perhaps on one of the Tahitian islands (Levy, 1973), subsisting on horticulture, fishing, and remittances from emigrated relatives. If so, they will spend much of their time in multi-age groups of children that include both sexes, assisting in subsistence, and the boys may anticipate an extended, unsettled post-adolescence period. Sibling relationships are unusually important and culturally elaborated in Polynesia.

Or are the imagined siblings living in Oaxaca, Mexico, migrating back and forth to Los Angeles each year for work? Or in the Guatemalan highlands, growing maize and weaving cloth and ropes for sale (Loucky, 1988)? If so, to assist family survival, their workloads may be extraordinarily high, and they will experience long and uncertain separations from close kin, and may be educated in schools in different countries. Each of these cultural places would have a profoundly different influence on the "human careers" of the siblings (Goldschmidt, 1990).

Once the cultural place is mentioned as an influence shaping development, its importance is rarely gainsayed. However, the role of the cultural place is often given only tacit, rather than explicit, recognition. The power of the cultural place to influence sibling relationships is not widely considered in the actual practice of research, even though it may be recognized as theoretically or conceptually important.

In this chapter, the author first defines ecology and culture, then presents some examples of the roles of siblings in the East African cultural place, and the ways in which a disability might influence these roles. Next, the topic of ethnography is covered, as much of the knowledge about different cultural places around the world has come primarily from ethnographic studies. Then a set of 12 features that shape human development is outlined. This set of characteristics should be useful in comparing children and their families in every cultural place, and has already been proven useful in cross-cultural research. The author and his colleagues have recently applied them to the study of developmentally delayed children and their families in Los Angeles.

One of the findings of the work comparing sibling relationships in different cultures is that the sibling group is usually more important in non–Euro-American cultures. Residential and subsistence ties among siblings are typically stronger, and the importance of the sibling relationship is more culturally elaborated than it is in Euro-American countries. The beliefs and practices of Euro-American culture regarding siblings also influence the lives of delayed children and their siblings. Data suggest that Euro-American parental concerns about treating siblings equally and their reluctance to involve siblings in too many domestic and caregiving tasks shape the ways in which parents respond to siblings. Both of these concerns ("equal" treatment and "excessive" caregiving responsibilities) are unusual from a cross-cultural perspective.

ECOLOGY, CULTURE, AND ETHNOGRAPHY

The *place* in which development occurs includes the ecology and the locally adapted environment in which the siblings and their family live. The *culture* includes the meanings, beliefs, values, and conventional practices learned and shared by members of a community. These two together define the ecocultural (ecology + culture) place within which human development takes place. Super and Harkness (1980, 1986) have used the term "developmental niche" to describe this environment for the child. The "ecocultural" niche refers to the family and community environment, as well as the child's developmental niche.

The cultural side of the ecocultural niche, according to D'Andrade (1984) includes three elements: 1) *representational* knowledge about the world (how the world is represented in an organized schema); 2) *norms for action,* which come from and organize one's participating in institutions like the family or church; and 3) *meanings* and felt experience (which shape members' social construction of the world) (D'Andrade, 1984, p. 116). These are analytically useful distinctions, but in actual practice the elements are merged together. Ethnographic and qualitative methods are essential to the study of cultural meaning systems in everyday life, in which representational knowledge, norms, and experience must be understood historically.

It is also useful to distinguish ethnicity and culture. Ethnicity is a politically and historically negotiated status or label. Ethnic status is often based on racial characteristics, immigrant status, language differences, conquests of one people by another, or other forms of inequality. Ethnic categories are often imposed from outside, and in fact may not even be recognized as fully legitimate by the group so labelled. For instance, the category "blacks" in North America incorporates descendents of slaves, recent immigrants from the Caribbean or Africa, and many other widely different contemporary cultural communities. Categories like "Asians" or "Hispanics" similarly include quite divergent groups who had no say in their being categorized together. Historically, ethnicity is one way modern nation states divided or reclassified the peoples they incorporated, or the immigrants they took in. Although ethnicity is profoundly important to cultural careers, it is not identical to culture.

A task as broad as the study of the cultural place in which human development occurs requires a comprehensive, holistic analysis. This holistic view suggests that families are not hapless victims of their circumstances, and do not necessarily passively accept the ecocultural world around them. They are, rather, proactive. The conception of external social and ecological forces pressing on individuals from without has been replaced by a model of an interactive relationship between individual members of a culture and their ecocultural niche.

Knowledge of a variety of cultural places will present researchers with new and surprising responses and solutions to the common problems faced by all families and children. Lambert (1971 [also cited in Weisner, 1984]) studied the socialization of aggression in six cultures, and concluded that:

> . . . we are going to be delighted as we travel about the world. We are always going to find some facet of human personality or of personality organization which glows with a serene excellence that we have never met before. And lying below the fact of that fresh, though partial and perhaps even fleeting, excellence, is new knowledge about how to make some future generation (and its parents) better, more happy, or more free. (p. 61)

Every culture provides its members with possible pathways for their life careers—not only in the sense of work or employment careers, but also in the wider sense of the "human career" (Goldschmidt, 1990). The human career includes familial, spiritual, work-related, and other life paths that are open to members of a culture. Siblings in North America, as compared to those in other cultural places, for example, have a limited range of culturally available "sibling life careers" available to them in their relationships with one another. Each cultural place provides siblings with certain normative life careers with one another, which are intertwined with other life careers.

Sibling roles are a more important part of the cultural definition of personhood in many other cultural places than they are in the West. Marshall (1983) comments that for the Pacific region the ideal social relationship is the relation between siblings, more so than between parents and children, or husband and wife. One becomes, and continues to be, identified as a distinctive person based on collective and shared exchanges of social and material resources between siblings in many parts of South Asia (Marriott, 1976). Euro-American family theory and media emphasize parent–child and couple/romantic relationships as the cultural ideals. "Brotherly" or "sisterly" roles are not unimportant, but they are subsidiary to parent–child, spouse, or even friendship relationships. A developmentally delayed child's life course will be different if the child is growing up in a culture in which brotherly and sisterly responsibilities, roles, myths, songs, legends, financial security, and even co-residence are more culturally elaborated than those of couple or parent–child relationships.

ECOCULTURAL VARIATIONS IN SIBLINGS' LIVES

Sibling Relationships in Eastern Africa

Sibling relationships in many sub-Saharan African societies are characterized by extensive cultural elaboration, ties of marriage and economic inheritance, and a closely intertwined cultural career. Consider Goldschmidt's (1976) depiction of the Sebei of Uganda in the 1950s. Sebei siblings are concerned with territory and land, age and gerontocracy, and gender differences. Brothers, who are clansmen cooperating, as well as rivals fighting to secure scarce resources, have to remain living with each other throughout their lives. They look on each other as potentially dangerous foes, but also as essential allies, since they will have to remain interdependent: they share their inheritance of land, cattle, or other valuable resources; they may well assist in one anothers' marriages; they are central figures in their own and their children's initiation and other major rituals; and they may care for each other's children in their homesteads.

Goldschmidt describes these relationships between brothers as inherently ambivalent:

> . . . they are enjoined on all occasions to be friendly and cooperative and are, of course, fellow clansmen and hence tied into the system of mutual support, yet

they are also in direct competition. Fratricide is not an infrequent occurrence. Rivalry between brothers is endemic. . . .
The relation between brothers and sisters is also characterized by antagonism, for the brother is deeply concerned with the marriage of his sister and, along with the father, may seek to force a liaison on her on the basis of his desires rather than hers. . . . Sisters on the other hand, are not put into a rivalrous relationship over property. The only expression of strong bonds that we observed between siblings was between sisters. When they marry [which must be outside of their natal community, due to clan exogamy], they are separated, but they frequently visit and regularly give gifts of food to one another when they do so. (1976, p. 98)

The imagined siblings mentioned above, if they lived in East Africa, would participate in this complicated and ambivalent life-long relationship system. They would also be a part of a much larger group of half-siblings and cousins; they would spend time living in others' households, whether as visitors, workers, or as fostered children "lent out" for varied periods of time. Older sisters and cousins would be taking care of the delayed sibling the majority of the time, under the direction of the mother or other adults. Grandparents, aunts, the mother, older boys, and hired nurses would all be probable caregivers (Weisner, 1982; Weisner & Gallimore, 1977). Indeed, in these homesteads children are nearly as likely to receive nurturance and assistance from their brothers and sisters as they are from their mothers. For instance, Weisner (1987) presented data based on over 11,000 individually coded interactions among children and adults in Abaluyia homesteads in Western Kenya. Behavior observations, consisting of continuous 30-minute accounts of the stream of interaction between children, showed that 41% of girls ages 3–8 were involved in sibling care interactions either as charge or caregiver, as were 15.8% of boys.

This pattern of sibling caregiving is clear in this story of a 40-year-old woman in Uganda in the 1980s. She comes from a polygynous Baganda family consisting of the 4 wives of her father and 25 siblings and half-siblings. Polygyny among the Baganda requires joint sibling responsibilities and sharing of resources. Sibling relationships are based on gender hierarchy, cooperation of co-wives, and the economic base of both a male protector and provider and the wives' agricultural and trading labor (Kilbride & Kilbride, 1990). Older siblings act as surrogate parents:

> It was my elder brother, however, who was very strict [unlike this woman's father]. With [my brother] it was all study and no time for playing! My elder sister was responsible for me in school. She made me do all things like eating, studying, and dressing. (p. 206)

Other cultural places in East Africa can offer surprising alternatives to the customs and beliefs of our own. In a number of East African communities in the not-too-distant past, for example, siblings and cousins from age 3 or 4 to their early teenage years might have lived with other children in their lineage, in a hut shared with an elderly woman delegated by the community to train the children, to teach them proper domestic conduct, and particularly to instruct them in, and manage, their sexual education and experiences (Cohen & Atieno-Odhiambo, 1989).

Among the Nyakyusa of Tanzania (Wilson, 1963) in the 1930s and 1940s, groups of youth left their natal village, and built and moved into their own "age village." The boys continued to work in their fathers' fields but reduced their time spent herding cattle for their fathers. Their sisters remained behind in their fathers' village, where the older girls often lived together in large huts, sometimes with older women co-resident with them. The sisters often visited their brothers' villages. These age villages grew larger until the older boys began to marry and left to establish their own new families.

How would this have shaped the life of a developmentally delayed Nyakyusa child? His or her movement to an age village would probably have been postponed, but he or she would have visited, and perhaps eventually found a place within it. Because of the concentration of children of multiple ages living together, and their sense of responsibility for each other, the child would have had caregivers available. Some of the subsistence tasks that boys and girls were expected to do in these villages could have been performed by most delayed children. They would probably be integrated into the age village peer and sibling group as a natural part of the Nyakyusa siblings' ecocultural career.

Beliefs about the etiology, treatment, or cure of disabling conditions are complicated in East Africa, and can't easily be understood out of context. In contemporary circumstances, medical reasons might be invoked for the delay, and Western medical clinics might be involved and consulted. Peltzer and Ng'andu (1989, p. 117) interviewed traditional healers in Zambia, for instance, and found that even among this group the cause of disabilities in children was attributed to natural causes (e.g., organic conditions, poor diet, infections, and problems with parental care), as well as supernatural causes (e.g., witchcraft and sorcery, spirit aggression, or violations of taboos). Thus, families might spend time and resources investigating witchcraft or sorcery, as well as natural causes, as a possible cause of the child's condition. Scheer and Groce (1988) in a review of cross-cultural attitudes toward birth and disability, concluded that the ". . . belief in the linkage between evil spirits and/or parental misconduct and the birth of a disabled newborn appears widespread" (p. 28). This link between spirits and disability often involves an analysis of any changes in social status, or disruptions in social relationships, which might have directly caused the disability, or which are thought to be associated with witchcraft or sorcery performed by others. In the case of a woman who gave birth to a delayed child, pregnancy events would immediately be scrutinized as a possible cause of the delay. Here, again, are the Nyakyusa in the 1930s (Wilson, 1963):

> . . . a pregnant woman is believed to have some of the attributes of a witch. . . [but] a pregnant woman is not spoken of as a witch unless she harms someone by neglecting the taboos connected with her state. . . .
> . . . impotence, sterility, lingering illnesses including paralysis, and sickly children, are not uncommon; . . . the penalty of sin is believed often to be delayed. . . . Parents are thought to be punished by the sickness of their children. . . . (p. 95)

An African family in the societies which have been described would not use a term equivalent to "delay." Such a term suggests that a child can or will catch up. A delayed child would more likely be labelled as handicapped, sickly, or retarded. There would be no euphemisms, but, rather, a frank admission of the limited life career that a disability allows in the community (Edgerton, 1976; Hanks & Hanks, 1948). Nor would the child be exempt from teasing, bad treatment, and other forms of dominance and even exploitation because of the delay. Special or compensatory status for such children would be unlikely. Frank recognition, and even harsh treatment, however, would be accompanied by social support and peer assistance during childhood. In studies of dyadic interaction among sibling groups in Kenya, dominance, aggression, nurturance, and social support have also been found to be bound together (Edwards & Whiting, in press; Weisner, 1989b).

UNIVERSALS AND DIVERSITY IN CROSS-CULTURAL LITERATURE ON SIBLINGS AND DISABILITY

The cross-cultural research literature reveals universally shared themes, as well as diversity. For instance, the beliefs that disabilities have social causes or might be caused by some action of the parents, whether intentionally or inadvertently, are certainly not notions found only among the Nyakyusa and other non-Western societies. The idea that social disruptions must be linked to the birth of such children is found widely around the world. These ideas appear in some Western theologies, in fact, and were widespread in the United States at one time. Here, for instance, is a report "On the Causes of Idiocy" (the author's colleague, Professor Keith Kernan, very kindly provided this text) commissioned in Massachusetts and published in 1848:

> We regarded idiocy as a disease of society: as an outward sign of an inward malady. It was hard to believe it to be in the order of Providence that the earth should always be cumbered with so many creatures in the human shape, but without the light of human reason. . . . It appeared to us certain that the existence of so many idiots in every generation *must* be the consequence of some violation of the *natural laws;*— that where there was so much suffering there must have been sin. [emphasis in original] (Howe, Byington, & Kimball, 1848, p. vi)

Many parents of delayed children in Euro-American culture are also concerned over the deeper meaning of their child's condition, although certainly not sharing the specific language, ideology, or 19th century cast of mind of Howe et al. (Weisner, Beizer, & Stolze, 1991). Worry over what the mother might have done or not done to cause her child's delay is common. Although siblings in Africa certainly have a very different life career than those in western societies, this does not mean that there are not shared common human concerns as well.

There may well be universal problems that every culture has to resolve in its own way, such as the fact that there seem to be "haves versus have-nots," or weaker and stronger individuals, including those with disabilities, in all communities (Shweder & Bourne, 1991). There are also common social-structural features of sibling groups that can form the basis for comparative work across cultures (Weisner, 1989a), such as their size, hierarchy, birth order, and gender differences, the degree of shared inheritance and monetary interdependence among siblings, and the emotionally and structurally ambivalent relationships among siblings, which often combine intense attachment and feelings of resentment. Comparisons across cultural places, then, lead not only to understanding diversity and difference, but also to the discovery of common concerns of families and siblings, universals in interaction (Whiting & Edwards, 1988), and often surprising similarities in cultural concerns regarding siblings.

Specific evidence regarding universals and cultural differences from the cross-cultural record on disabilities and delays is unfortunately thin, and recent evidence is also scanty. Hanks and Hanks (1948) reviewed ethnographic data in the Human Relations Area Files on persons with disabilities. They suggested that the social participation in everyday life of persons with disabilities (e.g., in work roles, some form of education, and community participation) is greater where cultural standards for success are relative, not absolute; where achievement criteria include individual ability, and not just status; and where economic living standards are higher. Scheer and Groce (1988) however, want to revise these generalizations. They argue that the treatment of people with disabilities is more variable across cultures than such summaries of "traditional cultures" would suggest. They report on a wide range of roles for persons with disabilities, including those that can be more supportive and incorporate individuals with disabilities into social life in traditional cultures.

Bowe (1990) points out that those in the field should be paying increasing attention to disability in cultural places throughout the non-Western world, if only because most of the world's persons with disabilities live there. Non-Western countries are home to over 80% of the world's people with disabilities and that figure is rising. The larger mean–completed family sizes in these countries suggests a potential for extensive family care and support. Since the mean age in such countries is so much lower than that in the West, and since childhood disabilities are more common than adult disabilities, the numbers of children with disabilities in these countries is far higher than that in the West.

More empirical research on ethnic and cross-cultural variations in the conditions and treatment of people with disabilities is needed, and this work will need to combine ethnographic methods with other systematic approaches (see Serpell, Nabuzoka, & Lesi, 1989, and Super, 1987 for two recent collections). The same considerations also apply to the need for increased understanding of ethnic groups in the United States.

ETHNOGRAPHIC METHODS IN THE STUDY OF THE CULTURAL PLACE

Ethnographic methods are essential to the study of the cultural place and the cultural careers of siblings. Ethnographic work involves the use of qualitative, holistic fieldwork methods—although complementary methods such as systematic behavior observations, structured interviews, or the use of text from folklore and myth are also used. The goal of ethnographic research is to describe and understand the cultural place. Ethnographic methods include the direct observation and interviewing—in naturalistic settings, and over long periods of time—of families in local communities. An ethnographic description, for example, should allow the reader to situate the sibling with developmental delays in a cultural place, and to predict the effects of that place on his or her life career. A good definition of a valid ethnographic account of a cultural place, or an activity going on in it, is that a researcher or visitor could read the account and go there and participate reasonably well in everyday life—or at least know what questions to ask in order to participate more competently. Ethnography describes a cultural place, provides an understanding and interpretation of that place, and assists in the reader's real or imagined performance in it.

Ethnographic research features participant observation and qualitative methods, and takes seriously the participants' own views of their cultural worlds. But ethnography is not limited to such an approach, as a perusal of any of the methods texts or articles in the field confirms. As with any other methodological approach in the social sciences, ethnographic research has an extensive literature covering all of the standard topics of concern to any methodology (Agar, 1980; Bernard, 1988; Edgerton & Langness, 1974; Levine, Gallimore, Weisner & Turner, 1980; Lofland & Lofland, 1984; Naroll & Cohen, 1970; Pelto & Pelto, 1978; Spradley, 1979, 1980; Werner & Schoepfle, 1987a, 1987b) including proven systematic ways to assess the reliability and bias of qualitative data (Miles & Huberman, 1984).

Ethnographic work often involves a sustained, long-term approach to research, with intense personal involvement by the researcher. This often makes the ethnographer a participant in events and an active constructor of the data being collected. Choices implicit in other methods are made explicit in ethnographic work. The buzzing confusion and complexity of everyday events come to the fore; neat analytical categories are tested by this intense exposure to varied, real activities. The meaning and interpretation of events is more accessible to the researcher. These characteristics of ethnographic work help make unique contributions to the study of human development, including the study of children with disabilities and their relationships with siblings.

Ethnographic work, like all methods, requires a complex set of skills that has been described in the literature of the field (Levine et al., 1980). These include managing one's fieldwork role, various note-taking skills, coding techniques for qualitative data, the use of field data recording techniques for systematic observation and sampling, the ability to use varying interviewing techniques, managing the memory requirements of field work, unique ethical and subject-protection issues, techniques for optimizing reliability and validity in field research, and strategies for writing and presenting ethnographic data. There is also evidence that such skills can be trained and improved, just as can other kinds of knowledge and techniques for doing research, such as test administration, selecting experimental designs, or clinical skills (Levine et al., 1980).

Ethnographic and qualitative methods have been widely used in research on siblings in non-Western cultures (Leiderman & Leiderman, 1977; Marshall, 1983; Nuckolls, in press; Weisner & Gallimore, 1977; Whiting & Whiting, 1975), as well as in Western societies (Dunn & Kendrick, 1982; Dunn & Plomin, 1990; Mendelson, 1990). Such methods have also been effectively used in work with families and siblings of children with disabilities (Brody & Stoneman, 1986; Crnic, Friedrich, & Greenberg, 1983; Edgerton, 1967, 1984; Langness & Levine, 1986; Lobato, 1983; Simeonsson & McHale, 1981; Stoneman & Brody, 1987). This literature is rich in multiple methods, including clinical and case materials, naturalistic observations and home visits, open-ended interviews, the use of literature and biography, and other rich qualitative techniques. The techniques of ethnography, naturalistic work, and qualitative data collection are widely accepted, used, and appreciated in this field.

EPISTEMOLOGICAL STATUS OF ETHNOGRAPHIC RESEARCH

Qualitative, ethnographic methods are complementary with other methods in the social sciences. The literature in the disabilities field illustrates this fact. However, the prevailing discourse elsewhere in the social sciences regarding methods does not make the complementary nature of ethnographic work clear.

Qualitative research is typically opposed to its presumed opposite, quantitative research. Naturalistic research is often paired with its presumed opposite: experimental research. Comparative research is contrasted with its assumed opposite of monocultural work. It is ironic that the terms of discourse and the cultural categories often used to define ethnographic as compared to other methods are part of the problem with placing ethnographic and qualitative cultural research within the social sciences. These conventional methodological dichotomies, however common they are in everyday parlance, are neither accurate nor useful. There is a different way to think about qualitative methods—a way that retains some important distinctions, but also focuses on their actual use in research contexts, rather than their presumed epistemological differences.

Quantitative versus Nominal Measurement

For example, the opposite of quantitative is nominal, not qualitative; that is, the opposite of quantitative measurement, which uses ranked categories, is nominal measurement, using unranked or unrankable categories. The term "quantitative" refers to a certain level of measurement, not to any necessary epistemology or general method. This distinction points toward the question of use: does one want nominal measurement, or other levels of measurement, for a particular research purpose?

Quantification thus bears no necessary or privileged relationship to positivism or to the generation of theory, for instance. In fact, Glaser and Strauss (1967, p. 9), in *Grounded Theory*, argue that the distinction is "useless for the generation of theory." In any case, ethnographic studies can and do routinely include statements regarding quantitative differences, in the sense of rank-ordered differences between people, behavior, and cultural beliefs. For instance, adults in an African clan are found to more often tell folktales to children than to one another, and adults in another culture rarely engage in co-equal question-framed discourse with children. Siblings in societies in which the scarce resources necessary for survival are jointly owned remain more socially interconnected than siblings in societies without such ownership patterns, and so on.

Qualitative/Holistic versus Particularistic Methods

Similarly, the opposite of qualitative work is not quantitative, but rather particularistic research. Qualitative work attempts to understand the whole of something; holism and qualitative work are close in meaning. (Of course, holism is the ideal; no single method—not even ethnography or quantitative models—allows the researcher to grasp the whole of a problem.) The goal is to understand and describe all the essential elements of a culture, a person, a community. Particularistic work, on the other hand, attempts to study only a part of something, to understand some discrete element or elements of the person or community.

Naturalistic versus Contrived Research

Similar semantic problems occur with terms like "naturalistic" field research. The opposite of naturalistic is not the usually associated term, experimental, but rather controlled or contrived research. Naturalistic field research focuses on the naturally occurring activities of everyday life as the locus of study, and does not actively attempt to intervene in, or structure these activities. Contrivance refers to explicit manipulation of situations for the purpose of inferring cause, or gaining an understanding of processes.

Field workers in ethnographic situations, of course, are not without influence on those they study, and vice versa. These influences include the historical circumstances of the study; the reciprocal roles and expectations of researcher and participants in the research; the discourse structure of the research interview; the mutual construction of the research process by both participants and researchers, and so forth. There are many ways to control for bias and reflexivity in ethnographic fieldwork. Miles and Huberman (1984) present a particularly good account of this topic, including lists of ways to control or understand such influences.

Experimental versus Correlational Designs in Research

The opposite of experimental designs is not naturalistic, but rather *correlational* designs. In correlational designs, the researcher attempts to make sense of "a cloud of correlated events to which we as human observers give meaning," to use Sandra Scarr's phrase (1985, p. 502). In correlational research, understanding results ultimately comes through the interpretation of patterns and processes, and not through causal proof. (Of course, correlations may be used in the analysis of experimental designs, and so assist in causal inferences.) In the great majority of cross-cultural work, understanding comes through correlation and interpretation, not through true causal experiments.

Ethnography and Comparative Research

Ethnographic research done in another cultural place always includes a comparison, whether explicit or implicit, with one's own cultural setting. Ethnographic work has the characteristic of forcing an awareness of the power of ecocultural factors, factors that would otherwise not be mentioned, or would be "controlled for" by focusing on individual differences within a single cultural community. Ethnographic research done in North American cultural settings, even if not directly culturally comparative, should equally strongly bring into explicit awareness the power of the cultural place. In this sense, there is no semantic opposite to comparative ethnographic research; *all* research methods have an implicit or explicit comparative frame. Ethnographic research simply brings that frame more clearly to the foreground.

ASSESSING THE CULTURAL PLACE: THE ECOCULTURAL NICHE AND FAMILIES WITH CHILDREN WITH DEVELOPMENTAL DELAYS

The Ecocultural Niche[1]

Ethnographic methods, along with other complementary methods, then, are important in assessing the cultural place. The belief that the cultural place or social setting around a child and family is a powerful influence on his or her development is, of course, a long-standing one in the social sciences (e.g., Bronfenbrenner, 1979). One version of this belief comes from *ecocultural* theory, which is derived from the psychocultural model developed by John and Beatrice Whiting (1975; B. Whiting, 1976, 1980; B. Whiting & Edwards, 1988) and their students and associates (LeVine, 1977; Munroe, Munroe, & Whiting, 1981; Super & Harkness, 1980, 1986; Weisner, 1984).

Ecocultural theory emphasizes that a major adaptive task for each family is the construction and maintenance of a daily routine through which families organize and shape their children's activity and development. The activities of the everyday routine create opportunities for development-sensitive interactions on which development partly depends. The conception of development-sensitive interactions and their activity contexts are derived from several sources, including the concept of behavior settings (B. Whiting, 1980; Whiting & Edwards, 1988), and the ideas of Vygotsky (1978), including his notion of the zone of proximal development, as described in recent research (Gallimore & Goldenberg, in press; Rogoff, 1990; Tharp & Gallimore, 1988; Weisner and Gallimore, 1985; Weisner, Gallimore, & Jordan, 1988; Wertsch, 1985; Wertsch, Minick, & Arns, 1984).

The everyday routines and the development-sensitive interactions occurring within them do not exist in a social vacuum; they are shaped by the surrounding ecocultural niche. A list of ecocultural features specific to families of children with developmental delays has been presented elsewhere (Gallimore, Weisner, Kaufman, & Bernheimer, 1989), and in summary form in Table 1. This list is adapted from a cross-cultural review of such features (Weisner, 1984). The features in Table 1 were gathered from field notes, ethnographic observations, and interviews with families with young developmentally delayed children.

---

[1]The following section is adapted and/or excerpted in part from several sources: Gallimore, Weisner, et al., in press; Gallimore, Weisner, Kaufman, and Bernheimer, 1989; Nihira, Weisner, and Bernheimer, in press; Weisner, 1984; Weisner and Gallimore, 1985; Weisner, Nihira, and Bernheimer, 1989. In these publications, we have outlined the ecocultural approach to the study of human development, with special reference to families with developmentally delayed children.

Through their management of daily routines, and the activities included in them, families can affect the impact of their ecocultural niche on children's activity and development. To do so, they use whatever resources are available to arrange their daily life, a process guided by their values and limited by ecological and other constraints. From this mix of constraints, resources, and values, families attempt to construct a sustainable, meaningful, and coherent everyday routine. The activities that this everyday routine of life comprises are the best, clearest, most immediate illustration of what the cultural place is, and how it is directly experienced by families and children.

Establishing this routine requires families to make many accommodations, (Bernheimer, Gallimore, & Weisner, 1990; Gallimore et al., 1989; Weisner et al., 1991), a process common to all families. They adapt, exploit, counterbalance, and respond to the many competing and sometimes contradictory forces that influence their everyday routine. Accommodation activity occurs frequently, although it may occur more during some periods of family life than others, and the level and focus of activity varies. Accommodations can be made in one or more ecocultural niche features (see Table 2 for ethnographic examples of accommodations at each level of the ecocultural niche).

Ecocultural Data and Families with Children with Developmental Delays: Project CHILD

The characteristics of the ecocultural niche in Tables 1 and 2 that are specific to families with delayed children come from a longitudinal study of 102 families with delayed children in the Los Angeles, California area (Project CHILD) (Gallimore et al., 1989). This longitudinal study focused on families with young children who exhibited developmental delays of unknown or uncertain cause (Bernheimer & Keogh, 1982, 1988; Gallimore, Weisner, Nihara, Keogh, Bernheimer, & Mink, 1983). The families in the cohort each had a child who had been judged to be developmentally delayed by a professional or an agency. Children were excluded from the sample if they were known to have chromosomal abnormalities and/or genetic conditions associated with mental retardation, or if the delay was associated with either known prenatal drug or alcohol usage, or with postnatal neglect or abuse.

Developmental delay is a term of relatively recent vintage, and it lacks definitional specificity (Bernheimer & Keogh, 1986). It is essentially a nonspecific clinical term with less ominous overtones for the future than "retarded." Although some children with early delays "catch up," the majority continue to lag behind age norms on standardized tests of development and cognition, and the majority are placed in special education classes once they enter school (Bernheimer & Keogh, 1988).

One hundred and three children from 102 families were recruited into the cohort for Project CHILD. Seventy-three different agencies in the greater Los

Table 1. Examples of representative ecocultural features, from interview and ethnographic data on 102 Euro-American families with children with developmental delays, age 3–4

1. **Family subsistence and financial base**
   a. Employment history of parents
   b. Hours worked and flexibility of hours
   c. Tenure and security of employment, stability & regularity of income sources
   d. Level of employment, occupational rank
   e. "Job" vs. "career" vs. "calling"
   f. Work done at home, or very near home
   g. Amount of unearned income
   h. Equity available to family
   i. Extent of self-direction of work, complexity or organization of work, control over work process or product (Kohn, 1977)

2. **Accessibility of health and educational services**
   a. Distance from home to employment, services, etc.
   b. Means and cost of transportation available and used
   c. Schedule juggling, problems in access (hours open, timing, family separation/integration)
   d. Flexibility of services (hours, location, etc.)
   e. Required or voluntary parent-group participation (as part of child services or otherwise)
   f. Child care provided in home for child by outside professionals
   g. Role of Regional Center for identified DD children

3. **Home and neighborhood safety and convenience**
   a. Yard vs. no yard, fencing, neighborhood play areas and accessibility for child
   b. Architectural issues, house safety and convenience (e.g., space available, one or two stories), interior organization and design, childproofing
   c. Neighborhood safety measures perceived by parents, judged by observers, and assessed by city statistics
   d. Use of neighborhood places and services by child and family (cf. Medrich et al., 1982)

4. **Domestic task and chore workload (excluding childcare) and family division of labor**
   a. Chore and task inventory: who does these, frequency and timing, level of family concern over work and cleanliness, etc.
   b. Absolute workload (number of persons in family, time spent, etc.)
   c. Perceived workload pressures on parents and children
   d. Complexity of chores and who does them, ages at which children take on work with responsible, self-managed sequences of tasks (Nerlove et al., 1974)
   e. Task sharing, complementarity, specialization of roles
   f. Exclusivity of work, or available alternatives to person with primary responsibility
   g. Children's work outside home (if any)
   h. Personnel available in family for aid (family size and composition, non-kin members)

5. **Childcare tasks**
   a. Personnel available and used (parents, grandparents, other kin, siblings, friends, neighbors)
   b. Number and variety of specific childcare jobs
   c. Amount of care and supervision time daily, degree of direct responsibility, control and monitoring required (Weisner & Gallimore, 1977)
   d. Additional childcare due to particular DD child's problems (vs. routine care for other children)
   e. Specialized settings or interactions created by child's problems (e.g., program requirements, reading, special babysitting skills)
   f. Extent of specialized *instrumental* childcare jobs, vs. *social* involvements, or training, etc.

(continued)

Table 1. (*continued*)

6. **Children's playgroups**
   a. Age, sex, and kinship category of playmates, including family, kin, and neighborhood groups
   b. Frequency of participation in playgroups
   c. Parent-organized and created playgroups; frequency, type, and hassle involved in participation in such groups
   d. Extent of parents' and/or older siblings' structuring of and intervention in peer play groups, degree of supervision and monitoring

7. **Marital role relationships**
   a. Quality of couple roles (companionate/intimate, degree of role separation, sharing of decisionmaking, domains of control and responsibility)
   b. Degree of task complementarity (fixed-role or shared functioning styles)
   c. Degree of socioemotional involvement and sharing in decisions involving DD child
   d. Decisionmaking style

8. **Networks and organizational involvement**
   a. Formal groups (church, organizations, parents' groups, etc.)
   b. Informal contacts (neighbors, kin, friends, casual contacts with professionals such as chats after school, etc), parents' contacts with other parents of children with disabilities
   c. Degree of instrumental vs. socioemotional involvement with such groups
   d. Degree of support by groups vs. aid given to others in group

9. **Role of mother and father in childcare**
   a. Degree of participation (see tasks, marital role, and childcare data)
   b. Organizational involvement in facilitating child care
   c. Quality of involvement with spouse re DD child (dominant, co-equal, supportive, avoidant)
   d. Non-biological father involved in home, roles of alternate male caregivers
   e. Focus of father involvement with DD child (instrumental, supervision and management, recreational, emotional, etc.)
   f. Sibling and other nonparental care replacing or complementing parental care

10. **Sources of child cultural influence**
    a. Overall TV viewing, games, organized sports and activities, family cultural activities, etc.
    b. Extent of parental management, control in presentation of information for child

11. **Sources of parental information and goals**
    a. Books, lectures, training, classes, required parent groups
    b. Special job, interest, or status giving access to information (e.g., mother is an RN and knows about programs; father knows psychologist in the field)
    c. Variety of alternative conceptions of treatment, etiology, etc., available to family (megavitamins, special programs, etc.); parents' level of awareness of ideas and developments regarding developmental delay.

12. **Community heterogeneity**
    a. Variety of social and cultural views of developmental delay, behavior and attitudes toward disabilities, etc. (see previous section)
    b. Social and cultural views and attitudes toward conventional success or achievement in community, the value of education, etc.
    c. Diversity of local community as a reference point for child's status, e.g., community is homogeneous and hence, child is unique, child significantly stands out on some dimensions and not others (appearance, speech, movement, cognitive ability, etc.); importance of these dimensions in the community.

From Gallimore, R., Weisner, T.S., Kaufman, S.Z., and Bernheimer, L.P. (1989). The social construction of ecocultural niches: Family accommodation of developmentally delayed children. *American Journal of Mental Retardation, 94*(3), 216–230; reprinted by permission.

Table 2. Examples of major accommodations across 12 ecocultural domains made by Euro-American families to children with developmental delays ages 3–4 and 6–7

1. **Family subsistence and financial base**
   a. Mother stayed home because child "needed" her, later went back to work to afford speech therapy.
   b. Father turned down contract for third year working abroad, in part to get child services in Los Angeles.
2. **Accessibility of health and educational services**
   a. Mother drives child an hour each way to intervention program, waits at grandmother's house while child is in program.
   b. Parents take time from work to allow for trips to doctor; arrange schedule "to the minute" so mother and father split responsibility for transportation—transfer child in the middle of the route.
3. **Home and neighborhood safety and convenience**
   a. Parents plan to move to larger house to accommodate wheelchair; father built special chairs and tables.
   b. Home is childproofed, nothing breakable; child's room allows for constant monitoring.
4. **Domestic task and chore workload for family**
   a. Mother put less priority on house and housework, higher priority on helping child.
   b. Mother gets up at 4 A.M. to do laundry, housework, has no paid help.
5. **Childcare tasks**
   a. Older sisters voluntarily assist—mother does not mobilize help outside family circle.
   b. Complex job assignments for childcare assumed by father, mother, grandmother, etc.
6. **Child playgroups and peers**
   a. Child may play only inside with sibling and sibling's friends, not outside with neighbor children
   b. Child plays well with siblings and mother also arranges for a playgroup in the neighborhood
7. **Marital role relationships**
   a. Father left family partially because he could not accept child with delays.
   b. Parents make all decisions jointly (e.g., parents sleep separately for 6 months due to child's sleeping problems).
8. **Social support**
   a. Extensive support networks are used (e.g., relatives, parents, church members, boy scouts).
   b. Mother lives rent-free with grandparents; grandfather helps teach child.
9. **Father's role**
   a. Father takes over domestic workload on weekends, as he commutes long distance and has long working hours during the week.
   b. Father quit job and now works out of home so he can be available to supervise childcare.
   c. Father's role is "breadwinner," father leaves all decisions regarding DD child to mother.
10. **Sources of child cultural influence**
    a. Mother feels sitter uses poor communication patterns with child, so trained sitter to use new communication patterns.
    b. Mother hired Montessori teacher for child and two others, for in-home school

(continued)

Table 2. (*continued*)

11. **Sources of parental information and goals**
    a. Father's former girlfriend is a speech therapist, led family to transfer child to her clinic.
    b. Grandmother is an RN; grandfather is a special educator; mother gets advice from former special education teacher.
12. **Community heterogeneity that influences family**
    a. Mother uses contacts with Native American groups for alternative treatment methods.
    b. Euro-American family lives in mostly Afro-American neighborhood; child stands out, but seems accepted.

From Gallimore, R., Weisner, T.S., Kaufman, S.Z., and Bernheimer, L.P. (1989). The social construction of ecocultural niches: Family accommodation of developmentally delayed children. *American Journal of Mental Retardation, 94*(3), 216–230; reprinted by permission.

Angeles metropolitan area assisted in the assembly of the cohort. Public schools and private intervention programs constituted two-thirds of the cooperating agencies. Only 5% of an original pool of 313 children were not included due to self-selection (i.e., the parents declined to participate, or the agency "decided" that the parents would not be interested). All the remaining cases initially mentioned or referred who did not eventually participate in the study did not participate because they did not meet the screening criteria. This suggests that selection bias was at an acceptable level of 5%.

At entry, the mean child chronological age (CA) was 41.8 months (standard deviation $[SD]=6.2$; range=32–55). The mean Gesell Developmental Quotient (DQ) was 72.32 ($SD=15.97$; range=38–117). All but 18 of the children had DQs below 90, and all 103 had significant delays in one or more areas (motor, speech, behavior, or cognition) in spite of some relatively high DQs. 58.3% of the children were boys.

The 102 families in the study cohort consisted predominantly of married, middle-class couples in their thirties; however, there was a wide range of variation and heterogeneity despite this central tendency, as seen in Table 3.

Ecocultural Influences in Families with Children with Developmental Delay_is

Ecocultural features of the families in Project CHILD were significantly related to children's developmental status, behavioral characteristics, and families' accommodations to their delayed children. For instance, the author and his colleagues have developed a psychometrically-based Ecocultural Scale (ECS) of 127 items (Weisner, Nihira, & Bernheimer, 1989). This scale is based on factor-analytically derived measures of family values and goals and ecocultural resources and constraints. This scale is significantly related to children's developmental scores (DQ), as well as other measures of proximal home environment, such as the Caldwell scale (Nihira, Weisner, & Bernheimer, in press). The author and his colleagues have also created systematic

Table 3. Sample description at entry

	Percent	Frequency
Marital status		
Parents married and living together	73.8	76
Separated/divorced	12.6	13
Single, never married	6.8	7
Divorced and remarried	2.9	3
Widowed	1.9	2
Mother's age		
Under 24 years of age	8.9	9
25–34 years of age	64.4	65
35–50 years of age	24.8	25
51 or more years of age	2.0	2
Unknown	2.0	2
Father's age		
Under 24 years of age	4.4	4
25–34 years of age	49.5	45
35–50 years of age	39.6	36
51 or more years of age	6.6	6
Unknown	11.8	12
Family annual income		
Under $10,000	9.8	10
$10,000–$19,999	7.8	8
$20,000–$29,999	17.6	18
$30,000–$49,999	34.3	35
$50,000–$74,999	16.7	17
$75,000–$100,000	7.8	8
Over $100,000	3.0	3
Missing	3.0	3
Number of siblings		
No siblings	15.5	16
1 sibling	53.4	55
2 siblings	22.3	22
3 siblings	7.8	8
4 siblings	1.0	1

measures of accommodations, and found that accommodation is related to the extent of the child's impact on the family's daily routine, and is affected by parental workload, socioeconomic status, and career orientations. Accommodation is unrelated to child DQ (Gallimore et al., in press). Parents' religious orientations also corresponded to a sense of "peace of mind" regarding their efforts (Weisner et al., 1991).

These studies show that the cultural place, as captured through the use of ethnographic field notes, interviews, and psychometrically developed scales such as the ECS, significantly influenced the CHILD families and their delayed children's developmental courses. Naturally, the range of variation in the single cultural place studied by Project CHILD (Euro-Americans in the Los Angeles area) does not begin to approach what would be found if additional samples were included—such as, for example, the different ethnic groups in North America, or other cultural samples from around the world. The possibilities for undertaking such systematic comparative work with both ethnographic and other methods are exciting.

Cultural Beliefs and the Siblings of Children with Delays: Ideas About Equality and Task Allocation

Recall that the cultural place exerts its influence on siblings by providing models for a cultural career as a sibling, and that being a sibling is, in turn, intertwined with other cultural careers. The parents in Project CHILD had a variety of ideas about sibling roles and cultural careers. Naturally, the ecocultural circumstances of each family in Project CHILD influenced sibling relationships with their delayed child—features such as workload, family size, age and sex of the sibling group, blended families and step-siblings, and others. But the beliefs and concerns of parents were also influential in how they accommodated their delayed children.

The following excerpts from extended interviews with families with developmentally delayed children age 3–4 or 6–7 illustrate how parents used such cultural beliefs and concerns. Two factors in particular seemed especially important to many of the parents in the study, and contrast with the parental concerns in other cultural places: 1) the importance of equal treatment of each child, and 2) low expectations for caregiving and domestic help by older siblings. Concern over equality of treatment is not as salient elsewhere in the world, and siblings are more often expected to assist the parents and one another.

Equality of Treatment One of the most often mentioned and deeply felt cultural beliefs is that each child should be treated equally or equivalently by the parents. Fifty-four percent of all CHILD families mentioned their concern over the equality of treatment of the children in their families—the second highest ranking (out of 18 such concerns that were coded) at age 3–4 and the 7th highest at age 6–7. The predominant theme regarding equality was the parents' concerns that they were not giving the typically developing siblings enough attention or resources, as compared to the delayed child, even though they felt that they should. Most parents' cultural assumption is that individual attention to each child is essential and should be equivalent according to some calculation, and parents struggle to achieve this.

Some parents have developed strategies to achieve equality of treatment by calibrating the time allocation, spending money, or stimulation and "quality time" spent with each child. Others recognize that they do not treat their children equally, but rationalize or explain this away in a variety of ways. Here are some data from ethnographic field notes, case summaries, and interview materials that illustrate these kinds of concerns:

> The delayed child in this family has a brother 2 years younger. "The mother is very concerned about not giving equal time to the younger brother; she wants to spend more time with the younger brother when the target child enters full-time school."

Another mother reports that she "tries to equalize money, time and activities for both children."

In another family, the younger sibling is going to be given piano lessons, and the mother is going to give the delayed child music lessons too, "to show that the delayed child is equally important."

Parents in another family try to equalize time each evening by splitting up—one goes with the delayed child, the other with the 6 1/2-year-old older brother. The parents continued doing this over 4 years of the study period.

The mother in another case was told that when her high-hassle, temper-tantruming delayed child acts out, she should strap the child into a car seat in the house. The mother, however, decides to do the same with the younger brother, so that she will "treat them the same."

One of the striking features of these examples is that the concerns match those of the Western cultural place. Euro-American parents did not easily accept, without question or guilt, the inequalities and (perceived) lost opportunities of the normal sibling due to their also having a delayed child. The frequent need to treat their children very differently clashed with their beliefs regarding equality and children's need for freedom and independence. Nor did the ecocultural circumstances of their daily lives make it very easy to live by their ideals of equality; parents often had to undertake significant accommodation efforts to try and attain this goal of equal treatment. The cultural value of equality of treatment of each sibling does not in itself prevent parents from rethinking the issue and making accommodations—but it does make these accommodations difficult and troubling for many.

Caregiving and Domestic Tasks of Siblings The Euro-American cultural expectation is that older siblings should not have too onerous a burden in caring for their younger siblings, nor do too many domestic chores. Many of the parents in the CHILD study worried about their children having too much work to do. Mentions of caregiving responsibilities—either as a burden and a concern, or as a part of sibling interactions—ranked 4th out of 18 rated concerns both at age 3–4 and 6–7. Twenty-five percent of the families of children of age 3–4 mentioned this, and 37% of those with children of age 6–7.

Parents in one family pay teenage sisters of the delayed child (ages 16 and 12) to babysit "so that they will not feel that it is an imposition on them." The mother says that it is harder to get her two daughters through their teenage years than it is to manage her delayed child, in part due to conflicts over such responsibilities.

A mother says that the older sister ". . . is very responsible for her age, and it makes her heart ache to realize that her childhood is being lost or stifled. . . . " [Mother's expectations are that the older sister should not caretake the delayed child, and that it is a deep loss to the sister to have done so. . . .]

In another case, parents do not expect child care from the older sibs of the delayed child, and state that they do not expect them to take care of the delayed child when grown. "Mother does not expect help with babysitting on a regular basis . . . there is less emphasis, as well, on sibs caring for the child later as an adult."

> An older sister in another family is a "typical teenager"—not rude, just focusing on her own activities. She is pleasant to the family, but spending time in her room and with her friends. As the older sister, she seems to lead a separate life. [The expectation here is that early teens lead their *own* lives, and are not expected to provide caretaking or other domestic assistance.]
>
> Another case has a mother who does not expect help from three older siblings because ". . . Mother does not have the energy to ride herd on them after dealing with the target child." [The expectation is that mother has to ride herd in order to have any sibling cooperation.]
>
> The older brother is very angry and frustrated with the delayed child's high-hassle behaviors, and that "he has to give in too often" to keep the peace. The parents are very worried about this . . . the parents do not think that the older child should be the one to provide nurturance, act prosocially and responsibly towards younger child—at least not too often, since it might be bad for the older child.

But not every parent displayed concerns over equality or domestic work, as the next two cases suggest.

> The delayed child in this family has two sisters who are 4 and 6 years older. The mother offers the sisters a choice: you can take care of the house, or do Doman-Delacato method patterning exercises with the target child. . . . The sisters chose patterning, but argue over who has to do it. Mother is *not* concerned with equal time for the older sisters, and treats this as a "matter of fact" issue.
>
> In another family, the fieldworker notes that "Mother has normal concerns about sibs getting along; she relies on the older sisters to supervise and provide a good influence for the target child."

No parents merely accepted, without raising the issue as a problematic cultural question, that older siblings would take care of the delayed child or assist the parent in domestic tasks. Of course, sibling participation in tasks occurred often in a number of families, and opinions varied among parents. But the practice did not occur naturally or easily, as a matter of normal sibling relationships, as it would in Kenya or India, for instance.

The cultural place and cultural meanings affected both the way in which families experienced having a delayed child and what they did as a result. This was true for the families' beliefs about equality, as well as those about issues surrounding caregiving and domestic workload. Parents reported feeling significant guilt and anxiety, for instance, over unequal treatment of their children. In many Kenyan or Indian families, the cultural concern would be over fostering sufficient *interdependence* among siblings, rather than autonomy or equality. Euro-American parents report making significant accommodation efforts in their attempts to rectify what they perceive as inequality. Similarly, mothers report that one of their most serious problems is the increased domestic workload that resulted from having a delayed child (Gallimore et al., 1989)—yet few report that siblings offer the kind of assistance that would be routine in other cultural places. Parents' social constructions of their circumstances—in these examples, constructions influenced by cultural beliefs about equality and appropriate caregiving roles for siblings—may well have influenced the developmental course of the delayed child and his or her siblings. These beliefs certainly influenced family responses to the delay as shown by the contrast between Euro-American and other cultures.

Parental Concerns and Reports of Sibling Roles Equality and caregiving were salient cultural concerns of the parents in the CHILD study, but not the only concerns mentioned. The author coded 18 distinct parental concerns about siblings and their delayed children, at child ages 3–4 and 6–7. These are listed in Figure 1 in descending order from those that increased in frequency of mention at age 6–7 (at the top of the figure) to those that decreased in frequency as the delayed children got older (at the bottom). The full labels for these concerns, corresponding to their order in Figure 1, are as follows:

Concern about having to act as mediators of conflicts between siblings (Parents as mediators of conflict)

Concern about how to communicate and explain the label for or status of the child with delays to the siblings (Communication of delayed label)

Concern about dominance problems of siblings over the child with delays (Dominance in interactions)

Concern over siblings "acting out" because of the delayed status of the child (Acting out by siblings)

Concern that interaction between the child with delays and siblings is uncooperative (Uncooperative interactions)

Concern that family should do things as a unit (Family should be a unit)

Concern about aggression between siblings and the child with delays (Aggression between siblings)

Concern about caregiving by siblings of the child with delays (Sibling caregiving for the child with delays)

Concern over using siblings' developmental status to make comparisons with the developmental status of the child with delays (Developmental comparisons using siblings)

Concern over having shared, equal goals for the child with delays and siblings (Goals for siblings are shared)

Concern over comparing expectations for the future of the child with delays with those for the siblings (Expectations at maturity)

Concern over siblings teaching the child with delays (Siblings teaching delayed child)

Concern over facilitating interaction between the child with delays and siblings (Facilitate sibling interaction)

Concern over using sibling as a role model to assist in managing the child with delays (Sibling as role model)

Concern about ensuring equality of treatment between siblings and delayed child (Equality of treatment)

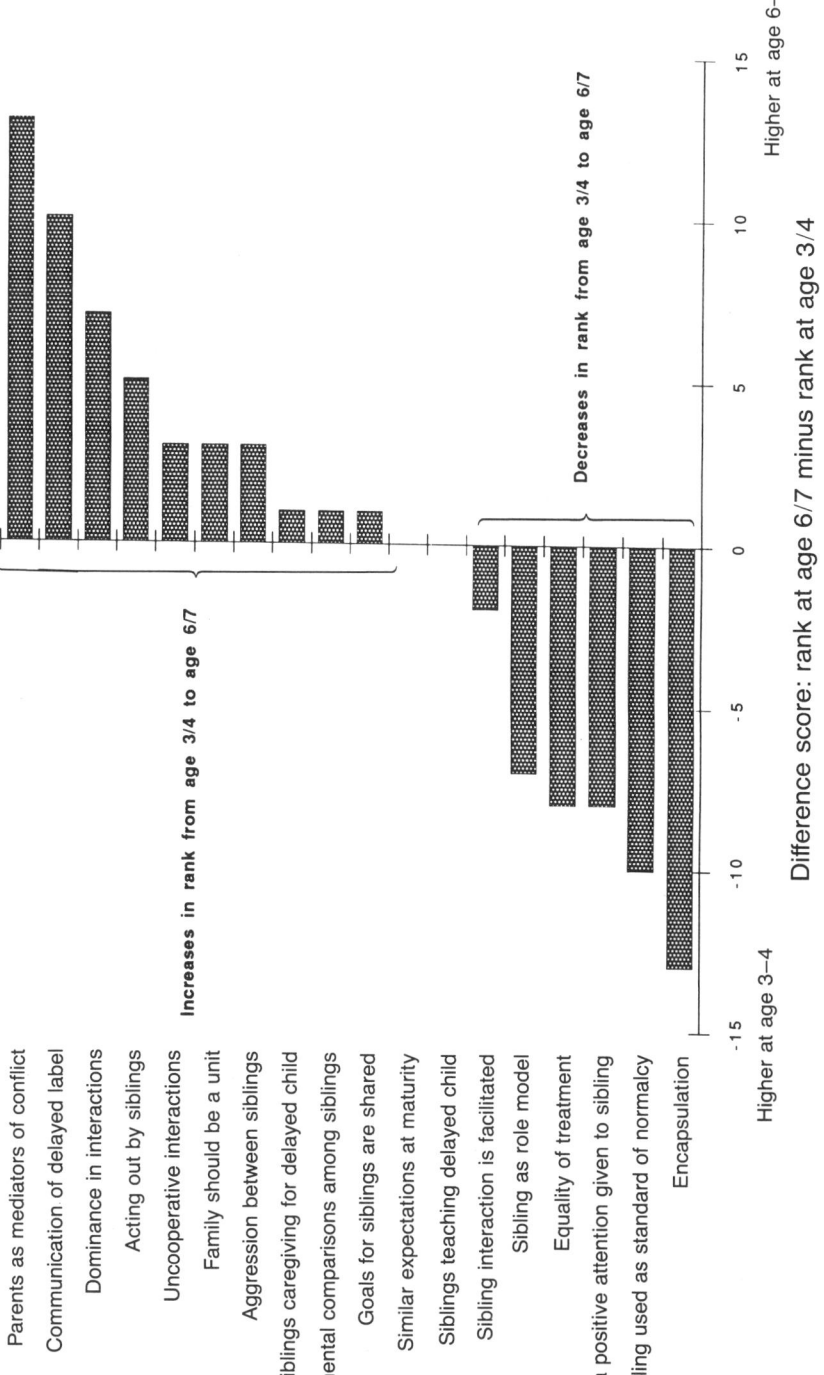

Figure 1. Change in ranking of parents' reports of their concerns regarding the relationships between their child with developmental delays and his or her siblings.

Concern about giving extra positive attention to siblings to compensate for the delayed child's needs (Extra positive attention to sibling)

Concern about siblings being used as a standard of normalcy by parents and the child with delays (Siblings used as standard of normalcy)

Concern about "encapsulating" the siblings from the delayed child, for example, separating the delayed child and his or her siblings in their schedules or friendships, and at home (Encapsulation: separate delayed child and siblings)

Figure 1 shows an increase in parental concerns regarding behavior and interactional problems at age 6–7, and a decline in concerns regarding developmental comparisons between the delayed child and siblings. For instance, the three most frequently mentioned parental concerns when the delayed children were age 3–4 were the following:

Using the siblings as a standard of normalcy to compare to the delayed child (56% of parents mentioned this at child age 3–4; 26% did so at age 6–7.)

Concerns over treating all the children equally (54% mentioned at child age 3–4; 26% at age 6–7.)

"Encapsulation" (54% mentioned this at child age 3–4, but only 9% at age 6–7.)

Each of these concerns has to do with the *developmental status* of the delayed child and with how to deal with the delayed child *in comparison* to the siblings.

At age 6–7, in contrast, the three most frequently mentioned concerns were focused more on *behavioral problems* of the delayed child and their effects on siblings and the family:

Concern over cooperative interactions between siblings and the delayed child (77% at age 6–7, but only 38% at age 3–4)

Concern over the family being together and the siblings and the child with delays doing things as a unit (42% at age 6–7, 25% at age 3–4)

Concern over having to mediate conflicts between siblings and the child with delays (42% at age 6–7, only 5% at age 3–4).

Parental discussion of encapsulation declined the most in number of mentions as children got older: it was ranked 2nd when children were 3–4, and 13th at age 6–7. By the time their child with delays reached age 6–7, parents were more interested in how to do things together. Concerns over using the siblings as a standard of normalcy with which to compare the delayed child and over giving extra positive attention to the siblings, declined substantially in frequency of mention between age 3–4 and 6–7.

Parents mentioned having to mediate conflicts significantly more often as children grew older; this topic increased from a rank of 15th at child age 3–4 to a rank of 3rd at age 6–7. Similarly, problems in discussing the delayed child's "label or status" (is the child "retarded," "slow," "handicapped," or perhaps none of these) increased in concern as the delayed child got older, moving from a rank of 11th to 5th. Problems with the older siblings "dominating" the child with delays also increased as a concern, from a rank of 14th to 9th.

The concerns of parents over developmental comparisons between siblings and the child with delays at age 3–4 seems due in part to uncertainty over the diagnosis and developmental condition of the delayed child at younger ages. Parents also worked harder to achieve overall equal treatment at younger ages than they did 3 or so years later. Parents turned away from this hoped-for equality and more towards ways to increase cooperation and shared experience as children grew older. The way many parents tried to provide equality during this later (age 6–7) period was often through separate-but-equal activities and interactions, including encapsulation, and not as often through joint activities.

By the beginning of their middle-childhood years, many delayed children were indeed significantly more of a behavioral and interactional problem for the siblings and the parents (Gallimore et al., in press). The mention of concerns over cooperation and conflict mediation increased substantially. Issues of equality and encapsulation declined overall, and "doing things together as a family" now began to be seen as the more appropriate way to provide "equality and balance" for the whole family. Worries over the effects of the child with delays on family solidarity and togetherness may also lie behind these concerns.

For most families, structural features such as birth order or age differences between the siblings, and the temperament of both the delayed child and the siblings, influenced how parents talked about their sibling-related concerns. In addition to such demographic and family-structure influences, the nature of the child's condition affected parents' concerns. However, the delayed child's DQ and developmental status did *not* correspond to parental concerns. Rather, behavioral and social problems of the delayed children were associated with different patterns of parental concerns. Parents and fieldworkers alike reported that in families with delayed children with high behavior problems that affected the functioning of the family, parents more often reported problems and concerns over mediation of conflict, doing things together or separately as a family, and problems in providing some form of equality of treatment for each sibling.

In summary, parents in the study had many different concerns regarding the siblings of their delayed children. These concerns were culturally familiar, and many are recognizable in all Euro-American families, not only in families with delayed children. They reflect more general Euro-American cultural concerns over equality of parental treatment of children, and the lack of a clear cultural norm regarding sibling caregiving. In many other cultural places, in contrast, sibling interdependence and differences in treatment are more widely accepted and expected, and sibling caregiving is a normal part of the siblings' life careers together.

There were also changes in concerns as the child with delays grew older. Developmental concerns and concerns over labelling declined in parental reports, and issues of behavior management and attempts to provide more shared family activities appeared more often. The delayed child's DQ did not influence concerns regarding siblings and the child with delays; rather, the family constellation and the child's behavioral and related problems influenced parental concerns.

More systematic exploration of similarities and differences in the lives of developmentally delayed children and siblings in different cultural places awaits further comparative work, empirical research, and testing. These comparisons should include a wide range of cultural and ethnic communities, include families with and without a child with disabilities, and use ethnographic and qualitative methods of study, in addition to other methods. Studying siblings in their varying cultural places around the world is not only of scientific value in understanding cultural diversity and universals in sibling relationships, it is essential in understanding our own cultural place.

REFERENCES

Agar, M. (1980). *The professional stranger.* New York: Academic Press.

Bernard, R.H. (1988). *Research methods in cultural anthropology.* Newbury Park, CA: Sage Publications.

Bernheimer, L.P., Gallimore, R., & Weisner, T.S. (1990). Ecocultural theory as a context for the Individual Family Service Plan. *Journal of Early Intervention, 14*(3), 219–233.

Bernheimer, L.P., & Keogh, B.K. (1982). *Research on early abilities of children with handicaps.* Los Angeles: University of California.

Bernheimer, L.P., & Keogh, B.K. (1986). Developmental disabilities in preschool children. In B.K. Keogh (Ed.), *Advances in special education* (Vol. 5, pp. 61–94). Greenwich, CT: JAI Press.

Bernheimer, L.P., & Keogh, B.K. (1988). The stability of cognitive performance of developmentally delayed children. *American Journal of Mental Retardation, 92,* 539–542.

Bowe, F.G. (1990). Disabled and elderly people in the first, second, and third worlds. *International Journal of Rehabilitation Research, 13,* 1–14.

Brody, G.H., & Stoneman, Z. (1986). Contextual issues in the study of sibling socialization. In J.J. Gallagher and P.M. Vietze (Eds.), *Families of handicapped persons: Research, programs, and policy issues* (pp. 197–219). Paul H. Brookes Publishing Co.

Bronfenbrenner, U. (1979). *The ecology of human development: Experiments by nature and design.* Cambridge, MA: Harvard University Press.

Cohen, D.W., & Atieno-Odhiambo, E.S. (1989). *Siaya: The historical anthropology of an African landscape.* Athens: Ohio State University Press.

Crnic, K., Friedrich, W.N., & Greenberg, M.T. (1983). Adaptation of families with mentally retarded children: A model of stress, coping and family ecology. *American Journal of Mental Deficiency, 88,* 125–138.

D'Andrade, R. (1984). Cultural meaning systems. In R.A. Shweder & R.A. LeVine (Eds.), *Culture theory: Essays on mind, self, and emotion* (pp. 88–119). Cambridge: Cambridge University Press.

deMunck, V.C. (in press). A study of cross-sibling relationships and the dowry in Sri Lanka. In C. Nuckolls (Ed.), *Siblings in South Asia: Brothers and sisters in cultural context.* New York: Guilford Publications.

Derne, S. (in press). Hierarchy and equality in the relationship of brothers: dynamics in the North Indian joint family. In Charles Nuckolls (Ed.), *Siblings in South Asia: Brothers and sisters in cultural context.* New York: Guilford Publications.

Dunn, J., & Kendrick, C. (1982). *Siblings: Love, envy and understanding.* Cambridge, MA: Harvard University Press.

Dunn, J., & Plomin, R. (1990). *Separate lives: Why siblings are so different.* New York: Basic Books.

Edgerton, R. (1967). *The cloak of competence: Stigma in the lives of the mentally retarded.* Berkeley: University of California Press.

Edgerton, R. (1976). *Deviance: A cross-cultural perspective.* Menlo Park, CA: Cummings Press.

Edgerton, R. (Ed.). (1984). *Lives in process: Mildly retarded adults in a large city.* Washington, DC: American Association on Mental Deficiency.

Edgerton, R., & Langness, L. (1974). *Methods and styles in the study of culture.* San Francisco: Chandler & Sharp Publishers, Inc.

Edwards, C., & Whiting, B. (in press). "Mother, older sibling and me": the overlapping roles of caregivers and companions in the social world of 2–3 year-olds in Ngeca, Kenya. In K.B. MacDonald (Ed.), *Parents and children playing.* Albany, NY: SUNY Press.

Gallimore, R., & Goldenberg, C.N. (in press). Activity settings of early literacy: home and school factors in children's emergent literacy. In E. Forman, N. Minick, & C.A. Stone (Eds.), *Education and mind: The integration of institutional, social, and developmental processes.* Oxford: Oxford University Press.

Gallimore, R., Weisner, T., Guthrie, D., Bernheimer, L., & Nihira, K. (in press). Family responses to young children with developmental delays: Accommodation activity in ecological and cultural context. *American Journal of Mental Retardation.*

Gallimore, R., Weisner, T.S., Kaufman, S.Z., & Bernheimer, L.P. (1989). The social construction of ecocultural niches: Family accommodation of developmentally delayed children. *American Journal of Mental Retardation, 94*(3), 216–230.

Gallimore, R., Weisner, T.S., Nihira, K., Keogh, B.K., Bernheimer, L.P., & Mink, I.T. (1983). *Ecocultural opportunity and family accommodation to developmentally delayed children.* Research proposal submitted to the National Institute of Child Health and Human Development, Sociobehavioral Research Group, Mental Retardation Research Center, University of California, Los Angeles.

Glaser, B., & Strauss, A. (1967). *The discovery of grounded theory: Strategies for qualitative research.* New York: Aldine de Gruyter.

Goldschmidt, W. (1976). *Culture and behavior of the Sebei: A study in continuity and adaptation.* Berkeley: University of California Press.

Goldschmidt, W. (1990). *The human career.* Cambridge, MA: Blackwell Publishers.

Hanks, J., & Hanks, L.M. (1948). The physically handicapped in certain non-Western societies. *Journal of Social Issues, 4*(4), 11–19.

Howe, S.G., Byington, H., & Kimball, G. (1848) (Republished in 1972). On the causes of idiocy. In Charles Rosenberg (Ed.), *Medicine and society in America* (pp. i–xvi, 1–37). New York: Arno Press.

Kilbride, P.L., & Kilbride, J.C. (1990). *Changing family life in East Africa: Women and children at risk.* University Park: Penn State University Press.

Kohn, M.L. (1977). *Class and conformity: A study in values* (2nd ed.). Chicago: University of Chicago Press.

Kolenda, P. (in press). Siblings in North, Central, and South India: A comparison. In Charles Nuckolls (Ed.). *Siblings in South Asia: Brothers and sisters in cultural context.* New York: Guilford Publications.

Lambert, W.W. (1971). Cross-cultural backgrounds to personality development and the socialization of aggression: findings from the Six Culture Study. In W.W. Lambert & R. Weisbrod (Eds.), *Comparative perspectives on social psychology* (pp. 49–61). Boston: Little, Brown.

Langness, L.L., & Levine, H.G. (Eds.). (1986). *Culture and retardation: Life histories of mildly retarded persons in American society.* Boston: D. Reidel.

Leiderman, P.H., & Leiderman, G. (1977). Economic change and infant care in an East African community. In P.H. Leiderman, S.R. Tulkin, & A. Rosenfeld (Eds.), *Culture and infancy: Variations in the human experience* (pp. 405–438). New York: Academic Press.

LeVine, R. (1977). Child rearing as cultural adaptation. In P. Leiderman, S. Tulkin, & A. Rosenfeld (Eds.), *Culture and infancy* (pp. 15–27). New York: Academic Press.

Levine, H.G., Gallimore, R., Weisner, T., & Turner, J. (1980). Teaching participant-observation research methods: A skills-building approach. *Anthropology & Education Quarterly, 11*(1), 38–54.

Levy, R.I. (1973). *Tahitians: Mind and experience in the Society Islands.* Chicago: University of Chicago Press.

Lofland, J., & Lofland, L.H. (1984). *Analyzing social settings: A guide to qualitative observation and analysis* (2nd ed.). Belmont, CA: Wadsworth.

Lobato, D. (1983). Siblings of handicapped children: A review. *Journal of Autism and Developmental Disorders, 13,* 347–364.

Loucky, J.P. (1988). *Children's work and family survival in Highland Guatemala.* Unpublished doctoral dissertation, University of California, Los Angeles.

Marriott, M. (1976). Hindu transactions: Diversity without dualism. In B. Kapferer (Ed.), *Transaction and meaning: Directions in the Anthropology of exchange and symbolic behavior* (pp. 109–142). Philadelphia: Institute for the study of human issues.

Marshall, M. (Ed.). (1983). *Siblingship in Oceania: Studies in the meaning of kin relations* (ASAO Monograph No. 8). Lanham, MD: University Press of America.

McGilvray, D. (1988). Sex, repression, and Sanskritization in Sri Lanka? *Ethos, 16*(2), 99–127.

Mendelson, M.J. (1990). *Becoming a brother: A child learns about life, family, and self.* Cambridge, MA: MIT Press.

Mendrich, E.A., Roizen, J.A., Rubin, V., & Buckley, S. (1982). *The serious business of growing up: A study of children's lives outside school.* Berkeley: University of California Press.

Miles, M., & Huberman, A.M. (1984, May). Drawing valid meaning from qualitative data: Toward a shared craft. *Educational Researcher,* pp. 20–30.

Munroe, R., Munroe, R., & Whiting, B. (Eds.). (1981). *Handbook of cross cultural human development.* New York: Garland STPM Press.

Naroll, R., & Cohen, R. (Eds.). (1970). *A handbook of method in cultural anthropology*. New York: Columbia Press.

Nerlove, S.B., Roberts, J.M., Klein, R.E., Yarbrough, C., & Habicht, J.P. (1974). Natural indicators of cognitive development: An observational study of rural Guatemalan children. *Ethos, 2*(3), 265–295.

Nihira, K., Weisner, T.S., & Bernheimer, L. (in press). Ecocultural assessment in families of children with developmental delays: Construct and concurrent validities. *American Journal of Mental Retardation*.

Nuckolls, C. (Ed.). (in press a). *Siblings in South Asia*: Brothers and sisters in cultural context. New York: Guilford Publications.

Nuckolls, C. (in press b). Sibling myths in a South Indian Fishing Village: a case study in sociological ambivalence. In C. Nuckolls (Ed.), *Siblings in South Asia: Brothers and sisters in cultural context*. New York: Guilford Publications.

Pelto, P., & Pelto, G. (1978). *Anthropological research: The structure of inquiry* (2nd ed.). Cambridge: Cambridge University Press.

Peltzer, K., & Ng'andu, K. (1989). The role of traditional healers towards children's mental handicap and developmental disabilities in Lusaka. In R. Serpell, D. Nabuzoka, & F.E.A. Lesi (Eds.), *Early intervention, developmental disability, mental handicap in Africa*. Lusaka, Zambia: Department of Psychology.

Ritchie, J., & Ritchie, J. (1979). *Growing up in Polynesia*. Sydney: George Allen and Unwin.

Rogoff, B. (1990). *Apprenticeship in thinking: Cognitive development in social context*. Oxford: Oxford University Press.

Rogoff, B., Newcombe, N., Fox, N., & Ellis, S. (1980). Transitions in children's roles and capabilities. *International Journal of Psychology, 15*, 181–200.

Scarr, S. (1985). Constructing psychology: Making facts and fables for our times. *American Psychologist, 40*(5), 499–512.

Scheer, J., & Groce, N. (1988). Impairment as a human constant: cross-cultural and historical perspectives on variation. *Journal of Social Issues, 44*(1), 23–37.

Serpell, R. (1989). Psychological assessment as a guide to early intervention: reflections on the Zambian context of intellectual disability. In R. Serpell, D. Nabuzoka, & F.E.A. Lesi (Eds.), *Early intervention, developmental disability, mental handicap in Africa*. Lusaka, Zambia: Department of Psychology.

Serpell, R., Nabuzoka, D., & Lesi, F.E.A. (Eds.). (1989). *Early intervention, developmental disability, mental handicap in Africa*. Lusaka, Zambia: Department of Psychology.

Shweder, R., & Bourne, E. (1991). Does the concept of the person vary cross-culturally? In R. Shweder (Ed.), *Thinking through cultures: Expeditions in cultural psychology* (pp. 113–155). Cambridge, MA: Harvard Press.

Simeonsson, R.J., & McHale, S.M. (1981). [Review of research on handicapped children: sibling relationships]. *Child: Care, health, and development, 7*, 153–171.

Spradley, J.P. (1979). *The ethnographic interview*. New York: Holt, Rinehart, & Winston.

Spradley, J. (1980). *Participant observation*. New York: Holt, Rinehart, & Winston.

Stoneman, Z., & Brody, G. (1987). Observational research on retarded children, their parents, and their siblings. In S. Landesman & P.M. Vietze (Eds.), *Living environments and mental retardation* (pp. 423–448). Washington, DC: American Association of Mental Deficiency (AAMD).

Super, C. (Ed.). (1987). *The role of culture in developmental disorder*. San Diego: Academic Press.

Super, C., & Harkness, S. (Eds.). (1980). *Anthropological perspectives on child development: New directions for child development* (No. 8). San Francisco: Jossey-Bass.

Super, C., & Harkness, S. (1986). The developmental niche: A conceptualization at the interface of child and culture. *International Journal of Behavioral Development, 9,* 1–25.

Tharp, R.G., & Gallimore, R. (1988). *Rousing minds to life: Teaching, learning, and schooling in social context.* Cambridge: Cambridge University Press.

Vygotsky, L. (1978). *Mind in society: The development of higher psychological processes.* Cambridge, MA: Harvard University Press.

Weisner, T.S. (1982). Sibling interdependence and child caretaking: A cross-cultural view. In M. Lamb & B. Sutton-Smith (Eds.), *Sibling relationships: Their nature and significance across the lifespan* (pp. 305–327). Hillsdale, NJ: LEA Press.

Weisner, T.S. (1984). Ecocultural niches of middle childhood: A cross-cultural perspective. In W.A. Collins (Ed.), *Development during middle childhood: The years from six to twelve* (pp. 335–369). Washington, DC: National Academy of Sciences Press.

Weisner, T.S. (1987). Socialization for parenthood in sibling caretaking societies. In J. Lancaster, A. Rossi, & J. Altmann (Eds.), *Parenting across the life span* (pp. 237–270). New York: Aldine Press.

Weisner, T.S. (1989a). Comparing sibling relationships across cultures. In Patricia Zukow (Ed.), *Sibling interactions across cultures* (pp. 11–25). Leiden: Springer-Verlag.

Weisner, T. (1989b). Social support for children among the Abaluyia of Kenya. In D. Belle (Ed.), *Children's social networks and social supports* (pp. 70–90). New York: John Wiley & Sons.

Weisner, T.S., Beizer, L., & Stolze, L. (1991). Religion and the families of developmentally delayed children. *American Journal of Mental Retardation, 95*(6), 647–662.

Weisner, T., & Gallimore, R. (1977). My brother's keeper: Child and sibling caretaking. *Current Anthropology, 18,* 169–191.

Weisner, T., & Gallimore, R. (1985, December). *The convergence of ecocultural and activity theory.* Paper presented at the annual meeting of the American Anthropological Association, Washington, DC.

Weisner, T.S., Gallimore, R., & Jordan, C. (1988). Unpackaging cultural effects on classroom learning: Hawaiian peer assistance and child-generated activity. *Anthropology and Education Quarterly, 19,* 327–353.

Weisner, T.S., Nihira, K., & Bernheimer, L. (1989, April). *Ecocultural assessment in families of children with developmental delay: Theoretical, methodological, and policy considerations.* Paper presented at the annual meetings of the Society for Research in Child Development, Kansas City.

Werner, O., & Schoepfle, G. (1987a). *Systematic fieldwork: Foundations of ethnography and interviewing* (Vol. 1). Newbury Park: Sage.

Werner, O., & Schoepfle, G. (1987b). *Systematic fieldwork: Ethnographic analysis and data management* (Vol. 2). Newbury Park: Sage.

Wertsch, J.V. (1985). *Vygotsky and the social formation of mind.* Cambridge: Harvard University Press.

Wertsch, J.V., Minick, N., & Arns, F.A. (1984). The creation of context in joint problem-solving. In B. Rogoff & J. Lave (Eds.), *Everyday cognition: Its development in social contexts* (pp. 151–171). Cambridge: Harvard University Press.

Whiting, B. (1976). The problem of the packaged variable. In K. Riegel & Meacham, T.A. (Eds.), *The developing individual in a changing world: Historical and cultural issues* (Vol. 1, pp. 303–309). Netherlands: Mouton.

Whiting, B. (1980). Culture and social behavior: A model for the development of social behavior. *Ethos, 8,* 95–116.

Whiting, B., & Edwards, C. (1988). *Children of different worlds: The formation of social behavior.* Cambridge: Harvard University Press.

Whiting, J., & Whiting, B. (1975). *Children of six cultures: A psychocultural analysis.* Cambridge, MA: Harvard University Press.

Wilson, M. (1963). *Good company: A study of Nyakyusa age villages.* Boston: Beacon Press.

Zukow, P. (Ed.). (1989). *Sibling interactions across cultures.* Leiden: Springer-Verlag.

CHAPTER 4

Issues and Interventions for Young Siblings of Children with Medical and Developmental Problems

Debra J. Lobato

The role that children's health and abilities play in the relationships that they develop with siblings and in the relationships that siblings develop with other family members and peers has been a subject of considerable interest to researchers since the early 1980s (e.g., Cadman, Boyle, & Offord, 1988; Lobato, 1990; Sourkes, 1980; Stoneman & Brody, 1987; Wagner, Schubert, & Schubert, 1985). As the care of children with illnesses and disabilities becomes increasingly family-centered, sibling influences and relationships deserve continued professional attention.

The issues and risks surrounding sibling relationships change over time as the children themselves develop and as the situations and pressures that they confront change. The purpose of this chapter is to examine the beginning stages of the relationship between siblings. Concerns more commonly encountered by young siblings (from infancy through the age of 7 years) of children with a variety of significant illnesses and disabilities are explored. Professional practices that influence young siblings and interventions that show promise in effectively addressing some of their unique concerns will be described. Thereafter, the special case of siblings of children with HIV infection will be examined, as these children make up a growing population of very young siblings who face a multitude of significant challenges.

CHARACTERISTICS AND VULNERABILITIES OF THE YOUNG SIBLING

Toddlers and preschoolers are, by nature, egocentric in their perspective, magical in their thinking, and reliant on appearances in their understanding of cause and effect. Their unique cognitive and emotional characteristics render them especially vulnerable to misunderstanding their brothers' and sisters' disease or disability, as well as the consequent emotional and utilitarian adaptations of their family and the community at large. To understand how young siblings may misconstrue their brothers' or sisters' condition and the stresses of illness that occur more commonly during early childhood, some of the literature pertaining to young children's concepts of disease, disability, and death is reviewed below.

Children's understanding of childhood diseases is characteristically vague and concrete; they tend to focus on only one or two functional and observable aspects of a condition at a time (Bibace & Walsh, 1980; Burbach & Peterson, 1986; Potter & Roberts, 1984). Their understanding of cause and effect is greatly influenced by the temporal relationship between events, even unrelated ones. Given that young siblings are less likely than older children to receive factual information about the child's disability or illness from professionals and parents (Townes & Wold, 1977), they are more likely to have to rely on their own unrelated experiences and imaginations when attempting to understand what has happened to their brother or sister. As such, young siblings, with their egocentric perspectives, are more likely than older children to perceive themselves as somehow instrumental in causing a child's problem. With their perceptions of adults as omnipotent, young siblings are also more likely to blame their parents for causing the brother's or sister's illness, or, at least, for having failed to protect the child from harm (Binger, 1973; Binger et al., 1969). Preschoolers are also more likely than others to consider a child's illness, disability, or death to be a form of divine punishment for the child's or parents' misbehavior (Perrin & Gerrity, 1981).

In attempting to understand the cause of an illness or disability, young children are particularly influenced by visible aspects of the condition (Lavigne & Ryan, 1979; Sourkes, 1980). Although preschool-age siblings of children with disabilities or chronic illnesses generally are no more likely than their peers to have major behavioral problems, in one investigation comparing siblings of children with visible and nonvisible disabilities, preschool siblings of children with visible impairments (i.e., cleft lip, cleft palate) were rated by mothers as exhibiting greater social withdrawal than siblings of children with cardiac problems and other terminal illnesses (Lavigne & Ryan, 1979).

The heightened incidental exposure to adults' conversations about illness and disability does not appear to offer much protection from misconception and misinterpretation for siblings of children with medical or developmental problems. Though there is wide variability in the accuracy of preschool siblings' beliefs about disease and disability, without intervention they tend to be able to provide no more information than their peers (Lobato, Barbour, Hall, & Miller, 1987).

Unfortunately, misinformation is not always attributable to the cognitive levels of preschoolers. It can also be perpetuated by a lack of information about or a stigmatization by a condition within a family or a professional community. Lack of information also stems from caregivers' confusion as to what information is appropriate to offer young children at what time. In fact, there are accounts of siblings who were well into adulthood before their parents informed them that they had a brother or sister with mental retardation who had been institutionalized at an early age (Grossman, 1972) or that the illness and treatments that had consumed family resources during the siblings' early childhood had been cancer (Gogan & Slavin, 1981). Although preschool siblings do not acquire more accurate information than peers through casual exposure, they can acquire more accurate information about their brother or sister, and about relevant medical diagnoses and treatments, through participation in family discussion (Townes & Wold, 1977) and developmentally appropriate didactic programs (Lobato, 1985; Oehler & Vileisis, 1990; Sahler & Carpenter, 1989). What is known is that, in the absence of an accurate, understandable explanation by caring adults, young siblings will create their own private explanations of what is happening to the child and family, only some of which resemble the understanding of the adults around them.

Of course, siblings' cognitive and emotional characteristics also influence the ways in which they interpret the alterations in family behavior and routines associated with a child's special medical or developmental needs. When a young sibling observes parental distress, especially when the ill or disabled child is not immediately present, there is a strong possibility that the preschooler will perceive him- or herself as having some role in the parents' distress. The sibling may feel that he or she has a responsibility to attempt to alleviate it by being "extra good" (Powell & Ogle, 1985).

Prolonged hospitalizations of a child for medical treatment often result in the isolation of siblings from their parents, as well as from their brother or sister, as the siblings are often cared for by others at home (Knafl & Dixon, 1983). Unlike school-age and adolescent siblings, preschoolers are at risk for greater behavioral distress during these times and for interpreting their reduced contact with parents as a form of emotional rejection or abandonment (Knafl & Dixon, 1983; Lindsay & MacCarthy, 1974; Sourkes, 1980). Young siblings cannot as easily substitute forms of contact such as telephone conversations, cards, and letters for face-to-face interaction. With their limited concepts of time and reliance on concrete evidence of parental and child involvement, preoperational siblings have fewer cognitive resources to assure themselves that the parents' and child's absence is only temporary, or that their own needs could be of concern to parents while they are gone (Koch, Hermann, & Donaldson, 1974).

Without a full understanding of the cause of a child's illness or the hospital treatment that allows the ill child to return home after prolonged absences, the preschool sibling is certainly vulnerable to confusion in the event of the child's death. The belief that this particular separation is no more final than previous ones is quite possible, since the finality of death is not a reality to most preschoolers (Furman, 1973). Indeed, the death of a brother or sister heightens young siblings' separation anxiety, temper tantrums, nightmares, school phobias, somatic complaints, depression, and developmental regression (Binger et al., 1969; Lindsay & MacCarthy, 1974; Sourkes, 1980). Understandably, because of their own grief and mourning, parents may be too overwhelmed to recognize and respond completely to the surviving sibling's needs.

PSYCHOSOCIAL CHARACTERISTICS OF YOUNG SIBLINGS

Given the cognitive and emotional characteristics of young siblings and the special stresses that a child's illness, disability, or death places on the family, it should not be surprising that empirical cross-sectional investigations across age ranges of siblings generally place preschool-age children within higher risk categories than older siblings in terms of behavioral adjustment (e.g., Binger et al., 1969; Ferrari, 1984; Gruszka, 1988; Knafl & Dixon, 1983; Lavigne & Ryan, 1979; Lindsay & MacCarthy, 1974). However, when young siblings (ages 3–7 years) of children with various developmental disabilities have been compared to a matched control group of children with healthy, nondisabled siblings, no differences have been found in their self-concepts and family perceptions. Differences between groups have been revealed in mothers' reports of more aggression and anxiety, but not more behavior problems in general (Lobato et al., 1987). While the interactions between experimental and control siblings have also been described as being quite similar, as a group, mothers of children with disabilities appear to display affection more freely, yet also deliver more commands to their nondisabled children (Lobato, Miller, Barbour, Hall, & Pezzullo, 1991).

Recognition that preschool-age siblings of children with special needs have unique experiences and concerns of their own is an important first step toward the goal of enhancing their adaptation and development. It is toward such issues of parental and professional practices that the author's attention now turns.

PRACTICES AND INTERVENTIONS

Hospitalization and Sibling Visitation

Newborn Nurseries For many people, some of their earliest and strongest memories are those of the events immediately surrounding the birth of their younger brother and sister. Even under routine conditions, when the child's birth and health status are free from complication, older siblings (especially firstborns) show an increase in whining, irritability, demandingness, temper tantrums, and sleep disturbance (Dunn & Kendrick, 1982; Robertson, 1971; Trause et al., 1981). Changes in older siblings' behavior at the time of a child's birth are probably due to a combination of family changes usually associated with late pregnancy and birth. These changes include anticipatory planning for the child's arrival with role and space reassignments, separation from the mother for childbirth, alterations in childcare figures and settings, and, finally, the introduction of, and adaptation to, the new family member.

Following the newborn's arrival home, an increase in oppositional and defiant behavior is common, especially during times when mothers are providing physical care to the infant (Dunn & Kendrick, 1982). Related differences in parents' behaviors toward first and other children have been documented as well. After a new child's birth, mothers typically talk to and play with their older children less. Interactions that occur with parents generally must be initiated by the child him- or herself.

For the most part, hospitals in the United States (Poster & Betz, 1987) and Canada (Alcock, 1977) now allow some form of visitation by siblings of newborns and children admitted for inpatient care; however, significant limitations are usually placed on sibling visitation practices, limitations that are especially relevant to preschool siblings. For example, most hospitals restrict sibling visitation to children over 12 years and limit direct sibling contact to particular visiting hours (Poster & Betz, 1987). The rationale hospitals use to justify restrictions on sibling visitation and contact include the control of infectious and communicable disease from sibling to patient; lack of supervision of visiting siblings and potential disruptions to other patients, families, and hospital staff; safety; and lack of emotional readiness for observing pediatric problems, treatments, and equipment (Poster & Betz, 1987).

While infection is the primary rationale for restricting sibling visitation, there is consistent evidence that neither brief nor extended direct contact with siblings during hospitalization is associated with any increase in normal newborn infection rates (Kowba & Schwirian, 1985; Solheim & Spellacy, 1987; Umphenour, 1980; Wranesh, 1982). When siblings are allowed to visit the newborn nursery, the visitation experience leads to increased sibling responsiveness to mothers and babies at the time of discharge (Trause et al., 1981). Routine sibling visits to the normal newborn nursery do not appear to have any appreciable effect on typical behavior problems (e.g., sleep disturbance, temper tantrums) in the first few weeks following the baby's homecoming (Trause et al., 1981). The effect of visitation practices on young siblings' sense of isolation or abandonment during hospitalization or on subsequent interactions has not been explored.

In contrast to the brief hospitalizations associated with an uncomplicated birth and delivery are the prolonged hospitalizations and separations from the baby and mother following birthing complications such as prematurity or newborn illness requiring intensive care. While normal newborns are likely to remain within the local hospital of their birth, babies requiring intensive care are frequently transported to distant neonatal intensive treatment centers. The separation experienced by the sibling, therefore, has a greater geographic and temporal reality.

Even with more recent acceptance and promotion of sibling visitation (American Academy of Pediatrics, 1985), many hospitals continue to restrict siblings under age 12 from neonatal intensive care units. Challenges to this policy have been raised by a few controlled investigations. Sibling visitation has been evaluated for its effects on newborn infection rates, sibling knowledge and behavioral adjustment, and overall family functioning (Ballard, Maloney, Shank, & Hollister, 1984; Maloney, Ballard, Hollister, & Shank, 1983; Oehler & Vileisis, 1990; Schwab, Tolbert, Bagnato, & Maisels, 1983). Siblings participating in these investigations have ranged in age from 2 to 19 years, with the average age being approximately 4½–5 years old. Newborns received intensive care for at least 3 weeks, primarily for prematurity and associated complications (e.g., respiratory distress, intraventricular hemorrhage), although other diagnoses and eventual lengths of stay were not fully reported. All siblings were in good health themselves and had not experienced recent exposure to chicken pox or other communicable diseases. Prior to contact with the baby, siblings were washed and gowned under supervision. "Visitation" was not well-defined in any of the studies, but appears to have involved one episode within the first week of birth, during which the sibling was permitted to hold the infant, if possible, or to touch it through incubator portholes for an unspecified amount of time. In one project, siblings met the infant's nurse to be briefed on the medical equipment found in the neonatal intensive care unit (Maloney et al., 1983). One or both parents and a staff member accompanied the sibling while visiting the newborn (Maloney et al., 1983; Schwab et al., 1983). Follow-up data were collected no more than 3 weeks following the child's birth and within two weeks of the siblings' visits.

In all reports, sibling visitation to the neonatal intensive care unit did not increase infection rates among the newborns and was not associated with any increase in sibling fears or anxieties about the medical conditions observed in the nursery (Ballard et al., 1984). It is amusing to note that possible increases in infection among the healthy siblings were not evaluated. These brief visits were associated with improvements in siblings' information about the new baby, siblings' expectations that caring for the baby would be a cooperative family effort, some reports of improvement in child behavior, and overall parental satisfaction with the policy (Maloney et al., 1983; Oehler & Vileisis,

1990; Renaud, 1981; Schwab et al., 1983). Undesirable outcomes for the hospitalized child, sibling, and parents have not been reported, perhaps because the visitation practices were highly structured and time was limited. Long-term effects of more frequent contact should be the subject of further investigation.

General Inpatient Care When children are hospitalized for acute illnesses or for recurrent treatments of chronic and terminal illnesses, there appears to be greater variation in sibling experiences than those observed during neonatal intensive care. There have been only a few controlled, prospective studies of siblings' reactions to these hospitalizations. Most are retrospective, and many are based on clinical interviews after the child's health stabilizes or the child has died. With short-term hospitalizations for acute illnesses, negative behavioral reactions among siblings are not usual, but occur most commonly in the 4- to 11-year-old group of siblings. This is especially true of those cared for outside of their own homes and separated from parents during the time of the child's hospitalization (Knafl & Dixon, 1983). Sibling reactions to a child's hospitalization for treatment of a life-threatening illness are difficult to disentwine from siblings' reactions to the illness itself, or to the child's death. Clinical lore promotes the recommendation that sibling visits occur when parents are present and when the hospitalized child is asleep or free from pain (Koch et al., 1974; Sourkes, 1980). Advocates of sibling visitation claim that it is of therapeutic value to the patient, facilitating his or her adaptation to the hospital setting and treatment and contributing positively to the child's attitude and recovery. Reductions in siblings' sense of abandonment, demystification of the hospital surroundings, and continuity of sibling relationships are some of the benefits reported anecdotally.

Sibling Information and Support Groups

To date, all available information suggests that siblings have much to gain when they are informed of their brother's or sister's illness and disability and encouraged to participate in their care in a manner respectful of the siblings' own developmental needs. Since the early 1980s, the potential value of providing information to siblings in a group format has been explored for both preschool-age (Lobato, 1985, 1990) and school-age (Meyer, Vadasy, & Fewell, 1985; Sahler & Carpenter, 1989) siblings of children with developmental disabilities and chronic illnesses.

While formats and frequency of sibling contact varies, all groups have the common goal of increasing siblings' understanding of their brother's or sister's medical and developmental problems and related treatments in order to dispel any misconceptions about etiology and personal responsibility and vulnerability. Group programs also provide a forum for expressing both the positive and negative emotional aspects of family situations to others who have shared similar experiences. Furthermore, when structured accordingly, groups offer siblings the opportunity to observe peers' methods of coping with a brother's or sister's illness or disability.

Evaluation of groups for siblings reveal that parent and sibling consumers perceive them to be enjoyable, which may be the most important ingredient in promoting consistent attendance. Group programs have also been effective in increasing sibling knowledge of developmental disabilities (Lobato, 1990) and illnesses (Sahler & Carpenter, 1989) and in improving siblings' understanding of themselves, their families, and illness-related experiences. Participation in the groups, however, has not been shown to have any short-term effect on parents' ratings of major aspects of their children's personality or behavioral traits (Lobato, 1990) but has been associated with improvements in ratings of mood (Sahler & Carpenter, 1989). The long-term impact of improvements in siblings' knowledge and understanding of their family situation has yet to be determined.

PEDIATRIC HIV: SPECIAL SIBLING ISSUES

When one considers the case of pediatric HIV infection from the perspective of the healthy sibling, it becomes obvious that the risk status and needs of these children are compelling. The issues that these children face overlap in every way with those faced by siblings of children with developmental disabilities and chronic illness, but also differ in some crucial dimensions that are difficult to ignore.

Most children with HIV infection acquired the virus prenatally from their mothers, the majority of whom are Hispanic or black and were infected via intravenous drug use or sexual contact with an infected sex partner (U.S. Surgeon General's Workshop on Children with HIV Infection and their Families, 1987). (The focus of this section is on the group of children with prenatally acquired HIV, rather than the population of children whose virus was contracted through blood transfusion.) Once the etiology of the child's infection is acknowledged, one must realize that these siblings will experience not only the illness and death of their younger brothers or sisters, but of their mothers, and perhaps their fathers as well. The social context of the healthy sibling is likely to be disrupted or chaotic, given the frequent conditions of low socioeconomic status, foster care, or sheltered living arrangements, along with compromises in parent functioning due to failing health and/or drug abuse. Aside from the potential for the child to experience isolation due to racial and ethnic factors, the child may also face rejection due to the highly stigmatizing nature of the HIV diagnosis.

In an effort to begin addressing some of these sibling issues within Rhode Island's pediatric HIV population, a survey was mailed nationally to professionals. Additionally, a small group of parents of children with HIV infection were interviewed about their concerns and plans for healthy siblings. Preliminary results of the survey and interviews are presented below.

National Survey

A questionnaire was developed (Lobato & Willis, 1991) to survey professionals working with pediatric AIDS populations across the United States regarding: 1) the existence of any educational and supportive services for siblings within their setting; 2) the type of AIDS-related information they believed to be appropriate to share with siblings in different age groups (i.e., preschool, elementary, junior/high); 3) their opinion as to how the information should be presented to siblings, by whom, and in what context; and 4) the possible beneficial or harmful effects to the patient, sibling, or parent of informing siblings of the child's and parent's diagnosis.

A total of 450 questionnaires were sent to directors of national and state AIDS service programs listed in the National Directory of Local AIDS services (United States Conference of Mayors, 1990). Also invited to participate were the Directors of Pediatrics, Social Work, and Psychology listed in the University Affiliated Program Directory. As of 1992, 95 questionnaires have been returned by professionals representing public health nursing, psychology, social work, medicine, and psychiatry. Of these 95, 71 respondents indicated that they were not providing any organized sibling services, while 21 reported offering ancillary types of services, such as counselling by referral.

Respondents showed a strong tendency toward restricting the type of information about HIV infection they would discuss with siblings in the preschool-age group. The majority of respondents indicated that information regarding HIV transmission was not appropriate until a sibling was of elementary or junior high school age. Only 10%–15% of the respondents reported that they would give information about transmission of the disease to preschoolers, while almost 40% believed they would share information regarding the likelihood of parental and child death. Approximately 75%–80% of the respondents felt that elementary school children should receive information regarding disease transmission, likelihood of parent and child death, possible social responses, and impact on the sibling's future.

For preschoolers, professionals were evenly divided as to whom they believed to be in the best position to provide AIDS information. Approximately one-third of the respondents believed parents or guardians alone should speak with youngsters, while the other two-thirds would opt for the parent or guardian with either a mental health professional or physician present for support. In contrast, 17% believed elementary and junior high school children should be informed by parents alone. The majority felt that parents would need assistance from physicians or mental health workers with this age group, as the siblings' questions may have required greater technical knowledge.

Based on prior reviews of the sibling literature, a list of possible benefits and goals of providing sibling information was generated and respondents were asked to indicate those that they believed would apply to siblings of different ages. Greater benefits were anticipated for older siblings in areas such as improved understanding of patient and family issues, reducing sibling feelings of isolation and increasing peer support, and opening discussion for the siblings' concerns and future. Interestingly, the majority of respondents believed that sibling groups might serve to prevent high-risk behaviors among siblings in the elementary and junior high school age ranges.

Generally, respondents anticipated that providing siblings with information about the HIV infection would be of greater benefit than harm for children. However, approximately 50% of those surveyed expressed concern over the possibility of negative emotional side effects such as anxiety, depression, preoccupation with illness, feelings of shame or guilt, and increased conflict or anger toward the parent or patient.

Parent Interviews

Parents of six children receiving care through a community-based agency for children and families with HIV infection were interviewed to obtain their views on sibling needs prior to developing a local sibling program. Interviews were conducted in their homes by a social worker or clinical psychology intern. The questions paralleled those of the professional survey noted above regarding parents' perceived need to inform siblings of different ages of the family HIV status, the parents' desire for professional assistance in doing so, and their interest in the development of sibling services. In addition, parents provided information about how they had been handling the situation thus far. While these interviews were only preliminary, they provide a sample of the concerns expressed by mothers who are attempting to deal with their own terminal illness as well as the developmental and health needs of their children.

As with professionals, mothers expressed ambivalence about sharing information concerning HIV infection and transmission with preschoolers. Most mothers viewed information regarding drug use and sexual contact as inappropriate for preschoolers and only conditionally appropriate for older children. A commonly cited criterion for when to provide information was the active questioning of the parent by the sibling regarding the cause of the disease. Thus, mothers would answer questions asked by the sibling, but would not volunteer this information spontaneously. However, one mother considered discussion of transmission as a necessary step toward her goal of preventing drug use by her children.

Three of the mothers interviewed had informed their children of their own HIV status, with the others planning to postpone sharing the information until the mothers or infected infants became symptomatic. None of the mothers of preschoolers had informed the sibling of the child's HIV status, which in some cases was still indeterminate, due to the child's age. Mothers of school-age children had begun discussions about the illness and its fatality, but not about modes of transmission. Mothers endorsed the notion of sibling support groups as a means providing information, dispelling misconceptions, and alleviating some of their own burden in helping the sibling cope with the diagnosis and prognosis.

CONCLUDING COMMENTS

All siblings of children with developmental disabilities and chronic illnesses have special needs of their own. As with older siblings and parents, when a child's health or development is at stake, very young siblings face unexpected changes in personal and family goals and routines. Yet, young siblings have different cognitive and emotional resources for understanding and adapting to the challenges they encounter. Although it appears that preschoolers are more vulnerable to behavioral adjustment problems than older siblings, they are not significantly different in psychosocial functioning from other preschoolers whose brothers and sisters do not have developmental or medical problems. The evidence compiled to date strongly suggests that very young siblings benefit from being provided with information about their brother's or sister's condition, whether it be an acute or chronic illness or a developmental disability. Medical, developmental, and relevant family information can be effectively disseminated to young siblings via open family communication, sibling visitation during hospitalizations, and participation in sibling support and information groups. All of these experiences have been associated with increased sibling knowledge and, in some instances, short-term improvements in ratings of sibling mood and behavior. Long-term effects of early sibling information and developmentally appropriate involvement have not yet been evaluated.

Siblings of children with HIV infection are facing considerable stresses and losses during their childhoods, many of which go beyond those suffered by other sibling groups. While preliminary responses of parents and professionals tend toward censorship of information given to very young siblings of children with HIV infection, this position is not supported by related clinical research with other populations. Continued exploration of the emotional, educational, and utilitarian needs of these siblings is needed.

REFERENCES

Alcock, D. (1977). Hey, what about the kids? *Canadian Nurse, 8,* 38–41.
American Academy of Pediatrics, Committee on Fetus and Newborn. (1985). Postpartum (neonatal) sibling visitation. *Pediatrics, 76,* 650.

Ballard, J.L., Maloney, M.M., Shank, M., & Hollister, L. (1984). Sibling visits to a newborn intensive care unit: Implications for siblings, parents, and infants. *Child Psychiatry and Human Development, 14,* 203–214.

Bibace, R., & Walsh, M. (1980). Development of children's concepts of illness. *Pediatrics, 66,* 912–917.

Binger, C. (1973). Childhood leukemia—emotional impact on siblings. In E.J. Anthony & C. Koupernik (Eds.), *The child in his family: The impact of disease and death* (pp. 195–210). New York: John Wiley & Sons.

Binger, C., Ablin, A., Feuerstein, R., Kushner, J., Zoger, S., & Mikkelsen, C. (1969). Childhood leukemia: Emotional impact on patient and family. *New England Journal of Medicine, 280,* 414–418.

Burbach, D.J., & Peterson, L. (1986). Children's concepts of physical illness: A review and critique of the cognitive-developmental literature. *Health Psychology, 5,* 307–325.

Cadman, D., Boyle, M., & Offord, D.R. (1988). The Ontario child health study: Social adjustment and mental health of siblings of children with chronic health problems. *Developmental and Behavioral Pediatrics, 9,* 117–121.

Dunn, J., & Kendrick, C. (1982). *Siblings: Love, envy, and understanding.* Cambridge, MA: Harvard University Press.

Ferrari, M. (1984). Chronic illness: Psychosocial effects on siblings—1. Chronically ill boys. *Journal of Child Psychology and Psychiatry, 25,* 459–476.

Furman, R. (1973). A child's capacity for mourning. In E.J. Anthony & C. Koupernik (Eds.), *The child in his family: The impact of disease and death* (pp. 225–232). New York: John Wiley & Sons.

Gogan, J.L., & Slavin, L. (1981). Interviews with brothers and sisters. In G.P. Koocher & J.E. O'Malley (Eds.), *The Damocles syndrome: Psychosocial consequences of surviving childhood cancer* (pp. 101–111). New York: McGraw-Hill.

Grossman, F.K. (1972). *Brothers and sisters of retarded children.* Syracuse, NY: Syracuse University Press.

Gruszka, M.A. (1988). *Family functioning and sibling adjustment in families with a handicapped child.* Unpublished doctoral dissertation, Kingston: University of Rhode Island.

Knafl, K.A., & Dixon, D.M. (1983). The role of siblings during pediatric hospitalization. *Issues in Comprehensive Pediatric Nursing, 6,* 13–22.

Koch, C., Hermann, J., & Donaldson, M.H. (1974). Supportive care of the child with cancer and his family. *Seminars in Oncology, 1,* 81–86.

Kowba, M.D., & Schwirian, P.M. (1985). Direct sibling contact and bacterial colonization in newborns. *Journal of Obstetric, Gynecologic and Neonatal Nursing, 14,* 412–417.

Lavigne, J.V., & Ryan, M. (1979). Psychologic adjustment of siblings of children with chronic illness. *Pediatrics, 63,* 616–627.

Lindsay, M., & MacCarthy, D. (1974). Caring for the brothers and sisters of a dying child. In L. Burton (Ed.), *Care of the child facing death* (pp. 189–206). London: Routledge and Kegan Paul.

Lobato, D. (1985). Preschool siblings of handicapped children—impact of peer support and training. *Journal of Autism and Developmental Disorders, 9,* 287–296.

Lobato, D.J. (1990). *Brothers, sisters, and special needs: Information and activities for helping young siblings of children with chronic illnesses and developmental disabilities.* Baltimore: Paul H. Brookes Publishing Co.

Lobato, D., Barbour, L., Hall, L.J., & Miller, C.T. (1987). Psychosocial characteristics of preschool siblings of handicapped and nondisabled children. *Journal of Abnormal Child Psychology, 15,* 329–338.

Lobato, D., Miller, C.T., Barbour, L., Hall, L.J., & Pezzullo, J. (1991). Preschool siblings of handicapped children: Interactions with mothers, brothers, and sisters. *Research in Developmental Disabilities, 12,* 387–399.

Lobato, D., & Willis, L. (1991). *Survey of service needs of siblings of children with HIV infection.* Manuscript submitted for publication.

Maloney, M.J., Ballard, J.L., Hollister, L., & Shank, M. (1983). A prospective, controlled study of scheduled sibling visits to a newborn intensive care unit. *Journal of the American Academy of Child Psychiatry, 22,* 565–570.

Meyer, D.J., Vadasy, P.F., & Fewell, R.R. (1985). *Sibshops.* Seattle: University of Washington Press.

Oehler, J.M., & Vileisis, R.A. (1990). Effect of early sibling visitation in an intensive care nursery. *Developmental and Behavioral Pediatrics, 11,* 7–12.

Perrin, E.C., & Gerrity, P.S. (1981). There's a demon in your belly: Children's understanding of illness. *Pediatrics, 67,* 841–849.

Poster, E.C., & Betz, L. (1987). Survey of sibling and peer visitation policies in southern California hospitals. *Children's Health Care, 15,* 166–171.

Potter, P.C., & Roberts, M.C. (1984). Children's perceptions of chronic illness: The roles of disease symptoms, cognitive development, and information. *Journal of Pediatric Psychology, 9,* 13–27.

Powell, T.H., & Ogle, P.A. (1985). *Brothers & sisters—A special part of exceptional families.* Baltimore: Paul H. Brookes Publishing Co.

Renaud, M.T. (1981). Parental response to family centered maternity care and to the implementation of sibling visits. *Military Medicine, 146,* 850–852.

Robertson, J. (1971). Young children in brief separation: A fresh look. *Psychoanalytic Study of the Child, 26,* 261–315.

Sahler, O.J.Z., & Carpenter, P.J. (1989). Evaluation of a camp program for siblings of children with cancer. *American Journal of Diseases of Childhood, 143,* 690–696.

Schwab, F., Tolbert, B., Bagnato, S., & Maisels, M.J. (1983). Sibling visiting in a neonatal intensive care unit. *Pediatrics, 71,* 835–838.

Solheim, K., & Spellacy, C. (1987). Sibling visitation: Effects on newborn infection rates. *Journal of Obstetric, Gynecologic and Neonatal Nursing, 17,* 43–48.

Sourkes, B.M. (1980). Siblings of the pediatric cancer patient. In J. Kellerman (Ed.), *Psychologic aspects of childhood cancer* (pp. 47–69). Springfield: Charles C Thomas.

Stoneman, Z., & Brody, G. (1987). Observational research on retarded children, their parents, and their siblings. In S. Landesman-Dwyer & P. Vietze (Eds.), *Living with retarded people* (pp. 423–448). Washington, DC: American Association on Mental Deficiency.

Townes, B.D., & Wold, D.A. (1977). Childhood leukemia. In E. Pattison (Ed.), *The experience of dying* (pp. 138–143). Englewood Cliffs, NJ: Prentice Hall.

Trause, M.A., Voos, D., Rudd, C., Klaus, M., Kennell, J., & Boslett, M. (1981). Separation for childbirth: The effect on the sibling. *Child Psychiatry and Human Development, 12,* 32–39.

Umphenour, J.H. (1980). Bacterial colonization in neonates with sibling visitation. *Journal of Obstetric, Gynecologic and Neonatal Nursing, 9,* 73–75.

United States Conference of Mayors. (1990). *The national directory of local AIDS services.* Washington, DC.

U.S. Surgeon General's Workshop on Children with HIV infection and their families. (1987, April). *Workgroup recommendations.* Philadelphia: The Children's Hospital of Philadelphia.

Wagner, M.E., Schubert, H.J.P., & Schubert, D.S.P. (1985). Effects of sibling spacing on intelligence, interfamilial relations, psychosocial characteristics, and mental and physical health. In H.W. Reese (Ed.), *Advances in child development and behavior, 19.* New York: Academic Press.

Wranesh, B.L. (1982). The effect of sibling visitation on bacterial colonization rate in neonates. *Journal of Obstetric, Gynecologic and Neonatal Nursing, 11,* 211–213.

CHAPTER 5

Adult Sibling Relationships of Persons with Mental Retardation

*Marsha Mailick Seltzer
and Marty Wyngaarden Krauss*

This chapter uses a lifespan perspective to examine sibling relationships in which one sibling has mental retardation. This perspective includes both predictable and unpredictable changes in the nature, intensity, and functions of sibling relationships that begin in childhood and extend through adulthood and old age. It is a particularly important perspective, because, although there is a great deal of literature on brothers and sisters of children with retardation, with few exceptions there is an astonishing silence in the literature about the adult relationships between sibling pairs when one has mental retardation. Thus, there is very little knowledge about the effects of early childhood experiences between such siblings on later-life relationships, about the extent to which findings from the "general" sibling literature have applicability in this context, or about the natural history of sibling relationships that are marked by such a salient difference in the siblings' abilities and roles.

There are at least three reasons to investigate the antecedents and consequences of adult sibling relationships when one sibling has mental retardation. First, it is now recognized that the vast majority of persons with mental retardation live with, or under the supervision of, their families throughout their lives (Seltzer, Krauss, & Heller, 1990). While parents are the primary

---

Support for the preparation of this paper was provided by the National Institute on Aging (R01 AG08768-01), the Andrus Foundation, the Retirement Research Foundation (12-225), the March of Dimes Birth Defects Foundation, and the National Institute of Disabilities and Rehabilitation Research.

care providers, it is often assumed that, upon their death or infirmity, one of their other children will take responsibility for the sibling with retardation (Krauss, 1990). Clearly, more information is needed about siblings' capacity to step into such roles, and about the potential consequences to them and to their relationship with their brother or sister with retardation.

Second, there is considerable evidence that some nondisabled siblings (particularly older girls) experience psychological distress in adolescence, including pathology in some subgroups, attributable to the atypical role demands placed on them in early childhood (Drotar & Crawford, 1985; Lobato, 1983). We have no information, however, about the durability or course of psychological distress among nondisabled siblings, or about the mechanisms by which stressful relationships in one period of life are either continued or mastered in subsequent periods of life.

Third, the marked increase in the life expectancy of persons with mental retardation means that it is now, and will continue to be, the norm for adults with mental retardation to survive long enough to enjoy sibling relationships in adulthood (Janicki & Wisniewski, 1985). Parents used to correctly assume that they would outlive their child with retardation; at the present time most adults with retardation outlive their parents, and may subsequently rely on their siblings for support, and possibly for direct care, during their mutual old age.

This chapter is divided into four sections. First, the theoretical perspectives that are relevant to the study of sibling relationships in adulthood and old age are examined. Second, a selective review of the research literature on adult sibling relationships in the general population is presented, focusing on the findings that are of particular relevance to adult sibling relationships when one sibling has mental retardation. The limited literature on the sibling relationships of adults with mental retardation is also reviewed. Third, the results of the research that the authors are conducting on aging families with an adult child with mental retardation are summarized, with a focus on patterns of sibling interaction in these families. Finally, avenues are suggested for future research on adult sibling relationships when one sibling has mental retardation.

THEORETICAL PERSPECTIVES

Lifespan Development

Theories of lifespan development seek to explain the extent to which behavior is constant or changing across the lifecourse, and to discover the factors that lead to either stability or discontinuity in human development (Baltes, 1987). Among these factors are normative and nonnormative events. Normative events are experienced with some predictability by most individuals, and these events are governed largely by biological maturation (e.g., puberty) or sociocultural timetables (e.g., entering school). In contrast, nonnormative experiences are unpredictable, unplanned, often unwanted, and are largely unshared. These events, for which individuals receive little prior socialization, are typically major life stressors such as physical disability, death of a loved one, or loss of a job (Seltzer & Ryff, in press). While having a sibling is a normative experience common to 85% or 90% of the population (Cicirelli, 1982), having a sibling with mental retardation or another developmental disability is a nonnormative experience.

The normative experience of having a sibling tends to be conceptualized in developmental terms, with an attempt to account for later development by examining earlier statuses or experiences. For example, Goetting (1986) conceptualized the extent of stability and change in the developmental tasks of normative siblingship during three stages over the life course: 1) childhood and adolescence, 2) early and middle adulthood, and 3) old age. According to Goetting, in childhood and adolescence the predominant sibling task is companionship and emotional support, with children (particularly sisters) having intense patterns of interaction with their siblings. Delegated caregiving and aid and direct services are tasks of lesser importance during this stage.

In early and middle adulthood, sibling ties are loosened and become more diffuse. Companionship and emotional support remain important developmental tasks in adulthood, but the relationship is less intense than in childhood, and may be characterized by a passive sense of concern. Additional tasks in adulthood are cooperation in the care of elderly parents, and aid and direct services provided by siblings to each other.

In old age, the sibling relationship persists autonomously, even though the family of origin is no longer intact. At this stage of life, the tasks of companionship and emotional support represent a reintensification of the emotional bonds between siblings, especially when one or both no longer is married. Other tasks of the siblingship in old age are shared reminiscence, the resolution of sibling rivalry, and aid and direct services.

It is noteworthy that, in Goetting's conceptualization, two tasks remain constant across the life course—companionship and emotional support, and aid and direct services. However, the behaviors that characterize these tasks and their importance relative to other tasks change as the siblings age. Thus, there is constancy as well as change in the sibling relationship across the life course.

It is clear from this review of Goetting's work that normative influences, including the life tasks of the siblingship, are conceptualized developmentally. In contrast, there has been very little theoretical analysis of the developmental consequences of nonnormative sibling relationships. Rather, having a brother or sister with retardation has been studied nondevelopmentally, with theoretical and empirical work using a cross-sectional, rather than a longitudinal, approach to compare siblings with and without a disabled brother or sister at a single point in time. The lifelong developmental sequelae of having a sibling with a disability have yet to be investigated.

Attachment

A second theoretical perspective relevant to lifelong sibling relationships is attachment theory. Although attachment has been linked almost universally to infancy, in recent years theorists have attempted to examine the implications of attachment across the lifespan. Ainsworth (1989) proposed that attachment extends beyond infancy into adulthood through affectional bonds, which she defined as "long-enduring tie(s) in which the partner is important as a unique individual and is interchangeable with none other" (p. 711). The sibling relationship is one example given by Ainsworth of affectional bonds that persist throughout the life course.

Lerner and Ryff (1978) also conceptualized attachment from a lifespan perspective. In their view, attachment has intrinsic lifespan properties because the early attachment relationship forms the basis for relationships that develop later in life. They noted, however, that the behaviors defining attachment differ at various stages of life, although the functions of these behaviors may remain constant. For example, proximity seeking, a hallmark of attachment, is achieved in later life through letters, visits, and phone calls exchanged by adults who have strong mutual affectional bonds (such as siblings). Similarly, at this stage of life, protective behaviors are expressed as mutual aid and caregiving (Cicirelli, 1985). As with Goetting's (1986) conceptualization, attachment between siblings persists across the lifecourse, even though the behaviors manifesting attachment change from stage to stage in age-appropriate ways. Empirical research is needed to clarify patterns of continuity or discontinuity in attachments across the lifecourse (Antonucci, 1976; Lerner & Ryff, 1978) and to study the ways in which attachment differs from the norm when one sibling has a lifelong disability.

Exchange Theory

A third theoretical perspective of relevance to sibling relationships in adulthood, especially when one sibling has mental retardation, is exchange theory. Exchange theory focuses on the interactions among people and explains social relationships in terms of give-and-take (Blau, 1964; Homans, 1961). Sahlins (1965) described three types of reciprocal relationships: generalized reciprocity (in which individuals give without the expectation of repayment, typically characteristic of the parent–child relationship), balanced reciprocity (which is characterized by an equitable pattern of exchanges, typically characteristic of sibling relationships), and negative reciprocity (in which the support given by one person is never reciprocated, even though reciprocity is expected).

Avioli (1989) noted that in the long run, sibling relationships are generally balanced in their reciprocity. However, when there are long-term inequities in the sibling relationship, one of two consequences may result. Either the siblings become estranged from one another, as with negative reciprocity, or the siblingship takes on the characteristics of generalized reciprocity, as with a parent–child relationship. Such shifts in patterns of interaction when one sibling does not reciprocate have implications for the analysis of the sibling relationship when one sibling has a disability.

In sum, general social and behavioral science theories as diverse as lifespan development, attachment, and exchange theories provide a framework for comparing the way that typical sibling relationships develop in adulthood and old age with the way that these relationships unfold when one sibling has a disability.

SIBLING RELATIONSHIPS IN ADULTHOOD AND OLD AGE: A REVIEW OF THE LITERATURE

Although research on sibling relationships in the general population has characteristically focused on the early childhood period, the recent influence of theories of lifespan development has resulted in an increased emphasis on patterns of sibling relationships at all stages (Lamb, 1982). Studies of the patterns of interaction and the affective ties among siblings during middle and old age confirm that these relationships remain important, even though they are expressed differently than in early childhood (Allan, 1977; Bedford, 1989; Cicirelli, 1988; Manney, 1975; Scott, 1990).

The sibling bond occupies a unique position within the range of family relationships. This bond is of potentially longer duration than any other human relationship (Cicirelli, 1982). Also, siblings share a common genetic, cultural, and experiential heritage, which has been described as a family life space (Ross & Dalton, 1981). Sibling relationships, especially in comparison with parent–child relationships, tend to be egalitarian rather than hierarchical (Avioli, 1989; Baskett & Johnson, 1982). Further, because the sibling role is ascribed rather than achieved, it remains a part of an individual's identity regardless of changes in marital status, place of residence, or financial well-being.

There are two demographic trends relevant to the study of sibling relationships in adulthood. The first trend is in the probability of having a sibling during adulthood and old age, given changes in the average size of the American family; the second relates to the probability of having a geographically close sibling during adulthood. With respect to the first trend, there has been a marked decline in the average size of the family. Whereas early in this century the average number of children per family who survived early childhood was between four and five, by the middle of the century the average family size included only two or three children (Treas & Bengtson, 1987). Given the age-related risks of morbidity and the longer lifespan characteristic of Americans today, the probability of having a surviving sibling throughout old age is now lower than it was in the past. To illustrate, Cicirelli (1979) found that adults in the 60–69 age range, who originally had an average of 4.6 siblings, had an average of 2.9 siblings still surviving. In contrast, those age 80 or older, who originally had almost as many siblings (4.2., on average), had only 1.1 surviving siblings. Currently, the average family size in childhood is only half of the original size of families of those age 80 or older. Thus, the chances of having a surviving sibling in old age may be much decreased, even though life expectancy has improved considerably. At the present time, however, most American adults have at least one living sibling (Cicirelli, 1982).

The second trend reflects the rise in geographic mobility, which has resulted in more widely dispersed families. Only about one-quarter to one-third of middle-age or older adults live in the same city as a brother or a sister (Cicirelli, 1982). Although available research indicates that bonds of affection may be characteristic of sibling relationships, even when the siblings live in different cities and even when face-to-face contact is limited, the possibility of direct instrumental assistance by a sibling to a brother or sister is obviously limited by factors such as the distance between their homes and the frequency of contact (Avioli, 1989). In spite of the rise in geographic mobility, however, it remains the norm for siblings to see each other at least several times each year (Cicirelli, 1982).

Most studies of the affective relationship between adult siblings indicate that these relationships are characterized by supportiveness, concern, and mutual affection (Allan, 1977; Cicirelli, 1982). Two important variables affect the quality of the sibling bond: gender and social class. Studies almost universally find that the bonds between sisters are stronger than either cross-sex sibling bonds or the bonds between brothers (Avioli, 1989; Rosenberg, 1982). Furthermore, the bonds between working-class siblings tend to be stronger than those between middle-class siblings (Allan, 1977; Brady & Noberini, 1987), possibly due to the greater geographic and social mobility of middle-class adults. The greatest degree of strife between brothers reportedly occurs when one attains a more prestigious occupational status than the other (Adams, 1968).

One noteworthy aspect of sibling relationships is that although these bonds tend to persevere longer than any other relationship, in adulthood they are ordinarily not as emotionally intense as during early childhood. It may well be that the simple existence of the sibling relationship is perceived to be more important than the actual aid that is exchanged between siblings. In fact, studies of the exchange of instrumental aid between siblings suggest that such assistance ordinarily is temporary in duration, received reluctantly, and accepted only if a spouse's or adult child's aid is not available (Avioli, 1989;

Cicirelli, 1982). As Avioli (1989) expressed, "siblings appear to function as an insurance policy for older persons. Although rarely called on for instrumental aid, there is comfort and satisfaction in knowing that a sibling is there (p. 52)." While there is a reintensification of the sibling bond in old age (Goetting, 1986), direct care by one sibling for another tends to be the exception rather than the rule, and is provided primarily in cases in which there is no spouse or adult child on whom to depend for support.

However, when one of the siblings has mental retardation, the nature of the sibling relationship across the lifespan is likely to be very different. In general, the results of research on the psychological effects on young children of having a brother or sister with mental retardation, chronic illness, or other type of disability suggest that some siblings of children with chronic disabling conditions are at risk for emotional morbidity, at least during the early childhood and adolescent periods (Breslau, 1982; Drotar & Crawford, 1985; Gath, 1972; Lobato, 1983; Poznanski, 1969; San Martino & Newman, 1974; Stoneman, Brody, Davis, Crapps, & Malone, 1991; Trevino, 1979; Wilson, Blacher, & Baker, 1989). The risk is assumed to be related largely to four factors: 1) the different amounts of time invested by parents in siblings with mental retardation, as compared to those who have no disability; 2) the propensity for increased caregiving responsibilities to be expected of nondisabled siblings (particularly older girls); 3) the family's socioeconomic status; and 4) the psychological impacts on siblings of anxiety or guilt over the etiology of their sibling's disabilities (Begun, 1989).

The long-term consequences of having a sibling with retardation have not been well studied. There is evidence, however, that many adult siblings of persons with retardation continue to be emotionally and instrumentally involved with their brother or sister throughout the lifespan. Cleveland and Miller's (1977) survey of adult siblings of institutionalized adults with mental retardation reported positive perceptions among siblings about their experiences growing up with their sibling with severe or profound retardation. They noted the importance of the attitudes and behaviors of their parents in creating a home environment that was not primarily focused on their brother or sister, but rather fostered the development of all family members.

In a more recent study, Zetlin (1986) used participation observation methods to study the sibling relationships of 35 adults with mild retardation. She identified five kinds of sibling relationships based on the affective quality of the relationships, frequency of contact, and level of involvement. The relationships ranged from siblings who assumed surrogate parent roles (paralleling the generalized reciprocity model discussed earlier) to siblings who maintained virtually no contact and had acrimonious relationships with their brother or sister with retardation (paralleling the negative reciprocity model). It was noteworthy that in Zetlin's research none of the five types of sibling relationships was balanced in the exchange of emotional and instrumental support, which is the norm in relationships between nondisabled siblings. Zetlin also found that sibling relationships involving a brother or sister with a disability were hierarchical, rather than egalitarian, sensitive to parental expectations and influences, and included a strong emotional dependency of the adult with retardation on his or her nondisabled sibling.

Begun (1989) studied the relationships between adolescent and adult females and their sibling with retardation. She found that these relationships were generally described as positive, but not intimate, supporting the affect-neutrality model offered by Miller (1974). She also reported that the quality of the sibling relationships was affected by the living arrangements of the siblings. Those who co-resided had higher levels of conflict than those who lived apart.

This review of the literature suggests that adult sibling relationships in which one sibling has mental retardation are very different from typical sibling relationships. While the latter tend to be egalitarian and are characterized by balanced exchanges of support, the former tend to be more imbalanced, being more similar to parent–child relationships in this regard. Furthermore, while the adult relationship between typical siblings tends to be of low intensity, more intense emotion appears to be a characteristic of the sibling bond when one sibling has a lifelong disability. Nondisabled siblings try to avoid the exchange of instrumental support, even though they are gratified to know that such support is available as needed. In contrast, siblings with a disability have a greater need earlier in life to receive instrumental support from their nondisabled brother or sister, and may be increasingly dependent on this support as they both age and as the parents are no longer able to provide primary care. As noted above, the lifespan developmental consequences of such atypical sibling relationships have not been studied in past research. However, theories of lifespan development would predict that having a sibling with a disability exerts a powerful influence on the personal development of the nondisabled siblings. Therefore, these influences and their consequences in adulthood and old age warrant examination in research on families with a member with retardation.

RESULTS FROM THE AUTHORS' RESEARCH ON SIBLING RELATIONSHIPS IN ADULTHOOD

The authors' longitudinal investigation of parental caregivers of adults with retardation who live at home (Seltzer & Krauss, 1989) also provided an opportunity to examine sibling relationships in adulthood (Seltzer, Begun, Seltzer, & Krauss, 1991). This 5-year study focused on 462 families who provide in-home care for an adult child with retardation. Families who participated met two criteria: 1) the mother was age 55 or older, and 2) the son or daughter with mental retardation lived at home with her at the time of study recruitment. About half of the families (277) lived in Massachusetts, and half in Wisconsin (235).

At the time of study enrollment, the mothers ranged in age from 55 to 85 (mean age=64.8 years). Their sons and daughters with retardation ranged in age from 15 to 66 (mean age=33.5 years). About three-fourths had either mild or moderate retardation, and more than one-third had Down syndrome. Most (80%) had always lived at home with their parent(s). Thus, these families had provided a lifetime of care for their member with retardation. While the study's primary goal was to understand how this life history had affected aging mothers and fathers, the importance of siblings as a support to both their brother or sister with retardation and to their parents has emerged quite clearly from the analyses. Indeed, there is rich evidence that the roles of adult siblings of persons with mental retardation are complex, determined, in part, by the emotional and social climate of the family, and an important influence on the well-being of multiple family members.

Regarding sibling relationships in these families, the authors have examined four issues: 1) the availability of siblings as potential sources of support to their brother or sister with mental retardation, 2) the nature of the support provided, 3) the influence of the family's social climate on the involvement of nondisabled siblings with their brother or sister with retardation, and 4) the effect on the mother of the relationship between her child with retardation and her other (nondisabled) children.

The quantitative and qualitative data for the cross-sectional analyses discussed below were collected during the first of four waves of data collection, through in-home interviews conducted with the mother, and through her responses to self-administered questionnaires. In the qualitative data reported below, all names have been changed to preserve the confidentiality of participating families. The research procedures have been described in detail elsewhere (Krauss, Seltzer, & Goodman, 1992; Seltzer, Begun, Seltzer, & Krauss, 1991; Seltzer & Krauss, 1989).

Availability of Siblings

In the authors' analyses of the older families who participated in our research, it was found that the siblings of the adults with mental retardation occupy a unique, active, and, in many families, a pivotal role. Specifically, consistent with the findings reported in the literature on the frequency of siblings in the general population (Cicirelli, 1982), nearly all of the adults with retardation in the sample (93.2%) had at least one living sibling. The average number of siblings per family (in those families in which there were siblings) was 2.9, in addition to the adult with retardation. These siblings averaged 36.6 years of age and half were female (50.3%). Most siblings were married (70.5%) and lived away from their parents' home. However, in 20.7% of the families, at least one other sibling lived in the parental home at the time of the study. Thus, the authors found that most adults with mental retardation have siblings who could potentially provide them with support.

Support Provided by Siblings

The authors also examined the extent to which instrumental and affective support was provided to the adult with retardation by his or her siblings. Consistent with the literature on the exchange of instrumental support between nondisabled siblings (Avioli, 1989), only about one-fifth of the adults with retardation in the sample (20.1%) received any instrumental support from their siblings, with the most frequent type of help being errands and home repairs (received by 9.1% and 8.2%, respectively, of those adults who needed help with these tasks). Rather, most instrumental support was provided by the parents. However, co-residence of siblings was clearly implicated in the provision of instrumental support; adults in families in which there was at least one sibling living at home were more likely to receive instrumental support from a sibling (40%) than adults in families in which no siblings still lived at home (14.5%). For example, one mother recounted the many skills that her nondisabled daughter had tried to teach her daughter with retardation:

> Andrea [nondisabled daughter] teaches Marilyn [daughter with retardation] to be with other people in a social setting, to have appropriate behavior and actions. Andrea also teaches Marilyn to dress properly. Marilyn now has a good sense of style and fashion so that she puts the correct color combinations together. Andrea teaches her housework and cleaning and stuff like that. There's a lot that she gives her.

In contrast, most adults with retardation (80.2%) were reported by their mothers to receive affective support from at least one sibling. On average, two-thirds (66.6%) of the siblings in a family were identified as members of the social support network of the adult with retardation. These findings are consistent with the literature on the exchange of affective support among nondisabled siblings (Bedford, 1989). One mother described the relationship between her nondisabled daughter and her son with retardation as follows:

> Well, you know there is a distance. Susan [nondisabled daughter] is married and has a family, so it's not an on-going, everyday thing where she does something for him all the time, but she was here last summer and she is very supportive and tries to devise ways to help him. I think if she were around, and they were closer in distance, she probably would do more that way.

The nature of the affective relationship between siblings and their brother or sister with retardation, however, had a number of qualities that differentiated it from typical sibling relationships. The authors' analyses indicated a generalized model of reciprocity (i.e., support provided without the expectation of equal repayment) rather than the balanced reciprocity characteristic of most relationships between nondisabled siblings (Sahlins, 1965). Specifically, of the six types of affective support examined that could be exchanged between siblings (i.e., serving as a confidante, providing reassurance, providing respect, providing care when ill, listening when one is upset, and discussing health matters), the nondisabled siblings in the sample provided an average of 2.9 types of support to the adult with retardation, who in turn provided only 1.3 types of support back to the sibling. This finding echoes those of Begun's (1989) and Zetlin's (1986) research on the lack of balanced reciprocity among siblings when one of them has a significant disability. Another mother described the relationship between her children as:

> a very friendly relationship. Ann [nondisabled daughter] tends to be very interested in what Sharon [daughter with retardation] is doing and what her work situation is. Ann enjoys being with Sharon, taking her shopping. She also protects her. Ann's the protector in the relationship.

For all families in which there was any affective support provided by a sibling to the adult with retardation, the authors identified one sibling who was "the most involved." The most involved sibling was defined as the sibling who provided the greatest number of affective supports to the adult with retardation. Consistent with the literature on nondisabled sibling involvements (Rosenberg, 1982), the most involved sibling in the family was more likely to be a sister (64.2%) than a brother (35.8%), and more likely to be of the same sex as the adult with retardation (54.4%) than of the opposite sex (45.6%). Among opposite-sex pairs, sisters were more likely to be the most involved sibling for a brother with retardation (71.4% of all opposite-sexed sibling pairs) than were brothers for a sister with retardation (27.8%). In about two-thirds of the cases (66.4%), the most involved sibling was older than the adult with retardation. It was generally the case (in 82.7% of the families) that the most involved sibling lived within a 1-hour drive of the family home, and most (75.6%) had at least weekly contact (in person or by telephone) with the adult with retardation. These findings contrast with the patterns of proximity and involvement reported in the literature among nondisabled siblings. As noted above, in the general population, only one-quarter to one-third of middle-age or older adults had a sibling living in the same city, and contact averaged only several times each year (Cicirelli, 1982). The impact on the nondisabled sibling and the sibling with retardation of having more frequent contact with one another than is typical in the general population is not yet understood.

Effect of the Family Environment on Sibling Relationships

As noted above, other studies (Cleveland & Miller, 1977; Grossman, 1972) have suggested that the characteristics of the family environment are important determinants of the ability of nondisabled brothers and sisters to adjust favorably to the unique contexts in which they grow up. The authors investigated whether attributes of the family environment—its emotional climate, the values or activities that were promoted within it, and its organizational style—corresponded to the level of involvement of siblings as adults with their brother or sister with mental retardation. On the one hand, it could be hypothesized that the effects of the qualities of family life would fade as siblings reach adulthood and develop their own lives, independent of their parent(s). In this case, one would not expect to find a relation between the family life space and the level of sibling involvement with their brother or sister with retardation in adulthood. On the other hand, one could hypothesize that the family life space is enduring, and continues to shape, support, and organize the interactions among family members throughout the lifespan.

The authors' analyses have revealed considerable evidence of the enduring effects of the family life space on the intensity of the relationships between siblings and their brother or sister with retardation. Specifically, the authors found that families in which there was an "involved" sibling (with respect to the provision of affective or instrumental support to the person with mental retardation) were characterized by high levels of expressiveness and more strongly held values on the importance of independence and active recreation. These values may be the manifestation of a commitment to the personal development of all family members and to an openness in communication within the family.

One mother noted how the openness in her family seemed to foster a close relationship between her children:

> There's a closeness there [between my children]. In so many cases we hear of brothers and sisters who are ashamed. We've never had to deal with that. They would bring friends in and there was no problem with acceptance or anything like that. We were proud of all our children and it just rubbed off, I guess.

In contrast, families in which none of the other children were reportedly "involved" with the member with retardation were characterized by significantly less expressiveness and more conflictual interactions. It appears that more constrained interactions among family members have a spill-over effect on the willingness or ability of adult siblings to maintain an active, ongoing, supportive relationship with their brother or sister with retardation.

These findings suggest an important link between the environment of the family and sibling interpersonal relationships, even through the later stages of life. Although most siblings were married, living away from the parental home, and nearing middle age, the social climate of their family of origin was found to correspond to their involvement with their brother or sister with retardation. In contrast, the literature on typical siblings clarifies that by middle age, the sibling relationship usually becomes autonomous of the family of origin (Goetting, 1986).

Effect of Sibling Involvement on Maternal Well-Being

The authors also examined the effect of sibling involvement on aging mothers. It was found that maternal reliance on nondisabled children is important in at least two respects. First, as the authors have reported elsewhere, mothers most often named one of their other children as the person who would assume responsibility, if necessary, for the care of their adult child with retardation when they were no longer able to continue in this role themselves (Krauss, 1990). While many mothers expressed deep-seated ambivalence about this expectation, the desire for continuity in family-based care and responsibility for the member with retardation was striking.

Second, the authors found that the well-being of the mother was strongly affected by the degree of involvement of her other children in the life of her son or daughter with retardation. Specifically, it was found that mothers whose adult children were affectively supportive of one another were significantly more satisfied with their lives, and felt significantly less stressed as parents of a child with retardation and less burdened by their caregiving responsibilities than did mothers whose adult children were less involved with one another. In contrast, the amount of instrumental support provided by the nondisabled sibling to the adult with retardation was not related to maternal well-being, suggesting that direct assistance in caregiving by the sibling to the adult with retardation was not as salient for the mother as was the emotional relationship between her children. As one mother said:

> It makes my heart easy when I watch them [her children] together. Because I know when something happens to me and I'm not there, Mark [her son with retardation] will have someone who loves him very much to take care of him.

In summary, the results suggest that non-normative roles—such as having a sibling with mental retardation—affect all family members in very distinct and enduring ways. Siblings of a person with mental retardation are often cast as the "vice president" of the family—as the person who may well inherit responsibilities traditionally assumed by the parents (most commonly the mother). Their level of involvement in adulthood with their brother or sister with retardation appears to be both similar to (i.e., characterized by a relatively low level of instrumental assistance) and different from (i.e., in regard to the salience of their involvement with respect to their mothers' well-being) patterns reported among typical siblings. Equally impressive, however, is the list of issues surrounding adult siblings of persons with retardation that remains unexplored, as discussed in the final section of this chapter.

AVENUES FOR FUTURE RESEARCH

Given the limited amount of research that has been conducted on sibling relationships during adulthood, there is a wide agenda of topics that warrant investigation. Much could be learned about the development of relationships between siblings and their brothers and sisters with mental retardation through the use of prospective, longitudinal studies. Specifically, the prevalence and durability of psychological morbidity among nondisabled siblings remains an immensely important issue from both a developmental and a public-policy perspective. While no one would discount the propensity of non-normative childhood experiences—such as having a sibling with mental retardation—for causing significant psychological ramifications, little is understood about the specific lifecourse consequences of this specific situation. Such knowledge is derived most readily from careful and artful tracking of individual changes over a period of decades, a "luxury" that requires a sustained commitment not only from investigators, but also from funding agencies.

In this regard, it is important to understand the effect of different life experiences of the sibling with retardation on his or her brothers and sisters without disability. Specifically, there is a need to investigate the effect of premature and postponed launching (Seltzer et al., 1990) of the individual with retardation into subsequent sibling relationships. Differences in the strength and diversity of the social networks of persons with retardation (Krauss et al., 1992) may also have profound implications for the dependency relationships between siblings with retardation and their nondisabled brothers or sisters. Extensive studies of these and other topics are needed, leading to analyses that determine the effects of gender, birth order, and family size, as these variables have been shown consistently in previous research to color and shape the nature of sibling relationships when one sibling has a disability.

It is clear that, within families who continue to provide direct care for an adult member with retardation, the nondisabled siblings provide an important protective layer of support—to both the adult with retardation (in the form of emotional support, and, less commonly, instrumental support) and indirectly to the parental caregivers (in the form of enhanced well-being). Further research is needed to determine the factors that promote and sustain active involvement by siblings in the lives of their brother or sister with retardation and why this involvement has such a salutary effect on their mothers.

There are policy issues that warrant investigation, as well. The authors' findings that siblings are the most likely replacement for the mothers suggests that greater attention should be given to finding ways to prepare siblings to assume this role and to encouraging their willingness to do so. Siblings may well worry whether their efforts will be matched or complemented by formal agencies charged with providing services to adults with retardation. It is likely that most siblings have an incomplete understanding of the community-based service system in their area, and may not have learned the advocacy skills that will be required of them should they assume a responsible role in the care of their family member with retardation.

Undoubtedly, siblings will also worry about the impact on their own lives—on their marriage, their children, their career, and their financial well-being—of assuming primary responsibility for a brother or sister with retardation. The development and evaluation of appropriate support services that are responsive to the concerns of siblings in adulthood is an important goal for the future.

Finally, it is vitally important that studies focus on the perspectives of adults with retardation with respect to their sibling relationships. Virtually nothing is known about the impact of nondisabled siblings on persons with retardation, at any life stage. Clearly, the perceived availability, quality, and functions of sibling relationships for adults with retardation are important, although poorly understood. The potential of these relationships to provide a foundation for long-term care planning and for contributing to the emotional well-being of adults with retardation is simply unknown.

REFERENCES

Adams, B.N. (1968). *Kinship in an urban setting*. Chicago: Markham Publishing.

Ainsworth, M.D.S. (1989). Attachments beyond infancy. *American Psychologist, 44*, 709–716.

Allan, G. (1977). Sibling solidarity. *Journal of Marriage and the Family, 39*, 177–184.

Antonucci, T. (1976). Attachment: A life-span concept. *Human Development, 19*, 135–142.

Avioli, P.S. (1989). The social support functions of siblings in later life. *American Behavioral Scientist, 33*, 45–57.

Baltes, P.B. (1987). Theoretical propositions of life-span development psychology: On the dynamics between growth and decline. *Developmental Psychology, 23*, 611–626.

Baskett, L.M., & Johnson, S.M. (1982). The young child's interactions with parents versus siblings: A behavioral analysis. *Child Development, 53*, 643–650.

Bedford, V.H. (1989). Understanding the value of siblings in old age: A proposed model. *American Behavioral Scientist, 31*, 33–45.

Begun, A.L. (1989). Sibling relationships involving developmentally disabled people. *American Journal on Mental Retardation, 93*, 566–574.

Blau, P.M. (1964). *Exchange and power in social life*. New York: John Wiley & Sons.

Brady, E.M., & Noberini, M.R. (1987, August). *Sibling support in the context of a model of sibling solidarity*. Paper presented at the 95th Annual Meeting of the American Psychological Association, New York.

Breslau, N. (1982). Siblings of disabled children: Birth order and age-spacing effects. *Journal of Abnormal Child Psychology, 10*, 85–96.

Cicirelli, V.G. (1979). *Social services for the elderly in relation to the kin network* (Report to the NRTA-AARP Andrus Foundation) West Lafayette, IN: Author.

Cicirelli, V.G. (1982). Sibling influence throughout the lifespan. In M.E. Lamb & B. Sutton-Smith (Eds.), *Sibling relationships: Their nature and significance across the lifespan* (pp. 267–284). Hillsdale, NJ: Lawrence Erlbaum Associates.

Cicirelli, V.G. (1985). The role of siblings as family caregivers. In W.J. Sauer & R.T. Coward (Eds.), *Social support networks and the care of the elderly* (pp. 93–107). New York: Springer.

Cicirelli, V.G. (1988). Interpersonal relationships among elderly siblings. In M.D. Kahn & K.G. Lewis (Eds.), *Siblings in therapy: Life span and clinical issues* (pp. 435–456). New York: W.W. Norton.

Cleveland, D.W., & Miller, N. (1977). Attitudes and life commitments of older siblings of mentally retarded adults: An exploratory study. *Mental Retardation, 15,* 38–41.

Drotar, D., & Crawford, P. (1985). Psychological adaptation of siblings of chronically ill children: Research and practice implications. *Developmental and Behavioral Pediatrics, 6,* 355–362.

Gath, A. (1972). The mental health of siblings of congenitally abnormal children. *Journal of Child Psychology and Psychiatry, 13,* 211–218.

Goetting, A. (1986). The developmental tasks of siblingship over the life cycle. *Journal of Marriage and the Family, 48,* 703–714.

Grossman, F.K. (1972). *Brothers and sisters of retarded children: An exploratory study.* Syracuse, NY: Syracuse University Press.

Homans, G.C. (1961). *Social behavior: Its elementary forms.* New York: Harcourt Brace Jovanovich.

Janicki, M.P., & Wisniewski, H.M. (Eds.). (1985). *Aging and developmental disabilities: Issues and approaches.* Baltimore: Paul H. Brookes Publishing Co.

Krauss, M.W. (1990, May). *Later life placements: Precipitating factors and family profiles.* Paper presented at the 114th Annual Meeting of the American Association on Mental Retardation. Atlanta, GA.

Krauss, M.W., Seltzer, M.M., & Goodman, S. (1992). Social support networks of adults with retardation who live at home. *American Journal on Mental Retardation, 96,* 432–441.

Lamb, M.E. (1982). Sibling relationships across the lifespan: An overview and introduction. In M.E. Lamb & B. Sutton-Smith (Eds.), *Sibling relationships: Their nature and significance across the lifespan,* (pp. 1–12). Hillsdale, NJ: Lawrence Erlbaum Associates.

Lawton, M.P. (1972). The dimensions of morale. In D. Kent, R. Kastenbaum, & S. Sherwood (Eds.), *Research planning and action for the elderly* (pp. 144–165). New York: Behavioral Publications.

Lerner, R.M., & Ryff, C.D. (1978). Implementation of the life-span view of human development: The sample case of attachment. In P.B. Baltes (Eds.), *Life-span development and behavior* (Vol. 1, pp. 2–44). New York: Academic Press.

Lobato, D. (1983). Siblings of handicapped children: A review. *Journal of Autism and Developmental Disorders, 13,* 347–364.

Manney, J.D. (1975). *Aging.* Washington, DC: Office of Human Development, Department of Health, Education, and Welfare, Government Printing Office.

McHale, S.M., & Gamble, W.C. (1989). Sibling relationships of children with disabled and nondisabled brothers and sisters. *Developmental Psychology, 25,* 421–429.

Miller, S.G. (1974). *An exploratory study of sibling relationships in families with retarded children.* Unpublished doctoral dissertation, Columbia University Teachers College.

Poznanski, E. (1969). Psychiatric difficulties in siblings of handicapped children. *Clinical Pediatrics, 8,* 232–234.

Rosenberg, B.G. (1982). Life span personality stability in sibling status. In M.E. Lamb & B. Sutton-Smith (Eds.), *Sibling relationships: Their nature and significance across the lifespan* (pp. 167–224). Hillsdale, NJ: Lawrence Erlbaum Associates.

Ross, H.G., & Dalton, M.J. (1981, August). *Perceived determinants of closeness in adult sibling relationships*. Paper presented at the American Psychological Association Convention, Los Angeles, CA.

Sahlins, S. (1965). Primitive exchange. In M. Banton (Ed.), *The relevance of models of social anthropology* (pp. 139–236). New York: Praeger.

San Martino, M., & Newman, M. (1974). Siblings of retarded children: A population at risk. *Child Psychiatry and Human Development, 4,* 168–177.

Scott, J.P. (1990). Sibling interaction in later life. In T.H. Brubaker (Ed.), *Family relationships in later life* (2nd ed.) (pp. 86–99). Beverly Hills, CA: Sage.

Seltzer, G.B., Begun, A., Seltzer, M.M., & Krauss, M.W. (1991). The impacts of siblings on adults with mental retardation and their aging mothers. *Family Relations, 40,* 310–317.

Seltzer, M.M., & Krauss, M.W. (1989). Aging parents with adult mentally retarded children: Family risk factors and sources of support. *American Journal on Mental Retardation, 94,* 303–312.

Seltzer, M.M., Krauss, M.W., & Heller, T. (1990, November). *Family caregiving over the life course*. Paper presented at the Roundtable on Aging and Developmental Disabilities, Boston, MA.

Seltzer, M.M., & Ryff, C. (in press). Parenting across the lifespan: The normative and nonnormative cases. In D.L. Featherman, R.M. Lerner, & M. Perlmutter (Eds.), *Life-span development and behavior* (Volume 12). Hillsdale, NJ: Lawrence Erlbaum Associates.

Stoneman, Z., Brody, G.H., Davis, C.H., Crapps, J.M., & Malone, D.M. (1991). Ascribed role relations between children with mental retardation and their younger siblings. *American Journal on Mental Retardation, 95,* 537–550.

Treas, J., & Bengtson, V.L. (1987). The family in later years. In M.B. Sussman & S.K. Steinmetz (Eds.), *Handbook of marriage and the family* (pp. 625–648). New York: Plenum.

Trevino, F. (1979). Siblings of handicapped children: Identifying those at risk. *Social Casework, 60*(8), 488–493.

Wilson, J., Blacher, J., & Baker, B.L. (1989). Siblings of children with severe handicaps. *Mental Retardation, 27,* 167–173.

Zetlin, A.G. (1986). Mentally retarded adults and their siblings. *American Journal of Mental Deficiency, 91,* 217–225.

CHAPTER 6

Siblings and Out-of-Home Placement

Jan Blacher

Today Noah leaves for OCC. . . I do not cry yet. I know there will be crying later. It is good that Foumi will be with me. If she cries, I cannot. One of us must remain dry-eyed in the presence of the other—and of Karl. He will be with us because I think he should see where we are putting Noah. He should have the same misgivings we have. (Greenfeld, 1986, p. 267)

In *A Client Called Noah,* Josh Greenfeld provides a prospective account of the out-of-home placement process for Noah, his son with autism. While Greenfeld's writing is first person, he takes his other son's (Karl's) perspective frequently:

I must say, with Noah gone Karl seems more relaxed, less moody, and happier. It is as if a great burden has been lifted from him. Or am I simply being more patient? Or just projecting?" (1986, p. 270). "But I do think with Noah gone Karl can't help but become more adult. It must be awfully hard trying to leave your own childhood behind when your sibling's childhood is perpetual. (1986, p. 265)

The subject of nondisabled siblings and out-of-home placement is a captivating one on which little is known. The sibling relationship is also an enduring one. Emmy Werner (1986) writes: "Among human relationships, the sibling relationship tends to be of the longest duration and may persist for 80 or 90 years, outlasting the bonds between parent and child or husband and wife" (p. 56). Such bonds take on special meaning when one sibling has a disability, especially when that sibling has been placed outside of the family home. Personal accounts such as Greenfeld's (1970, 1978, 1986) provide a valuable glimpse of the issues surrounding siblings and placement. Interest in

---

The author appreciates the support for researching and writing this paper provided by NICHD grant #HD 21324.

this topic was aroused recently by the revival of a relationship between a young adult with autism and his brother in the hit movie *Rainman*. Yet researchers have given little attention to this topic.

This chapter focuses on the issue of nondisabled persons and the out-of-home placement of their siblings who have mental retardation. Although many children, for various reasons, live apart from their families (National Commission on Children, 1991), the focus of this chapter is on individuals with moderate or severe mental retardation, who often have accompanying disabilities (i.e., the population at highest risk for placement) (Meyers, Borthwick, & Eyman, 1985). It is important to note that although at present most professionals encourage parents to keep children with mental retardation at home, a great many such children and adolescents continue to be placed. Moreover, placement is becoming normative for young adults with mental retardation. In short, many individuals must face the experience of their brother or sister with mental retardation moving from the family home to some type of program. For the purposes of this chapter, out-of-home-placement is defined as living arrangements outside of the natural family for persons with disabilities. Placements can be arranged along a continuum based on the degree to which the setting resembles a typical home environment, roughly as follows: foster care, group homes, intermediate care facilities, and large state hospitals or institutions (Baker, Seltzer, & Seltzer, 1977). Adoption is probably the most homelike type of placement, but it represents unusual circumstances and will not be included in the definition for this chapter (Blacher & Bromley, 1990; Glidden, 1990).

The remainder of this chapter comprises three sections. The first focuses on the rationale for studying siblings and out-of-home placement, addressing reasons that the topic has been neglected in the past and why it should be an area of focus for researchers in the future. The second section outlines a conceptual framework for the study of placement and siblings that combines both ecological and developmental perspectives. The final section concludes with a proposed research agenda for the study of nondisabled siblings and out-of-home placement.

OUT-OF-HOME PLACEMENT AND THE SIBLING PERSPECTIVE: RATIONALE FOR FOCUSED STUDY

Siblings have rarely been the focus of research on out-of-home placement. The author will note historical reasons for this, as well as developments that suggest that greater attention must now be given to siblings and placement. Several subjects will be considered, including: 1) conceptual models that emphasize the family context, 2) the influence of evolving service delivery models, 3) the implications of the increased life expectancy of persons with retardation, 4) increased preplacement involvement of siblings, and 5) benefits of postplacement sibling involvement for the individual with retardation.

Ecological Perspectives on Child and Family

Siblings have become important subjects of study in their own right (Dunn, 1985; Dunn, Kendrick, & MacNamee, 1981; Werner, 1986) and as members of a broader family system (Skrtic, Summers, Brotherson, & Turnbull, 1984). The more systems-oriented view of development, popularized by Bronfenbrenner (1979), emphasizes the interrelations among major settings that contain, or affect, the developing child. Hence, rather than continuing to focus on studies of children with mental retardation in isolation, or on children and their mothers, researchers have begun to look at the entire family system—the target child, mother, father, and siblings.

Grossman's (1972) study of college-age brothers and sisters of children with retardation notwithstanding, most of the literature on siblings of children with disabilities is of recent vintage (e.g., Brody, Stoneman, Davis, & Crapps, 1991; Lobato, 1990; Powell & Gallagher, 1992; Simeonsson & McHale, 1981; Stoneman & Brody, 1984; Stoneman, Brody, Davis, & Crapps, 1989). As such, it benefits from current findings on the development of typical siblings. The ecological perspective has influenced much of this research as well (Crnic, Friedrich, & Greenberg, 1983; Dyson, Edgar, & Crnic, 1989) and may prove vital to understanding siblings and out-of-home placement.

An adaptation of Bronfenbrenner's (1979) original model will be explained in the next section and used to conceptualize the impact of placement on nondisabled siblings. Here the authors merely note that contextual influences are important for understanding child development, for understanding families with children who have disabilities, and for understanding out-of-home placement. As this volume shows, siblings are a fundamental component of the disabled child's environment, and very likely remain so even after out-of-home placement.

From Models of Permanent Care to Community Residence

The shift from institutional to community-based models of service delivery also has implications for sibling involvement. Most children with retardation who were placed a generation or more ago moved into institutions that were large, stable, generally custodial, and seen as a permanent placement. Caldwell and Guze (1960) interviewed siblings 30 years ago and found that they believed that the institution "would be there forever." The community residence movement has replaced the custodial model with a more promising developmental one, but has also brought a degree of impermanence. Indeed, the community residence movement renders much of the earlier research on the impact of institutionalization somewhat irrelevant (Farber 1959, 1960, 1963; Farber, Jenne, & Toigo, 1960; Farber & Ryckman, 1965). The developmental model invites greater involvement of families in programming. But the lack of permanence of many group homes and residences in the community (Halpern, Close, & Nelson, 1986) also forces families to be more involved and to assume a greater role as advocates for their child's or sibling's normalized life style (Baker & Blacher, 1988; Turnbull, Turnbull, Bronicki, Summers, & Roeder-Gordon, 1989). Thus, a more community-based approach to serving persons with disabilities is providing opportunities and needs for the greater involvement of families, including siblings.

Shifting the Burden of Care Across the Lifespan

> Noah is an experience he [i.e., Karl, the nondisabled son] will share with us until our deaths. And then, even to his greater misfortune, afterward. (Greenfeld, 1986, p 267)

Josh Greenfeld recognized the likely possibility that his autistic son, Noah, would outlive him. For many reasons, the life expectancy of persons with mental retardation is much longer today than it was several decades ago (Carter & Jancar, 1983). When persons with retardation outlive their parents, or their parents become infirm, the burden of care shifts to their siblings. The life expectancy of all individuals is increasing (Rice & Feldman, 1985), resulting in an expanding population of aging parents of adult offsprings with mental retardation (Seltzer & Krauss, 1990). Seltzer and Krauss write poignantly of the dual challenges of aging parents who still care for their son or daughter with retardation at home—coping with the deficits and discomforts of their own age and with the care and management of their "child."

In the normal course of events, adult children look after their aging parents (Carter & McGoldrick, 1989; Neugarten 1976). However, adults who have a sibling with mental retardation face a dual challenge—that of continued emotional and instrumental involvement with both their aging parents (Seltzer, Begun, Seltzer, & Krauss, in press) and their sibling who is retarded (Begun, 1989; Cleveland & Miller, 1977; Zetlin, 1986). The nondisabled sibling may become involved with two types of out-of-home placements—a facility to provide care for an aging parent, and another to provide programming and vocational opportunities for a sibling. Thus, shifts in the burden of care as the family moves through the lifespan have particularly important implications for siblings of adults with retardation (Goetting, 1986).

Siblings without Disabilities (Pre- and Post-Public Law 94-142)

Longitudinal research on siblings has been scarce; there are a few studies that have monitored changes in sibling relationships, but these have focused primarily on infancy and early childhood (Lamb, 1978; Pepler, Abramovitch, & Corter, 1981). There are, as yet, few studies documenting changes in sibling relationships during childhood and adolescence, or on relationships between persons with disabilities and their nondisabled siblings. However, analysis of existing studies does suggest differences between sibling experiences for children growing up before the 1975 Education for All Handicapped Children Act (PL 94-142) and those growing up after its passage, particularly when one sibling is severely disabled.

Much of what is known about the impact of out-of-home placement on siblings is derived from studies conducted a decade and a half before Public Law 94-142, when placement nearly always meant institutionalization. Parents of children who had severe disabilities were routinely offered the option of institutionalization for their child (Caldwell & Guze, 1960; Moroney, 1986). Because of the lack of available resources, schooling, and knowledge about how to care for and integrate such a child into the home and community, many families availed themselves of that option. Thus, nondisabled siblings were often denied the opportunity to get to know their special brother or sister. Caldwell and Guze (1960) found that for some of these siblings, there was an air of mystery about the placement, which they did not understand for years. And while many of these children were presumably placed, in part, for the good of the family, including the typical siblings (Lobato, 1990), there are only a few studies that have looked at the impact of placement or institutionalization on the nondisabled sibling's adjustment (Caldwell & Guze, 1960; Farber, 1959, 1960; Fotheringham, Skelton, & Hoddinott, 1971).

Farber and his colleagues (Farber 1959, 1960, 1963; Farber et al., 1960; Farber & Ryckman, 1965) compared families who had institutionalized a child with retardation to families who had kept a similar child at home. They interviewed parents about the impact of the child who was retarded on their nondisabled children, and found that older sisters whose sibling with retardation lived at home felt more of the burden of care. This expansion of the daughter's role to assist the mother produced more points of conflict between mother and child. These effects were dulled in families with older daughters who placed the child with retardation. The impact of institutionalization had almost an opposite effect on sons; parents who had placed a child expected more of their nondisabled son; they were presumably more permissive when the child with retardation was at home. Note Josh Greenfeld's thoughts on this subject after placing Noah:

> A friend asked me how we were getting along. I told him I never realized how much of a pain Karl was until after Noah left home.(1986, p. 272)

In her novel *Family Pictures,* Sue Miller elaborates:

> When you read about families like ours, where one member is very ill—special, they're sometimes called now—you discover that often when the problem is removed—because the ill person is sent away, or dies, or gets cured—someone else in the family takes on that role. And maybe that's all it was: that after

Randall left, there was suddenly room for Mack and me to go crazy, to be as mad, as bad, as we wanted. (1990, p. 247)

To the author's knowledge, the only study on this topic that involved interviews with children themselves was conducted by Caldwell and Guze (1960). The purpose of this study was to determine whether mothers and siblings in families where institutionalization was chosen differed in personal adjustment from mothers and siblings in families who kept the child with retardation at home. It is of note that no significant differences in adjustment of siblings were found. Explanations for the lack of differences included methodological difficulties (i.e., one-time interviews; not enough objective measures; the possibility that children were disguising their real feelings) as well as the possibility that the two groups were actually really one group. The authors felt that although placement had already occurred for one group of families, the other group may have contained many "potential" placements.

Adjustment, though, is only one indicator of postplacement impact on nondisabled siblings. Another dimension is involvement with the placed brother or sister. Older studies do not separate sibling involvement from overall family involvement. They indicate, however, that the typical resident receives few visits, phonecalls, or other contacts (Baker & Blacher, 1988; Hill, Rotegard, & Bruininks, 1984; Lei, Nihira, Sheehy, & Meyers, 1981). However, as the authors have noted elsewhere (Blacher & Baker, 1992), a child born with severe mental retardation in 1975 will be a young adult in the 1990's. The parents most likely will have been active participants in his or her education and activities (Meyers & Blacher, 1987). Many parents will have acquired teaching skills and become accustomed to a meaningful role in advocacy and decisionmaking for their child. It is reasonable that parents so deeply involved would continue to be so after placement, to ensure a smooth transition for the child and for themselves and the family members at home.

Siblings, too, may enjoy a unique role in the post–Public Law 94-142 era. The authors found, for example, that siblings not only voiced positive benefits of having a brother or sister with retardation, but showed very high levels of responsibility toward, awareness of, and involvement with the child with disabilities (Wilson, Blacher, & Baker, 1989). Very recent research has shown that younger siblings of children with retardation at home assume childcare roles that are usually reserved for older children in the family, without any negative impact on their relationship with the child with retardation or on their own social life (Stoneman, Brody, Davis, Crapps, & Malone, 1991). As with their parents, one would expect continued high rates of involvement by siblings with brothers and sisters who are subsequently placed out-of-home. Indeed, Stoneman and Crapps (1990) recently reported that family care providers perceived sibling–client relationships to be closer than parent–client relationships.

Benefits of Sibling Involvement for the Placed Individual

Friendships and social relationships are important for individuals with mental retardation, and have been shown to develop in out-of-home placement settings (Landesman-Dwyer, Berkson, & Romer, 1979). Affiliation with family members is equally important for individuals with mental retardation who live outside the natural home:

> Family members are virtually the only constant figures in the developmentally disabled person's life. No service provider will follow him or her throughout life or across a multiple range of needs. Only a family has a broad enough perspective to take in the total picture of service needs. (Brotherson, Backus, Summers, & Turnbull, 1986, p. 37)

Other benefits of family involvement also accrue to the placed individual, including a sense of enduring relationships (Taylor, Lakin, & Hill, 1989), access to physical and financial assistance, and advocacy (Winik, Zetlin, & Kaufman, 1985). Even care providers report significantly less stress as a result of frequent visits by nondisabled siblings to their brother or sister with retardation (Stoneman & Crapps, 1990). Presumably, a less-stressed provider delivers better care.

Sibling involvement can be subsumed under family involvement. Much of the literature on postplacement family involvement assumes parents as the main actors (Baker & Blacher, 1988), yet nondisabled siblings should be considered as well. The individual in out-of-home placement may reap all of the benefits of sibling involvement over a lifetime, long after his or her parents have become infirm or passed away. Zetlin (1986) looked at adult sibling relationships in a sample of 35 fairly independent, community-based adults with mild retardation. She found that in the majority of sibling–client relationships, siblings provided help and support for their less capable brothers and sisters. Relationships ranged from very warm with extensive involvement to resentful with minimal involvement. In response to the question, "What do you think brothers and sisters should give each other?" a 15-year-old girl with mental retardation who lives in a residential facility said, "He should see me more and call me more. Brothers and sisters should be my friends" (T. McCool, personal communication, March 8, 1991).

Summary: Rationale for Study

Siblings and out-of-home placement is a new issue for the 90's, due to changes in philosophy about out-of-home placement, in education and services available, and in ideas about permanency planning and the role of families. To summarize, there are several overriding reasons to study siblings and out-of-home placement at this time. The growing interest in sibling relationships in all families has stimulated the development of conceptual models that take into account the entire family context. Smaller, more normalized, and geographically closer facilities are potentially more accessible to parents and siblings. More intensive involvement by nondisabled siblings with their brothers and sisters while they are living at home sets the stage for more concerted involvement with them in out-of-home settings. Since persons who are mentally retarded are living longer, nondisabled siblings are more likely to assume some advocacy and other responsibilities. Finally, data on family involvement highlights the potential benefits of sibling involvement for the individual who is placed.

A CONTEXT FOR RESEARCH

In this section the author offers two conceptual approaches for guiding and interpreting research on siblings and out-of-home placement. These approaches are not mutually exclusive; both could be used in planning a program of research.

An Ecological Perspective

The study of siblings and out-of-home placement can be conceptualized within a broader framework that incorporates institutional or facility influences, family interactions, societal norms, and public policy. Other studies of families of children with disabilities have incorporated versions of this ecologically oriented view (Crnic et al., 1983; Dyson et al., 1989; Kazak, 1986), which is adapted from Bronfenbrenner's (1979) "systems" approach. The conceptualization of development depicted in Figure 1 shows the "emanative effects" on the child within the context of a series of four concentric circles (adapted from Whalen & Henker, 1980). Changes in any level, or circle, affect others; research focused too narrowly at one level could lead to a misinterpretation of findings. The top portion of the figure depicts the interactive effects of the child, the family, the immediate social environment, and cultural influences when the child is living at home. The lower portion shows how these interrelationships may change when the child is placed.

The inner circle on the lower figure represents the child, including his or her characteristics and behaviors, in the placement setting. The second level represents relationships among the child with disabilities, the immediate environment, and persons in that environment. For the child who is still at home, the second level represents interactions with the family; for the child who is placed, the second or next immediate level is with careproviders. Research on patterns of relationships in the placement setting (Berkson & Romer, 1980; Romer & Berkson, 1980) or in the immediate community (Edgerton, 1967; Edgerton & Bercovici, 1976; Halpern et al., 1986) would be reflective of level two. Also included in level two would be relationships between the placed child and the staff or personnel at the placement setting.

(a) Pre-placement

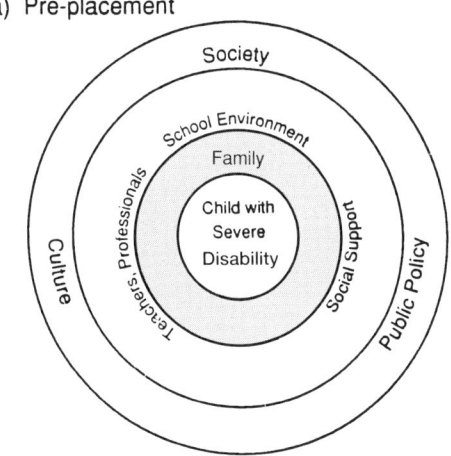

(b) Post-placement

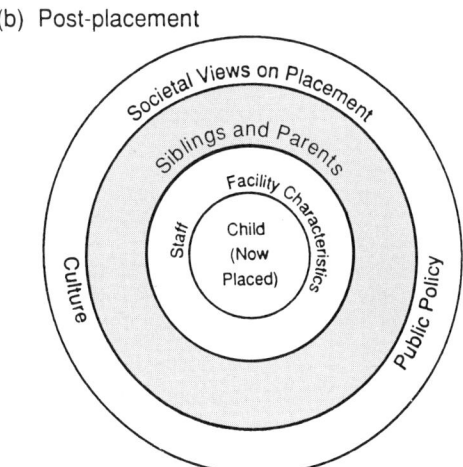

Figure 1. An ecological perspective on siblings and placement. (Adapted from Blacher [1984] and Blacher and Bromley [1990].)

The third level represents the family, typically siblings and parents. For the child who is still at home, the third level includes the school environment, teachers, and social support for the child and family. For the child who is placed, parents and siblings are more removed, conceptually, from the child. They are more likely to have to interact with members of level two in maintaining relationships with the child. Parents' interactions with careproviders and other members of the service delivery system may have an effect on nondisabled siblings as well as the placed child. Indeed, McKeever (1983) noted that parents whose disabled children are still at home often have longstanding relationships with the service delivery system, which may in turn have an effect on nondisabled siblings. For example, whether the child with disabilities is at home or not, families often relocate simply to be near better services (Greenfeld, 1970, 1978), a move that changes the environment and roles of all family members and may be acutely felt by siblings.

Studies of the interrelationships among the staff of an out-of-home placement facility, the child with disabilities, and family members at home would involve levels one, two, and three. Policies or procedures regarding out-of-home placement that dictate the form, function, or duration of family involvement would be part of this system. For example, researchers don't yet know how the care provided in the placement setting will affect the families' (and particularly the typical siblings') subsequent interest in and involvement with the child. Out-of-home placements themselves create their own patterns and subcultures that may or may not be welcoming of family involvement (Blacher & Baker, 1992) or, more specifically, of sibling involvement. Studies of nondisabled siblings' involvement with their brother or sister who lives in a facility should go beyond simply recording the nature and amount of involvement to asking what extent of involvement the placement setting itself will allow.

The fourth level refers to the broader culture or subculture and can include or reflect economic, social, educational, legal or political trends. For example, Public Law 94-142, with its educational provisions and concomitant services to parents, promotes keeping a child with severe disabilities at home. Prolonging the years that a severely disabled child spends in the natural home is presently viewed by most professionals and policymakers as philosophically justifiable to themselves, developmentally helpful to the child, and economically beneficial to society (Blacher, 1986). This particular view has made out-of-home placement increasingly less likely for young children. Furthermore, social and educational policies currently in place make services to families increasingly more likely. Still undetermined is the impact on nondisabled siblings of such prevailing philosophies and norms (especially when a placement is chosen despite the prevailing views), and any cultural influences on postplacement involvement.

From an ecological perspective, there are several broader issues that might affect the study of siblings and out-of-home placement. First, public policy that is antiplacement may put additional stress on parents and siblings with respect to lifestyle and coping; it reduces options for families and creates more need for in-home supports or respite, two services that are in short supply and high demand. Second, the full course of normalization may not actually be in the best interest of women and nondisabled siblings (see Farber, 1959; Moroney, 1986). Deinstitutionalization has primarily meant returning clients to the care or advocacy of mothers and older sisters. Even younger siblings of children with mental retardation at home may assume childcare responsibilities and roles that exceed those of their peers who don't have an older sibling who is retarded (Stoneman et al., 1991). The social ecology of these nondisabled siblings would surely change dramatically upon placement.

Placement Across the Lifespan

Another, though not incompatible, perspective on nondisabled siblings and placement is developmental, and involves conceptualizing relationships across the lifespan. Here the author will consider the impact of out-of-home placement at three points during the life of the child with disabilities: childhood, adolescence, and beyond adolescence. In doing so, the author will also consider the sibling relationship to the child who is mentally retarded at these different stages. The impact of placement at or during infancy will not be considered, for two reasons: years ago, parents who were told to place infants usually did so in order that the child would be "out of sight, out of mind;" today, when infants are placed, it is usually for the purpose of receiving specialized medical care. In either case, opportunities for involvement by nondisabled siblings would be rare.

During Childhood Placing a child, any child, out of the natural home during the childhood period constitutes an off-cycle transition for the family and can be expected to produce additional stress for family members (Birenbaum, 1971; Farber, 1959; Neugarten, 1976). The typical stressors of the childhood period or childbearing years have been identified in the literature (Turnbull, Summers, & Brotherson, 1986), but arranging for out-of-home placement is not usually one of them. Parents placing a child during this period may feel guilt, as well as a sense of sadness or loss. Yet nondisabled siblings may have very different cognitions and feelings about placement at this time. In remarking about his nondisabled son's reaction to the thought of placing Noah, Josh Greenfeld writes: "Kids are real. Kids are hard. Before going to sleep last night Karl said, 'I don't mind if you put Noah in an institution, as long as you adopt a new brother for me'" (Greenfeld, 1978, p. 33).

The impact of placement during childhood on nondisabled siblings was studied by Caldwell and Guze (1960), who directly assessed siblings' adjustment following the placement of a brother or sister with disabilities. The authors have noted that the siblings of the institutionalized children did not differ significantly from the other siblings with brothers and sisters with retardation at home on any measures of adjustment. However, their anecdotal reports were revealing and did differ for the two groups. For example, when asked whether it was better for children with mental retardation to live at home or in a training school, the children whose sibling lived out of home gave answers that reflected the existing family policy (i.e., they recommended an institution if their sibling was already in one). Their responses also reflected the beliefs of those times (e.g., that their brother or sister with retardation would be happier in an institution, could learn more there, would be with his or her "own kind"). The answers of children whose sibling with disabilities lived at home were reported to be more equivocal and evasive.

A related question for further study is how much nondisabled siblings actually influence the parents' decision to place a child. Very little is known on this subject. Parents, both before and after Public Law 94-142, consistently report that the feelings or lives of their other children are a consideration when deciding on placement. In a post–Public Law 94-142 study conducted with parents who had recently placed their child (Bromley & Blacher, 1991), parents were asked to check items on a questionnaire that influenced their placement decision. Items were presented in a Likert format, ranging from "no influence" to "strong influence." The third most frequently checked item as a strong reason for placement was "feelings of my nonhandicapped children." This finding held true regardless of the age of the child with disabilities when placed; children were between the ages of 2 and 16 at the time of placement, and the interviews occurred no more than 23 months after the placement.

Using the same sample in a study of the factors that delay the placement decision (Bromley & Blacher, 1989), the item, "My nonhandicapped children get along with their handicapped sibling" was a strong delayer of placement. (It was ranked 6 out of 20 in a list of possible delayers, also presented in a Likert format.) This is consistent with recent findings reported by Stoneman et al. (1991) suggesting that "parents may be considering the quality of the sibling relationship when placing the younger sibling in a variety of surrogate parent roles, assigning these responsibilities only when siblings are able to interact with a minimum of conflict" (p. 547). Parents' own perceptions of such sibling behaviors may indeed affect their decisions regarding placement during the childhood years.

Adolescence Many parents wait until their child with disabilities reaches adolescence before considering placement:

> I watch Noah guardedly. It is only a question of time before we will have to put him away. He is simply too retarded, too unable to take care of himself on an elementary level. The decision will somehow make itself. As Karl gets older it will just be easier for him to accept Noah's departure from the family picture. (Greenfeld, 1978, p. 29)

The normal lifespan progression includes a shift of responsibilities from parents to offspring, and ultimately to the offspring's own extrafamilial system (Turnbull et al., 1986). In adolescence, this shifting begins with more household and childcare chores being handed down. Farber's early work highlighted the increased caregiving burden on adolescent girls with brothers or sisters with disabilities, especially those in families of low socioeconomic status (1959; 1960).

"Adolescence is something that happens to a family, not just to an individual child" (Carter & McGoldrick, 1989, p. 14). Families of children who are disabled report feeling saddened by, and fearful of, the transition to adolescence. While parents of typical adolescents also worry about the teenage years, their fears are very different—arguments, drugs, driving, pregnancy. For those with severe retardation, however, the normal developmental tasks of adolescence (Erikson, 1968) may be far off; the parents and families of such children are confronted with the reality that their child, who in many cases still functions like an infant, now has an adult body (Rowitz, 1988). There are many implications. At a practical level, caregiving demands (especially for older daughters) may increase, and respite care and socialization programs will be more difficult to locate. On a psychological level, as the child ages without significant progress, some remaining expectations and dreams must be let go. The typical transitions of adolescence—proms, graduations, and college applications—never come, and the "chronic sorrow" Olshansky (1962) theorized about may become even more real. This is also the time when grandparents may pass away and parents may begin to reflect on their own aging. As implied by Rossi (1980), the risk for adjustment difficulties may well be greater for parents in their middle years than for the adolescent him or herself.

Unfortunately, almost nothing is known about the period of adolescence in families with children who have severe disabilities, or about the mutual influence that the child with disabilities and parents have on one another during this period (Wallander, 1990). Donovan (1988) suggests that the "more pervasive the impact of a handicapping condition on development the more stressful the adolescent is on family life" (p. 507).

Evidence suggests that the risk of out-of-home placement is heightened at this point in the family lifespan. There is reason to believe that both behavior problems and daily care needs of an individual with severe disabilities become more intense in adolescence, leading to increased stress for families (Farber, 1979; Shapiro, 1988) and increased need for placement (Blacher & Bromley, 1990; Farber et al., 1960; Seltzer & Krauss, 1984). Moreover, the family may find placement more acceptable for the late adolescent as nondisabled adolescents are also in the process of moving out on their own. Thus, the stress of the placement decision may reasonably be expected to be less. However, professionals know little about the correlates and consequences of placing an adolescent with disabilities and the impact that this could have on nondisabled siblings, many of whom will also be adolescents.

This is a time when adolescents typically set distance between themselves and family, so some distancing for nondisabled siblings of children with retardation could be expected as part of their own development. They may not be concerned with decisions that don't directly affect them. The egocentrism characteristic of teenagers perhaps buffers some of the impact of placement during this period: "And so what seemed of greatest importance to her during these three or four months when so much was happening to them was that she inherited Randall's room" (Miller, 1990, p. 230).

Beyond Adolescence The authors would not expect findings for children or adolescents to generalize to families further along in the lifespan (Rowitz, 1988; Seltzer & Krauss, 1989). For example, the role of the nondisabled sibling certainly changes over time. Parents indicate that siblings' reactions are only a moderate influence on the decision to place the young child with disabilities (Bromley & Blacher, 1991), but siblings often play a crucial role in decisions about adults with mental retardation (Seltzer et al., in press).

There are really three populations of adults with retardation living in out-of-home placements today. The first comprises elderly individuals placed several decades ago, many at birth or shortly thereafter. Most of these early-institutionalized individuals are unlikely to have ongoing relationships with their families—their parents are now deceased, and nondisabled siblings have long since drifted away and are engrossed in their own lives and families.

A second group is made up of older adults more recently placed out of their family home, those who were previously living with aging caregivers. Seltzer and Krauss (1990) recognize this population as being at "high risk" for out-of-home placement once the caregiver becomes infirm or passes away. They have reported that nondisabled siblings make up about one-fourth of the support network of adults with mental retardation while they are still living at home with their parents (Krauss & Seltzer, 1989). Furthermore, the nondisabled siblings' involvement with their brother or sister with mental retardation corresponded closely to their mother's well-being. As parents confront their own mortality and the natural declines that come with aging, they look toward future living arrangements for their children. Aging mothers frequently name one of their nondisabled children as the future caregiver or person responsible for the retarded adult sibling (Krauss, 1990; Schatz, 1983).

The third population of adults with retardation in out-of-home placement is the post–Public Law 94-142 group, who now enjoy "the right to grow up" (Summers, 1986) and to participate in the launching process experienced by their nondisabled siblings and nearly everyone else. While the *zeitgeist* includes the idea that all children with mental retardation or severe disabilities should live at home with their families, the prevailing view is that young adults with disabilities should live in the community (Elder, 1988). Thus, the transition to an out-of-home placement is viewed as normative. For these younger adults, there may be much variability in sibling involvement. Zetlin (1986) proposed that relationships between nondisabled siblings and young adults with mental retardation in the community have their own developmental cycle. For example, younger adolescents still at home who were close to their brother or sister with retardation before placement continued to have a special relationship after placement. The young adult nondisabled sibling living on his or her own might be absorbed in his or her own education or career and be less dependable from the placed sibling's perspective. Furthermore, his or her parents might still take active responsibility for the placed sibling. However, middle-age nondisabled siblings with stable lifestyles were found to be available, consistent supporters of the young adult living independently in the community.

It is appropriate, then, to consider the topic of sibling involvement and out-of-home placement from a lifespan perspective. Preplacement relationships between siblings will undoubtedly affect postplacement relationships, an axiom recognized by Stoneman and Crapps (1990) in their study of family involvement with placed individuals. Furthermore, the age and developmental level of the person with retardation have been shown to affect preplacement levels of involvement (Stoneman et al., 1991), while the age of the nondisabled siblings has been shown to affect levels of postplacement involvement (Zetlin, 1986). The age of the child (or adult) when placed may influence both the effects of the "child" with disabilities on the nondisabled sibling and their subsequent relationship.

The following conclusion outlines a research agenda for the 1990's that specifically addresses many of the issues raised in this, and previous, sections.

A PROPOSED RESEARCH AGENDA

Below are several particularly salient questions, derived from considerations already raised, that can begin to establish a research agenda for the 1990's on siblings and out-of-home placement.

1. *What attitudes do nondisabled siblings express toward the idea of out-of-home placement?* It seems reasonable to begin by finding out what siblings think of the idea of placement, and whether their attitudes do more than simply reflect the beliefs of their parents. The early work reported by Caldwell and Guze (1960) indicated that children's thoughts and opinions about placement did indeed mirror their parents' views. However, 3 decades later, today's children with disabilities are growing up in a rather different environment, one that is more responsive to them and more supportive of their families. Professional and parental thinking about placement has changed in meaningful ways. So researchers must ask whether nondisabled siblings are more or less receptive to the idea of out-of-home placement of the person with mental retardation than they were 3 decades ago.

2. *How are siblings affected by the out-of-home placement of their brother or sister?* A vast amount of the past research on siblings of children with retardation and other severe disabilities (as attested to by this volume) focused on the impact on nondisabled siblings of the child with disabilities who lives at home. This is an important topic for both theoretical and practical reasons; however, impact continues even when the child with disabilities no longer lives at home. As one parent dolefully said to the author after placing her 9-year-old son:

> Nobody wants to hear from parents anymore after they place a child. It's as if there is no more impact, no more interaction.
>
> The parents of handicapped children at home don't relate to us anymore, there aren't any support groups for us, and now even the researchers don't want us in their studies!

The field needs studies of impact that encompass family adjustment and coping both before and after placement. Studies that have compared adjustment in families who have placed versus that in families who have not placed have been plagued by the possible confound of initial differences between the two groups. Only prospective, longitudinal studies will allow researchers a systematic look at the ways that placement affects nondisabled siblings.

The authors have recently expanded their own model for understanding the process of out-of-home placement for children with severe disabilities. Unlike models of placement that treat the placement itself as the end of a decisionmaking process (e.g., Cole, 1986), the authors specifically look at postplacement adjustment of family members and at the phenomenon of "detachment." The term detachment is used here to refer to the loosening of ties between family and the child with disabilities once the child is placed (Baker & Blacher, 1991). While the term derives its meaning from Bowlby (1980), the authors have hypothesized cognitive, emotional, and behavioral components of detachment that are manifested by families after placement. While mothers have been the main source of information on placement correlates and consequences, valuable information could be obtained from nondisabled siblings as well.

3. *Does the impact of out-of-home placement on nondisabled siblings differ if the sibling with disabilities is placed as a child, or at subsequent times in the family lifespan?* In the not-too-distant past many children with moderate to severe retardation were placed out of the home as infants; siblings had little or no awareness of the process. Many other individuals with mental retardation spent their lifetime at home, only to be placed when parents became infirm or died; siblings seem to have figured prominently at this point, though little is known about the decisionmaking processes that occurred. Today, placement at both age extremes is discouraged; moving out of the natural home in late adolescence or early

adulthood is considered normal and desirable. (Thus, the mean age of placement may be similar to that in previous decades, but the variance is decreased.)

Nonetheless, there is still sufficient variability in the point in time in which individuals with retardation and their families decide on an alternative living arrangement, and it seems meaningful to ask whether the impact on siblings and their involvement in the decisionmaking and planning varies at different points in the family lifespan. As mentioned above, by the time of adolescence siblings are feeling in some ways responsible for their brother or sister with disabilities. It might be hypothesized that placement at this stage would reduce siblings' feelings of responsibility, whereas placement when the person with mental retardation is an older adult will increase the siblings' sense of responsibility, as the process makes them most acutely aware that their parents' involvement will of necessity diminish.

4. *What is the nature of postplacement sibling involvement? And how is it influenced by the sex of the sibling, the stage in the family lifespan, and opportunities provided by the facility?* Today, siblings appear to have higher levels of preplacement involvement with their brothers and sisters who are disabled. This is true not only for teenagers but for younger children as well (Brody et al., 1991; Stoneman, Brody, Davis, & Crapps, 1987; Wilson et al., 1989). With or without a role reversal whereby siblings younger than the child with retardation take on childcare roles and share in household tasks (Farber, 1959, 1960; Stoneman et al., 1991), involvement levels are high. Nondisabled siblings interviewed in one study (Wilson et al., 1989) showed striking consistency in their familiarity with their brother's or sister's schooling, respite care, and home management, along with considerable involvement in caregiving. Their attitudes and involvements were interpreted as reflecting not only familial values, but also the new, post–Public Law 94-142 social realities of persons with mental retardation being more visible and less stigmatized. Moreover, Werner (1986) has noted greater sibling involvement in childcare, even in families without a special needs child, driven mainly by increases in the number of working mothers.

Siblings who are initially more deeply involved can be predicted to maintain higher involvement with their brothers or sisters with disabilities across the lifespan than have siblings in previous generations. Researchers need to study the nature of such involvements and the benefits that accrue to the child with disabilities and also to the nondisabled sibling. There is also a need to study the predictors of sibling involvement, which will most likely include characteristics of the siblings with and without disabilities, but may also include facility characteristics as well. In a recent study of family involvement with their child in the two years after placement, for example, it was found that the facility's opportunities for involvement more strongly influenced involvement than did parent or child characteristics, or even the time the child had been placed (Baker & Blacher, 1991). It is known that siblings play different roles than parents with respect to their brother or sister with disabilities. Because staff in out-of-home placement facilities will most likely have different perceptions of siblings than they do of parents, siblings may be less threatening, and in some respects their involvement may be more welcome.

With regard to the detachment phenomenon mentioned earlier, a brief review of the literature on the placement of senile dementia patients into nursing homes revealed some interesting parallels. In these cases, detachment did not occur upon placement, but rather, upon the death of the senile family member. This literature indicates that placement does not relieve the family of burden in this case—it merely changes the nature of the burden (Zarit & Zarit, 1982). Families have been shown to take on active patterns of visitation and interaction with staff. These activities, when regularly pursued, are probably maintaining attachment, rather than contributing to detachment. All of this is to say that opportunities for sibling involvement may be different from those of parents, and completely different patterns of involvement and detachment may emerge for siblings than for parents.

5. *Does the impact of a child with mental retardation vary with culture? Specifically, is there a difference in the United States between Anglo and Hispanic families in decisionmaking concerning out-of-home placement, in reactions to placement, or in the reactions and roles of nondisabled siblings?* By the turn of the century, Hispanics will be the largest minority group in the United States (Chan, 1991). It is critical that service delivery decisions be based on culturally appropriate information (Gartner, Lipsky, & Turnbull, 1991; Keefe, Padilla, & Carlos, 1979; Vega & Miranda, 1985). Yet little is known about how the Hispanic family responds to disabling conditions, in terms of either these families' strengths or stresses. Nearly all that is known about out-of-home placement, including the little that is known about siblings and out-of-home placement, derives primarily from research with Anglo, middle-class populations.

Studies in California indicate that placement rates for Hispanic individuals who are mentally retarded at all ages and levels of ability are lower than for Anglo or Black groups (Blacher, Hanneman, & Rousey, 1992; Borthwick-Duffy, Eyman, & White, 1987; Meyers et al., 1985). From a family-ecology perspective (Crnic et al., 1983; Harrison, Wilson, Pine, Chan, & Buriel, 1990), potential placement in Hispanic families might be affected by such issues as parents' relationship to community agencies and professionals, language barriers, uncertain immigrant status, or level of acculturation.

There is a need for research that addresses the relationship between siblings with and without disabilities in Hispanic families, both before and after placement. These siblings' language ability and level of acculturation often exceed those of their parents. Hence, they may play a more crucial role in postplacement involvement and interaction with service delivery systems than do Anglo siblings.

6. *What is the impact of the death of a child with disabilities on his or her siblings?* The death of a sibling with disabilities, whether he or she has been living at home or elsewhere, is a special circumstance about which little is known. Are there parallels between the death of a child with disabilities and out-of-home placement in terms of feelings of loss experienced by nondisabled siblings? Many children with severe and profound disabilities have medical complications; for them, shorter life spans are expected. This ultimate separation is, of course, more severe and permanent than placing the child out of the home. Yet some dimensions of the impact may be similar (e.g., relief of burden and consequent feelings of guilt). Both clinicians and researchers need to learn more about the death of a sibling with disabilities and its impact on surviving brothers and sisters.

CONCLUDING COMMENTS

The author has focused primarily on the child with mental retardation who is placed outside of the natural home. Yet we need to keep in mind that a great many children live outside of their natural families for reasons beyond those under consideration here. These include: medical risk (e.g., AIDS, other chronic illness, disabling conditions in intellectually normal children); court orders (e.g., delinquency, victims of child abuse, drug addicted babies); mental health considerations (e.g., substance abuse, schizophrenia); social considerations (e.g., homelessness, runaways); lack of parent figures (e.g., foster care, adoption); and parental request for alternative residences for children with special behavior problems and care demands (e.g., dual diagnosis, severe emotional disturbance). Most of these, of course, can also co-exist with the problem of retardation. In any event, there is a pressing need for more empirical study on the effects of such placements on the child's development, and on the family. Consistent with the theme here, the author concludes by noting that it is critical to determine how these diverse placements affect brothers and sisters remaining at home, as sibling involvement may prove crucial to rehabilitation.

REFERENCES

Baker, B.L., & Blacher, J. (1988). Family involvement with community residential programs. In M.P. Janicki, M.W. Krauss, & M.M. Seltzer (Eds.), *Community residences for persons with developmental disabilities: Administrative and program handbook* (pp. 173–188). Baltimore: Paul H. Brookes Publishing Co.

Baker, B.L., & Blacher, J.B. (1991, May). *Involvement of families post-placement: Patterns, influences, and changes over time.* Paper presented at the 115th Annual Meeting of the American Association on Mental Retardation, Washington, DC.

Baker, B.L., Seltzer, G.B., & Seltzer, M.M. (1977). *As close as possible.* Boston: Little, Brown.

Begun, A.L. (1989). Sibling relationships involving developmentally disabled people. *American Journal on Mental Retardation, 93,* 566–574.

Berkson, G., & Romer, D. (1980). Social ecology of supervised communal facilities for mentally disabled adults: I. Introduction. *American Journal of Mental Deficiency, 85,* 219–228.

Birenbaum, A. (1971). The mentally retarded child in the home and family cycle. *Journal of Health and Social Behavior, 12,* 196–206.

Blacher, J. (1984). A dynamic perspective on the impact of a severely handicapped child on the family. In J. Blacher (Ed.), *Severely handicapped young children and their families: Research in review.* Orlando, FL: Academic Press.

Blacher, J. (1986). *Placement of severely handicapped children: Correlates and consequences* (Grant No. HD21324). Washington, DC: National Institute of Child Health and Human Development.

Blacher, J., & Baker, B.L. (1992). Toward meaningful family involvement in out-of-home placement settings. *Mental Retardation, 30,* 35–43.

Blacher, J., & Bromley, B.E. (1990). Correlates of out-of-home placement of handicapped children: Who places and why? In L.M. Glidden (Ed.), *Formed families: Adoption of children with handicaps* (pp. 3–40). NY: The Haworth Press.

Blacher, J., Hanneman, R., & Rousey, A.M. (1992). Out-of-home placement of children with severe handicaps: A comparison of approaches. *American Journal on Mental Retardation, 96,* 607–616.

Borthwick-Duffy, S.A., Eyman, R.K., & White, J.F. (1987). Client characteristics and residential placement patterns. *American Journal of Mental Deficiency, 92,* 24–30.

Bowlby, J. (1980). *Attachment and loss, Volume III: Loss, sadness, and depression.* London: The Hogarth Press.

Brody, G.H., Stoneman, Z., Davis, C.H., & Crapps, J.M. (1991). Observations of the role relations and behavior between older children with mental retardation and their younger siblings. *American Journal on Mental Retardation, 95,* 527–536.

Bromley, B., & Blacher, J. (1989). Factors delaying out-of-home placement of children with severe handicaps. *American Journal on Mental Retardation, 94,* 284–291.

Bromley, B., & Blacher, J. (1991). Parental reasons for out-of-home placement of children with severe handicaps. *Mental Retardation, 29,* 275–280.

Bronfenbrenner, U. (1979). *The ecology of human development: Experiments by nature and design.* Cambridge, MA: Harvard University Press.

Brotherson, M.J., Backus, L.H., Summers, J.A., & Turnbull, A.P. (1986). Transition to adulthood. In J.A. Summers (Ed.), *The right to grow up: An introduction to adults with developmental disabilities* (pp. 17–44). Baltimore: Paul H. Brookes Publishing Co.

Caldwell, B.M., & Guze, S.B. (1960). A study of the adjustment of parents and

siblings of institutionalized and non-institutionalized retarded children. *American Journal of Mental Deficiency, 64,* 845–861.
Carter, G., & Jancar, J. (1983). Mortality in the mentally handicapped: A 50 year survey at the Stoke Park group of hospitals (1930–1980). *Journal of Mental Deficiency Research, 27,* 143–156.
Carter, B., & McGoldrick, M. (1989). Overview: The changing family life cycle—A framework for family therapy. In B. Carter & M. McGoldrick (Eds.), *The changing family life cycle: A framework for family therapy* (2nd ed.) (pp. 3–28). NY: John Wiley & Sons.
Chan, S. (1991). *Asian Americans: An interpretive history.* Boston: Twayne Publishers.
Cleveland, D.W., & Miller, N. (1977). Attitudes and life commitments of older siblings of mentally retarded adults: An exploratory study. *Mental Retardation, 15,* 38–41.
Cole, D.A. (1986). Out-of-home placement and family adaptation: A theoretical framework. *American Journal of Mental Deficiency, 91,* 226–236.
Crnic, K., Friedrich, W.N., & Greenberg, M.T. (1983). Adaptation of families with mentally retarded children: A model of stress, coping, and family ecology. *American Journal of Mental Deficiency, 88,* 125–138.
Donovan, A.M., (1988). Family stress and ways of coping with adolescents who have handicaps: Maternal perceptions. *American Journal of Mental Retardation, 92,* 502–509.
Dunn, J. (1985). *Sisters and brothers.* Cambridge, MA: Harvard University Press.
Dunn, J., Kendrick, C., & MacNamee, R. (1981). The reaction of firstborn children to the birth of a sibling: Mothers' reports. *Journal of Child Psychology and Psychiatry, 22,* 1–18.
Dyson, L., Edgar, E., & Crnic, K. (1989). Psychological predictors of adjustment by siblings of developmentally disabled children. *American Journal on Mental Retardation, 94,* 292–302.
Edgerton, R.B. (1967). *The cloak of competence.* Berkeley: University of California Press.
Edgerton, R.B., & Bercovici, S.M. (1976). The cloak of competence: Years later. *American Journal of Mental Deficiency, 80,* 485–497.
Elder, J.K. (1988). Foreword. In B.L. Ludlow, A.P. Turnbull, & R. Luckasson (Eds.), *Transitions to adult life for people with mental retardation—principles and practices* (pp. xi–xii). Baltimore: Paul H. Brookes Publishing Co.
Erikson, E.H. (1968). Identity and identity diffusion. In C. Gordon & K.J. Gergen (Eds.), *The self in interaction* (Vol. 1, pp. 197–205). New York: John Wiley & Sons.
Farber, B. (1959). Effects of a severely mentally retarded child on family integration. *Monographs of the Society for Research in Child Development, 21*(75).
Farber, B. (1960). Family organization and crisis: Maintenance of integration in families with a severely mentally retarded child. *Monographs of the Society for Research in Child Development, 25*(75).
Farber, B. (1963). Interactions with retarded siblings and life goals of children. *Marriage and Family Living, 25,* 96–98.
Farber, B. (1979). Sociological ambivalence and family care: The individual proposes and society disposes. In R.H. Bruininks & G.C. Krantz (Eds.), *Family care of developmentally disabled members: Conference proceedings.* Minneapolis: University of Minnesota.
Farber, B., Jenne, W., & Toigo, R. (1960). Family crisis and the decision to institu-

tionalize the retarded child. *Council for Exceptional Children, Research Monograph Series, A*(1).

Farber, B., & Ryckman, D. (1965). Effects of severely mentally retarded children on family relationships. *Mental Retardation Abstracts, 2,* 1–17.

Fotheringham, J.B., Skelton, M., & Hoddinott, B.A. (1971). *The retarded child and his family: The effects of home and institution* (Monograph No. 11). Ontario, Canada: The Ontario Institute for Studies in Education.

Gartner, A., Lipsky, D.K., & Turnbull, A.P. (1991). *Supporting families with a child with a disability: An international outlook.* Baltimore: Paul H. Brookes Publishing Co.

Glidden, L.M. (1990). *Formed families: Adoption of children with handicaps.* NY: The Haworth Press.

Goetting, A. (1986). The developmental tasks of siblingship over the life cycle. *Journal of Marriage and the Family, 48,* 703–714.

Greenfeld, J. (1970). *A child called Noah.* San Diego: Harcourt Brace Jovanovich.

Greenfeld, J. (1978). *A place for Noah.* San Diego: Harcourt Brace Jovanovich.

Greenfeld, J. (1986). *A client called Noah.* San Diego: Harcourt Brace Jovanovich.

Grossman, F.K. (1972). *Brothers and sisters of retarded children.* NY: Syracuse University Press.

Halpern, A.S., Close, D.W., & Nelson, D.J. (1986). *On my own: The impact of semi-independent living programs for adults with mental retardation* Baltimore: Paul H. Brookes Publishing Co.

Harrison, A.O., Wilson, M.N., Pine, C.J., Chan, S.Q., & Buriel, R. (1990). Family ecologies of ethnic minority children. *Child Development, 61,* 347–362.

Hill, B.K., Rotegard, L.L., & Bruininks, R.H. (1984). The quality of life of mentally retarded people in residential care. *Social Work, 29,* 275–280.

Kazak, A.E. (1986). Families with physically handicapped children: Social ecology and family systems. *Family Process, 25,* 265–281.

Keefe, S.E., Padilla, A.M., & Carlos, M.L. (1979). The Mexican-American extended family as an emotional support system. *Human Organization, 38,* 144–152.

Krauss, M.W. (1990). *Later life placements: Precipitating factors and family profiles.* Paper presented at the 114th Annual Meeting of the American Association on Mental Retardation, Atlanta, GA.

Krauss, M.W., & Seltzer, M.M. (1989). *The social networks of adults with mental retardation: Extensiveness, independence, and reciprocity.* Paper presented at the 113th Annual Meeting of the American Association on Mental Retardation, Chicago, IL.

Lamb, M.E. (1978). The development of sibling relationships in infancy: A short-term longitudinal study. *Child Development, 49,* 1189–1196.

Landesman-Dwyer, S., Berkson, G., & Romer, D. (1979). Affiliation and friendship of mentally retarded residents in group homes. *American Journal of Mental Deficiency, 83,* 571–580.

Lei, T., Nihira, L., Sheehy, N., & Meyers, C.E. (1981). A study of small family care for mentally retarded people. In R.H. Bruininks, C.E. Meyers, B.B. Sigford, & K.C. Lakin (Eds.), *Deinstitutionalization and community adjustment of mentally retarded people* (Monograph No. 4). Washington, DC: American Association on Mental Deficiency.

Lobato, D.J. (1990). *Brothers, sisters, and special needs: Information and activities for helping young siblings of children with chronic illnesses and developmental disabilities.* Baltimore: Paul H. Brookes Publishing Co.

McKeever, P. (1983). Siblings of chronically ill children: A literature review with

implications for research and practice. *American Journal of Orthopsychiatry, 53,* 209–218.
Meyers, C.E., & Blacher, J. (1987). Parents' perceptions of schooling for their severely handicapped child: Home and school variables. *Exceptional Children, 53,* 441–449.
Meyers, C.E., Borthwick, S.A., & Eyman, R.K. (1985). Place of residence by age, ethnicity, and level of retardation of the mentally retarded/developmentally disabled population of California. *American Journal of Mental Deficiency, 90,* 266–270.
Miller, S. (1990). *Family pictures.* New York: Harper & Row.
Moroney, R.M. (1986). Family care: Toward a responsive society. In P.R. Dokecki & R.M. Zaner (Eds.), *Ethics of dealing with persons with severe handicaps: Toward a research agenda* (pp. 217–232). Baltimore: Paul H. Brookes Publishing Co.
National Commission on Children. (1991). *Beyond rhetoric: A new American agenda for children and families.* Washington, DC: U.S. Government Printing Office.
Neugarten, B. (1976). Adaptation and the life cycle. *The Counseling Psychologist,* 6(1), 16–20.
Olshansky, S. (1962). Chronic sorrow: A response to having a mentally defective child. *Social Casework, 43,* 191–194.
Pepler, D.J., Abramovitch, R., & Corter, C. (1981). Sibling interaction in the home: A longitudinal study. *Child Development, 52,* 1344–1347.
Powell, T.H., & Gallagher, P.A. (1993). *Brothers and sisters—A special part of exceptional families* (2nd ed.). Baltimore: Paul H. Brookes Publishing Co.
Rice, D.P., & Feldman, J.J. (1985). Living longer in the United States: Demographic changes and health needs of the elderly. In M.P. Janicki & H.M. Wisniewski (Eds.), *Aging and developmental disabilities: Issues and approaches* (pp. 9–26). Baltimore: Paul H. Brookes Publishing Co.
Romer, D., & Berkson, G. (1980). Social ecology of supervised communal facilities for mentally disabled adults: II. Predictors of affiliation. *American Journal of Mental Deficiency, 85,* 229–242.
Rossi, A. (1980). Aging and parenthood in the middle years. In P. Baltes & O. Brim (Eds.), *Lifespan development and behavior* (Vol. III, pp. 138–205). NY: Academic Press.
Rowitz, L. (1988). The forgotten ones: Adolescence and mental retardation. *Mental Retardation, 26,* 115–117.
Schatz, G. (1983). The problem of preparing mentally retarded people for the future. *International Journal of Rehabilitation Medicine, 6,* 197–199.
Seltzer, G.B., Begun, A., Seltzer, M.M., & Krauss, M.W. (1991). Adults with mental retardation and their aging mothers: Impacts of siblings. *Family Relations, 40,* 310–317.
Seltzer, M.M., & Krauss, M.W. (1984). Placement alternatives for mentally retarded children and their families. In J. Blacher (Ed.), *Severely handicapped young children and their families: Research in review* (pp. 143–175). Orlando, FL: Academic Press.
Seltzer, M.M., & Krauss, M.W. (1989). Aging parents with adult mentally retarded children: Family risk factors and sources of support. *American Journal on Mental Retardation, 94,* 303–312.
Seltzer, M.M., & Krauss, M.W. (1990). *Aging mothers of retarded adults: Impacts on caregiving.* (NIA Grant No. RO1AG08768 [1990–1994]).
Shapiro, J. (1988). Stresses in the lives of parents of children with disabilities: Providing effective caregiving. *Stress Medicine, 4,* 77–93.

Simeonsson, R.J., & McHale, S.M. (1981). Review: Research on handicapped children: Sibling relationships. *Child: Care, Health, and Development, 7,* 153–171.

Skrtic, T.M., Summers, J.A., Brotherson, M.J., & Turnbull, A.P. (1984). Severely handicapped children and their brothers and sisters. In J. Blacher (Ed.), *Severely handicapped young children and their families: Research in review* (pp. 215–246). Orlando, FL: Academic Press.

Stoneman, Z., & Brody, G.H. (1984). Research with families of severely handicapped children: Theoretical and methodological considerations. In J. Blacher (Ed.), *Severely handicapped young children and their families: Research in review* (pp. 179–214). Orlando, FL: Academic Press.

Stoneman, Z., Brody, G.H., Davis, C.H., & Crapps, J.M. (1987). Mentally retarded children and their older same-sex siblings: Naturalistic in-home observations. *American Journal on Mental Retardation, 92,* 290–298.

Stoneman, Z., Brody, G.H., Davis, C.H., & Crapps, J.M. (1988). Childcare responsibilities, peer relations, and sibling conflict: Older siblings of mentally retarded children. *American Journal on Mental Retardation, 93,* 174–183.

Stoneman, Z., Brody, G.H., Davis, C.H., & Crapps, J.M. (1989). Role relations between mentally retarded children and their older siblings: Observations in three in-home contexts. *Research in Developmental Disabilities, 10,* 61–77.

Stoneman, Z., Brody, G.H., Davis, C.H., Crapps, J.M., & Malone, M. (1991). Ascribed role relations between children with mental retardation and their younger siblings. *American Journal on Mental Retardation, 95,* 537–550.

Stoneman, Z., & Crapps, J.M. (1990). Mentally retarded individuals in family care homes: Relationships with the family-of-origin. *American Journal on Mental Retardation, 4,* 420–430.

Summers, J.A. (1986). (Ed.). *The right to grow up: An introduction to adults with developmental disabilities.* Baltimore: Paul H. Brookes Publishing Co.

Taylor, S.J., Lakin, K.D., & Hill, B.K. (1989). Permanency planning for children and youth: Out-of-home placement decision. *Exceptional Children, 55,* 541–549.

Turnbull, A.P., Summers, J.A., & Brotherson, M.J. (1986). Family life cycle: Theoretical and empirical implications and future directions for families with mentally retarded members. In J. Gallagher & P. Vietze (Eds.), *Families of handicapped persons: Research, programs, and policy issues* (pp. 45–66). Baltimore: Paul H. Brookes Publishing Co.

Turnbull, H.R., Turnbull, A.P., Bronicki, G.J., Summers, J.A., & Roeder-Gordon, C. (1989). *Disability and the family: A guide to decisions for adulthood.* Baltimore: Paul H. Brookes Publishing Co.

Vega, W.A., & Miranda, M.R. (Eds.). (1985). *Stress & Hispanic mental health: Relating research to service delivery.* Rockville, MD: National Institute of Mental Health.

Wallander, J. (1990). *Mentally retarded adolescents' stress and coping.* Grant proposal submitted to NIH, University of Alabama at Birmingham.

Werner, E.E. (1986). *Childcare: Kith, kin, and hired hands.* Baltimore: University Park Press.

Whalen, C.K., & Henker, B. (1980). The social ecology of psychostimulant treatment: A model for conceptual and empirical analysis. In C.K. Whalen & B. Henker (Eds.), *Hyperactive children. The social ecology of identification and treatment.* NY: Academic Press.

Wilson, J., Blacher, J., & Baker, B.L. (1989). Siblings of severely handicapped children. *Mental Retardation, 27,* 167–173.

Winik, L., Zetlin, A.G., & Kaufman, S.Z. (1985). Adult mildly mentally retarded persons and their parents: The relationship between involvement and adjustment. *Applied Research in Mental Retardation, 6,* 409–419.

Zarit, S.H., & Zarit, J.M. (1982). Families under stress: Interventions for caregivers of senile dementia patients. *Psychotherapy: Theory, research and practice, 19,* 461–471.

Zetlin, A.G. (1986). Mentally retarded adults and their siblings. *American Journal of Mental Deficiency, 91,* 217–225.

SECTION II

RESEARCH PERSPECTIVES

CHAPTER 7

Siblings of Persons with Mental Retardation
A Historical Perspective and Recent Findings

*Glenna C. Boyce
and W. Steven Barnett*

This chapter presents a review of research on siblings of persons with retardation. The review takes an explicitly historical perspective in which research since the 1960s is seen as evolving in response to both an internal dynamic and external change. This perspective helps the reader to understand that the changes in questions, assumptions, methods, and findings over the years are more than simply a matter of scientific competence or random fluctuation.

This field of study began with relatively simple theories and questions, as most do. (Farber's work [1959, 1960], drawing on sociological traditions, is largely an exception.) As the field of study grew, more elaborate and complex theories developed, and new questions and variations replaced the old ones. The initial stimulus for research on siblings of persons with retardation appears to have come from clinicians who discovered that these siblings were having problems. Negative psychological outcomes were also noted in case studies of siblings (Kaplan, 1969; Poznanski, 1969; San Martino & Newman, 1974).

The clinical view of "expected impairment" became the framework for research on families of children with retardation, and remained so until some studies unexpectedly found positive effects for siblings of these children (Graliker, Fishler, & Koch, 1962; Grossman, 1972). Reviewers then noted that some researchers had limited their findings by using measures that al-

---

This research was supported in part with funds from NICHD (Grant # R01H0 22999) and from the U. S. Office of Special Education Programs (#s 300-85-0173 and HS90010001).

lowed only for negative replies (Bristol & Gallagher, 1986); the field responded by developing research approaches and instruments that allowed for both positive and negative findings (e.g., McHale & Gamble's [1989] use of measures of children's self-esteem, anxiety, depression, sibling interaction, and sibling satisfactions).

Theoretical developments from outside of the field have been imported by researchers, providing stimuli for developing new research designs. Bronfenbrenner's ecological systems theory (1979), the family lifespan and developmental-stage theory, and the stress and coping theory have all influenced the development of research (Crnic, Friedrich, & Greenberg, 1983; Crnic & Leconte, 1986; Foster & Berger, 1985; Gamble & McHale, 1989; Simeonsson & McHale, 1981). These theories have facilitated the development of more intricate, bi-directional models of effects on siblings (e.g., direct observation of sibling interaction by Abramovitch, Stanhope, Pepler, & Corter, 1987, and by Stoneman, Brody, Davis, & Crapps, 1987; time-use survey methods used with national data sets by Barnett, 1987).

Similarly, the development of computer capabilities and new statistical techniques have made it practical to investigate more complicated multivariate models, such as those of systems theory, and have influenced the research designs and analyses. Multiple regression analysis, analysis of covariance, and other complex analyses have been used to measure interaction effects in recent research (Boyce, Barnett, & Miller, 1991; McHale & Gamble, 1989; Stoneman et al., 1987).

Finally, societal changes have had a profound influence on the research. Families have changed and become much more diverse. The early studies of siblings of children with retardation investigated large families, which are no longer the norm. Today, families are not only smaller, but are often one-parent families, or families in which both parents are employed outside of the home, or in which neither parent is employed outside the home. Other changes include the postponement of marriage and childbirth and increased longevity, especially for persons with disabilities.

Societal attitudes and practices have also changed as to the appropriate care or place in society of individuals with retardation. Raising the child with retardation in the home is now the norm, having taken the place of institutionalization. Today, children with retardation are usually educated in the public schools, and are often being mainstreamed into regular classrooms. The federal government's passage of Public Laws 94-142 and 99-457 mandated preschool intervention programs for children with disabilities. Special Olympics are held nationwide. Such changes may have influenced the attitudes not only of family members, but also of society at large, and may have altered the situations or contexts that siblings of children with retardation previously found to be problematic. For example, there may be less caregiving by siblings if the child with disabilities participates in special programs or regular schools. However, the sibling may find contact with peers more problematic if the child with disabilities is in contact with them at both home and school (McHale, Sloan, & Simeonsson, 1986).

SAMPLE

The authors have interpreted the findings of the research on siblings of children with retardation for the last 30 years, keeping in mind the potential influence of internal dynamics and external changes. Over 50 primary studies and 10 reviews published during this time period were found (see Table 1). Four of these studies reported group intervention/discussion programs for siblings (Chinitz, 1981; Kaplan & Fox, 1968; Lobato, 1985; Schreiber & Feeney, 1965) and three discussed clinical case studies (Kaplan, 1969;

Table 1. Literature reviewed

Primary research studies	
Abramaovitch, Stanhope, Pepler, & Corter (1987)	Kaplan & Fox (1968)
Begun (1989)	Kirk & Bateman (1964)
Bergreen (1971)	Kirkman (1983)
Boyce (1990)	Lauterbach (1974)
Boyce, Barnett, & Miller (1991, April)	Lloyd-Bostock (1976)
Brody, Stoneman, Davis, & Crapps (1991)	Lobato (1985)
Caldwell & Guze (1960)	Lobato, Barbour, Hall, & Miller (1987)
Carr (1988)	Lonsdale (1978)
Carver & Carver (1972)	McConachie & Domb (1983)
Chinitz (1981)	McHale & Gamble (1987, 1989)
Cleveland & Miller (1977)	McHale, Sloan, & Simeonsson (1986)
Dittman (1962)	Miller (1974)
Dupont (1980)	O'Connor & Stachowiak (1971)
Dyson, Edgar, & Crnic (1989)	Poznanski (1969)
Dyson & Fewell (1989)	San Martino & Newman (1974)
Farber (1959, 1960, 1963)	Schipper (1959)
Farber & Jenne (1963)	Schreiber & Feeley (1965)
Fowle (1968)	Seltzer, Begun, Seltzer, & Krauss (1991)
Gamble & McHale (1989)	Stoneman, Brody, Davis, & Crapps (1987, 1988, 1989)
Gath (1972, 1973, 1974)	Stoneman, Brody, Davis, Crapps, & Malone (1991)
Gath & Gumley (1987)	Summers, Summers, Ascione, & Braeger (1989, April)
Graliker, Fishler, & Koch (1962)	Wilson, Blacher, & Baker (1989)
Grossman (1972)	Zetlin (1986)
Holt (1958)	
Kaplan (1969)	
Kaplan & Colombatto (1966)	
Reviews	
Brody & Stoneman (1983)	McHale, Simeonsson, & Sloan (1984)
Correa, Silberman, & Trusty (1986)	Simeonsson & Bailey (1986)
Crnic & Leconte (1986)	Simeonsson & McHale (1981)
Gallagher & Powell (1989)	Vadasy, Fewell, Meyer, & Schell (1984)
Hannah & Midlarsky (1985)	
Lobato (1983)	Wasserman (1983)

Poznanski, 1969; San Martino & Newman, 1974). The other studies will be discussed in detail later in the text. The most frequently cited studies are those of Bernard Farber (Farber, 1959, 1960; Farber & Jenne, 1963), Frances Kaplan Grossman (Grossman, 1972; Kaplan & Colombatto, 1966; Kaplan & Fox, 1968; Kaplan, 1969) and Ann Gath (Gath, 1972, 1973, 1974). The sample sizes ranged from 21 to over 200 siblings. Over half of the studies involved comparison groups, with the early studies often comparing families who had institutionalized their children with those who had not.

Eleven reviews of research on siblings of children with disabilities were found. The inclusion criteria were that they had been published in the United States and had reviewed 20 or more primary studies of siblings or families of children with disabilities. These reviews have summarized findings, advocated theoretical perspectives, discussed methodological limitations, and given direction to future research—thus providing an internal force in the development of the research. Table 2 provides an outline of these reviews.

The studies reported during the last five years are too recent to have been discussed in the reviews. Table 3 briefly describes these recent studies. All of the samples include persons with mental disabilities, but some samples also include persons with other types of disabilities.

Within this sample of literature, which covers 30 years of research on siblings of children with disabilities, certain themes tend to be repeated. The variables that have been studied can be divided into 5 categories: 1) psychological distress/well-being, 2) self-concept, 3) activities/time use, 4) the sibling interactional relationship between the siblings with and without disabilities, and 5) stress and coping. In addition, much of the research has been concerned with the child and family characteristics that influence the effect of the presence of a child with disabilities in the family. Examples of these mediating variables are the age and gender of the siblings and the children with disabilities, functional level of the child with disabilities, and family size. These will also be discussed.

PSYCHOLOGICAL DISTRESS/WELL-BEING

The psychological adjustment of siblings of children with mental disabilities has been a primary focus of the research in this field throughout the last 3 decades. Early investigators attempted to measure siblings' psychological distress (e.g., resentment, embarrassment, shame) or deviant behaviors (e.g., antisocial, neurotic) that resulted from having a brother or sister with a disability. Recent research has examined the psychological well-being (using scales to measure both adaptation and maladaptation). This section will give a chronological review of these studies, followed by a discussion of the findings.

Early Investigations

Some of the early findings on the subject came from studies that surveyed families with children with disabilities, ascertaining their problems and strengths. These surveys revealed that some of the siblings were experiencing resentment, embarrassment, shame, or other problems, but that most of the siblings were adjusting well (Dupont, 1980; Holt, 1958; Lloyd-Bostock, 1976; Schipper, 1959).

Farber, in his landmark study (Farber, 1959, 1960; Farber & Jenne, 1963), specifically investigated siblings' feelings (role tension) and the conditions that affected the amount of role tension siblings felt. He defined role tension as subjective feelings of frustration, tension, or anxiety. The amount of role tension that siblings experienced was based on maternal ratings of ten personality traits (e.g., gets angry easily, stubborn, jealous, irritable). Farber (1959) found that siblings had higher role-tension scores when the child with disabilities was highly dependent, rather than less dependent. (Dependency was measured by the Vineland Maturity Scale, using a median split to determine levels of dependency.) He also found that siblings who interacted frequently with the brother or sister with mental disabilities had higher role-tension scores than did siblings who interacted infrequently. Sisters experienced more role tension than did brothers when the child with disabilities lived at home. Fowle's (1968) findings confirmed that siblings' role tension was higher when the child with mental disabilities lived at home and that oldest sisters had greater role tension than did oldest brothers.

The early British investigations by Ann Gath (1972, 1973, 1974) of school-age siblings of children with Down syndrome tended to support Farber and Fowle's conclusions about sisters who were older than the child with a mental disability. Her studies, some of the first ones in the field to include a comparison group of siblings, assessed the effect of growing up with a child with disabilities by having parents and teachers rate the children's deviant behaviors as measured by the Behavioural Rating Scales (Rutter, Tizard, and Whitman, 1970). The first study, a comparison of siblings of children with cleft-palates, Down syndrome, or no disability, did not show any differences in behavior problems, but the subsequent study (Gath, 1973, 1974) suggested that sisters of children with Down syndrome had more behavioral difficulties, and that sisters more than 3 years older than the child with Down syndrome and from a large family were at greatest risk for behavioral difficulties.

In contrast, Graliker et al. (1962) interviewed 21 adolescent siblings of preschool-age children with disabilities. They concluded from the interviews that the siblings had good relationships within the home, had adequate social relationships with peers, and accepted their younger brother or sister who was severely mentally disabled.

Table 2. Reviews focusing on sibling effects

Review	Year	Type of disability	Family members affected	Purpose of review
Simeonsson and McHale	1981	Varied	Siblings	Examines the bi-directionality of effects in sibling relationships
Brody and Stoneman	1983	Mental retardation, sensory deficits	Siblings	Summarizes literature on sibling relations of atypical children
Lobato	1983	Varied	Siblings	Critically reviews and evaluates literature on siblings of children with disabilities and identifies mediating variables
Wasserman	1983	Mental retardation	Siblings	Reviews literature to identify needs of siblings of children with disabilities and encourages intervention for siblings
McHale, Simeonsson, and Sloan	1984	Varied	Siblings	Integrative review of literature on relationships among disabled and nondisabled siblings
Vadasy, Fewell, Meyer, and Schell	1984	Varied	Siblings (also mothers and fathers to some extent)	Reviews literature on siblings of children with disabilities, identifying variables related to sibling vulnerability to stress, and calls for more study of the dynamic variables involved in family interaction

Hannah and Midlarsky	1985	Varied, also chronic illness	Siblings	Reviews literature on sibling effects for school psychologists
Correa, Silberman, and Trusty	1986	Visual impairment (some varied disabilities)	Siblings	Reviews literature for those working with families of children with visual impairments
Crnic and Leconte	1986	Varied	Siblings	Addresses issues surrounding the relationship between disabled and nondisabled siblings and suggests the use of a coping and adaptation framework
Simeonsson and Bailey	1986	Varied	Siblings	Reviews research on families of children with disabilities in an attempt to identify general effects attributable to sibling relations and determine to what extent the effects are a function of the context and role of sibling relations
Gallagher and Powell	1989	Varied	Siblings	Outlines the major findings and future issues surrounding research on sibling relationships, with emphasis on those involving a child with a disability

Table 3. Recent studies of siblings of persons with mental disabilities

Reference	Purpose of study	Sample size	Age[a] of siblings	Age[a] of target child[b]	Diagnostic category of target child	Research design	Variables measured
Abramovitch, Stanhope, Pepler, and Corter (1987)	• Examine generality of research with normative samples • Explore responses to children's disabilities • Determine what special problems might exist	31 sibling dyads at Time 1, 20 at Time 2	1–11	1–10	Down syndrome	Longitudinal design Direct observation	Coded observations into prosocial, agonistic, & imitation/interaction categories
Begun (1989)	• Investigate nature of sibling relationship • Investigate mediating effects of developmental status, siblingship constellation variables, situation variables, characteristics of person with disabilities	46 sisters with 46 disabled siblings and 78 nondisabled siblings	12–69 $\bar{x} = 30.1$	Disabled sibs 8–69 $\bar{x} = 27.2$ Nondisabled sibs 12–82 $\bar{x} = 32.4$	Moderate to profound developmental disability	Cross-sectional comparison within families Mailed questionnaire	Nature of sibling relation
Boyce, Barnett, Miller (1990)	• Compare time use and perceptions of well-being of siblings of children with/without disabilities	120 (60 + 60)	10–17 $\bar{x} = 13$	1–27	Down syndrome	Cross-sectional comparison Telephone survey (2 times in one year)	Time use/activities, attitudes
Brody, Stoneman, Davis and Crapps (1991)	• Observe interaction of sibling pairs when older child has mental retardation, focusing on role relationships/affect	32 sibling pairs (16 with older child with mental retardation)	7	10	7 Down syndrome 1 birth injury 8 unknown etiologies	Cross-sectional group comparison Observation and interview/questionnaire	Sibling roles (manager, teacher, helper) Affect Interaction (playmate, interactor, solitary) in three

	• Determine effect of competence of older child with MR on the interaction • Determine effect of play context on interaction • Determine effect of relative ages on interaction				contexts (play, snack, TV watching) Competence of child with mental retardation
Carr (1988)	• Longitudinally compare the development and family effect of children with and without Down syndrome	Families of 54 infants with Down syndrome. Control group matched for age, sex, and social class	—	21 yrs., at last data collection Down syndrome	Longitudinal design w/individual cohort Interview/questionnaire	Problem behavior difficulties Health Benefits of sibling, plus child with Down syndrome and family variable
Dyson, Edgar, and Crnic (1989)	• Study adjustment of siblings in light of psychological predictors (e.g., parent attitude, family psychological environment, and child) • See if predictors would vary for siblings of children with and without disabilities.	110 (55 + 55)	8–15 x̄ = 9.7	Under 7 x̄ = 4.4 Mixture 18 mental retardation 22 physical/sensory disabilities 8 speech disorders 3 learning disability 4 developmental delay	Cross-sectional design Mailed questionnaire	Self-concept Behavior problems Social competence
Dyson and Fewell (1989)	• Investigate self-concept in siblings of children with and without disabilities • Investigate mediating effects of sex of sibling, type of disability, and SES.	74 (37 + 37)	7–14 x̄ = 10	1–16 x̄ = 7.5 Mixture 18 mental retardation 5 severe behavior disability 9 physical/sensory disabilities	Cross-sectional design Questionnaire	Self-concept

(continued)

Table 3. (continued)

Reference	Purpose of study	Sample size	Age[a] of siblings	Age[a] of target child[b]	Diagnostic category of target child	Research design	Variables measured
Gamble and McHale (1989)	• Examine the adjustment processes of children with younger siblings with mental disabilities • Investigate problems in sibling relationships • Examine relationships between stressors, coping, and adjustment	62 older siblings (31 + 31)	8–14 m = 12	3–11	4 Down syndrome 7 spina bifida 14 cerebral palsy, brain damaged, and other rare syndromes 3 developmental delay 2 speech disorders	Cross-sectional design Home visits with questionnaire	Stressor events Stress Coping appraisals Self-Concept, depression, anxiety
Gath and Gumley (1987)	• Differences in behavior and competence between sibling pair • Whether problems of normal siblings are related to problems of child with retardation • School behavior of siblings of child with retardation • Parents' treatment of sibling pair • How siblings of child with Down	183 sibling pairs 183 classroom controls	x̄ = 11	x̄ = 11	Mental retardation 95 Down syndrome 88 others with retardation	Cross-sectional group comparison within families and with classroom controls Interview and questionnaire	Behavior and competence of both siblings in dyad and classroom control

	syndrome differ from siblings of children with other forms of retardation • Effect of mediating variables on sibling				
Lobato, Barbour, Hall, and Miller (1987)	• Examine psychosocial functioning of siblings of children with and without disabilities	46 (24 + 22)	$\bar{x} = 5$ preschoolers	$\bar{x} = 4$ (1–11) Significant disability 3 Down syndrome 2 spina bifida 1 profound hearing loss 7 cerebral palsy 1 blindness 1 William syndrome 5 global develop. delay 1 multiple due to head injury 1 hydrocephalus 2 unknown etiology	Cross-sectional group comparison Interview and questionnaire	Psychosocial functioning, including: self-perception, empathy, verbalized affect toward family, understanding disabilities, behavioral functioning, home routines
McHale and Gamble (1989)	• Compare siblings as to daily activities and psychological well-being	62 older siblings (31 + 31)	8–14 school age	3–11 Mental retardation 4 Down syndrome 7 spina bifida 14 cerebral palsy, brain damaged and other rare syndromes	Cross-sectional group comparison Home interview, telephone surveys (7 times within 3-week period)	Daily activities Psychological well-being Family processes (i.e., amount of caregiving and house tasks, extent of sibling conflict and mother/child conflict, children's perception of favoritism)
McHale, Sloan, Simeonsson (1986)	• Compare sibling relationship	90 (30 + 30 + 30)	6–15 $\bar{x} = 11.2$	19 older than sibling and 11 Autism Mental retardation	Cross-sectional group comparison	Attitudes and perceptions of sibling

(continued)

Table 3. (continued)

Reference	Purpose of study	Sample size	Age[a] of siblings	Age[a] of target child[b]	Diagnostic category of target child	Research design	Variables measured
	• Examine correlates of individual differences in quality of sibling relationships with siblings of children with disabilities group		school age	younger than sibling in each group		Interview/ questionnaire	relationship
Seltzer, Begun, Seltzer, and Krauss (1991)	• Describe instrumental and affective involvement of siblings of adults with mental retardation • Determine how involvement varies with differences in "family life space" • Determine if there is a direct relationship between level of sibling involvement and maternal well-being	411 families, 93% had siblings	x̄ = 37	15–66 x̄ = 34	Mental retardation, over ⅓ with Down syndrome	Cross-sectional analysis Interview and questionnaires with mother	Adult with mental retardation well-being functional abilities health level of retardation Family well-being Maternal well-being health life satisfaction burden of care
Stoneman, Brody, Davis, and Crapps (1987)	• Compare sibling pairs to ascertain frequency of interaction, type of activities, roles, and affect • Investigate interactions of siblings with parents • Investigate the correlation between severity of	32 sibling pairs (16 with younger child with mental retardation, 16 with younger child without mental retardation)	10 school age 6–12	6 4–8	7 Down syndrome 4 organic brain damage 5 mental retardation	Cross-sectional group comparison Interview/ questionnaire and observation	Roles: manager, teacher, playmate, interaction Affect negative position Other behaviors: solitary, compliance

Stoneman, Brody, Davis, and Crapps (1988)	• Assess time use of older siblings of children with and without mental retardation • Assess the association between sibling childcare responsibilities and degree of conflict in the sibling relationship • Assess effects of age, income, and competencies of disabled sibling on amount of older sibling's responsibilities	32 sibling pairs (16 + 16) (same as above)	6–12	7 Down syndrome 4 organic brain damage	Cross-sectional Interview/questionnaire/in-home observation	Interaction of sibling pairs Household tasks and childcare Peer contacts Out-of-home activities Competency of child with mental retardation
Stoneman, Brody, Davis, and Crapps (1989)	• Compare interaction, role relationships, and affect of dyads with younger siblings with and without mental retardation • Determine effect of language and adaptive skills of younger child w/mental retardation on role relationships	32 sibling pairs (16 with younger child with mental retardation)	10 school age	7 Down syndrome 4 organic brain damage 5 other mental retardation	Cross-sectional group comparison Observation and interview/questionnaire	Sibling roles (manager, teacher, helper) Affect Interaction (playmate, interactor, solitary) in 3 contexts (toy play, snack, TV watching) Competency of child with mental retardation

(continued)

Table 3. (continued)

Reference	Purpose of study	Sample size	Age[a] of siblings	Age[a] of target child[b]	Diagnostic category of target child	Research design	Variables measured
Stoneman, Brody, Davis, Crapps, and Malone (1991)	• Determine effect of difference in relative age on role relationships • Compare ascribed roles (responsibilities) of younger siblings of older children with and without mental retardation • Determine effect of level of competency of older sibling with mental retardation on family responsibilities • Determine effect of compliance behaviors of older sibling with mental retardation on childcare responsibilities • Determine effect of childcare responsibility on observed sibling interaction • Investigate out-of-home activities of siblings in dyad	32 sibling pairs (16 with younger child with mental retardation)	7	10	7 Down syndrome 1 birth injury 8 unknown etiologies	Cross-sectional group comparison Observation and interview/questionnaire	Household tasks and childcare Peer contacts Out-of-home activities Verbal and adaptive skills of child with mental retardation Interaction of sibling pairs

Study	Purpose	Sample	Sibling age	Target age	Disability	Method	Variables
Summers, Summers, Ascione, and Braeger (1989)	• Compare sibling dyads in which one of the pair has a disability to sibling dyads in which neither of the pair has a disability	95 (60 disabled + 35 nondisabled)	2–11 x̄ = 9	3–6 x̄ = 4	19 hearing impaired 17 Down syndrome 24 cognitive/language disability	Cross-sectional observations of siblings Mothers' surveys	Categories of interactional behaviors (imitation, agonism, dominance, prosocial behavior) Family stress Sibling relationship
Wilson, Blacher, and Baker (1989)	• Explore school age siblings' perceptions of and feelings about family life. • Assess the nature and extent of interactions between siblings and children with severe mental retardation	24 older siblings from 20 families	9–13	6.5	Severe mental retardation	Cross-sectional Semistructured interview with questionnaire	Caregiving Interaction Sense of responsibility Impact (pos./neg.) Denial
Zetlin (1986)	• Determine the nature of the adult sibling relationship of community-based adults with mild retardation and their nonretarded siblings	35 mildly retarded adults and siblings, making 74 pairs	—	23–60 x̄ = 34	Mildly retarded	Participant observation techniques used for 18 months Structural life history Interviews with parents or sibling	Sibling relationship now Sibling relationship while growing up Relationship dimensions (warmth, frequency of contact, and degree of involvement)

[a] Ages rounded to nearest year.
[b] "Target child" refers to child with disabilities or comparison counterpart.

Grossman (1972) found that 45% of young adult college students, remembering their childhoods, felt that they had suffered from being a sibling of a person with mental disabilities. They reported feeling guilt, shame, neglect, defectiveness, and having negative feelings toward the brother or sister with mental disabilities. An equal percentage felt that they had benefitted from the experience, citing increased understanding, tolerance, compassion, and appreciation of their own good health and intelligence.

The findings vary greatly across these early studies, but with the great variety in methods, variables, measures, ages of siblings, and quality of studies, differences are to be expected. All the studies indicate that some siblings experience adjustment problems, but the factors influencing the siblings' adjustment other than having a brother or sister with mental disabilities are not clearly delineated.

Recent Investigations

Recent studies have again examined the adjustment problems of siblings of children with disabilities. Gath and Gumley (1987) have replicated and extended Gath's earlier studies through comparisons of three groups: 1) children with mental disabilities (about half of whom had Down syndrome), 2) their siblings, and 3) classroom controls for the siblings. The siblings of the children with mental disabilities were not found to have significantly greater behavioral problems than did the comparison siblings. The authors concluded that the findings demonstrated little evidence of detrimental effects of being a sibling of a child with a mental disability.

Another British investigator, Janet Carr (1988), has been following children with Down syndrome, matched comparison children, and their families since the children with Down syndrome were born. Data were collected from the mothers when the children with Down syndrome were 4, 11, and 21 years of age. The siblings of children with Down syndrome were reported to have fewer behavioral problems than did the comparison siblings. (The only exception was at the testing at age 21, when 4 comparison families with particular problems could not be traced.) Behavior problems were also measured by the Rutter Behavioral Scale (mothers completed the scale) when the children with Down syndrome were 11. No sibling of the children with Down syndrome reached the clinical cut-off point, indicating that none demonstrated severe behavior problems, whereas three of the comparison siblings did. These findings indicate that while the child with Down syndrome was growing to adulthood, the mothers perceived their other children to be adjusting fairly well.

In this country, two recent investigations examined the adjustment of siblings of children with disabilities, one studying preschool siblings (Lobato, Barbour, Hall, & Miller, 1987), and the other studying school-age siblings who were older than their brothers or sisters with disabilities (McHale &

Gamble, 1989). Both studies used comparison groups, measures of self-concept, and measures of psychological stress. The results revealed that for both age groups, the siblings of children with disabilities had poorer adjustment scores than did siblings of children who were not disabled; however, the gender differences were not consistent. The preschool brothers of children with disabilities had significantly higher depression and aggression scores (from maternal ratings) than did sisters of children with disabilities or the brothers and sisters in the comparison group. Sisters of children with disabilities had higher aggression scores than the comparison sisters (Lobato et al., 1987).

In the school-age study (McHale & Gamble, 1989), siblings of children with disabilities reported higher depression and anxiety than did the comparison siblings. Sisters of children with disabilities reported the highest depression scores. (The results of the perceived competence will be reported in a later section.) However, even though the differences between the groups were significant for anxiety and depression, all but two scores of the school-age siblings fell below the clinical cut-off point, indicating that although the adjustment problems of the school-age siblings were more severe than were those of the comparison children, they were within the normal range.

As with the earlier studies, the findings on adjustment problems were not consistent across studies. The American studies (Lobato et al., 1987; McHale & Gamble, 1989) found that the siblings had more adjustment problems than the comparison siblings, as measured by measures of psychological functioning, but the British studies (Gath & Gumley, 1987) found no difference in behavioral problems between the siblings of disabled children and the comparison siblings. Also, the findings of more frequent depression for preschool brothers of children with disabilities (Lobato et al., 1987) and for school-age sisters (McHale & Gamble, 1989) is intriguing. These differences could reflect the use of different measures, sampling fluctuations, or could be associated with age-related–gender-role expectations. The fact that the findings do differ in these well-controlled studies needs to be addressed in further research.

SELF-CONCEPT

The influence of the presence of a child with a disability on the sibling's self-concept was not measured directly in early studies. Grossman, however, was concerned with the likelihood that siblings, especially younger siblings, defined themselves in terms of the brother or sister with a disability (i.e., took on characteristics of the child with disabilities) (Grossman, 1972; Kaplan, 1969). Items in her measures of coping effectiveness used with college-age siblings of persons with retardation addressed this question of over-identification with a child with a disability (Grossman, 1972). Clinical case studies also documented cases in which younger siblings over-identified with their disabled sibling (San Martino & Newman, 1974).

Studies investigating self-concept of siblings appeared in related research during the late 1970s and early 1980s. Self-concept of siblings of children with cystic fibrosis (Gayton, Friedman, Tavormina, & Tucker, 1977), physical disabilities (Harvey & Greenway, 1984), and chronic illness (Ferrari, 1984) were reported. The results of these studies varied.

Four studies investigated the self-concept of siblings of children with disabilities in the late 1980s. One of these studies used a sample of preschool children (Lobato et al., 1987), and the others used school-age siblings (Dyson, Edgar, & Crnic, 1989; Dyson & Fewell, 1989; McHale & Gamble, 1989). Preschool siblings of children who were disabled and nondisabled were given the Pictorial Scale of Perceived Competence and Social Acceptance (Harter & Pike, 1983), which included four self-report subscales (cognitive competence, physical competence, peer acceptance, and maternal acceptance). No differences between the groups were found for any of the four measures (Lobato et al., 1987); the siblings' feelings of self-competence did not appear to be affected by having a brother or sister with a disability. Dyson and Fewell (1989), likewise, found no differences between the self-concepts of school-age siblings of children who were disabled and nondisabled using the Piers-Harris Children's Self-Concept Scale (Piers-Harris, 1969). Not only did the siblings of children with disabilities do as well as the others, the mean of the group was in the top range of the norms of the self-concept measure. Also, in these groups, sisters tended to score higher than brothers ($p = .09$). Scores ranged widely for both groups, with a few siblings in either group having extremely low self-concepts. In a second study of a larger sample, Dyson and her associates (Dyson et al., 1989) again found no difference in self-concept for siblings of children who were disabled and nondisabled. This study went on to investigate the antecedents of adjustment. Self-concept was one of the measures of adjustment. The antecedents of self-concept were found to be different for siblings of children with disabilities than for the comparison siblings.

Conversely, McHale and Gamble (Gamble & McHale, 1989; McHale & Gamble, 1989) found that school-age siblings of younger children with disabilities had lower self-esteem, as measured by the Perceived Competence Scale (Harter, 1982). The gender findings also differed from the previous studies. Sisters of children who were disabled had significantly lower self-esteem scores than did brothers of children with disabilities, or brothers or sisters of children who were not disabled. Why the findings from these two studies differ so much is perplexing, as the ages of the siblings and children with disabilities and the types of disabilities in the samples were fairly similar.

Both measures of self-concept reported are widely used and have adequate reliability and validity. Again, further investigation seems to be needed.

ACTIVITIES AND TIME USE

Childcare and Household Tasks

Early studies tried to identify the variables associated with negative psychological effects on the siblings. One of the variables thought to cause negative effects was the burden of physical care of the child with mental retardation. The research of Farber (1959, 1960), Gath (1972, 1973, 1974), and Grossman (1972), by identifying time spent performing household tasks and caring for a sibling with mental retardation as being related to negative effects, helped to focus the research and identify time use as a concern.

In trying to understand the effects of children with retardation on families, Farber (1959, 1960; Farber & Jenne, 1963) studied the role tension of siblings. Sibling role tension, defined as a subjective feeling of frustration, tension, or anxiety resulting from having to assume responsibilities for the child with retardation, is a score based on the mother's rating of 10 personality traits of the sibling (e.g., gets angry easily, stubborn, jealous). Farber (1959), in interpreting his findings, suggested that the sister's roles in the home expanded to include many adult responsibilities when the child with retardation lived at home and was highly dependent. The sister shared the burden of care with her mother.

Gath's studies (1972, 1973, 1974) in England supported the concern over sibling (especially sister) stress caused by the need for physical care of a child with retardation. The measures used in the studies were the Rutter Behavioral Scale A (mother form) and B (teacher form) (Rutter et al., 1970) that measured the degree of the siblings' psychiatric disorder. The first study (Gath, 1972) found no difference in neurotic and antisocial disorders among three groups (siblings of children with Down syndrome, with cleft palate, and with no disabilities). However, the second study (Gath, 1973, 1974) found that significantly more siblings of children with Down syndrome were rated as deviant than were siblings of children without disabilities. The differences in the findings of the two studies (Gath, 1972, 1973) were thought to possibly be due to the difference in sample size—in the 1972 study, the experimental groups included 36 and 35 subjects and the control group included 71, while in the 1973 study the experimental and control groups were each made up of 174 subjects.

Gath's (1974) analysis focused separately on the sisters and brothers of children with Down syndrome. Her analysis looked at types and levels of schooling, family (siblingship) size, socioeconomic status, birth order, and spacing. Fewer sisters with four or five siblings were rated as deviant than were those from larger or smaller families. Birth order and birth spacing both appeared to affect sisters (but not brothers), with sisters at least 3 or more years older than the child with Down syndrome appearing to be at the greatest risk. Ann Gath concluded that "the ill effects of having a mentally disabled brother or sister are shared unequally amongst the other children in the family. The brunt of the burden appears to be borne by the sisters" (p. 145).

Grossman (1972) interviewed college-age siblings of persons with mental retardation, studying siblings from community colleges and private universities in a socioeconomic comparison. Through the interviews, they recalled their feelings concerning their childhood relationships with the brother or sister with mental retardation. One of the findings dealt with the physical care issue. Sisters of children with retardation had higher anxiety scores than did brothers, and sisters from lower socioeconomic levels coped better when the physical disability was less severe. Grossman (1972) thought these findings reflected the amount of physical caregiving involved. In other words, sisters had higher anxiety than brothers because they devoted a greater amount of time to the physical care of their sibling with a disability. Also, sisters in the lower socioeconomic group (community college) had more problems when the physical involvement of the child with retardation was more severe and the child could do fewer things for him- or herself. Other early studies also indicated a relationship between caring for the child with retardation and negative sibling effects, at least for some of the siblings (Cleveland & Miller, 1977; Dupont, 1980; Fowle, 1968; Graliker et al., 1962; Holt, 1958; Lloyd-Bostock, 1976).

The more recent study of Gath and Gumley (1987), which was similar in design to the earlier Gath studies, reported conflicting findings. The sample included 183 in each of the three groups (children with retardation, their siblings, and classmates of the siblings). This time, they did not find any evidence of increased domestic burden on older sisters of children with retardation. In fact, they reported "little evidence of direct detrimental effect of a child with mental retardation upon the siblings" (Gath & Gumley, 1987, p. 729). They explained that the earlier finding on the burden placed on older sisters was possibly due to the effect of membership in a lower socioeconomic level and in a large (5+ children) family (Gath, 1973, 1974).

None of the studies reviewed above attempted to measure actual time spent in household tasks, childcare, or other activities for the siblings of children who were retarded. Schwirian (1976) (for her study of older siblings of preschoolers who were hearing impaired) developed a frequency rating scale to study childcare responsibilities, general home responsibilities, degree of independence, and extent of social activities. Although older siblings of children with hearing impairments performed more childcare and had lower levels of social activity than the comparison siblings, the majority of the variance was explained by differences in the age and gender of the sibling.

Frequency Rating Scales Three recent investigations (Lobato et al., 1987; Stoneman, Brody, Davis, & Crapps, 1988; Stoneman, Brody, Davis, Crapps, & Malone, 1991) used adaptations of Schwirian's scale to study household tasks and childcare responsibilities. All of these studies used comparison groups of siblings of children without disabilities. Lobato and her associates (1987) studied preschool siblings of children with disabilities, including children with mental retardation and other disabilities. The sisters of the children with disabilities did have the greatest degree of responsibility for household tasks and childcare when compared with brothers of children with disabilities, and with sisters and brothers of nondisabled children, but the difference was not statistically significant. The young age of these siblings may have affected these findings.

Two Stoneman and Brody studies investigated the activities of either older (Stoneman et al., 1988) or younger (Stoneman et al., 1991) siblings of children with mental retardation using the same research design in both studies. In the study of older siblings of children with and without retardation, participation in household tasks was found to follow traditional sex-role patterns, with older sisters in both groups having significantly more responsibilities in personal and adaptive tasks and meal preparation, and older brothers having significantly more responsibilities in outside yard work. The older sisters of children with retardation did significantly more babysitting and caring for the child with retardation than any of the other four groups. Older sisters of comparison children and older brothers of children with retardation performed about the same amount of babysitting, and the older brothers of comparison children did the least amount of babysitting. Correlational analyses revealed that for siblings of children with retardation, more childcare responsibilities were associated with less observed positive interaction and more conflict between siblings, indicating a relationship between childcare by siblings and negative outcomes. Conversely, performing more household tasks was associated with less sibling conflict. Also, within the group of siblings of children with retardation, more demands for family responsibilities were directly related to decreased time for being with friends and participating in out-of-home activities.

In the study of younger siblings of children with and without retardation (Stoneman et al., 1991), the younger siblings of children with retardation assumed childcare responsibilities (as measured by the variables of babysitting, monitoring child, and helping with care) for the older child with retardation, as did the older siblings of children with retardation in the previous study. The younger comparison siblings performed significantly less total childcare and never babysat their older siblings. Conversely, the younger comparison siblings performed significantly more household tasks than did the younger siblings of the children with retardation. In examining the childcare provided by younger siblings for their older brothers or sisters who were retarded, it was found that those who performed more childcare also performed the helper role more and the playmate role less in the observed interaction, demonstrating greater role reversal. However, negative affect was not associated with more childcare, as it was in the study of older siblings caring for younger children with retardation (Stoneman et al., 1988). More childcare was given when the competency of the child with retardation was lower.

Gender differences were also found for these younger siblings of older children with and without disabilities. Performance of household tasks generally followed traditional sex roles (with sisters performing significantly more adaptive tasks, meal preparation, and cleaning), but the brothers did not do more yard work.

Other Time-Use Methodologies Two types of time-use methodology that were developed in other disciplines were used in recent investigations. McHale and Gamble (1989) investigated the impact of siblings' (ages 6–15) childcare and household tasks using a cued-recall procedure with 62 older siblings of children with and without mental retardation. They phoned the siblings on seven nights over a 3-week period after the initial interview. Mothers also reported the household tasks of the siblings and younger children (retarded or comparison). Group and gender effects were found. Siblings of children with disabilities and girls did more caregiving and household tasks. Caregiving was found to correlate with greater sibling anxiety, but not with depression or self-competence.

Boyce et al. (1991) compared the time use of 60 siblings (ages 10–17) of children with Down syndrome and 60 siblings of nondisabled children using the time-use methodology devised by Juster and Stafford (1985) at the Survey Research Center of the Institute for Social Research. The samples were matched case by case. This time-diary methodology detailing 24 hours (1,440 minutes) of activities for the previous day were collected twice, once on a weekday and once on a weekend day. These were combined into a "synthetic week" of activities (weekday × 5 + weekend × 2), which was coded into 223 categories and then reduced to 10 composite categories (work for pay, household tasks, childcare, shopping, personal care, educational activities, organizational activities, social activities, entertainment, active leisure, and passive leisure). Fourteen more specific categories (isolated out of the composite categories) were also analyzed. Siblings of children with Down syndrome performed more childcare for family members than did the siblings of children without Down syndrome. Within the group of siblings of children with Down syndrome, only siblings older than the child with Down syndrome performed childcare, and sisters tended to provide care for longer periods of time than did brothers. This childcare finding substantiates those of the previous studies, but the interesting fact is that very little time of the synthetic week was spent in childcare. In a synthetic week of 10,080 minutes (60 minutes × 24 hours × 7 days), the Down syndrome group averaged 44 minutes, and the comparison group 16 minutes, of childcare. Only 23 (of 60) siblings of children with Down syndrome and 8 comparison siblings reported spending time caring for children in the family. The amount of time spent varied from several minutes to more than 3 hours in a week. (This amount of time spent in childcare included childcare of any child in the family, not just the child with retardation.) In this study, no significant group difference or gender difference in time spent in household tasks was found, but the category of household tasks included both inside and outside chores.

Other Activities

In families of children with retardation, Farber and Jenne (1963) found that activities of sisters of children who were retarded were limited because of their responsibilities. Brothers, however, were found to seek interactions outside the home to avoid the tension there. Stoneman et al. (1988) investigated these same variables by asking the older school-age siblings of children with and without retardation about their friendships and activities. Their findings differed from those of Farber and Jenne. Concerning visiting patterns, older brothers of children with retardation had friends over to their homes to visit more frequently, had more different friends over, and visited homes of more different friends than did the brothers of the comparison siblings or the sisters of either group.

Few group (with or without a younger sibling with retardation) differences were detected for out-of-home activities. The two groups of siblings participated in sports, clubs, and church similarly, but siblings of younger children with retardation took part in fewer music-related activities than did comparison siblings. In both groups, older brothers participated in church and sports more than older sisters did. The findings of the study of younger siblings of older children with and without retardation (Stoneman et al., 1991) also differed from those of Farber and Jenne. The younger siblings of children with retardation had as many friendship contacts and out-of-home activities as the comparison younger siblings. In both studies (Stoneman et al., 1988, 1991) the children with retardation had fewer out-of-home friendships and activities than did the comparison siblings.

Boyce et al. (1991) did not investigate out-of-home activities per se, but, using the time-diary methodology, studied all of the activities of the siblings, and in doing so found some unexpected differences between siblings of children with and without Down syndrome. Siblings of children with Down syndrome spent less time in school ($p = .01$). In the category of leisure activities, the siblings of children with Down syndrome spent more time watching TV ($p = .01$) and less time working on hobbies ($p = .10$). However, there were no statistically significant differences in other activities (e.g., shopping, personal care, sports, playing, reading, social activities).

What, then, has been found about activities of siblings of children with retardation? Generally, childcare was performed more by siblings of children with retardation than by the comparison siblings and for school-age siblings (Boyce et al., 1991; McHale & Gamble, 1989; Stoneman et al., 1988, 1991), these differences were significant. Gender-role expectations seem to be an influence, because in all three studies sisters performed more childcare than brothers. However, both McHale and Gamble (1989) and Stoneman et al. (1987) reported that older brothers of children with retardation performed about as much caregiving as did older sisters of children who were not retarded. Likewise, in their within-group analysis, Boyce (1990) found that 12 older sisters and 11 older brothers performed childcare, but that sisters spent more time doing so.

These findings suggest that when help was needed, the roles of older brothers changed. Relative age of the siblings may also be a factor. Siblings older than the child with retardation reported giving childcare (Boyce et al., 1991; McHale & Gamble, 1989; Stoneman et al., 1987; Stoneman, Brody, Davis & Crapps, 1989), but the findings for siblings younger than the child with retardation varied (Boyce, 1990; Stoneman et al., 1991). The differences may be due to differences in the measures used in the studies. However, the time use study reported that no siblings younger than the child with Down syndrome reported that time was spent giving childcare (Boyce, 1990), and the findings from the rating scale report of frequency of household and childcare tasks (Stoneman et al., 1991) demonstrated that younger siblings provided some care for their older brothers and sisters with retardation. On the adapted Schwirian (1976) rating scale, the siblings rated the childcare items 1) never, 2) very infrequently, 3) several times a month, 4) about once a week, 5) several times a week, and 6) daily. The frequency of childcare by these siblings younger than the children with retardation was less than it was for the siblings in a similar study who were older than the children with retardation. The mean score for babysitting of older children with retardation was 1.56 for sisters and 1.36 for brothers (Stoneman et al., 1991). The mean score for babysitting of younger children with retardation was 3.94 for sisters and 2.71 for brothers (Stoneman et al., 1988).

In sum, the presence of a sibling with mental retardation appears to be a powerful caregiving stimulus that influences the behavior of siblings, to paraphrase Brody, Stoneman, Davis, and Crapps (1991). Older siblings of children with retardation have increased childcare responsibilities; the normal role of older siblings caring for younger siblings is magnified by the presence of the disability. For younger siblings of children with retardation, roles are not magnified, but roles may be reversed, with the younger sibling taking on roles that he or she would not experience in a family where there was no older child with a disability. However, these non-normative roles do not appear to negatively influence the affective relations of siblings and the child with retardation, or the siblings' out-of-home social activities (Stoneman et al., 1991).

Another consideration is the amount of time siblings of children with disabilities spend providing childcare. McHale and Gamble (1989) reported that siblings of children with disabilities spent about twice as much time caring for their younger brothers or sisters as did comparison siblings. The findings of Boyce et al. (1991) agreed; in their study, siblings of children with disabilities spent almost three times as long providing childcare as did comparison siblings. However, the total estimated time spent by siblings of children with Down syndrome in childcare activities was 44 minutes in a week. Although only the Boyce et al. (1991) study measured the amount of time spent in childcare, findings from other studies also appear to indicate limited childcare. McHale and Gamble (1989) investigated siblings' time use through a series of seven telephone calls over a 3-week period. Using a checklist approach, frequencies and duration of caregiving were reported; the mean frequency was 1.7 for both brothers and sisters, and 17.9 minutes for brothers and 25.2 minutes for sisters. The rating-scale means in the studies of Stoneman and associates (1988, 1991) discussed above also appear to indicate limited childcare. This finding of limited time spent performing childcare deserves further study. Possibly due to smaller families and the school-based intervention programs that are now available, siblings seem not to be needed to help as much with childcare as they were needed from the 1950s through the 1970s, when Farber and Gath conducted their original investigations. As Gath and Gumley concluded in their 1987 study, there is now no convincing evidence that the siblings in this group of families are presently bearing an undue domestic burden.

Nevertheless, among families of children with retardation, there seem to be large individual differences in the amount of childcare responsibilities siblings are given. When these responsibilities are great, the siblings may be negatively affected, as evidenced by increased conflict and decreased positive interactions (Stoneman et al., 1987).

SIBLING RELATIONSHIPS

Research into the interactional sibling relationship between the sibling with a disability and the sibling without a disability seems to have begun with Miller's study (1974). In this study, the children were interviewed about their activities with their siblings with disabilities and with their other siblings, the affect expressed, and their perceptions of parental expectation concerning their activities and affect. The respondents generally reported more activities of an instrumental nature (helping) with their brother or sister with a disability and more activities of an expressive nature (playing together) with their nondisabled siblings. They reported expressing less negative and more positive affect to their disabled siblings than to the other siblings, partly due to the responses of the disabled child and partly due to their perception of parents' expectations. Miller concluded that the children's perception of their relationship with siblings with and without disabilities appeared to be different.

During the early 1980s, reviewers (Brody & Stoneman, 1983; Simeonsson & McHale, 1981) urged researchers to study the bi-directionality of effects between siblings in the interactional process, and to use methodologies that would focus on interaction. During the latter part of the 1980s, 12 papers on relationships between disabled and nondisabled siblings appeared in the literature. Most of the papers reported findings for children, primarily of school age, but three reported on relationships of adult siblings.

Studies of Childhood Sibling Dyads

In the studies of children, the data collection included observations of the sibling pair (Abramovitch et al., 1987; Stoneman et al., 1987, 1989, 1991; Summers, Summers, Ascione, & Braeger, 1989) and home visits with questionnaires (Gamble & McHale, 1989; McHale & Gamble, 1989; McHale et al., 1986; Wilson, Blacher, & Baker, 1989). The Stoneman, McHale, and Wilson studies investigated the relationships of older siblings and younger children with disabilities. Stoneman and Brody also investigated the relationship between younger siblings and older children with disabilities (Brody et al., 1991). The observational studies coded for somewhat different aspects of the interaction. Abramovitch et al. (1987) coded initiation and response behaviors (as to whether they were prosocial or agonistic) and imitative behaviors. Summers et al. (1989) coded four types of behaviors for both siblings (i.e., agonism, prosocial, dominance, and imitation). Stoneman and associates (1987, 1989, 1991) coded the relationship roles of manager, helper, and teacher, as well as those of playmate, interactor, and solitary player, and the affective tone of the interaction. All of these studies of children, with the exception of a study by Wilson et al. (1989), included comparison groups of siblings and typical children. The findings of this interview study of siblings of children with severe disabilities substantiated the findings of the comparison-group studies.

Overall, the findings were generally consistent across studies and supported Miller's (1974) initial findings. Interaction was as high for the pairs of siblings in which one was disabled as it was for the comparison siblings or normative sample, except for the sibling pairs that included a child with hearing impairment (Abramovitch et al., 1987; Brody et al., 1991; Stoneman et al., 1987, 1989; Summers et al., 1989). The activity contexts (e.g., toy play, snack time, and TV watching) were found to influence the amount of interaction (Stoneman et al., 1989). The relationships were generally positive in nature (Abramovitch et al., 1987; Brody et al., 1991; McHale & Gamble, 1989; Stoneman et al., 1987, 1989; Wilson et al., 1989); however, McHale & Gamble found that the siblings' and mothers' ratings of the interactions were more positive (warmer and less aggressive) than the time-use reports indicated they were. The relationship in the disabled/nondisabled pairs was reported by all to be asymmetrical, with the nondisabled sibling being dominant in the interaction (i.e., the teacher, leader, or manager); whereas, in the interaction of the two nondisabled siblings, there was more joint play, and the comparison sibling more often took the role of playmate instead of teacher. School-age siblings with disabilities initiated less interaction (either prosocial or agonistic) and responded less often to overtures, but imitated more than did the siblings without disabilities (Abramovitch et al., 1987). Preschool siblings with disabilities imitated less and displayed more agonistic behavior than did comparison preschool siblings (Summers et al., 1989).

The findings of these studies demonstrated that sibling pairs that include children with disabilities were similar to other sibling pairs in the amount of interaction and the affect demonstrated. However, the role relationships in sibling pairs with one sibling with a disability were more asymmetrical, with the nondisabled sibling demonstrating more helping, teaching, managing, and dominating behaviors. Possibly, the siblings who were nondisabled were "scaffolding" their behaviors in order to make interaction work.

Developmental status of either the child with disabilities or the sibling may also affect sibling interaction. Preschool-age children ($\bar{x} = 4$ years) with disabilities imitated less than nondisabled preschool children (Summers et al., 1989), but the siblings with Down syndrome ($\bar{x} = 9$ years) imitated their siblings more than did the 9-year-old (mean age) comparison children (Abramovitch et al., 1987). Begun (1989) also reported developmental status differences. Adolescent sisters reported more conflict with their siblings with disabilities than did adult sisters. The ways in which sibling interactions change with age need to be investigated further.

Studies of Adult Sibling Dyads

Three studies of adult siblings support the research on sibling relationships reported previously. Zetlin's study (1986) brings a different research design to the literature on siblings of persons with disabilities. Participant observation was conducted over an 18-month period with 35 adults with mild retardation. Structured life-history interviews (lasting 6–9 hours over 2 or 3 interview sessions) were conducted with one or both parents, or, if parents were deceased, with a sibling. The interview data and field notes were independently rated for each sibling pair on a 5-point continuum that reflected warmth, frequency of contact, and degree of involvement (i.e., dependency/reciprocity). The second study (Begun, 1989) used a design similar to Miller's study (1974). Questionnaires were mailed to sisters ($N = 46$) closest in age to the sibling with a disability, asking them to rate (on a 5-point scale) 16 dimensions of their relationship with their sibling with a disability ($N = 46$) and with their other siblings ($N = 78$). The third study (Seltzer, Begun, Seltzer, & Krauss, 1991) included interviews with the mothers of adults with retardation ($N = 411$, with 93% also having other, nondisabled children) concerning the sibling relationships of their adult children.

From these three studies, the researchers learned that most of the adults were involved with their adult brother or sister with retardation (Seltzer et al., 1991; Zetlin, 1986) and that the sibling relationships were usually viewed in a positive light (Zetlin, 1986). The siblings viewed these relationships as being similar to their relationships with their other siblings in terms of affection and companionship (Begun, 1989). However, the relationships between the siblings with and without disabilities were hierarchical, or, in Stoneman and Brody's words, "asymmetrical" (Stoneman et al., 1989, p. 61), with the sibling who was not disabled providing help and support for the sibling with a disability (Begun, 1989; Seltzer et al., 1991; Zetlin, 1986). The fact that the siblings with disabilities attempted to reciprocate by giving help in return (e.g., babysitting for the nondisabled sibling's family) is interesting (Zetlin, 1986). Seltzer and associates (1991) reported that within the adult sibling relationship, the mothers perceived that more affective support than instrumental help was given. There was also less competition in the disabled/nondisabled relationship than in the relationships with other siblings (Begun, 1989), but the relationships with other siblings were viewed as being closer and more intimate than the relationship with the sibling with disabilities (Begun, 1989).

STRESS AND COPING

Only one investigation (Gamble & McHale, 1989) was found that investigated how older siblings of children with and without retardation coped with stress in the sibling relationship. Stress was measured by frequency and affect appraisals of stress (feeling mad). The stresses were reported as being generally similar in kind for both groups, except that the younger children in the comparison group "teased or bugged" (Gamble & McHale, 1989, p. 361) their older siblings significantly more often than did the younger children with retardation. Likewise, both groups reported similar feelings of anger when having problems with their younger brothers and sisters, but siblings of children with disabilities tended to report being more upset when the child "got hurt or sick."

Differences were also found in coping behaviors. Siblings of children with disabilities and sisters (in a comparison of sisters vs. brothers) used "other-directed cognitions" (Gamble & McHale, 1989, p. 368) (e.g., placing blame on others) more frequently than did siblings of nondisabled children or brothers. Group differences were also found in adjustment for the variables of depression, anxiety, and general self-worth, with the siblings of children who were disabled being more depressed and anxious and having perceptions of lower self-competence than comparison siblings.

A different trend was observed in the siblings' ratings of their relationship with their younger brothers and sisters. Siblings of children with disabilities rated their behaviors toward their younger brother or sister more positively than did the comparison siblings, but the two groups of children rated their satisfaction with the sibling relationship equally.

Analyses were performed to investigate the relationships between stressor of effect and coping, and siblings' adjustment and sibling relationship measures. The multiple-regression analyses revealed that group membership (i.e., siblings of children with versus those without disabilities) and self-cognition coping accounted for a significant portion of the variance of sibling feelings of depression and anxiety, but not for feelings of general self-worth. However, group membership did not account for a significant portion of the variance in either sibling relationship measure (satisfaction with sibling relationship or behavior ratings), although the frequency of stressors and the coping measures used did account for a significant portion of the variance. This investigation of sibling stress and coping seems fruitful, and further replicative research with various age groups would be productive.

MEDIATING VARIABLES

Suomi (1982) identified certain factors that influence patterns of sibling interaction and caregiving across nonhuman primates as well as across all groups of humans. These factors included age differences in the sibling group and within dyads, the sex of the participants, the availability of other peers who enter into the sibling group interactions, the developmental stage of the individuals, and the features of the local social structure. Starting with Farber (1959, 1960), researchers studying siblings of children with disabilities have attempted to investigate some of these factors, along with the developmental level or functional abilities of the child with a disability. The attempt has been to understand what factors (mediating variables) influence the sibling's reaction to living with a brother or sister with a disability. Reviewers (e.g., Simeonsson & McHale, 1981) have attempted to integrate the findings, noting methodological problems and confounds in the research. Table 4 lists those characteristics that have been studied and the tentative conclusions reached by the reviewers. The recent research adds to the evidence of the influence of those mediating variables.

Gender

Gender was most frequently investigated, and the findings indicate that gender differences, which are probably due to gender role expectations, exist.

Table 4. Characteristics of sibling, family, and child with disability

Reference	SES	Family size	Gender of sibling	Age and/or[a] relative age of sibling	Gender × age	Age of child with disabilities	Gender of child with disability	Type of disability	Severity/ functioning level
Crnic and Leconte (1986)	X	—	—	First born[b]	Younger brothers[c]	Grows older[c]	—	—	—
Gallagher and Powell (1989)	Middle SES[b] (more resources)	Larger[b]	Same sex[c]	Younger[c] (with small birth gap) Older[b] (with large birth gap)	Older sisters[c]	Grows older[c]	—	Type not crucial except ambiguous w/high SES[c]	Severe[c]
Hannah and Midlarsky (1985)	Lower SES[c]	Smaller[c]	Female[c]	—	Contradictory findings	—	—	—	Severe[c] Least severe[c] Moderate[b]
McKeever (1983)	X	More than one sibling and child with retardation[b]	Female	Conflicting findings	Younger brothers	—	—	—	—
Simeonsson and McHale (1981)	X	Smaller[c] (with one child) Larger[b]	Female[c] Male[b]	Younger[c] Older[b]	—	Older[c] Younger[b]	Male[c] Female[b] Same sex[c]	Ambiguous[c] Visible[b]	Severe[c]

[a]Age and relative age are confounded in the research.
[b]Less affected (more positive adjustment).
[c]More affected (less positive adjustment).
—Not discussed in review.

X = a qualitative difference for SES. The presence of a child with retardation in the family was seen as a coping crisis, one of providing physical care with few resources, for the lower class. For the middle-class family, it was a crisis of destroyed expectations.

Sisters have more caregiving responsibilities than do brothers, but brothers of persons with disabilities also perform caregiving (Boyce et al., 1991; McHale & Gamble, 1989; Seltzer et al., 1991; Stoneman et al., 1988; Zetlin, 1986). However, in the study of siblings of children with severe disabilities, gender did not correlate with caregiving (Wilson et al., 1989). Sisters manage and direct more frequently in their relationships with younger siblings than do brothers (Stoneman et al., 1987). They report experiencing more negative interaction with their mothers and with siblings, including teasing, hitting, etc. (Gamble & McHale, 1989). However, no gender differences were found for the interaction variables of imitation, dominance, agonism, or prosocial behaviors by Summers and associates (1989).

Age/Developmental Status

Age is a common marker for developmental stages. This sample of studies, which have appeared in the literature in the last 5 years, includes studies of preschool, school-age, adolescent, and adult siblings. Because no study compares siblings across these ages, it is impossible to know how similarly or differently siblings of different developmental stages react to, or are affected by, having a brother or sister with a disability. The indications in the studies so far are that developmental stages do affect psychological well-being, activities, and the relationship itself. For example, adolescent sisters reported more conflicts with their brothers or sisters with retardation than did adult sisters (Begun, 1989). Also, middle-age siblings with stable lifestyles were perceived by their siblings with retardation as being better supporters than young adult siblings (Zetlin, 1986).

Relative Birth Order

Early studies investigated how the relative birth order of the siblings mediated the influence of the one sibling's disability. For instance, Gath (1974) found that older sisters took on many of the mothering responsibilities, and Farber (1960) found that the roles of the child with disabilities and younger sibling "crossed over," with the child with disabilities eventually assuming the position and roles of the younger child and the younger child assuming the roles of the older sibling. The majority of the more recent studies limited their sample to older siblings of children with disabilities (McHale & Gamble, 1989; Stoneman et al., 1987, 1988); however, Brody et al. (1991) also used a sample of younger siblings of older children with and without retardation. They found that siblings who were younger than the children with disabilities took on the roles of teaching, helping, and managing their older siblings with disabilities.

Limited investigation of the influence of the relative birth order and the sibling relationship in adulthood has found varied results. Seltzer and associates (1991) found that the most involved sibling (with the adult with retardation) was likely to be older and of the same sex. However, Zetlin (1986) found that younger siblings were more likely than older siblings to act as caregivers.

In some of the recent studies, the relative birth order has not been found to influence the outcome measures of self-concept (Dyson & Fewell, 1989); overall time use, general attitudes, or attitudes toward children with retardation (Boyce et al., 1991); vulnerability to deviant behaviors (Gath & Gumley, 1987); or maternal reports of sibling acceptance, hostility, support, or embarrassment. The one exception was that the siblings younger than the child with a disability reported more feelings of rejection toward the brother or sister with a disability than did the siblings who were older (e.g., McHale et al., 1986).

Another piece of the relative birth order puzzle is whether the siblings are born consecutively. Seltzer et al. (1991) found that siblings most likely to be involved with the adult with retardation had consecutive birth order positions. Stoneman and Brody and associates have limited their investigations to siblings of consecutive birth order (Brody et al., 1991; Stoneman et al., 1989). Further studies are needed to examine the effect of nonconsecutive birth order.

Competence of Sibling with a Disability

The functional level of the child with a disability appears to influence the relationship between the siblings in some ways, but the findings do not all agree. When the child with a disability has a higher functional level, the sibling relationship is warmer and closer, but more competitive (Begun, 1989); there is less solitary play and greater family interaction (Stoneman et al., 1987), more joint toy play and increased symmetry in roles, and less childcare (Stoneman et al., 1991, 1988). Factors related to the extent of disability (e.g., helplessness or intrusive behavior) were found to influence the extent of psychiatric problems seen in siblings (Gath & Gumley, 1987). However, McHale and Gamble (1989) found no direct connections between the abilities of the child with disabilities and sibling well-being (e.g., measures of depression, anxiety, and self-competence).

Age and Gender of the Child with Disabilities

Few of these studies investigated any characteristic of the child with disabilities other than competence level. Wilson and associates (1989) did find that, generally, the characteristics of the child (e.g., age and sex) with disabilities were unrelated to the various sibling scale scores. The sex of the child with disabilities related to only the interaction score, which indicated that the siblings interacted more with boys with disabilities.

Family Social-Process Variables

Reviewers have also urged the investigation of family social-process variables and have conjectured that these process variables may affect the siblings more than do variables such as age and gender (e.g., Vadasy, Fewell, Meyer, & Schell, 1984).

An initial investigation revealed that certain sibling concerns (e.g., worries about the future, or parental favoritism) and certain parent attitudes did affect the sibling relations with the child with a disability (McHale et al., 1986). In a later study, the family-process variables of differential treatment and maternal negativity accounted for a significant portion of the variance in sibling depression and anxiety, while sibling caregiving, sibling negativity, and household chores did not (McHale & Gamble, 1989).

Dyson and associates (Dyson et al., 1989) also identified "family psychological variables" and found that different groupings of these variables influenced siblings of children with and without disabilities differently. They concluded that parental stress and some dimensions of the family social environment were the most significant predictors of adjustment of siblings of children with disabilities. The study of family psychological or process variables also seems to be a promising area of investigation.

Other Mediating Variables

Investigations have thus far shown that certain contexts affect the sibling interactions of persons with disabilities. Adults with retardation received more support from siblings who were more geographically accessible (Seltzer et al., 1991; Zetlin, 1986). Begun (1989) found that cohabitation influenced sisters' feelings about their sisters with disabilities. Stoneman, Brody, and associates (Stoneman et al., 1987, 1989, 1991) found that the context of the activity (toy play, snack time, and TV watching) influenced the amount of interaction and the roles of school-age siblings.

CONCLUDING COMMENTS

What is the state of the research on siblings of children with mental disabilities? In 1984 Vadasy et al. referred to the findings on siblings of children with disabilities as "bits of information" that are tempting to use in estimating sibling effects (p. 165). It seems that in 1992 a more complete understanding of sibling relationships, activities, and well-being is available. Methodologically sound research has been completed in the last half of the 1980s. The interplay between internal dynamic growth within the research field of siblings of children with disabilities and societal, theoretical, and methodological influences from outside the field has contributed to the richness of this research.

Relationships Similar, But Different

In many ways, including frequency of interactions and positive exchange, the relationship between a child with a disability and his or her sibling is much like the relationships between nondisabled siblings, but atypical relationships seem to be qualitatively different in that they are characterized by a greater frequency of caregiving, teaching, and dominating behaviors by the nondisabled sibling. Research using comparison groups and direct observation, as well as other methodologies, has aided in this line of investigation.

Similar Activity Patterns with Some Exceptions

Research on time use generally indicates similar patterns of activities for siblings of children with and without disabilities. Throughout childhood, age and gender influence children's activities, but, for certain activities, having a brother or sister with mental disabilities does seem to influence children's time use (e.g., childcare of family members). Other activities have recently been investigated, and time in school and watching television have been found to be influenced by having a brother or sister with retardation. These findings await confirmation by replicative research.

The linkage between childcare responsibilities and negative outcomes, either in the sibling interaction or sibling psychological adjustments, is indicated by some, but not all studies. In order to effectively counsel families, it is essential to more completely understand this relationship between home responsibilities and negative sibling outcomes. Consequently, more research delineating this link is needed.

Psychological Adjustment and Family-Process Variables

The psychological adjustment of siblings of children with disabilities remains a puzzle; findings from studies using different research designs don't agree. The self-esteem studies have added a new component to understanding of the psychological well-being of siblings, but the findings of these studies also differ. The fact that siblings of children with disabilities, in one study using a sound methodological design with a comparison group, were found to report more anxiety and depression may indicate that many of these siblings experience mild levels of disturbance (McHale & Gamble, 1989). The interplay of the family-process variables (e.g., the mother's negativism, the perception of parental differential treatment) and sibling interaction adjustment is most intriguing.

Mediating Influences of Child and Family Characteristics

The mediating influence of gender has been studied frequently and seems to follow the gender-role expectations of the culture, with the exception that brothers of children with disabilities seem to respond to the needs of the family and are more involved in childcare than typical brothers. (Brothers are, nevertheless, still less involved than are sisters of children with disabilities.) Much of the recent research has investigated outcomes for siblings older than the child with a disability, but further research needs to be focused on siblings who are younger than the child with a disability. The influence of the birth gap or spacing (i.e., amount of age difference between siblings) and the developmental stage (e.g., preschool, adolescent) of siblings both with and without disabilities have yet to be clearly delineated.

Future Research Directions

It is perhaps a pat answer to simply call for further research, but in this field much will be learned if the body of research continues to grow based on the thoughtful use of findings within the research field and changes in contexts outside the field of research. As was said earlier, much more is known now than 5 years ago, but much is left to be learned. What then is important to investigate next? The following questions need to be addressed: Do the siblings of children who are mentally disabled experience elevated levels of depression and anxiety? Is time spent on childcare an important factor in the well-being of the siblings when it appears that, on the average, siblings spend only limited time performing childcare (e.g., an average of 44 minutes per week [Boyce et al., 1991])? Are there other activities that are significantly affected by having a brother or sister who is mentally disabled? Exactly which family processes affect sibling relationships and attitudes?

Additionally, four other aspects of research in this field should also be investigated. First, as with normative child and sibling research, the descriptive, normative research on siblings needs to be complemented with studies of individual differences. Researchers have found indications of great variability among siblings of persons with mental retardation in terms of relationships, activities, and psychological well-being (Dyson & Fewell, 1989; McHale & Gamble, 1989; McHale et al., 1986). Knowing what variables affect these sibling outcomes is extremely important if preventive interventions are going to be designed for these families of children with disabilities.

Second, reviewers, beginning with Simeonsson and McHale (1981) have called for examination of the bi-directional nature of the sibling relationship between a child with disabilities and his or her siblings. Other than effects of interventions that involve a sibling teaching the child with a disability, no one has yet studied the effects on children with disabilities of living with normally developing children. The only exception is the in-depth interviewing of adult persons with mild retardation by Zetlin (1986) about their relationship with their siblings. Measuring the effects on the sibling with a disability is difficult, and new measures and techniques may need to be developed, but how the nondisabled sibling affects the sibling with a disability is an essential question for those who are implementing intervention programs for these families. Questions relating to how the interaction with normally developing siblings influence the psychological well-being, self-esteem, developmental status, and activities of the child with disabilities need to be investigated. The interactional effects of mediating family-process variables on the child with disabilities also need to be addressed.

Third, the studies thus far have primarily investigated sibling relationships in Caucasian families. Whether these findings can be generalized to families of other ethnic groups is not known. Cultural expectations for sibling interaction, roles, and responsibilities, as well as for coping with the presence of a disability in a family member, may differ markedly among different ethnic groups, and interventionists need to know how best to help families of each of these groups. Studies of siblings of different ethnic groups (e.g., African American, Hispanic, Asian American and Native American) need to be performed.

Finally, sibling dyads, usually of consecutive birth order and often of the same sex, have received most of the investigative attention thus far. Many families include more than two siblings. Some early researchers concluded that siblings fared better if there were more siblings in the family to share the caregiving responsibilities and meet parental expectations (Simeonsson & McHale, 1981). Gath's (1974) findings that sisters at least 3 years older than the child with Down syndrome were at the greatest risk for behavioral problems suggest that certain ascribed roles are not based on age relative to the child with disabilities, but may be ascribed by the birth order of all the siblings living in the household. Indeed, Stoneman and associates (1991) found in post hoc analysis that the childcare role of a younger sibling for an older child with disabilities was mediated by the presence of a sister who was older than either of the sibling pair. They, too, concluded that, in the future, research needs to move beyond the sibling pair.

REFERENCES

Abramovitch, R., Stanhope, L., Pepler, D., & Corter, C. (1987). The influence of Down's syndrome in sibling interaction. *Journal of Child Psychology and Psychiatry, 28,* 865–879.

Barnett, S. (1987). *Time use in families of retarded children and adults.* Proposal funded by the National Institute of Child Health and Human Development. (Available from author, Rutgers Graduate School of Education.)

Begun, A.L. (1989). Sibling relationships involving developmentally disabled people. *American Journal on Mental Retardation, 93*(5), 566–574.

Bergreen, S.M. (1971). A study of the mental health of the near relatives of twenty multihandicapped children. *Acta Paediatrica Scandinavia* (Suppl. 215), 1–24.

Boyce, G.C. (1990). *Time use and attitudes among siblings: A comparison in families of children with and without Down syndrome.* Unpublished doctoral dissertation, Utah State University, Logan.

Boyce, G.C., Barnett, S., & Miller, B.C. (1991, April). *Time use and attitudes among siblings: A comparison in families of children with and without Down syndrome.* Poster presented at the Biennial Meeting of the Society for Research in Child Development, Seattle, WA.

Bristol, M.M., & Gallagher, J.J. (1986). Research on fathers of young handicapped children: Evolution, review, and some future directions. In J.J. Gallagher & P.M. Vietze (Eds.), *Families of handicapped persons: Research, programs, and policy issues* (pp. 81–100). Baltimore: Paul H. Brookes Publishing Co.

Brody, G.H., & Stoneman, Z. (1983). Children with atypical siblings: Socialization outcomes and clinical participation. In B.B. Lahey & A.E. Kazdin (Eds.), *Advances in clinical child psychology* (Vol. 6, pp. 285–326). New York: Plenum.

Brody, G.H., Stoneman, Z., Davis, C.H., & Crapps, J.M. (1991). Observations of the role relations and behavior between older children with mental retardation and their younger siblings. *American Journal on Mental Retardation, 95*, 527–536.

Bronfenbrenner, U. (1979). *The ecology of human development: Experiments by nature and design*. Cambridge, MA: Harvard University Press.

Caldwell, B.M., & Guze, S.B. (1960). A study of the adjustment of parents and siblings of institutionalized and noninstitutionalized retarded children. *American Journal of Mental Deficiency, 64*, 845–861.

Carr, J. (1988). Six weeks to twenty-one years old: A longitudinal study of children with Down's syndrome and their families. *Journal of Child Psychology and Psychiatry, 29*(4), 407–431.

Carver, J.N., & Carver, N.E. (1972). *The family of the retarded child*. Syracuse, NY: Syracuse University Press.

Chinitz, S.P. (1981 November–December). A sibling group for brothers and sisters of handicapped children. *Children Today*, pp. 21-23.

Cleveland, D.W., & Miller, N. (1977). Attitudes and life commitments of older siblings of mentally retarded adults: An exploratory study. *Mental Retardation, 15*, 38–41.

Correa, V.L., Silberman, R.K., & Trusty, S. (1986). Siblings of disabled children: A literature review. *Education of the Visually Handicapped, 18*(1), 5–13.

Crnic, K.A., Friedrich, W.N., & Greenberg, M.T. (1983). Adaptation of families with mentally retarded children: A model of stress, coping, and family ecology. *American Journal of Mental Deficiency, 88*(2), 125–138.

Crnic, K.A., & Leconte, J.M. (1986). Understanding siblings needs and influences. In R.R. Fewell & P.F. Vadasy (Eds.), *Families of handicapped children: Needs and support across the life span* (pp. 75–98). Austin, TX: PRO-ED

Dittman, L.L. (1962). The family of the child in an institution. *American Journal of Mental Deficiency, 66*, 759–765.

Dupont, A. (1980). A study concerning the time-related and other burdens when severely handicapped children are reared at home. *Acta Psychiatrica Scandinavica, 62*(Suppl. 285), 249–257.

Dyson, L., Edgar, E., & Crnic, K. (1989). Psychological predictors of adjustment of siblings of developmentally disabled children. *American Journal of Mental Retardation, 94*(3), 292–302.

Dyson, L., & Fewell, R.R. (1989). The self-concept of siblings of handicapped children: A comparison. *Journal of Early Intervention, 13*(3), 230–238.

Farber, B. (1959). Effects of a severely mentally retarded child on family integration. *Monographs of the Society for Research in Child Development, 24*(2).

Farber, B. (1960). Family organization and crisis: Maintenance of integration in families with a severely retarded child. *Monographs of the Society for Research in Child Development, 25*(1).

Farber, B. (1963). Interaction with retarded siblings and life goals of children. *Journal of Marriage and Family, 25*, 96–98.

Farber, B., & Jenne, W.C. (1963). Family organization and parent–child communication: Parents and siblings of a retarded child. *Monographs of the Society for Research in Child Development, 28*(7).
Ferrari, M. (1984). Chronic illness: Psychosocial effects of siblings and chronically ill boys. *Journal of Child Psychology and Psychiatry, 25*(3), 459–476.
Foster, M.A., & Berger, M. (1985). Research with families with handicapped children: A multilevel systemic perspective. In L. L'Abate (Ed.), *The handbook of family psychology and therapy* (Vol. 2, pp. 741–780). Homewood, IL: The Dorsey Press.
Fowle, C.M. (1968). The effect of the severely mentally retarded child on his family. *American Journal of Mental Deficiency, 75*(3), 468–473.
Gallagher, P.A., & Powell, T.H. (1989). Brothers and sisters: Meeting special needs. *Topics in Early Childhood Special Education, 8*(4), 24–37.
Gamble, W.C., & McHale, S.M. (1989). Coping with stress in sibling relationships: A comparison of children with disabled and nondisabled siblings. *Journal of Applied Developmental Psychology, 10*, 353–373.
Gath, A. (1972). The mental health of siblings of congenitally abnormal children. *Journal of Child Psychology and Psychiatry, 13*, 211–218.
Gath, A. (1973). The school-age siblings of mongol children. *British Journal of Psychiatry, 123*, 161–167.
Gath, A. (1974). Sibling reactions to mental handicap: A comparison of the brothers and sisters of mongol children. *Journal of Child Psychology and Psychiatry, 15*, 187–198.
Gath, A., & Gumley, D. (1987). Retarded children and their siblings. *Journal of Child Psychology and Psychiatry, 28*(5), 715–730.
Gayton, W.F., Friedman, S.B., Tavormina, J.F., & Tucker, F. (1977). Children with cystic fibrosis: 1. Psychological test findings of patients, siblings & parents. *Pediatrics, 59*(6), 888–894.
Graliker, B.V., Fishler, K., & Koch, R.K. (1962). Teenage reactions to a mentally retarded sibling. *American Journal of Mental Deficiency, 66*, 838–843.
Grossman, F.K. (1972). *Brothers and sisters of retarded children: An exploratory study.* Syracuse, NY: Syracuse University Press.
Hannah, M.E., & Midlarsky, E. (1985). Siblings of the handicapped: A literature review for school psychologists. *School Psychology Review, 14*(4), 510–520.
Harter, S. (1982). The perceived competence scale for children. *Child Development, 53*, 87–97.
Harter, S., & Pike, R. (1983). *The pictorial scale of perceived competence and social acceptance for children.* Denver: University of Denver.
Harvey, D.H.P., & Greenway, A.P. (1984). The self-concept of physically handicapped children and their nonhandicapped siblings: An empirical investigation. *Journal of Child Psychology and Psychiatry, 25*(2), 273–284.
Holt, K.S. (1958). The home care of severely retarded children. *Pediatrics, 22*, 744–755.
Juster, F.T., & Stafford, F.P. (1985). *Time, goods, and well-being.* University of Michigan: Survey Research Center.
Kaplan, F. (1969). Siblings of the retarded. In S.B. Sarason & J. Doris (Eds.), *Psychological problems in mental deficiency.* New York: Harper & Row.
Kaplan, F., & Colombatto, J. (1966). Head start project for siblings of retarded children. *Mental Retardation, 4*, 30–32.
Kaplan, F., & Fox, E. (1968). Siblings of the retarded: An adolescent group experience. *Community Mental Health Journal, 4*, 499–508.

Kirk, S.A., & Bateman, B.D. (1964). *10 years of research at the Institute for Research on Exceptional Children*. Urbana: University of Illinois.

Kirkman, M. (1983). Adult siblings of the handicapped: Early family relationships. *Australian Research Conference, 5*, 171–200.

Lauterbach, C.G. (1974). *Sociobehavior adaptation of siblings of the mentally handicapped child*. Scranton, PA: Print-Shop.

Lloyd-Bostock, S. (1976). Parents' experiences of official help and guidance in caring for a mentally handicapped child. *Child: Care, Health and Development, 2*, 325–338.

Lobato, D. (1983). Siblings of handicapped children: A review. *Journal of Autism and Developmental Disorders, 13*(4), 347–364.

Lobato, D. (1985). Brief report: Preschool Siblings of Handicapped Children—Impact of Peer Support and Training. *Journal of Autism and Developmental Disorders, 15*(3), 345–350.

Lobato, D., Barbour, L., Hall, L.J., & Miller, C.T. (1987). Psychosocial characteristics of preschool siblings of handicapped and nonhandicapped children. *Journal of Abnormal Child Psychology, 15*(3), 329–338.

Lonsdale, G. (1978). Family life with a handicapped child: The parents speak. *Child: Care, Health and Development, 4*, 99–120.

McConachie, H., & Domb, H. (1983). An interview study of 20 older brothers and sisters of mentally handicapped and non-handicapped children. *Mental Handicap, 11*, 64–66.

McHale, S.M., & Gamble, W.C. (1987). Sibling relationships and adjustment of children with disabled brothers and sisters. In F.F. Schacter & R.K. Stone (Eds.), *Practical concerns about siblings: Bridging the research–practice gap* (pp. 131–158). New York: Haworth.

McHale, S.M., & Gamble, W.C. (1989). Sibling relationships of children with disabled and nondisabled brothers and sisters. *Developmental Psychology, 25*(3), 421–429.

McHale, S.M., Simeonsson, R.J., & Sloan, J.L. (1984). Children with handicapped brothers and sisters. In E. Scholpler & G.B. Mesibov (Eds.), *The effects of autism on the family* (pp. 327–342). New York: Plenum Press.

McHale, S.M., Sloan, J., & Simeonsson, R.J. (1986). Sibling relationships of children with autistic, mentally retarded, and nonhandicapped brothers and sisters. *Journal of Autism and Developmental Disorders, 16*(4), 399–413.

Miller, S.G. (1974). An exploratory study of sibling relationships in families with retarded children (Doctoral dissertation, Columbia University, 1974). *Dissertation Abstracts International, 35*, 2994B–2995B.

O'Connor, W.A., & Stachowiak, J. (1971). Patterns of interaction in families with low adjusted, high adjusted, and mentally retarded members. *Family Process, 10*(2), 229–241.

Piers, E.V., & Harris, D.B. (1969). *The Piers-Harris Children's Self-Concept Scale (The Way I Feel About Myself)*. Nashville: Counselor Recording & Tests.

Poznanski, E. (1969). Psychiatric difficulties in siblings of handicapped children. *Clinical Pediatrics, 8*(4), 232–234.

Rutter, M., Tizard, J., & Whitmore, K. (1970). *Education, health, and behavior*. London: Longman.

San Martino, M., & Newman, M.B. (1974). Siblings of retarded children: A population at risk. *Child Psychiatry and Human Development, 4*(3), 168–177.

Schipper, M.T. (1959). The child with mongolism in the home. *Pediatrics, 24*, 132–144.

Schreiber, M., & Feeley, M. (1965). Siblings of the retarded: A guided group experience. *Children, 12*(6), 221–225.

Schwirian, P.M. (1976). Effects of the presence of a hearing-impaired preschool child in the family on behavior patterns of older "normal" siblings. *American Annual of the Deaf, 121,* 373–380.

Seltzer, G.B., Begun, A., Seltzer, M.M., & Krauss, M.W. (1991). The impacts of siblings on adults with mental retardation and their aging mothers. *Family Relations, 40,* 310–317.

Simeonsson, R.J., & Bailey, D.B., Jr. (1986). Siblings of handicapped children. In J.J. Gallagher & P.M. Vietze (Eds.), *Families of handicapped persons: Research, programs, and policy issues* (pp. 67–80). Baltimore: Paul H. Brookes Publishing Co.

Simeonsson, R.J., & McHale, S.M. (1981). [Review of *Research on handicapped children: Sibling relationships*]. *Child: Care, Health and Development, 7,* 153–171.

Stoneman, Z., Brody, G.H., Davis, C.H., & Crapps, J.M. (1987). Mentally retarded children and their older same-sex siblings: Naturalistic in-home observations. *American Journal on Mental Retardation, 92*(3), 290–298.

Stoneman, Z., Brody, G.H., Davis, C.H., & Crapps, J.M. (1988). Child care responsibilities, peer relations, and sibling conflict: Older siblings of mentally retarded children. *American Journal on Mental Retardation, 93*(2), 174–183.

Stoneman, Z., Brody, G.H., Davis, C.H., & Crapps, J.M. (1989). Role relations between children who are mentally retarded and their older siblings: Observations in three in-home contexts. *Research in Developmental Disabilities, 10,* 61–76.

Stoneman, Z., Brody, G.H., Davis, C.H., Crapps, J.M., & Malone, D.M. (1991). Ascribed role relations between children with mental retardation and their younger siblings. *American Journal on Mental Retardation, 95,* 537–550.

Summers, M., Summers, C.R., Ascione, F., & Braeger, T. (1989, April). *Observations of siblings' social interactions: Comparing families with and without a handicapped child.* Paper presented at the biennial meeting of the Society for Research in Child Development, Kansas City, MO.

Suomi, S.J. (1982). Sibling relationships in nonhuman primates. In M.E. Lamb & B. Sutton-Smith (Eds.), *Sibling relationships: Their nature and significance across the lifespan* (pp. 329–356). Hillsdale, NJ: Lawrence Erlbaum Associates.

Vadasy, P.F., Fewell, R.R., Meyer, D.J., & Schell, G. (1984). Siblings of handicapped children: A developmental perspective on family interactions. *Family Relations, 33,* 155–167.

Wasserman, R. (1983). Identifying the counseling needs of the siblings of mentally retarded children. *The Personnel and Guidance Journal, 61*(10), 622–627.

Wilson, J., Blacher, J., & Baker, B.L. (1989). Siblings of children with severe handicaps. *Mental Retardation, 27*(3), 167–173.

Zetlin, A.G. (1986). Mentally retarded adults and their siblings. *American Journal of Mental Deficiency, 91*(3), 217–225.

CHAPTER 8

Siblings of Children with Physical Disabilities and Chronic Illnesses
Studies of Risk and Social Ecology

George W. Howe

If children have siblings with chronic, physically disabling conditions caused by illness or trauma, how are they affected? This question, a deceptively simple one, has generated a small but growing body of research. Most work in this area has reduced the question to one of risk: are siblings of children with a chronic illness or physical disability at increased risk for psychopathology, or for increased levels of subclinical adjustment problems? Individual studies have often taken the question a step further by asking: are all such siblings at increased risk, or is this true only for certain subgroups? That is, are there different levels of risk for boys and girls, or for children older than or younger than the affected sibling, or for siblings of children with severe or mild disabilities, or for children in isolated families as opposed to those in families with strong ties to friends or extended kin?

Questions about subgroup differences naturally lead the investigator on to questions of risk and protective factors, and from there on to questions of causal process. For example, Breslau (1982), in her study of children with congenital disabilities, found two groups of siblings to be at increased risk for aggressive behavior and symptoms of depression and anxiety: male siblings younger than, and female siblings older than, the child with disabilities. She hypothesized that these two groups may be at increased risk for different reasons. Siblings born before the child with disabilities may be more likely to be pressed into service as caregivers, particularly if the older child is female, and this increased burden may overwhelm the sibling and lead to increased distress. And siblings born after the impaired child may be subject to a lack of attention from parents responsible for the care of the child with disabilities. Breslau suggested that such inattention would be more disruptive to development in infancy, and found evidence that younger males close in age to the child with disabilities show more aggressiveness than do males born more than 2 years after the child. Breslau was unable to account for the absence of increased aggression in younger female children.

From this example it should be clear that risk-factor research can be fertile ground for the identification of promising causal hypotheses about risk and protection. Most risk-factor research is limited, however, when it comes to studying such causal processes in detail. Breslau's hypotheses about older females and younger males are clearly inferential and not based on measurement of the family processes she describes. To study these processes directly would require a different research paradigm that included more elaborate measurement of interactions within the family. Such studies would be organized around the question: what family, peer, teacher, or individual psychological reactions are shaped by the presence of a child with a physical disability or chronic illness and how do these reactions lead to increases in sibling disturbance or psychopathology? Very few researchers have as yet attempted such a study. Examples include the work of Hilliard and colleagues on goal-setting and levels of aspiration in the parents of children with siblings who have asthma or diabetes (Hilliard, Fritz, & Lewiston, 1982, 1985) and a study of lowered performance expectations of teachers for children with learning-disabled siblings in the same school (Richey & Ysseldyke, 1983).

Both risk-factor research and causal-process studies are essential for furthering understanding of how sibling development is affected by the presence of a sister or brother with physical disabilities or a chronic illness. Risk-factor research asks *population-based* questions, and the answers to these questions can be seen as defining the *boundary conditions* for causal-process studies. At the most general level, the presence of physical disability is assumed to be a boundary condition that places limits on the adjustment of siblings. To the extent that this hypothesis is supported (i.e., that populations include siblings of children with physical disabilities or chronic illnesses who show increased risk), researchers can have greater confidence that causal-process studies will uncover something of practical relevance. Careful attention to subgroups within the population of families that include children with physical disabilities or chronic illnesses can further sharpen the field's knowledge of risk, and will have concomitant benefits in defining the parameters of causal-process research, as Breslau's studies have demonstrated. Causal-process research asks questions about *psychological* and *small group influ-*

ence. It answers questions that are of direct relevance to specific treatment or preventive interventions, questions that are difficult if not impossible to answer with risk-factor designs.

The remainder of this chapter is concerned with these two different research paradigms and their integration in the study of siblings with physical disabilities or chronic illnesses. It has three goals. First, literature on risk-factor research will be reviewed, with particular attention given to the boundary conditions that research to date seems to place on the field. Second, causal-process studies will be discussed. Finally, the author will advance some observations about the ways in which these two paradigms might be more directly linked. This chapter is limited to research on samples of children having siblings with chronic illness or physically based disabilities.

RISK-FACTOR RESEARCH

As in most areas of the field, risk-factor research involving siblings of children with physical disabilities or chronic illnesses has been characterized by a number of stages of increased attention to rigor and method. Early case-study reports of sibling maladjustment (Binger, 1973) were followed by case-series studies using impressionistic assessment (Turk, 1964), and then by studies using norm-referenced measures or matched comparison groups and more sophisticated measures of child adjustment. In this review the author will focus only on this last group of studies, since levels of risk can only be accurately assessed through comparison to baseline risks of similar children who do not have siblings with physical disabilities or chronic illnesses. Earlier comprehensive reviews that include clinical case reports and case series may be found in Lobato, Faust, and Spirito (1988); McKeever (1983); and Shapiro (1983). This review will include studies of children having siblings with disabilities caused by chronic illnesses such as juvenile arthritis, by congenital conditions such as cerebral palsy, or by physical trauma. It will also include issues surrounding chronic conditions such as epilepsy, progressive renal disease, and cystic fibrosis that can lead to periodic restriction of activities. Several groups were excluded: siblings of children with mental retardation (although some of the conditions reviewed here include subgroups that fit the criterion for retardation), siblings of the learning disabled, and siblings of children with autism or pervasive developmental delay.

A search of the research literature in psychology, social science, and pediatrics journals, including computer-based searches of the Psychological Abstracts and iterated searches based on the reference lists of relevant studies, identified 21 studies of adjustment of siblings of children with physical disabilities or chronic illness that included either control groups of healthy children or the use of measures for which data from normative reference groups were available. Sixteen of these studies have been published within the last decade.

Design Issues

Table 1 compares these studies based on several aspects of sampling design. Researchers have usually studied homogeneous groups characterized by particular disabling conditions, although in four instances groups were constituted of children with a variety of mixed conditions (Breslau, 1982; Breslau, Wietzman, & Messenger, 1981; Cadman, Boyle, & Offord, 1988; Harvey & Greenway, 1984; Lobato, Barbour, Hall, & Miller, 1987), and in other cases groups were selected from specialty clinics serving children with a variety of conditions (Daniels, Miller, Billings, & Moos, 1986; Drotar et al., 1981; Lavigne & Ryan, 1979). As a group, these studies include index children with a wide range of conditions. None of the conditions have been studied frequently; diabetes has been the subject of five studies, and cystic fibrosis the subject of four studies, with the remainder of the conditions included in no more than two studies. Lobato et al. (1988) have noted that chronic conditions vary in a number of dimensions, including rate of onset, presence of genetic etiology, stable or fluctuating course, and prognosis of fatality, and have suggested that such differences in the characteristics of diseases or disabilities may have profound effects on sibling reactions and adjustment. Given the limited number of studies on each condition, little can be said, as yet, concerning this general hypothesis.

Sampling Methods As Table 1 summarizes, the majority of studies (14 of 21) have used clinic-based sampling to identify index cases. Two studies (Harvey & Greenway, 1984; Neuhaus, 1958) identified children with physical disabilities or chronic illnesses through the schools, and two other studies (Cadman et al., 1988; Tew & Laurence, 1973) have conducted epidemiological surveys of all cases within a defined geographic region. Clinic-based sampling has clearly been the most common method for pragmatic reasons, given the relatively small number of children with each particular condition. However, clinic samples are not necessarily representative of the populations in question. Specialty clinics are often in university hospital centers that tend to serve families with fewer financial resources. And because specialty clinics serve large regions, they may be less likely to attract patients from more distant rural areas. Utilization of these clinics, particularly by families of children with milder forms of a condition, can be confounded with family motivation or proactive attitudes toward healthcare. Families with such attitudes may therefore be over-represented, particularly for less severe cases where parental discretion plays a greater part in the decision to use services. These issues are salient to the study of sibling risk to the degree that variables such as family financial resources or parent motivation may be related to sibling adjustment in the general population.

Studies also varied in the method of selecting siblings for participation. A number of studies (7 of 21) have identified a sample of children with physical disabilities or chronic illness and then assessed adjustment in all siblings

Table 1. Sample characteristics of risk factor studies

Study	Date	PD/CI types	Source of index cases	Sibling selection rules	Sibling ages	Number of siblings
1. Breslau, Wietzman, and Messenger and Breslau and Prabucki	1981, 1987	Cystic fibrosis, cerebral palsy, myelodysplasia, mixed congenital	Hospital clinics	Single sibling, random	6–18	Cystic fibrosis: 46, Cerebral palsy: 75, Myelodysplasia: 47, Mixed congenital: 53
2. Cadman, Boyle, and Offord	1988	Mixed	Random sample	All siblings in family	4–16	260
3. Cowen, Mok, Corey, MacMillan, Simmons, and Levinson	1986	Cystic fibrosis	Hospital clinics	All siblings in family	2–19	238
4. Daniels, Miller, Billings, and Moos and Daniels, Moos, Billings, and Miller	1986, 1987	Rheumatic diseases	Hospital clinics	Single sibling, nearest in age, same sex if possible	2–19	72
5. Drotar, Doershuk, Stern, Boat, Boyer, and Mattews	1981	Cystic fibrosis, mixed pulmonary (mostly asthma)	Hospital clinics	Siblings of children with cystic fibrosis only, selection not specified	3–13	17

(continued)

Table 1. (continued)

Study	Date	PD/CI types	Source of index cases	Sibling selection rules	Sibling ages	Number of siblings
6. Ferrari	1984	Diabetes	Not specified	Single sibling, cell sampling	9–12	16
7. Ferrari	1987	Diabetes	Not specified	Single sibling, cell sampling	7–12	30
8. Fielding, Moore, Dewey, Ashley, McKendrick, and Pinkerton	1985	Progressive renal disease	Hospital clinics	All siblings in family		15
9. Harvey and Greenway	1984	Mixed congenital with disabilities (spina bifida, cerebral palsy: limb or bowel deficiency)	Schools	Single sibling, nearest in age	7–15	33
10. Hoare	1984	Epilepsy (newly diagnosed & chronic)	Hospital clinics and private pediatricians	Not specified		Newly diagnosed epilepsy: 23, Chronic epilepsy: 23
11. Kazak and Clark	1986	Myelomeningocele	Hospital clinics	All siblings in family	33	
12. Klein and Simmons	1979	Kidney disease	Hospital clinics	Single sibling, closest in age	—	44
13. Lavigne and Ryan	1979	Plastic surgery (mostly cleft lip or palate), congenital heart defects, leukemia and other cancers	Hospital clinics	Up to 2 siblings, younger and older than PD/CI child	3–13	Plastic surgery: 37, Chronic heart defects: 57, Cancer: 62
14. Lavigne, Traisman, Marr, and Chasnoff	1982	Diabetes	Private pediatrician	Single sibling, closest in age	6–16	41

	Authors	Year	Condition	Source	Siblings	Age	N
15.	Lobato, Barbour, Hall, and Miller	1987	Mixed congenital with disabilities (spina bifida, cerebral palsy, Down syndrome, hearing or vision impaired)	Not specified	Not specified	3–7	24
16.	Neuhaus	1958	Asthma, cardiac	Schools	All siblings in family	8–14	Asthma: 25, Cardiac: 24
17.	Tew and Laurence	1973	Spina bifida	Regional sampling	All siblings in family	2–15	44
18.	Treiber, Mabe, and Wilson	1987	Sickle cell anemia	Hospital clinics	Single sibling, method unspecified	8–17	13
19.	Tritt and Esses	1988	Diabetes, rheumatoid arthritis, gastrointestinal	Hospital clinics	Single sibling, method unspecified	—	Diabetes: 11, Rheumatoid arthritis: 10, Gastro-intestinal: 6
20.	Vance, Fazan, Satterwhite, and Pless	1980	Nephrotic syndrome	Hospital clinics	All siblings in family	—	79
21.	Wood, Boyle, Watkins, Nogueira, Zimand, and Carroll	1988	Crohn's disease, Ulcerative colitis	Hospital clinics	Single sibling, closest in age	—	Crohn's disease: 41, Ulcerative colitis: 24

PD/CI = physical disability/chronic illness.

in the family. As Breslau (1983a) has pointed out, this method can produce confounds if sibling adjustment measures are correlated with family size, as is often the case. In addition, if sibling adjustment is correlated within the same family, risk rates may be inflated by the inclusion of multiple children from the same family. While statistical techniques can be used to adjust for the lack of independence of sibling scores, only one of the studies reviewed here used such techniques (Cadman et al., 1988).

In about half of the studies (10 of 21), a single sibling was chosen, usually the sibling closest in age and of the same gender, when possible. This method reduces the age difference between the sibling and the child with a physical disability or chronic illness to allow for more meaningful comparisons between the two on adjustment measures. Other methods have included random sampling of a single sibling (Breslau et al., 1981), sampling of all siblings from a regional random sample of families that included both children with physical disabilities or chronic illnesses and healthy children (Cadman et al., 1988), and cell sampling (Ferrari, 1984, 1987). Ferrari has used cell sampling to study the effects of relative birth order and gender on sibling risk. Sibling pairs were sampled from the pool of families having a child with physical disabilities or a chronic illness and at least one healthy sibling. Families were selected to fill four cells in the design: families of affected children with younger female siblings, with younger male siblings, with older female siblings, and with older male siblings. This method provides for more accurate tests of hypotheses about risk in sibling subgroups, particularly if families can be matched across cells based on important demographic and illness characteristics.

Control Procedures and Measurement Table 2 compares studies on the bases of control procedures and measurement method. Most of these studies (17 of 21) included control groups of children from families with no chronic illness; only 4 relied entirely on normative data as a baseline against which to assess risk. Comparison to norms is a less rigorous approach, and the results of this method are more suspect. Even if norms are available on a national representative sample (and they rarely are), families with physical disabilities or chronic illnesses may not be representative, due to sampling biases introduced by clinic sampling, as discussed earlier, or because many conditions are not distributed evenly throughout the population. For example, cystic fibrosis is more prevalent in children of Jewish background, sickle cell anemia is more prevalent in African-American children, and juvenile rheumatoid arthritis is found more frequently in girls. Since measures of adjustment often vary with gender or ethnicity (Sandberg, Meyer-Bahlburg, & Yager, 1991), overall norms do not provide a valid baseline for comparison in many instances.

Control groups were recruited from a number of sources, including local physicians, schools, scout leaders, and by conducting representative regional sampling. Except for the four studies using representative sampling techniques (Breslau et al., 1981; Cadman et al., 1988; Daniels et al., 1986; Klein & Simmons, 1979), investigators used samples of convenience and relied on matching procedures to equate groups according to important demographic characteristics, or used covariance procedures to remove the effects of demographic and other characteristics if groups were found to differ. Two of these studies used particularly problematic control selection procedures. Neuhaus (1958) restricted sampling such that index control children were free of psychological problems, and Kazak and Clark (1986) restricted their control sample to children with no chronic psychological problems. These procedures bias the study toward finding increased risk in siblings of children with physical disabilities or chronic illness by eliminating extreme cases of adjustment problems in the control but not the group that included children with physical disabilities or chronic illnesses. The findings in the Kazak and Clark study are not compromised to as great an extent by this bias, since results were in the opposite direction from the bias (siblings of children with physical disabilities or chronic illnesses did not differ from controls on measures of self-esteem); however, they did contradict the findings of Neuhaus, which held that siblings of children with physical disabilities or chronic illnesses were at increased risk for neurotic symptoms and feelings of insecurity.

Four studies used more rigorous sampling procedures for identifying control groups. Breslau et al. (1981) used a regional sampling of households, randomly selected one child as an index child, and, in households with more than two children, randomly selected a second child as a sibling of the index child. Daniels et al. (1986; Daniels, Moos, Billings, & Miller, 1987) drew comparison families from a regional representative sample, and parents rated their children's behavior as a whole, so siblings were not matched for gender or age. Klein and Simmons (1979) relied on a two-stage random sample of urban school children, with no attempt to restrict the sample by sibling status. Cadman et al. (1988), in the most rigorous epidemiologic study to date in this area, used a stratified, clustered, random sampling from the 1981 census file of all households in the Province of Ontario, Canada. Ninety-one percent of all eligible households participated, and data were collected on the physical and psychological functioning of all children between the ages of 4 and 16 in these households. Since 17.7% of all children in this sample had some form of disability or chronic illness, the sample could yield a set of siblings in households with such children, and a second set of siblings in households without childhood disability or chronic illness.

Measurement techniques have shown some consistency in this series of studies. Almost half (9 of 21) of the studies used children as respondents in order to assess self-concept or self-esteem, usually with the Piers-Harris Children's Self-Concept Scale (Piers & Harris, 1969). Twelve studies used parents to assess symptom levels with symptom checklists, and seven studies used

Table 2. Control and measurement procedures of risk factor studies

Study	Control method	Source of control sample	Selection methods	Measurement sources	Measurement methods
1. Breslau, Weitzman, and Messenger (1981)	Control group, normative data	Regional sample	Three-stage random sample	Parent Child	Symptom checklist Diagnostic interview
2. Cadman, Boyle, and Offord (1988)	Control group	Regional sample	Stratified random sample	Parent, child, teacher	Symptom checklist modified for diagnosis
3. Cowen, Mok, Corey, MacMillan, Simmons, and Levinson (1986)	Normative data			Parent Child	Symptom checklist Self-concept measure
4. Daniels, Miller, Billings, and Moos (1986)	Control group	Regional sample	Random sampling of index child	Parent Child	Symptom checklist Symptom checklist
5. Drotar, Doershuk, Stern, Boat, Bajer, and Mattews (1981)	Control group	Local pediatricians	Not specified	Parent Teacher	Symptom checklist Symptom checklist
6. Ferrari (1984)	Control group	Not specified	Not specified	Parent Child Teacher	Symptom checklist Self-concept measure Symptom checklist, self-concept rating
7. Ferrari (1987)	Control group	Not specified	Matched sibling pairs	Child	Self-concept measure
8. Fielding, Moore, Dewey, Ashley, McKendrick, and Pinkerten (1985)	Normative data			Teacher	Symptom checklist
9. Harvey and Greenway (1984)	Control group	Leaders of guides and scouts movement	Matched sibling pairs	Child	Self-concept measure
10. Hoare (1984)	Control group	Teachers selected from same classroom	Matched sibling pairs	Teacher	Symptom checklist

11. Kazak and Clark (1986)	Control group	Local pediatricians, pediatric clinics, ads	Not specified	Child	Self-concept measure
12. Klein and Simmons (1979)	Control group (from earlier study)	Schools	Two-stage random survey (same measures)	Child	Self-concept measure
13. Lavigne and Ryan (1979)	Control group	Schools	Identification unspecified; parents rated youngest & eldest	Parent	Symptom checklist
14. Lavigne, Traisman, Marr, and Chasnoff (1982)	Control group	Pediatric clinic	Matched on index child	Parent	Symptom checklist
15. Lobato, Barbour, Hall, and Miller (1987)	Control group	Daycare centers, preschools, Head Start classes, pediatricians	Matched sibling pairs	Parent Child	Symptom checklist Self-concept measure
16. Neuhaus (1958)	Control group	Not specified	Matched sibling pairs	Child	Personality inventory
17. Tew and Laurence (1973)	Control group	Not specified	Families matched, all siblings included	Teacher	Symptom checklist
18. Treiber, Mabe, and Wilson (1987)	Normative data			Child	Depression scale
19. Tritt and Esses (1988)	Control group	Local physicians	Not specified	Parent Child	Symptom checklist Self-concept measures
20. Vance, Fazan, Satterwhite, and Pless (1980)	Control group	Families attending HMO	Matched sibling pairs	Parent Teacher Child	Symptom checklist Symptom checklist Self-concept measure
21. Wood, Boyle, Watkins, Nogueira, Zimand, and Carroll (1988)	Normative data			Parent	Symptom checklist

teacher reports with similar measures. Breslau and Prabucki's (1987) study was unique in using a diagnostic interview with the child to assess symptomatology, although Cadman et al. (1988), Daniels et al. (1986), Neuhaus (1958), and Treiber, Mabe, and Wilson (1987) used questionnaires completed by children to assess symptomatology. Nine of the 21 studies used multiple sources of information about child functioning (parent, child, teacher).

Summary Almost all research to date is based on case-control designs using clinic records to identify index cases of children with physical disabilities or chronic illnesses and samples of convenience to identify matched controls. Such studies are much easier to conduct, given the relative rarity of any particular form of disability or chronic illness in the general population, but are likely to introduce sampling biases that can seriously reduce confidence in findings. Since the question of risk is an epidemiologic or population-based question, more rigorous sampling methods would do much to advance work in this area. These have been used successfully to identify and sample representative control groups in four of the studies reviewed here; the works by Breslau and by Cadman et al. stand out as exemplars of this technique. Only two studies used such methods for the sampling of siblings of children with physical disabilities or chronic illnesses, however. Finally, measurement techniques have greatly improved over those used in early studies on this subject, although investigators have continued to rely too heavily on single sources for data on adjustment.

Findings on General Levels of Risk

Table 3 summarizes the findings on risk for siblings across a variety of indicators of adjustment. Given findings that children with conditions affecting the central nervous system are more consistently at risk for adjustment problems than children with conditions that do not affect the brain (Howe, Feinstein, Reiss, Molock, & Berger, 1991), study results have been summarized separately for siblings of children with these two different sets of conditions. In instances where index children have had both types of conditions and results were not reported separately for each condition, studies have been grouped with those involving only neurologic conditions.

Self-Concept Of the nine studies measuring child self-concept, only three found significant decrements: these included studies of conditions involving diabetes (Ferrari, 1987), a mixture of congenital disabling conditions (Harvey & Greenway, 1984), and nephrotic syndrome (Vance, Fazan, Satterwhite, & Pless, 1980). Ferrari and Harvey both found that decrements in total self-concept scores were due to the intellectual and school status subscale of the measure used in the study. Vance noted that, while the siblings in his study showed significantly lower scores as a group, none scored more than one standard deviation below the mean when compared to normative data, sug-

Table 3. Levels of risk for siblings of children with PD/CI in various areas of functioning[a]

	Non-neurologic conditions			Neurologic conditions or mixed		
	Lower risk	No difference	Higher risk	Lower risk	No difference	Higher risk
Self-concept		3, 6, 12, 19	7, 20		11, 15	9
Internalizing conditions		4, 5, 6, 13[a], 14, 18	1[a], 2, 13[a], 16, 19		15	1[a]
Externalizing conditions	20	4, 5, 6, 13[a], 14, 19	1[a]			1[a], 2, 15
General symptom levels	5	4, 6, 8, 13[a], 20	1[a], 3, 13[a], 21		15	1[a], 10, 17
Deficits in social competence	6	13[a], 14			2	
Deficits in school performance		14	20		2	

PD/CI = physical disability or chronic illness; numbers refer to studies listed in Table 1.

[a] Study separately reported effects for more than one condition, allowing for comparisons based on each.

gesting that the decrements were mild. There appear to be no differences in risk levels between neurological and non-neurological conditions.

Internalizing Symptoms Symptom patterns that might be labelled internalizing (including depression, anxiety, withdrawal, and somatic complaints) demonstrated significantly increased risk levels in 4 of 11 studies that measured them. Breslau and Prabucki (1987) found an increased risk of depression symptoms (but not of clinical levels of diagnosed major depression) and social isolation in their study of siblings of children with congenital disabilities and chronic illness. Findings on anxiety were mixed: parents reported higher levels of regressive anxiety, but interviews with children revealed no increased risk of anxiety symptoms or diagnosable anxiety disorders. This longitudinal follow-up study indicated that siblings maintained symptom levels across a 5-year period, and became more symptomatic relative to control siblings. Parent-reported levels of social isolation increased across the period for siblings of children with physical disabilities or chronic illnesses, but stayed the same for control siblings. These findings are consistent with studies by Lavigne and Ryan (1979), who found an increased risk of social withdrawal in siblings of children attending a plastic surgery clinic for cleft palate, cleft lip, and other disfigurements. Lavigne and Ryan did not find increased risk for siblings of children with congenital heart defects or with leukemia, however. They are also consistent with Tritt and Esses' (1988) finding of higher personality-problem scores (but not of inadequacy-immaturity) in preschool siblings of children with diabetes, arthritis, and gastrointestinal problems, and with Neuhaus's (1958) finding of higher neurotic scores and deeper feelings of insecurity for siblings of children with asthma or a heart condition that restricted activity. The findings of Neuhaus must be interpreted with caution, however, given the potential sampling bias discussed earlier.

It is worth noting that the epidemiologic study by Cadman et al. (1988) found that emotional disorders including depression and over-anxious or obsessive-compulsive diagnoses were more than twice as likely for siblings of children with chronic health problems as for those of healthy children (7.8% of the sample, as compared to 3.9%). However, this was only a tendency in the data, since the 95% confidence interval for the odds ratio ranged from 0.9 to 3.2. These findings were not influenced by covariates such as age, sex, siblingship, size, or family income. They do reflect differences in the occurrence of diagnosable conditions, rather than in mean symptom levels, and so may lead to underestimating differences in subclinical manifestations of internalizing problems.

Of the 11 studies assessing internalizing symptoms, 6 found no increased risk; these included siblings of children with non-neurological conditions, including rheumatic diseases (Daniels et al., 1986), diabetes (Ferrari, 1984; Lavigne, Traisman, Marr, & Chasnoff, 1982), and sickle cell anemia (Treiber et al., 1987). It also included Lobato et al.'s (1987) study of mixed congenital conditions involving spina bifida and cerebral palsy, as well as vision and hearing impairment and Down syndrome.

Externalizing Symptoms Evidence for externalizing patterns involving aggressiveness, conflict with family, and conflict with peers appears to show differential risk for neurological conditions (although the number of studies is limited). Of the eight studies of non-neurological conditions, only one shows increases in the risk of externalizing symptoms (Breslau's sample of siblings of children with cystic fibrosis), while Vance's study of siblings of children with nephrotic syndrome provides evidence of reduced conflict with siblings in contrast to control children. Two studies using mixed samples of children, the majority with neurologically based conditions, show increased risk of externalizing in siblings. Both Breslau and Prabucki (1987) and Lobato et al. (1987) found that parents of siblings reported increased rates of aggressive behavior compared to controls, and Breslau found that older siblings themselves (age 11–17) in her sample reported engaging in more oppositional behaviors, although Breslau found no increased risk of a clinical level of an oppositional behavior syndrome. The findings of Cadman et al. (1988) are more complex. This epidemiologic study aggregated data from siblings of children with a wide range of chronic conditions, many of them neurologically based. As a whole, this group of siblings had lower rates of diagnosed conduct disorder and attention deficit disorder than comparison siblings, but these differences were not significant, even for this large sample of siblings.

However, siblings of children with physical disabilities or chronic illnesses were at significantly higher risk for problems in getting along with peers, a component of externalizing disorders. The odds ratio for this last difference was 1.6, indicating that the effect was modest.

Several studies reported only general levels of symptoms, without differentiating among externalizing or internalizing dimensions, while other studies reported findings at both levels. Of the 12 studies reporting general symptom levels, 6 showed increased symptoms for siblings of children with physical disabilities or chronic illnesses. These include studies of siblings of children with cystic fibrosis (Breslau & Prabucki, 1987; Cowen, Mok, Corey, Mac-Millan, Simmons, & Levinson, 1986), chronic epilepsy (Hoare, 1984), disfigurement requiring plastic surgery (Lavigne & Ryan, 1979), spina bifida (Breslau & Prabucki, 1987; Tew & Laurence, 1973), Crohn's disease (Wood et al., 1988), and mixed neurologically based congenital conditions (Breslau & Prabucki, 1987). Studies that found no increase in general symptoms included samples with arthritis (Daniels et al., 1986), diabetes (Ferrari, 1984), progressive renal disease (Fielding et al., 1985), congenital heart defects and leukemia (Lavigne & Ryan, 1979), mixed congenital disabling conditions (Lobato et al., 1987), and nephrotic syndrome (Vance et al., 1980). Drotar et al. (1981) found that siblings of children with cystic fibrosis and asthma scored as more highly adjusted than the normative sample on a behavior checklist completed by parents.

Five studies have gone beyond symptom checklists and self-concept measures to assess risk in other domains of functioning. Lavigne and Ryan (1979) found no increased risk of decrements in prosocial skills, and Ferrari (1984) found that siblings of diabetic children scored higher on teacher reports of prosocial behavior and parent reports of social competence than did controls. Vance et al. (1980) found that parents reported siblings of children with nephrotic syndrome as lower in school performance, and their teachers were likely to rate the group as having both more underachieving and more overachieving children than teachers of controls. Lavigne et al. (1982) found no evidence of increased decrements in school performance or social relations in their study of siblings of children with diabetes, and Cadman et al. (1988) found no differences in ratings of social competence, isolation, participation in leisure or recreational activities, or in risk for repeating a grade in school.

Taken as a whole, these studies do provide evidence of increased risk for siblings of children with physical disabilities or chronic illnesses, but this risk appears to depend on the domain of symptomatology and perhaps on the presence of neurologically based conditions. Problems in self-concept are not found very frequently, and, when reported, tend to be mild. Increased risk of internalizing symptoms was found in about half the studies, and, while risk of externalizing symptoms was found less often, it was found mostly in studies including neurologically based conditions, and infrequently in all other samples. General symptom levels (to some degree reflecting the aggregation of these two general domains of symptoms) again showed increased risk in about half the studies.

Sample Size Effects It is important to ask whether negative findings of these studies could be due to insufficient sample sizes, since studies with small groups often lack the power to detect all of the effects that are actually present. Eight of the 21 studies had sibling groups of less than 25 (including studies by Harvey and Greenway (1984), Hoare (1984), and Lavigne et al. (1982), in which findings are reported only on subsets of the total group of siblings: in Hoare, on siblings of chronic, as opposed to newly diagnosed, cases of epilepsy; in Harvey & Greenway, on siblings of children in normal schools as opposed to those in special schools; and in Lavigne et al., on male and female siblings within different age categories). Eliminating studies with low sample sizes would lead to stronger evidence of the presence of symptoms in both non-neurological and neurological conditions, since studies with samples of under 25 disproportionately result in findings of no increased risk or of decreased risk.

This raises both a methodological and a substantive issue. New studies will probably be more likely to detect risk with larger samples. However, the level of risk detected may not be of substantive concern. Half of the studies (10 of 21) addressed this question by analyzing data not just in terms of mean differences in symptom counts, but also by identifying clinical levels of symptomatology, in most cases by applying previously established cutoff scores to symptoms counts. Table 4 compares these findings with those for simple symptom counts. In the table, studies are counted as demonstrating increased risk in symptom counts or in clinical cases if any measure in the study showed increased risk.

Clinical Levels of Symptomatology Only one of five studies on non-neurological conditions showed an increased risk of clinical levels of symptomatology. Wood et al. (1988) compared parent ratings on the Child Behavior Checklist (Achenbach & Edelbrock, 1983) to norms for the mea-

Table 4. Levels of risk for siblings of children with PD/CI for symptom counts and clinical syndromes

	Non-neurologic conditions			Neurologic conditions or mixed		
	Lower risk	No difference	Higher risk	Lower risk	No difference	Higher risk
Symptom or behavior counts	6, 20	4, 5, 8, 12, 14, 18	3, 7, 13, 16, 19, 20, 21		11	1, 2, 9, 15
Syndrome or above clinical cutoffs	5	4, 8, 20	21		1	2, 10, 15, 17

PD/CI = physical disability or chronic illness; numbers refer to studies listed in Table 1.

sure. They found that 24% of the children who had a sibling with Crohn's disease scored above the 98th percentile on the total scale, commonly used as a clinical cutoff for severe disorder. However, only 4% of siblings of children with ulcerative colitis, another inflammatory bowel disease with many symptoms in common with Crohn's disease, were above this cutoff. Increased disorder in siblings was not found to be related to greater acute activity of the disease.

Neurological and mixed-group studies reporting data on clinical cutoffs showed stronger evidence of sibling risk, with four of the five studies reporting such information showing increased risk levels. Hoare (1984) found higher rates of severe symptomatology in siblings of children with chronic epilepsy according to both parent and teacher reports. Siblings of children with newly diagnosed epilepsy did not differ from controls in rates of severe disorder. Lobato et al. (1987), using mother ratings on the Child Behavior Checklist, found that over twice as many preschool siblings of children with congenital disabilities had at least one subscale score over the 98th percentile cutoff when compared to control children. Tew and Laurence (1973), in their study of siblings of children with spina bifida, found these siblings to be four times as likely to score above cutoff levels on teacher reports of behavior problems at school.

Findings by Breslau and Cadman et al. add to the complexity of this issue. In her initial study of siblings of children with mixed conditions, Breslau (Breslau et al., 1981; Breslau, 1982) found no increased risks for severe conditions using cutoffs based on parent reports on the Brief Symptom Inventory (Langner et al., 1976). When follow-up was conducted 5 years later, siblings were found to be at increased risk using the same measure (Breslau & Prabucki, 1987). However, structured diagnostic interviews using the Diagnostic Interview for Children found no evidence of increased risk of any diagnosable condition, including major depression, anxiety disorders, or oppositional disorder. For this reason this study is included in the "no increased risk" column of Table 4. These results suggest that cutoff scores on symptom checklists may be problematic when used to reflect levels of diagnosable disorders, a point reinforced by other recent research on child-behavior checklists (Sandberg et al., 1991).

Cadman et al. (1988) administered a modified version of the Child Behavior Checklist to parents, and, when appropriate, to children and teachers. These data were used by the investigators to approximate clinical diagnosis by developing cutoffs based on psychiatric diagnosis of a subset of children from the same sample. Four general diagnostic categories were studied: conduct disorder, attention deficit disorder-hyperactivity (ADD-H), emotional disorder (aggregating over-anxious disorder, depression, and obsessive-compulsive disorder), and somatization disorder. Siblings of children with physical disabilities or chronic illnesses were at small (statistically nonsignificant) risk for having one or more of these diagnoses (odds ratio of 1.4). These siblings were not at significantly increased risk for conduct disorder, ADD-H, or somatization disorder, and while they were twice as likely to have a reported emotional disorder, this finding represented only a tendency toward significance. These findings are of particular interest because of the rigorous epidemiological design used in this study and because of the large sample sizes involved.

Summary of Findings As a group, these studies provide evidence that siblings of children with physical disabilities or chronic illnesses are at increased risk for mild adjustment problems. Children of siblings with neurologically based conditions appear to be at heightened risk for externalizing symptoms, while siblings of children with non-neurological conditions do not seem at risk for increased aggression. Increased risk is by no means uniform across the population, however, and may likely vary according to other factors such as etiology, course, and prognosis of the disabling condition, although there are too few studies as yet to determine differential risk associated with such factors. Siblings of children with physical disabilities or chronic illnesses are much less at risk for severe forms of disorder, but those with brothers or sisters having neurologically based conditions may be more so. Findings on the neurological/non-neurological distinction must be considered highly tentative, since the number of studies on neurological conditions is small, and these studies may differ from those on non-neurological conditions in a variety of ways other than etiology of impairment.

Findings on Boundary Conditions

If risk to siblings is not uniformly distributed across the population of families with children with physical disabilities or chronic illnesses, what boundary conditions might define the limits of increased risk? Only a few of the studies reviewed here attended to this issue, so any conclusions concerning such conditions would be premature. Therefore, boundary conditions that have been studied will be presented with no attempt at summarizing findings. Rather, these variables will be advanced to provide some direction for future risk research, and to suggest some avenues to pursue in studying more specific causal processes that mediate the relationship between the presence of a disability or illness and sibling adjustment problems.

Family Constellation Several studies have examined the effects of family constellation variables on sibling risk levels. These have included age of sibling, gender of sibling, gender match between sibling and affected child, and relative birth order. Cowen et al. (1986) found increased risk of behavior problems in preschool siblings (ages 1–5), but not for older siblings (ages 6–15), of children with cystic fibrosis. Breslau and Prabucki (1987), in their 5-year follow-up of siblings of congenitally disabled children, found increases in depression and social isolation across 5 years for the group as a whole, but the largest increases were in children who were ages 6–9 at the first assessment and 11–14 at the second. Oppositional behavior was higher than the control group only for siblings of ages 11–17 at the time of the second assessment. Lavigne and Ryan (1979) found increased risk of overall disturbance in preschool siblings (ages 3–6) of children receiving plastic surgery for disfigurement, but not for preschool siblings of children with cancer or congenital heart defects. Tew and Laurence (1973) found no age effects for siblings (ages 2–15) of children with spina bifida. Thus, while two studies found increased risk for preschool children when compared to older children (bolstered by the finding of increased aggression in preschool siblings of congenitally disabled children by Lobato et al., 1987) two other studies failed to corroborate this finding.

Gender effects have also emerged in some studies but not others. Lavigne and Ryan (1979) found that for siblings of children with congenital heart defects, males age 7–13 showed much higher levels of overall disturbance than females, as compared to control male and female siblings. This pattern did not emerge for siblings of children with cancer or for those of children receiving plastic surgery for disfigurement. Breslau found no differential effects for males or females, nor did Kazak and Clark in their study of children with siblings with spina bifida. However, Breslau and others have reported differential risk for more complex factors involving both gender and relative birth order (younger or older than the child with a physical disability or chronic illness). Breslau found more adjustment problems in younger male and older female siblings of children with physical disabilities or chronic illnesses, with no similar pattern emerging in her community control sample. She was also able to demonstrate that the increased risk to younger males was attenuated by greater age spacing, such that younger males whose siblings with physical disabilities or chronic illnesses were more than 2 years older were less at risk than younger siblings born within 2 years of the child. Ferrari (1987) did not find that younger siblings of children with diabetes were more at risk, but did find that male siblings of male children with diabetes were at the highest risk.

Characteristics of the Child with a Physical Disability or Chronic Illness Several studies in this group have looked at characteristics of the disability or illness as possible moderators of influence on sibling adjustment. Hoare (1984) studied chronicity of epilepsy, finding that siblings of children with established chronic epilepsy were at increased risk for adjustment problems, while siblings of children with newly diagnosed epilepsy did not differ from controls. Breslau and Prabucki's (1987) finding that siblings of children with congenital disabilities maintained or increased symptom levels across 5 years, while siblings of healthy children showed reductions in symptom levels, is consistent with this finding. However, Lavigne and Ryan (1979) found no correlation between chronicity ratings and sibling adjustment for any of the non-neurological conditions that they studied (cancer, congenital heart defects, or disfigurement requiring plastic surgery). In addition, Lavigne et al. (1982) found decreases in male sibling externalizing symptoms as the length of illness increased.

Tew and Laurence (1973) assessed the effects of the severity of disabilities on sibling adjustment in families with children with spina bifida and found a curvilinear relationship. Siblings of children with moderate levels of disability fared best, while siblings of children with mild or severe disabilities had the poorest adjustment. However, four studies have found no relationship between severity indicators (such as extent of disability or illness severity) and sibling adjustment, (e.g., Breslau et al., 1981; Cadman et al., 1988; Lavigne & Ryan, 1979; Lavigne et al., 1982).

Summary of Findings A few studies have begun to map out possible relationships between subsample variables such as sibling age, sibling gender, relative birth order, and chronicity or severity of the disability or illness. These appear to be promising avenues for future study, yielding findings on both boundary conditions that could sharpen the field's understanding of risk levels for this population of siblings, and on factors that can point toward more specific causal processes that mediate the influence of chronic conditions on sibling adjustment, to which the author now turns.

CAUSAL PROCESS RESEARCH

As noted earlier, researchers studying sibling risk have ventured a number of hypotheses on the causal mediators of adjustment problems, based on subgroup analyses of boundary-condition factors. As an example, consider the findings on gender, age, and relative birth order described above. Two factors have been advanced as possible causes of adjustment problems: *parental unavailability* and the *burden of caregiving*. Young children, particularly children younger than the child with a physical disability or chronic illness, may be more at risk because their parents are not available to provide the quality and constancy of parenting necessary to support the child's social and emotional development. As Lobato (1990) has pointed out, this hypothesis does not take into account the wide variability in parenting resources that families bring to this situation. Thus, a more adequate test of the hypotheses would not assume a uniform effect for all families with a child with a physical disability or chronic illness, but would actually measure indicators of parent availability within a group of these families and within a group of families with only healthy children. The hypothesis would be supported if parents of children with physical disabilities or chronic illnesses were found to be less available for their other children than control parents, and if availability was found to correlate with sibling adjustment.

A similar study of family process could be conducted to test the hypothesis that older children, particularly females, are given more of the burden of caregiving for the child with a physical disability or chronic illness, leading to increased stress and resultant symptomatology in those siblings. Adequate controls in this area of research are essential. In one of the few studies to directly test this hypothesis, Schwirian (1976) found that in families of hearing-impaired children, older siblings were given greater childcare responsibilities and had fewer social activities than did controls, but when age, gender, and family size were statistically controlled, these differences almost disappeared.

If research into causal mediators is to be undertaken, what directions are most likely to prove fruitful? Early models of sibling impact focused on "direct effects." Siblings were seen as identifying with the child with a physical disability or chronic illness, and therefore developing self-concepts that included reduced feelings of self-worth. More recent research has examined "indirect effects." The chronic condition is seen as putting increased demands on parents, such that the parent's relationship with the healthy sibling suffers. Several investigators have advanced the thesis that indirect effects might best be placed in a more general framework that studies child development within the context of family systems or social ecologies (Bristol, Gallagher, & Schopler, 1988; Kazak, 1989; Newbrough, Simpkins, & Maurer, 1985).

Principles of Social Ecology

Kazak (1989) has begun to elaborate on how social ecology (Bronfenbrenner, 1979) and family systems (Minuchin, Rosman, & Baker, 1978) concepts might advance the study of families with chronically ill children. Four general principles from this perspective can provide some guidance in research on siblings. These involve *embeddedness, units of study, system boundaries*, and *bidirectionality.*.

First, sibling development is seen as being embedded within an interlocking web of relationships among the sibling and parents, the child with a physical disability or chronic illness, other children in the family, peers, teachers, and extended family. Figure 1 gives a graphic representation of this set of relationships. Second, because of this embeddedness, the unit of study in any research into influences on sibling adjustment can range from simple dyads (such as sibling–sibling interactions between the sibling and the child with a physical disability or chronic illness) or triads (such as parent–parent interactions that involve the sibling), or even larger groupings, including the nuclear family in relation to the extended family. Third, the units of study can vary for a particular question or process. Ecological and systems models have been criticized because they assume that everything influences everything else, making it impossible to study the internal workings of the system. More

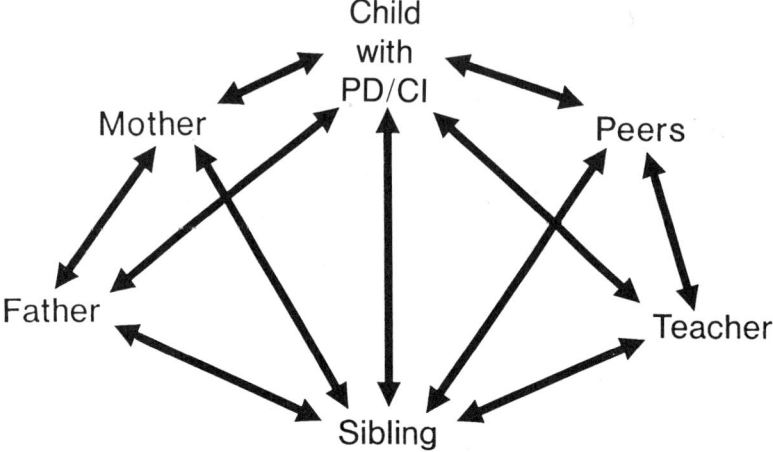

Figure 1. Linkages in the social ecology of a sibling of a child with a physical disability or chronic illness (PD/CI).

sophisticated systems models, however, include the concept of boundary. Subgroups within an ecology or within a family are often conducting daily business in relative isolation from other components of the system. Boundaries limit cross-group influence, and are most likely essential to the successful operation of many aspects of family life. Thus, researchers need to look for naturally occurring boundaries that demarcate the limits of important social influence processes within the overall set of social relationships experienced by the sibling.

Finally, ecological and systems models assume that, while it is possible that influences can be unidirectional, they are often bidirectional or mutual. Bidirectional influences can be simultaneous (child anxiety and parent depression growing together over time, for example, with neither taking precedent) or phasic (parent withdrawal leading to child demandingness at a later time, leading to increased parental depression still later, for example).

Applications in Sibling Research

While very few studies have attempted to measure relationship patterns and determine their effects on sibling adjustment, a number of researchers have studied aspects of sibling ecology in families with children with physical disabilities or chronic illnesses. These studies have usually included only subsets of the relationships depicted in Figure 1.

Studying the relationship between the child with a physical disability or chronic illness and the healthy sibling, Vance et al. (1980) found no differences between families of children with nephrotic syndrome and control families in parental reports of healthy siblings' expressions of anger, jealousy, overprotectiveness, lack of interest, negative feelings, or positive feelings toward the index sibling. Siblings of children with physical disabilities or chronic illnesses were reported to have experienced more embarrassment over their sibling, and were reported to fight less frequently with their sibling, as compared to controls. Sibling jealousy and overprotectiveness have been reported as frequent problems in uncontrolled studies, such as Phillips, Bohannon, Gayton, and Friedman's (1985) survey of families with children with cystic fibrosis. Whether such factors have any bearing on sibling adjustment is an open question.

An important issue in the area of sibling relationships is reciprocity. Since physically disabled children have fewer resources than their siblings, and are more likely to be viewed, because of their disability, as the child needing the most attention, their relationships with siblings may be restricted to patterns of "caregiver–patient" or "parental child–younger child." Overprotective behavior by the healthy sibling may be only one side of a relationship pattern that is reinforced by both parties, as well as supported by the rest of the family. The presence of reciprocally supportive relationships has not been studied as yet, but such relationships may provide protective resources for healthy siblings, rather than just reflecting the absence of a stressful burden. Mattson and Gross (1966) found such patterns of mutual support in their uncontrolled interview study of families with children having hemophilia when they assessed relationships in which both siblings had the medical condition.

Sibling–sibling relationships may be profoundly influenced by other family members, particularly parents. The triad of parent, healthy sibling, and child with physical disability or chronic illness has been studied from a number of perspectives. As noted earlier, risk researchers have attempted to study indirect indications of two such processes: parental unavailability and parental reinforcement of caregiving, particularly for older female children. There have as yet been no attempts to directly study the relationship between the parent and healthy sibling, either in the general context of having a child with a physical disability or chronic illness in the family, or in terms of direct observation of triadic interaction. Processes involved in a lack of parent availability have been studied indirectly, however. Breslau (1983b) has provided evidence that a child with disabilities can have a profound impact on parents' emotional adjustment. Increased depression in parents, particularly mothers, has in other populations been linked with increased risk of maladjustment in children. Breslau's data indicate that this process is mediated by the impact on family cohesion and by economic loss. In poorer families where economic losses due to treatment demands are more severe, disability is associated with losses in family cohesion and increased maternal depression, while in families with more financial resources the economic effects are less pronounced and family cohesion and maternal well-being are less affected.

Data from a study of families with a child with Duchenne Muscular Dystrophy (Firth, Gardner-Medwin, Hosking, & Wilkinson, 1983) suggest that relationships in this triad will have an impact on the healthy sibling not only during childhood but also later in life. Parents in this study reported that adult siblings living away from home continued their involvement with the care of the affected sibling, offering practical and even financial help to the parent. The impact of such a continuing relationship on the sibling, whether imposing extra financial or time burdens, or reinforcing a sense of connectedness with the family of origin, warrants further study.

A third unit of interaction in the ecology of siblings involves the four-way relationship among mother, father, nondisabled sibling, and the child with a physical disability or chronic illness. Indirect evidence of the importance of this unit comes from research on the effects of child disability on the marriage. Sabbeth and Leventhal (1984) recently reviewed this research and concluded that the presence of a child with a chronic illness or physical disability does not increase the risk of divorce or separation. However, they found evidence that parents of such children express more dissatisfaction with their marriages, and argue and disagree more. Since marital conflict has been associated with child adjustment problems in other populations, and is a major risk factor in maternal depression, which itself is predictive of child adjustment difficulties, these findings suggest that child disability may indirectly influence sibling adjustment through its impact on the marriage and on the emotional health of the parents. This is consistent with Breslau's finding that disability was linked to problems in family cohesion and maternal depression, although her data indicated this was true primarily when the disability led to economic loss.

While marital quality may be one mediator of effect, other pathways involving this constellation of relationships have been advanced in the literature. Bristol et al. (1988) studied allocation of parenting responsibilities in families with children with severe developmental disabilities. They found, contrary to hypothesis, that fathers of children with disabilities assumed significantly less responsibility for childcare than did fathers of nondisabled children. However, this was restricted to responsibility for care of the child with a disability; fathers in both groups provided equivalent amounts of care to nondisabled siblings. Thus, redistribution of parental responsibilities for childcare may be a factor in sibling adjustment, although Bristol et al.'s data suggest that the central tendency in families with children with physical disabilities or chronic illness involves doubly increased demands on mothers (due to reduction in father involvement with care of the child), even when the mothers are employed.

Child ecologies increasingly come to include relationships with persons outside the family as the child grows older. Relationships with peers may be affected in a number of ways by the presence of a sibling with a physical disability or chronic illness. Some studies have found increased social activity with peers for siblings of children with physical disabilities or chronic illness (Ferrari, 1984), perhaps reflecting attempts to compensate for the absence of a satisfying reciprocated friendship at home. Other researchers have suggested that siblings of children with physical disabilities or chronic illness may be stigmatized by peers, and Voysey (1972) has presented data suggesting that parents reinforce typical children for withholding information about their sibling with disabilities from peers, neighbors, and relatives outside of the immediate family in order to project an image of normalcy. Richey and Ysseldyke (1983) have provided evidence that stigmatization may occur within school settings as well. They had teachers rate younger siblings of children with learning disabilities and nondisabled children who had been in their classes, and found that teachers held significantly lower expectations for the former group of siblings.

Summary

Research has increasingly begun to follow ecological-systems principles, and a number of researchers have begun to look in detail at various relationships within the family and at the general social ecology of siblings. No single pathway looms as the most likely avenue for increased or decreased risk in these children, and evidence is pointing to a number of social interaction patterns that can be shaped by the presence of a child with a physical disability or chronic illness and that can have important influences on the development and adjustment of siblings in the family. These various pathways may be overlapping: parents may reinforce certain sibling–sibling interactions, for example, and marital conflict may influence parent–child interaction. Boundaries that establish the limits of influence among these subsystems have yet to be identified. Nor have researchers as yet attended to possible bidirectional influence among individuals or subsystems.

CONCLUDING COMMENTS

This chapter approaches the issue of sibling adjustment in families that include a child with a physical disability or chronic illness from two rather different points of entry. Risk-factor research is essentially epidemiologic in its focus; that is, it raises questions of risk about various populations or subpopulations. Causal-process research (at least as defined here) is more microanalytically focused; it is concerned with uncovering and describing those patterns of social relationship and social influence that lead to increased risk.

The paradigmatic study in this review has been the clinic-based study of adjustment with matched control samples of convenience. This method has severe limitations in identifying risk factors; those researchers that have used more population-based sampling techniques have provided findings that inspire much greater confidence (Breslau et al., 1981; Cadman et al., 1988; Daniels et al., 1986). More such studies are needed. Risk-factor research in general has supported the notion that some siblings of children with physical disabilities or chronic illnesses are at risk for adjustment problems, but risk is clearly not constant across this population, and may be limited to mild levels of symptomatology for a substantial portion of this group.

Clinic-based samples may provide a better means of studying more specific causal processes, particularly those involving patterns of interaction within the social ecology of the nondisabled sibling. Brody and Stoneman (1983) have called for more direct observation of sibling social environments, and the ecological model advocated here would be greatly advanced by such work, which is still lacking for this particular population.

While risk-factor and causal-process research are contrasted in this review, recent research efforts in what might be termed the "epidemiology of social ecologies" suggest that direct integration of rigorous methods from these two traditions is not out of the question. Kellam (1990) has pioneered the synthesis of rigorous cluster sampling techniques with direct observation of schoolroom ecologies to assess social processes influencing the mental health of children, and Reiss et al. (in press) have surveyed a national sample of families in order to study family ecologies and sibling interaction through direct observation techniques. While requiring substantial resources, the application of such methods to the study of family ecologies involving children with physical disabilities or chronic illnesses and their siblings may hold great promise for advancing knowledge in this area.

Risk-factor and causal-process research are the two sources that together will provide the information necessary to determine which children and families are most likely to need further supports in order to prevent adjustment problems, along with information on which particular social processes may need to be targeted for preventive intervention. These twin agendas, while leading to different research paradigms, are both essential to furthering understanding of the worlds of siblings of children with physical disabilities and chronic illnesses.

REFERENCES

Achenbach, T.M., & Edelbrock, C. (1983). *Manual for the Child Behavior Checklist and Revised Child Behavior Profile*. Burlington: University of Vermont, Department of Psychiatry.

Binger, C. (1973). Childhood leukemia: Emotional impact on siblings. In E. Anthony & C. Koupernik (Ed.), *The child in his family: The impact of disease and death* (pp. 195–210). New York: John Wiley & Sons.

Breslau, N. (1982). Siblings of disabled children: Birth order and age-spacing effects. *Journal of Abnormal Child Psychology, 10*, 85–96.

Breslau, N. (1983a). Family care: Effects on siblings and mothers. In G.H. Thompson, I.L. Rubin, & R.M. Bilenker (Ed.), *Comprehensive management of cerebral palsy* (pp. 299–309). New York: Grune & Stratton.

Breslau, N. (1983b). The psychological study of chronically ill and disabled children: Are healthy siblings appropriate controls? *Journal of Abnormal Child Psychology, 11,* 379–391.

Breslau, N., & Prabucki, K. (1987). Siblings of disabled children. Effects of chronic stress in the family. *Archives of General Psychiatry, 44,* 1040–1046.

Breslau, N., Wietzman, M., & Messenger, K. (1981). Psychologic functioning of siblings of disabled children. *Pediatrics, 67,* 344–353.

Bristol, M.M., Gallagher, J.J., & Schopler, E. (1988). Mothers and fathers of young developmentally disabled and nondisabled boys: Adaptation and spousal support. *Developmental Psychology, 24,* 441–451.

Brody, G.H., & Stoneman, Z. (1983). Children with atypical siblings: Socialization outcomes and clinical participation. In B.B. Lahey & A.E. Kazdin (Ed.), *Advances in clinical child psychology* (Vol. 6, pp. 285–321). New York: Plenum.

Bronfenbrenner, U. (1979). *The ecology of human development: Experiments by nature and design.* Cambridge, MA: Harvard University Press.

Cadman, D., Boyle, M., & Offord, D.R. (1988). The Ontario Child Health Study: Social adjustment and mental health of siblings of children with chronic health problems. *Journal of Developmental and Behavioral Pediatrics, 9,* 117–121.

Cowen, L., Mok, J., Corey, M., MacMillan, H., Simmons, R., & Levinson, H. (1986). Psychological adjustment of the family with a member who has cystic fibrosis. *Pediatrics, 77,* 743–753.

Daniels, D., Miller, J.J., Billings, A.G., & Moos, R.H. (1986). Psychosocial functioning of siblings of children with rheumatic disease. *Journal of Pediatrics, 109,* 379–383.

Daniels, D., Moos, R.H., Billings, A.G., & Miller, J.J.I. (1987). Psychosocial risk and resistance factors among children with chronic illness, healthy siblings, and healthy controls. *Journal of Abnormal Child Psychology, 15,* 295–308.

Drotar, D., Doershuk, C.F., Stern, R.C., Boat, T.F., Boyer, W., & Matthews, L. (1981). Psychosocial functioning of children with cystic fibrosis. *Pediatrics, 67,* 338–343.

Ferrari, M. (1984). Chronic illness; Psychosocial effects on siblings—I. Chronically ill boys. *Journal of Child Psychology and Psychiatry and Allied Disciplines, 25,* 459–476.

Ferrari, M. (1987). The diabetic child and well sibling: Risks to the well child's self-concept. *Children's Health Care, 15,* 141–148.

Fielding, D., Moore, B., Dewey, M., Ashley, P., McKendrick, T., & Pinkerton, P. (1985). Children with end-stage renal failure: Psychological effects on patients, siblings, and parents. *Journal of Psychosomatic Research, 29,* 457–465.

Firth, M., Gardner-Medwin, D., Hosking, G., & Wilkinson, E. (1983). Interviews with parents of boys suffering from Duchenne Muscular Dystrophy. *Developmental Medicine and Child Neurology, 25,* 466–471.

Harvey, D., & Greenway, A. (1984). The self-concept of physically handicapped children and their non-handicapped siblings: An empirical investigation. *Journal of Child Psychology and Psychiatry, 25,* 273–284.

Hilliard, J.P., Fritz, G.K., & Lewiston, N.J. (1982). Goal-setting behavior of asthmatic, diabetic, and healthy children. *Child Psychiatry and Human Development, 13,* 35–47.

Hilliard, J.P., Fritz, G.K., & Lewiston, N.J. (1985). Levels of aspiration of parents for their asthmatic, diabetic, and healthy children. *Journal of Clinical Psychology, 41,* 587–597.

Hoare, P. (1984). Does illness foster dependency? A study of epileptic and diabetic children. *Developmental Medicine and Child Neurology, 26,* 20–24.

Howe, G.W., Feinstein, C., Reiss, D., Molock, S., & Berger, K. (1991). *Adolescent adjustment to chronic physical disorders: I. Comparing neurological and non-neurological conditions.* Manuscript submitted for publication.

Kazak, A.E. (1989). Families of chronically ill children: A systems and social-ecological model of adaptation and challenge. *Journal of Consulting and Clinical Psychology, 57,* 25–30.

Kazak, A.E., & Clark, M.W. (1986). Stress in families of children with myelomeningocele. *Developmental Medicine and Child Neurology, 28,* 220–228.

Kellam, S. (1990). Developmental epidemiological framework for family research on depression and aggression. In G. Patterson (Ed.), *Depression and aggression in family interaction* (pp. 11–48). Hillsdale, New Jersey: Lawrence Erlbaum Associates.

Klein, S.D., & Simmons, R.G. (1979). Chronic disease and childhood development: Kidney disease and transplantation. In R.G. Simmons (Ed.), *Research in Community and Mental Health* (Vol. 1). Greenwich, CT: JAI Press.

Langner, T.S., Gersten, J.C., McCarthy, E.D., Eisenberg, J.G., Greene, E.L., Herson, J.H., & Jameson, J.D. (1976). A screening inventory for assessing psychiatric impairment in children 6 to 18. *Journal of Consulting and Clinical Psychology, 44,* 286–296.

Lavigne, J.V., & Ryan, M. (1979). Psychological adjustment of siblings of children with chronic illness. *Pediatrics, 63,* 616–627.

Lavigne, J.V., Traisman, H.S., Marr, T.J., & Chasnoff, I.J. (1982). Parental perceptions of the psychological adjustment of children with diabetes and their siblings. *Diabetes Care, 5,* 420–426.

Lobato, D.J. (1990). *Brothers, sisters, and special needs: Information and activities for helping young siblings of children with chronic illness and developmental disabilities.* Baltimore: Paul H. Brookes Publishing Co.

Lobato, D., Barbour, L., Hall, L.J., & Miller, C.T. (1987). Psychosocial characteristics of preschool siblings of handicapped and nonhandicapped children. *Journal of Abnormal Child Psychology, 15,* 329–338.

Lobato, D., Faust, D., & Spirito, A. (1988). Examining the effects of chronic disease and disability on children's sibling relationships. *Journal of Pediatric Psychology, 13,* 389–407.

Mattson, A., & Gross, S. (1966). Social and behavioral studies on hemophiliac children and their families. *Journal of Pediatrics, 68,* 952–964.

McKeever, P. (1983). Siblings of chronically ill children: A literature review with implications for research and practice. *American Journal of Orthopsychiatry, 53,* 209–218.

Minuchin, S., Rosman, B., & Baker, L. (1978). *Psychosomatic families.* Cambridge, MA: Harvard University Press.

Neuhaus, E.C. (1958). A personality study of asthmatic and cardiac children. *Psychosomatic Medicine, 20,* 181–186.

Newbrough, J.R., Simpkins, C.G., & Maurer, H. (1985). A family development approach to studying factors in the management and control of childhood diabetes. *Diabetes Care, 8,* 83–92.

Phillips, S., Bohannon, W.E., Gayton, W.F., & Friedman, S.B. (1985). Parent interview findings regarding the impact of cystic fibrosis on families. *Developmental and Behavioral Pediatrics, 6*, 122–127.

Piers, E.V., & Harris, D.B. (1969). *The Piers-Harris Children's Self-Concept Scale*. Nashville, TN: Counselor Recordings and Tests.

Reiss, D., Plomin, R., Hetherington, M., Howe, G.W., Rovine, M., Tryon, A., & Stanley, M. (in press). The separate social worlds of teenage siblings. In M. Hetherington, D. Reiss, & R. Plomin (Eds.), *The separate social worlds of siblings: Impact of nonshared environments on development*. Hillsdale, NJ: Lawrence Erlbaum Associates.

Richey, L.S., & Ysseldyke, J.E. (1983). Teachers' expectations for the younger siblings of learning disabled students. *Journal of Learning Disabilities, 16*, 610–615.

Sabbeth, B.F., & Leventhal, J.M. (1984). Marital adjustment to childhood illness: A critique of the literature. *Pediatrics, 73*, 762–768.

Sandberg, D.E., Meyer-Bahlburg, H.F.L., & Yager, T.J. (1991). The Child Behavior Checklist nonclinical standardization samples: Should they be utilized as norms? *Journal of the American Academy of Child and Adolescent Psychiatry, 30*, 124–134.

Schwirian, P.M. (1976). Effects of the presence of a hearing-impaired preschool child in the family on behavior patterns of older "normal" siblings. *American Annals of the Deaf, 121*, 373–380.

Shapiro, J. (1983). Family reactions and coping strategies in response to the physically ill or handicapped child: A review. *Social Science and Medicine, 17*, 913–931.

Tew, B., & Laurence, K.M. (1973). Mothers, brothers and sisters of patients with spina bifida. *Developmental Medicine and Child Neurology, 15*(6, suppl. 29), 69–76.

Treiber, F., Mabe, P.A.I., & Wilson, G. (1987). Psychosocial adjustment of sickle cell children and their siblings. *Children's Health Care, 16*, 82–88.

Tritt, S.G., & Esses, L.M. (1988). Psychosocial adaptation of siblings of children with chronic medical illnesses. *American Journal of Orthopsychiatry, 58*, 211–220.

Turk, J. (1964). Impact of cystic fibrosis on family functioning. *Pediatrics, 34*, 67–71.

Vance, J.C., Fazan, L.E., Satterwhite, B., & Pless, I.B. (1980). Effects of nephrotic syndrome on the family: A controlled study. *Pediatrics, 65*, 948–955.

Voysey, M. (1972). Impression management by parents of disabled children. *Journal of Health and Social Behavior, 13*, 180–189.

Wood, B., Boyle, J.T., Watkins, J.B., Nogueira, J., Zimand, E., & Carroll, L. (1988). Sibling psychological status and style as related to the disease of their chronically ill brothers and sisters: Implications for models of biopsychosocial interaction. *Developmental and Behavioral Pediatrics, 9*, 66–72.

CHAPTER 9

Siblings of Children with Chronic Illnesses
A Categorical and Noncategorical Look at Selected Literature

*Agatha M. Gallo
and Kathleen A. Knafl*

> I think that the kid that doesn't have it is the one who's most affected. They've got to accept a lot of things. Like the one with the diabetes, the illness, gets a little more attention sometimes and the other one doesn't understand why this is. Sometimes they have to give things up too. Sometimes we have to cancel plans because of the diabetes.
>
> I think the other children are more open to other people having problems, whether it's someone with diabetes or something else. They may be more responsible than other children in their age bracket, but I don't think it's much different. They still lead a normal life as far as I can tell.
> (Two mothers of children with diabetes, as quoted in Knafl, Breitmayer, Gallo, & Zoeller, 1987)

In spite of the growing interest across disciplines in siblings of children with various health problems, there is little agreement about how best to conceptualize and investigate the impact on a child of having a sibling with chronic illness. Moreover, research to date has produced inconsistent findings on the nature and extent of the impact on siblings.

In general, studies of siblings have conceptualized the child's chronic illness as a stressor that affects the behavioral, psychological, and cognitive development of the nondisabled sibling. Earlier studies relied heavily on anecdotal accounts and typically used single-group designs with no control or comparison group, and they frequently reported negative effects on siblings (Drotar & Crawford, 1985; Lobato, Faust, & Spirito, 1988). More recent studies have incorporated better controls, as well as a wider variety of valid, reliable measures of sibling adjustment. Such studies have reported less dramatic rates of sibling maladjustment, with some authors noting only minimal adjustment problems (Daniels, Miller, Billings, & Moos, 1986; Ferrari, 1984; Lavigne, Traisman, Marr, & Chasnoff, 1982; Menke, 1987) and others noting emotional and psychological benefits to siblings (Breslau, Weitzman, & Messenger, 1981; Ferrari, 1984; Taylor, 1980; Tritt & Esses, 1988). These studies suggest that siblings respond to a child's chronic illness in a variety of both positive and negative ways. However, relatively little is known about how these varying responses correspond to individual and environmental factors.

In these sibling-response studies, several authors have emphasized the characteristics of the child's illness (Brett, 1988; Drotar & Crawford, 1985; Lobato et al., 1988; McKeever, 1983; Tritt & Esses, 1988). For example, in outlining a model for selecting and evaluating sibling-research variables, Lobato et al. (1988) noted that, "the characteristics of disabilities vary greatly, but few researchers have hypothesized or tested specific relationships between these characteristics and outcome" (p. 400). In a similar vein, Drotar and Crawford (1985) recommended that "studies should begin to consider the role of illness-related variables (e.g., treatment regimens, duration of disease) in sibling adjustment" (p. 361).

Linking the nature of the disease to outcomes for siblings raises fundamental questions about the salience of traditional disease categories for illuminating such linkages. In other words, are specific diseases associated with specific psychosocial outcomes for siblings, or are there characteristics that cut across diseases and play an important role in shaping the response of siblings to chronic illness? The authors' intent in this chapter is to undertake an integrative review of the literature on siblings of chronically ill children, with a focus on the contributions of both disease entity and illness characteristics in determining how siblings respond to chronic illness.

CATEGORICAL AND NONCATEGORICAL APPROACHES

For researchers of childhood chronic illness, an enduring issue has been the relative importance of disease categories in understanding child adjustment. In recent years, it has been addressed in terms of the relative merits of taking a categorical (disease entity) or noncategorical (general illness characteristics) approach to studying the impact of illness on individuals and family members. As early as 1975, Pless and Pinkerton argued:

> The chronicity of the illness and the impact that it has on the child, his parents, and his siblings, is more significant than the specific character of the disorder, be it diabetes, cerebral palsy, hemophilia, etc. In other words, there are certain problems common to all chronic illness over and above the particular challenges posed by individual needs. (p. 52)

Building on Pless and Pinkerton's work (1975), various authors have attempted to identify underlying characteristics that pose unique psychosocial challenges to children with chronic illness and their families. While most authors have focused on the child with chronic illness, the characteristics that they have identified provide a useful starting point for exploring the possible existence of similar characteristics for siblings of the child.

Frameworks for Categorizing Illness

As shown in Table 1, authors have postulated a wide variety of characteristics as cutting across disease categories. Individual authors' justifications for including specific characteristics range from cursory statements to more fully elaborated supportive arguments. For example, in their initial presentation of the noncategorical approach, Stein and Jessop (1982) stated:

> The essence of a noncategorical approach is that children face common life experiences and problems based on generic dimensions of their conditions rather than on idiosyncratic characteristics of any specific disease entity. The lives of children and their families are affected by whether the condition is visible or invisible; whether it is life threatening, stable, or characterized by unpredictable

Table 1. Comparison across psychosocial frameworks for categorizing illness

Stein and Jessop (1982)	Rolland (1984)	Jessop and Stein (1985)	Pless and Perrin (1985)	Lobato, Faust, and Spirito (1988)
Visibility		Visibility	Visibility	Visibility
Disease course	Course	Change expected	Course of illness	Course or phase
Cosmetic aspect				
Sensory/motor/ cognitive functioning	Incapacitation	Functional status	Sensory/motor/ cognitive functioning	Functional implications
Treatment demands				
	Onset		Time necessary for diagnosis	Onset
	Outcome			Prognosis
			Prevalence	
			Age at onset	
			Genetic component	
			Amount of medical supervision	
				Etiology
		Surgical procedures		

crises; and whether it involves mental retardation, has a cosmetic aspect, affects sensory or motor systems, or requires intrusive or demanding routines of care. (pp. 354–355)

In contrast to this succinct listing of noncategorical characteristics, their later, revised breakdown of salient illness attributes is based on a study of 209 mothers of children with a chronic illness (Jessop & Stein, 1985). In this study, providers reported information on 17 characteristics of the child's illness, and analysis of-variance techniques were used to explore the impact of these illness characteristics on children's social and psychological characteristics and health behaviors. Only 4 of the 17 characteristics (functional status, child's appearance, major surgical procedures, and expectation of change) yielded consistently significant results across outcome measures. The authors discussed these four characteristics in terms of the amount of uncertainty in characterizing the illness.

While not empirically based, Rolland (1984) and, to a lesser extent, Pless and Perrin (1985) provided well-developed justifications for the illness characteristics they identified. Rolland (1984) maintained that his characteristics direct attention to the psychosocial demands of the illness, and he stated that they are "hypothesized to be the most significant at the interface of the illness and the individual or family" (p. 248). Pless and Perrin (1985) argued in favor of what they called a "partial categorical approach." The characteristics they identified were meant to balance what they saw as an overemphasis on the unique qualities of individual diseases. They acknowledged the importance of both categorical and noncategorical considerations, saying:

> From the point of view of either service or research, a strong case can be made for viewing all chronic conditions, regardless of their individual characteristics, as one group having many problems in common, although it is true that, in some disorders, the elements shared with other conditions are heavily outweighed by those that are unique to that condition. (p. 42)

Lobato et al. (1988) are the only authors identified in Table 1 who focused explicitly on sibling research. Their proposed model for studying the impact of childhood disease or disability on siblings included both family-background factors and disease and disability characteristics. They described the characteristics as an adaptation of Rolland's framework and suggested that it is important for investigators to explicitly describe the characteristics of the diseases included in their samples. Like Pless and Perrin (1985), they acknowledged the importance of recognizing both characteristics that cut across diseases and those that are unique to a particular disease.

Although varied, the frameworks summarized in Table 1 reflect some common themes. All authors identified disease-course and functional implications as important illness characteristics; four authors noted the importance of visibility; and three mentioned illness onset. These common characteristics are discussed below.

Noncategorical Illness Characteristics

Disease Course Rolland (1984) emphasized the importance of disease course, which he maintained could take three forms: progressive, constant, or relapsing/episodic. In a similar vein, Pless and Perrin (1985) differentiated between static and dynamic illnesses. While static illnesses are characterized by a "fixed deficit," the dynamic illnesses change over time. They added:

> The dynamic disorders may be further categorized as to whether the course is predictably toward improvement or decline or whether it is marked by exacerbations, with times the child may be relatively healthy and others when she or he might be quite ill. (p. 46)

Jessop and Stein (1985) found poorer outcomes for both children with illness and their families when there was an expectation that the child's condition would change. In their application of Rolland's framework to siblings, Lobato et al. (1988) stated, "Fluctuating and episodic illnesses, such as colitis or asthma, produce demands and stressors that differ widely from steadily progressive or stable diseases. One would expect these contrasts to be expressed in differing psychological effects on siblings" (p. 402). All authors identified the relative stability and predictability of the illness as factors that were likely to shape the ill person's and the family's response to the experience.

Functional Factors In spite of some variation across authors, *functional* factors are generally conceptualized as the ill person's ability to fulfill usual social roles. Rolland (1984) addressed functional issues by distinguishing between incapacitating and nonincapacitating illnesses. He noted that incapacitation can result from impairment of cognition, sensation, movement or energy production, or from disfigurement, and that different types of impairment required different adjustments for the family. Rolland concluded:

> The sum effect of incapacitation on a particular individual or family depends on the interaction of the type of incapacitation with the pre-illness roles occupied by the ill member. However, it may be the presence or absence of *any* significant incapacitation that constitutes the principal dividing line relevant to a first attempt to build a model. (p. 251)

Lobato et al. (1988) concluded that the particular type of functional incapacity may "create common stresses, complaints, or rewards for siblings" (p. 402). Pless and Perrin (1985) discussed functional issues in terms of mobility–activity, cognitive functioning, and sensory functioning. They maintained that impairments in cognitive and sensory functioning are likely to be linked with distinct patterns of development and psychological adjustment. Mobility–activity impairments, however, "may prevent children from participating in sports and other activities with their peers and separate them from siblings at home as well" (p. 46). This last statement clearly implies that functional aspects of the illness may have implications for siblings as well as children with chronic illness themselves. Jessop and Stein (1985) conceptualized functional status in terms of the child's ability to perform usual day-to-day activities.

Visibility With the exception of Rolland, all the authors listed on Table 1 identify visibility as an important characteristic of the illness. Pless and Perrin (1985) noted that visibility is likely to have its greatest negative effect on peer relationships. Jessop and Stein (1985), however, found poorer outcomes for children and families when the appearance of the child was not affected by the illness. In either case, visibility appears to be an important illness characteristic. Deviating from Rolland's framework, Lobato et al. (1988) list visibility as an important characteristic to consider in sibling research, but do not elaborate on its significance. Although Rolland (1984) does not identify visibility as an illness characteristic, he does list disfigurement as a type of incapacitation. The different ways in which illnesses become visible to others (e.g., disfigurement, treatment regimen) were not discussed by these authors.

Onset Three authors identified onset as an important illness characteristic. Rolland (1984) discussed onset in terms of the symptomatic presentation of the illness and categorized illness onset as either gradual or acute. Lobato et al. (1988) distinguished between sudden and gradual illness onset, and added that sudden onset can be either traumatic or congenital. They emphasized the importance of this illness characteristic noting that: "time of onset likely exerts a strong and direct effect on the sibling relationship" (p. 401). In particular, they highlighted the presence or absence of an established sibling relationship prior to the onset of illness. Pless and Perrin (1985) identified age of onset as an important issue with likely implications for the adjustment of both the ill child and his or her family.

The following review of the literature on sibling response to chronic illness addresses the extent to which this research has been characterized by a categorical versus noncategorical approach. In addition, the authors highlight both disease categories and noncategorical characteristics. These two sets of factors are explored in the context of the conceptual and methodological underpinnings of the research that is reviewed.

STRATEGIES FOR REVIEWING SIBLING LITERATURE

This review was limited to research studies on siblings of children with chronic illness published in major journals between 1960 and 1990. For the purposes of this chapter, a chronic illness is defined as any anatomical or physiological impairment that interferes with the child's ability to function fully in the environment (Rose & Thomas, 1987). A chronic illness is characterized by three factors: 1) it has a stable or progressive course, 2) it may allow a relatively normal lifespan despite impairment, and 3) it requires active management by family members to minimize serious consequences (Knafl,

Breitmayer, Gallo, & Zoeller, 1987). Studies of chronic illnesses (including oncologic and neurologic disorders) and developmental disabilities were excluded because they are discussed in other chapters in this volume. However, studies that included these and other illnesses as part of their total sample were retained. Several methods were used to obtain the sample of studies for review. First a library computer search was conducted (Medline, Psychological Abstracts, Sociological Abstracts), then the reference lists of those studies yielded additional citations. The purpose and focus of each study were examined, and one study was excluded from the review because it focused on childrearing practices. All other studies addressed the effects of childhood chronic illness on siblings. The final sample consisted of 20 research articles.

The analysis of each research article included five dimensions: 1) date published; 2) the purpose of the article, including focus and conceptual framework; 3) the sample, including size and sample selection; 4) method of data collection, including content of questionnaires; and 5) findings, including descriptions of sibling psychological adjustment and discussion of characteristics that influence sibling adjustment. Descriptions of dimensions for each study are presented in Table 2.

This chapter's first author read each article and recorded information about the five dimensions on a one-page review form created by both authors. A doctoral graduate student then compared the information on the review forms with that in the abstracts of the studies. If discrepancies were found, the study was reviewed a third time.

OVERVIEW OF STUDIES ON SIBLINGS

Methodology

All the studies focused primarily on the psychosocial effects of childhood chronic illness on siblings. However, five of the studies (Fielding et al., 1985; Gayton, Friedman, Tavormina, & Tucker, 1977; Phillips, Bohannon, Gayton, & Friedman, 1985; Turk, 1964; Vance, Fazan, Satterwhite, & Pless, 1980) explicitly included other members of the family (parents and all children with illnesses) in their titles. Eleven studies (Breslau, 1983; Crain, Sussman, & Weil, 1966; Daniels et al., 1986; Ferrari, 1984; Fielding et al., 1985; Gayton et al., 1977; Harder & Bowditch, 1982; Lavigne et al., 1982; Treiber, Mabe, & Wilson, 1987; Turk, 1964; Vance et al., 1980) included other members of the family in the focus of the article. Eight articles focused on the siblings alone (Breslau, 1982; Breslau et al., 1981; Cadman, Boyle, & Offord, 1988; Lavigne & Ryan, 1979; Menke, 1987; Taylor, 1980; Tritt & Esses, 1988; Wood et al., 1988).

While only one study was organized around a biopsychosocial conceptual framework (Wood et al., 1988), three others used either family systems

Table 2. Dimensions of research on the effects of childhood chronic illness on well siblings

Author/year	Focus	Sample	Measures	Findings
Turk (1964)	Effects of cystic fibrosis on family	25 families	Interview—25 mothers, 3 fathers	Parents described deprivations and communication issues, restrictions of siblings' activities, use of attention seeking devices.
Crain, Sussman, and Weil (1966)	Behavior and family interaction in diabetes	19 diabetics, 16 well siblings (8–11 years)	Observation of mother/child interactions; questionnaires—child	Psychosocial functioning of diabetics did not differ from that of siblings. Mother–child relationship markedly different for diabetic child than for sibling. Mothers' behavior not related to sibling self-esteem, satisfaction with own behavior, academic achievement, or level of aspiration.
Gayton, Friedman, Tavormina, and Tucker (1977)	Psychological evaluation of families with a child with cystic fibrosis	29 fathers, 43 mothers, 33 children with illness, 31 siblings (5–11 years)	Interview and questionnaires—mother, father, child with illness, sibling	Evidence of negative psychological impact on sibling was lacking; decreased family satisfaction and family adjustment.
Lavigne and Ryan (1979)	Effects of chronic illness on siblings	203 siblings (3–13 years): plastic surgery (37), heart (57), hematology (62), healthy children (46)	Questionnaire—mothers, fathers, stepparents	Siblings showed more symptoms of irritability and social withdrawal. Younger siblings (ages 3–6) of children who had plastic surgery showed higher levels of psychopathology. Male siblings of patients with blood dyscrasias showed more significant signs of emotional distress than female siblings. There were no group differences in measures of aggression or learning problems. There were significant interactions among sex and age and social withdrawal, inhibition, immaturity, and irritability.

Taylor (1980)	Descriptions of the effects of long-term illness on siblings	25 siblings (7–12 years): asthma, cystic fibrosis, congenital heart conditions	Interview—siblings	Correlations of severity and chronicity of illness with behavior scales were not significant. Siblings described both negative and positive effects. Number of positive and negative effects were equal regarding diagnosis, severity, and duration of illness.
Vance, Fazan, Satterwhite, and Pless (1980)	Frequency of psychosocial problems in children and parents in nephrosis	nephrotics (36), healthy siblings (79), healthy children (79)	Interview—parents; questionnaires—parents, children, teachers	Stress on family members was less than generally assumed. Areas of increased sibling vulnerability were: social confidence, self-acceptance, poorer academic performance.
Breslau, Weitzman, and Messenger (1981)	Psychological adjustment of siblings of children with disabilities	239 siblings: cystic fibrosis (49), cerebral palsy (79), myelodysplasia (54), multiple disabilities (57), well children (6–18 years) (1034)	Questionnaires—mothers	Siblings of children with illness did not differ from normative sample, but scored higher on mentation problems, fighting, and delinquency subscales. Type and level of disability, severity of illness, sibling sex and age were not related to sibling adjustment. Younger male siblings and older female siblings had more psychological impairment.
Breslau (1982)	Effects of birth order on sibling adjustment	237 siblings: cystic fibrosis (49), cerebral palsy (77), myelodysplasia (54), multiple disabilities (57), healthy children (248) (6–18 years)	Questionnaires, interview—mother	Younger male siblings, specifically those closer in age to child with disabilities, scored higher on psychological impairment than other male siblings. Female siblings were better psychologically adjusted than older siblings, and age spacing did not relate to adjustment in this group.

(continued)

Table 2. (continued)

Author/year	Focus	Sample	Measures	Findings
Lavigne, Traisman, Marr, and Chasnoff (1982)	Psychological adjustment of children with diabetes and their siblings	Diabetics (41), well siblings (41), well children (35), well siblings (35) (6–16 years)	Questionnaires—parents	Families did not differ on divorce rate or level of marital adjustment. For both male and female siblings of diabetics, there was no difference from controls on behavior problems or social competence. Male siblings were lower than diabetics and control on school performance. Level of illness control was unrelated to adjustment. Behavior symptoms increased for male diabetics with length of illness, and tended to decrease for male siblings. For siblings, there were no differences in behavior among groups for degree of illness control.
Harder and Bowditch (1982)	Perceptions of the impact of cystic fibrosis on siblings and families	Well siblings (19) (6–16 years)	Interview—siblings	Exploratory study: found only minimal negative effects on family life; positive effects identified.
Breslau (1983)	Appropriateness of use of siblings as controls in psychological assessment of children with chronic illness and disabilities	206 child–sibling pairs: cystic fibrosis (42), cerebral palsy (68), myelodysplasia (45), multiple handicaps (51), healthy children (222) (6–18 years)	Questionnaire—parents	Children with disabilities differed significantly from siblings on total scores and mentation problems and isolation. Matched comparison of controls and siblings did not differ. Children with cystic fibrosis were not at increased risk for psychopathology. Children with disabilities and siblings were more aggressive, regressed, and anxious than randomly selected controls.

Ferrari (1984)	Psychological adjustment of siblings/parents	48 siblings of male children: developmental delay, diabetes, healthy children	Interview and questionnaires—mother, father, sibling	Few group differences on self-concept or behavior problems were found. Siblings of same-sex children with illness had more adjustment problems. Relative youth at diagnosis, longer time elapsing since diagnosis, more maternal social support, and better dyadic adjustment were all related to less behavior problems and more self-esteem in well siblings.
Fielding, Moore, Dewey, Ashley, McKendrick, and Pinkerton (1985)	Psychological effect of end stage renal disease	32 children with illness, siblings, parents	Questionnaires—parents, ill child, teacher	Study showed high levels of anxiety and depression in parents as compared to normative sample, but these were not related to increased worsening condition of ill child. There was no difference on school performance between ill children and siblings and controls.
Phillips, Bohannon, Gayton, and Friedman (1985)	Impact of cystic fibrosis on family	94 siblings (5–21 years)	Interview—parents	Majority of parents reported minor behavioral problems in siblings.
Daniels, Miller, Billings, and Moos (1986)	Psychosocial functioning of siblings of children with rheumatic diseases	Children with illness and well siblings (72), healthy children (60) (2–17 years)	Questionnaires—mothers, siblings	Siblings generally functioned as well as siblings of healthy children, but reported more allergies and asthma. Family cohesiveness and expressive family environment promoted better sibling adjustment. Siblings had more physical and psychological problems when child with illness had more dysfunction and mothers reported more medical problems. Severity of illness and extent of disability did not predict sibling adjustment.

(continued)

Table 2. (continued)

Author/year	Focus	Sample	Measures	Findings
Treiber, Mabe, and Wilson (1987)	Psychological adjustment of children with sickle cell disease and their healthy siblings during a non-crisis period	13 children with illness, 13 well siblings (8–17 years)	Questionnaires—children with illness, siblings	Healthy siblings, as compared to the children with illness, were found to be at increased risk for adjustment problems. Distress levels were associated with ill children's reports of problems and with maternal depression and anxiety. No differences found for depression between groups.
Menke (1987)	Impact of childhood chronic illness on school-age siblings	53 families, 72 siblings (6–12 years): cancer (20), cystic fibrosis (15), congenital heart (14), myelomeningocele (12), burns (11)	Interview—siblings	Majority of siblings expressed worries about child with illness. Siblings of children with myelomeningocele worried most. None of siblings of children with myelomeningocele and burns worried about themselves. Siblings of children with cancer and cystic fibrosis mentioned that worrying about the ill child was most difficult. For siblings of children with myelomeningocele, limitations were most difficult. Differences in worry depended on age and diagnosis (prognosis and limitations).
Cadman, Boyle, and Offord (1988)	Associated health problems and mental health of siblings of children with chronic illness	General population survey of 3,294 children in Ontario (4–16 years): disability (3.7%), no disability (14%),	Questionnaire—mother, child with illness, sibling, teacher	Siblings of children with illness had a twofold risk of emotional disorders (anxiety, depression, obsessive-compulsive disorders) and a 60% increase in poor peer relationships compared to siblings of well children.

			healthy (82.3%)	Study found no increased risk of conduct disorders, somatization, attention deficit hyperactivity, social isolation, or low competence in activities and school. No difference was found in associations of sibling problems between children with chronic illness and disabilities and those with chronic illness but no associated disabilities
Wood, Boyle, Watkins, Nogueira, Zimand, and Carroll (1988)		Relationship between disease type and disease activity and psychosocial adjustment of siblings	Well siblings of children with Crohn's disease (CD) (41), ulcerative colitis (UC) (24) (6–17 years)	Questionnaire—parents	CD siblings had more psychological disorder than UC siblings, independent of disease acuity. As a group, siblings of the sickest CD patients displayed more "internalizing behaviors," whereas siblings of the healthiest CD patients displayed more "externalizing" behaviors. UC siblings, who were psychologically healthier, displayed more "externalizing" behaviors regardless of disease activity.
Tritt and Esses (1988)		Behavioral and emotional adjustment of siblings	Well siblings of children with diabetes (11), juvenile rheumatoid arthritis (10), gastrointestinal disorders (6), healthy children (27)	Questionnaires—parents, siblings; interview—siblings	Siblings of children with illness had greater incidence of withdrawal and shyness than controls. Self-concept did not differ.

(Breslau, 1982; Tritt & Esses, 1988) or intrafamily processes (Crain et al., 1966) as organizing themes. As guiding frameworks, Menke (1987) and Cadman et al. (1988) explicitly referred to noncategorical "models," such as those developed by Pless and Pinkerton (1975), Rolland (1984), and Stein and Jessop (1982).

Of these 20 studies, 10 limited their samples to siblings of children with a single chronic illness in common (Crain et al., 1966; Daniels et al., 1986; Fielding et al., 1985; Gayton et al., 1977; Harder & Bowditch, 1982; Lavigne et al., 1982; Phillips et al., 1985; Treiber et al., 1987; Turk, 1964; Vance et al., 1980), and 10 drew on two or more chronic illness groups (Breslau, 1982; Breslau, 1983; Breslau et al., 1981; Cadman et al., 1988; Ferrari, 1984; Lavigne & Ryan, 1979; Menke, 1987; Taylor, 1980; Tritt & Esses, 1988; Wood et al., 1988). Nine of these studies included the child with chronic illness as part of the sample. Because of the increased emphasis on using typical children as comparison groups, 10 of the studies included such a group.

Eight studies clearly identified noncategorical illness characteristics that the researchers used to select their samples. In 1979, Lavigne and Ryan's research was the first of these studies to select a multidisease sample based on illness characteristics such as visibility, severity, and chronicity of the illness. For sample selection, the seven other studies used these characteristics: visibility (Ferrari, 1984; Tritt & Esses, 1988), stage of illness or disease activity (Fielding et al., 1985; Treiber et al., 1987; Wood et al., 1988), illness trajectory (Menke, 1987; Tritt & Esses, 1988), and limitation of function (Cadman et al., 1988).

Of the 20 studies, most used questionnaires focusing on child and parent psychosocial functioning to collect data. Ten studies used questionnaires only (Breslau, 1983; Breslau et al., 1981; Cadman et al., 1988; Daniels et al., 1986; Fielding et al., 1985; Lavigne & Ryan, 1979; Lavigne et al., 1982; Treiber et al., 1987; Tritt & Esses, 1988; Wood et al., 1988), five used semistructured interviews only (Harder & Bowditch, 1982; Menke, 1987; Phillips et al., 1985; Taylor, 1980; Turk, 1964), four combined questionnaires and interviews (Breslau, 1982; Ferrari, 1984; Gayton et al., 1977; Vance et al., 1980), and one combined observation and questionnaires (Crain et al., 1966).

Nine of the studies collected data from both the parents and children with illness and siblings (Cadman et al., 1988; Crain et al., 1966; Daniels et al., 1986; Ferrari, 1984; Fielding et al., 1985; Gayton et al., 1977; Treiber et al., 1987; Tritt & Esses, 1988; Vance et al., 1980), eight collected data from parents only (Breslau, 1982; Breslau, 1983; Breslau et al., 1981; Lavigne & Ryan, 1979; Lavigne et al., 1982; Turk, 1964; Wood et al., 1988), and three interviewed only the siblings (Harder & Bowditch, 1982; Menke, 1987; Taylor, 1980). Four of the studies also collected data from teachers (Cadman et al., 1988; Ferrari, 1984; Fielding et al., 1985; Vance et al., 1980).

Presence or Absence of Effects of Illness on Siblings

Table 2 summarizes, in its far-right column, major findings for each study. The following summary of the findings includes: 1) the effects of chronic illness on siblings, and 2) noncategorical characteristics related to sibling adjustment.

Each study was reviewed to identify the presence or absence of effects of chronic illness on siblings. Of the 10 single-illness studies, 8 reported little evidence of major effects on siblings (Crain et al., 1966; Daniels et al., 1986; Fielding et al., 1985; Gayton et al., 1977; Harder & Bowditch, 1982; Lavigne et al., 1982; Phillips et al., 1985; Vance et al., 1980). Only one study, which compared well siblings and children with sickle cell anemia in a noncrisis period (Treiber et al., 1987), found that siblings experienced greater emotional distress and behavior difficulties than the children with illnesses. While most of these studies found only minimal effects of illness on siblings, three studies reported areas of increased sibling vulnerability: poorer school performance (Lavigne et al., 1982; Vance et al., 1980), behavior problems (Turk, 1964), and decreased social confidence and self-acceptance (Vance et al., 1980). Two other studies reported that related areas of vulnerability included the mother-sibling relationship (Crain et al., 1966) and family satisfaction and adjustment (Gayton et al., 1977).

Unlike the majority of single-disease studies, all 10 of the multiple-disease studies reported selected effects on siblings. For example, eight studies reported significant disease-category differences in areas including emotional and behavioral difficulties (Breslau, 1983; Cadman et al., 1988; Ferrari, 1984; Lavigne & Ryan, 1979; Tritt & Esses, 1988; Wood et al., 1988), sibling worry (Menke, 1987), and difficulties getting along with peers (Cadman et al., 1988). However, five studies also reported no group differences in areas including self-concept (Ferrari, 1984; Tritt & Esses, 1988) and emotional and behavioral difficulties (Breslau, 1983, Cadman et al., 1988; Ferrari, 1984; Lavigne & Ryan, 1979).

Because these studies involved more than disease category, the investigators inferred that the effect of chronic illness on siblings was related to the demands of the different illnesses. For instance, Menke (1987) suggests that clear differences in sibling worry may be caused by potentially poorer prognosis (e.g., cancers) or by the severe physical limitations that the illness places on the child (e.g., mylomeningocele). Lavigne and Ryan (1979) found that siblings of patients undergoing plastic surgery demonstrated the highest irritability of all groups, perhaps because of the visibility of the child's condition. While finding few global group differences, Ferrari (1984) reported that siblings of children with diabetes were more likely to complain of somatic symptoms than were siblings of other groups; and siblings of developmentally delayed children exhibited more internalizing behaviors than did other groups. Ferrari attributes these group differences to the notion that different chronic illnesses may predispose siblings to different sorts of psychosocial adjustment problems. While Wood et al. (1988) found that siblings of patients with Crohn's disease had more problems than siblings of children with ulcerative-colitis, the difference was independent of the acuity of the illness.

Studies using multidisease categories and comparison groups also found differences between the siblings of children with chronic illness and siblings of healthy children. For instance, Cadman et al. (1988) reported increased depression, anxiety, and obsessive-compulsive behavior, and poorer peer relationships for siblings of children with chronic illness, as compared to other siblings. Breslau (1983) found that siblings of children with chronic illness exhibited more anxiety, aggression, and regressive behavior than did siblings of healthy children. Tritt and Esses (1988) found increased withdrawal and shyness in siblings of children with rheumatic illnesses, diabetes, and gastrointestinal disorders. And finally, Lavigne and Ryan (1979) found the highest irritability in siblings of children in all illness groups when compared to those of healthy children.

Of the 20 studies, 5 reported positive effects, including increased self-esteem, cooperation, and empathy (Harder & Bowditch, 1982; Taylor, 1980), increased family activities and closeness (Daniels et al., 1986; Harder & Bowditch, 1982), greater social integration in school (Daniels et al., 1986), greater prosocial behavior in school (Ferrari, 1984), and increased assertiveness and less intimidation reported by older siblings (Tritt & Esses, 1988).

Noncategorical Characteristics Related to Sibling Adjustment

Each study was also reviewed to identify the effect of noncategorical characteristics on sibling psychological adjustment to their brother or sister's chronic illness. As seen in Table 3, seven studies explicitly discussed sibling adjustment in terms of sociodemographic, family, and/or illness characteristics. Three studies related sociodemographic variables to sibling adjustment (Breslau et al., 1981; Daniels et al., 1986; Ferrari, 1984). Five studies related individual and family-functioning variables to sibling adjustment (Crain et al., 1966; Daniels et al., 1986; Ferrari, 1984; Lavigne et al., 1982; Treiber et al., 1987). And only five studies related noncategorical illness characteristics, such as severity and chronicity of illness (Breslau et al., 1981; Daniels et al., 1986; Lavigne & Ryan, 1979), degree of illness control (Lavigne et al., 1982), and amount of time elapsed since diagnosis (Ferrari, 1984), to sibling adjustment.

Because the number of studies reporting noncategorical characteristics was limited and a variety of different characteristics were used for each study,

Table 3. Relationship of characteristics to sibling adjustment

Author(s)	Related	Unrelated
Crain, Sussman, and Weil (1966)	Mother's behavior related to mother–sibling relationship.	Mother's behavior not related to sibling self-esteem and satisfaction.
Lavigne and Ryan (1979)		Severity and chronicity of illness not related to behavior.
Breslau (1981)		Type and severity of illness, and sex, age, and birth order not related to sibling psychological functioning.
Lavigne, Traisman, Marr, and Chasnoff (1982)	Increased length of illness related to decreased behavioral problems in male siblings.	Marital adjustment not related to behavioral problems. Degree of illness control not related to behavioral problems.
Ferrari (1984)	Relative youth of child at diagnosis, length of time elapsed since time of diagnosis, increased maternal social support and dyadic adjustment all related to less behavioral problems and more self-esteem in siblings.	Birth order, SES, family size, father's dyadic adjustment and social support not related to behavior problems or self-esteem in siblings.
Daniels, Miller, Billings, and Moos (1986)	Increased family cohesiveness, expressive family environment, better functioning of child with illness and mother's health related to fewer sibling-adjustment problems.	Family composition and status, severity of illness, and extent of disability not related to sibling adjustment.
Treiber, Mabe, and Wilson (1987)	More problems in the functioning of the ill child and increased maternal depression and anxiety related to more sibling problems.	

comparing the findings was difficult. However, sibling adjustment was not found to correspond to severity of illness in the studies of Breslau et al. (1981), Lavigne and Ryan (1979), or Daniels et al. (1986). In two other studies, sibling adjustment was found to improve with the passage of time since the ill child's diagnosis (Ferrari, 1984; Lavigne et al., 1982). And in another two studies, by Daniels et al. (1986) and Treiber et al. (1987), sibling adjustment was found to relate to the functioning of the child with illness and the mother's health.

AN AGENDA FOR NONCATEGORICAL RESEARCH

This review reveals that research on the effects of a child's chronic illness on siblings has primarily focused on disease categories. But while still working within these disease categories, researchers have begun to incorporate noncategorical illness characteristics in their designs. In regard to single-disease category studies, siblings were generally found to be at little risk for psychosocial adjustment problems when compared to children with illness or to other siblings. However, some of these single-disease studies identified areas of sibling vulnerability. As a result of such findings, researchers designed studies to includes multidisease categories in order to compare the effects of a child's chronic illness on siblings based on differences among disease categories. Hence, researchers then selected multidisease samples based on noncategorical illness characteristics.

With this promising trend, sibling research gained a greater understanding of the complexity and subtleties of the effects of childhood chronic illness on siblings. While only seven of the studies reviewed related noncategorical characteristics to sibling adjustment, these findings suggest that length of time since diagnosis, family communication, and the functioning of the mother and the child with illness may mediate the effects on siblings. For example, Menke (1987) specifically selected her multidisease sibling sample to obtain divergent experiences based on disease trajectory as reflected in prognosis and degree of incapacitation. Like other researchers using multidisease samples, she presented her findings using these illness characteristics to highlight differences among disease categories.

In a large survey study that included children with many different chronic illnesses, Cadman et al. (1988) sampled using three levels of physical limitation. Sibling adjustment was associated with the same variables whether the child who was ill had physical limitations or not. When the researcher compared a single category of "siblings with chronic illness problems" with physically healthy siblings, they found little evidence of increased risk for sibling maladjustment. However, they noted in siblings a trend of increased emotional, internalizing, and peer-interaction problems. Cadman et al. (1988), like Menke (1987), explicitly referred to the noncategorical characteristics to explain their sample selection and report their findings.

Over time, studies have become more methodologically sophisticated. At the same time, few researchers have employed conceptual models to guide their research questions. Future studies on sibling adjustment would be enhanced by conceptual grounding in models that include noncategorical characteristics. While using disease categories is pragmatic and useful, researchers need to capture the subtle similarities and differences in risk among disease categories by explicitly defining the samples' illness characteristics. As research in the field progresses, investigators will then be able to utilize and test available noncategorical models by relating such noncategorical characteristics to sibling adjustment.

REFERENCES

Breslau, N. (1982). Siblings of disabled children: Birth order and age-spacing effects. *Journal of Abnormal Child Psychology, 10,* 85-95.

Breslau, N. (1983). The psychological study of chronically ill and disabled children: Are healthy siblings appropriate controls? *Journal of Abnormal Child Psychology, 11,* 379-391.

Breslau, N., Weitzman, M., & Messenger, K., (1981). Psychologic functions of siblings of disabled children. *Pediatrics, 67,* 344-353.

Brett, K. (1988). Sibling response to chronic childhood disorder: Research perspectives and practice implications. *Issues in Comprehensive Pediatric Nursing, 11,* 43-57.

Cadman, D., Boyle, M., & Offord, D. (1988). The Ontario Child Health Study: Social adjustment and mental health of siblings of children with chronic health problems. *Developmental and Behavioral Pediatrics, 9*(3), 117-121.

Crain, A.L., Sussman, M.B., & Weil, W.B. (1966). Family interaction, diabetes, and sibling relationships. *International Journal of Social Psychiatry, 12,* 35-43.

Daniels, D., Miller, J.J., Billings, A.G., & Moos, R.H. (1986). Psychosocial functioning of siblings of children with rheumatic disease. *The Journal of Pediatrics, 109,* 279-383.

Drotar, D., & Crawford, P. (1985). Psychological adaptation of siblings of chronically ill children: Research and practice implications. *Developmental and Behavioral Pediatrics, 6,* 355-362.

Ferrari, M. (1984). Chronic illness: Psychological effects on siblings—I. Chronically ill boys. *Journal of Child Psychology and Psychiatry, 25,* 459-476.

Fielding, D., Moore, B., Dewey, M., Ashley, P., McKendrick, T., & Pinkerton, P. (1985). Children with end stage renal failure: Psychological effects on patients, siblings and parents. *Journal of Psychosomatic Research, 29,* 457-465.

Gayton, W.F., Friedman, S.B., Tavormina, J.F., & Tucker, F. (1977). Children with cystic fibrosis: Psychological test findings of patients, siblings, and parents. *Pediatrics, 59,* 888-894.

Harder, L., & Bowditch, B. (1982). Siblings of children with cystic fibrosis: Perceptions of the impact of the disease. *Children's Health Care, 10,* 116-120.

Jessop, D., & Stein, R. (1985). Uncertainty and its relation to the psychological and social correlates of chronic illness in children. *Social Science and Medicine, 20,* 993-999.

Knafl, K., Breitmayer, B., Gallo, A., & Zoeller, L. (1987). *How families define and manage a child's chronic illness* (Grant # NR01594). Funded by the National Center for Nursing Research, Public Health Service.

Lavigne, J.V., & Ryan, M. (1979). Psychologic adjustment of siblings of children with chronic illness. *Pediatrics, 63,* 616-627.

Lavigne, J.V., Traisman, H.S., Marr, T.J., & Chasnoff, I.J. (1982). Parental perceptions of the psychological adjustment of children with diabetes and their siblings. *Diabetes Care, 5,* 420-426.

Lobato, D., Faust, D., & Spirito, A. (1988). Examining the effects of chronic disease and disability on children's sibling relationships. *Journal of Pediatric Psychology, 13,* 389-407.

McKeever, P. (1983). Siblings of chronically ill children: A literature review with implications for research and practice. *American Journal of Orthopsychiatry, 53,* 209–218.

Menke, E.M. (1987). The impact of a child's chronic illness on school-aged siblings. *Children's Health Care, 15,* 132–140.

Phillips, S., Bohannon, W., Gayton, W., & Friedman, S. (1985). Parent interview findings regarding the impact of cystic fibrosis on families. *Journal of Developmental and Behavioral Pediatrics, 6,* 122–127.

Pless, I., & Perrin, J. (1985). Issues common to a variety of illnesses. In N. Hobbs & J. Perrin (Eds.), *Issues in the care of children with chronic illness* (pp. 41–60). San Francisco: Jossey-Bass.

Pless, I., & Pinkerton, P. (1975). *Chronic childhood disorder: Promoting patterns of adjustment.* London: Henery Kimptom.

Rolland, J. (1984). Toward a psychosocial typology of chronic and life-threatening illness. *Family Systems Medicine, 2,* 245–262.

Rose, M.H., & Thomas, R.B. (1987). *Children with chronic conditions.* New York: Grune & Stratton, Inc.

Stein, R., & Jessop, D. (1982). A noncategorical approach to chronic childhood illness. *Public Health Reports, 97,* 354–362.

Taylor, S.C. (1980). The effect of chronic childhood illness upon well siblings. *Maternal–Child Nursing Journal, 9,* 109–116.

Treiber, F., Mabe, P.A., & Wilson, G. (1987). Psychological adjustment of sickle cell children and their siblings. *Children's Health Care, 16,* 82–88.

Tritt, S.G., & Esses, L.M. (1988). Psychosocial adaptation of siblings of children with chronic medical illnesses. *American Journal of Orthopsychiatry, 58,* 211–219.

Turk, J. (1964). Impact of cystic fibrosis on family functioning. *Pediatrics, 34,* 67–71.

Vance, J.C., Fazan, L.E., Satterwhite, B., & Pless, I.B. (1980). Effects of nephrotic syndrome on the family: A controlled study. *Pediatrics, 65,* 948–955.

Wood, B., Boyle, J.T., Watkins, J.B., Nogueira, J., Zimand, E., & Carroll, L. (1988). *Developmental and Behavioral Pediatrics, 9*(2), 66–72.

CHAPTER 10

Siblings of Children with Learning Disabilities

Lily L. Dyson

A major development in special education in recent years is the belated recognition of the needs of siblings of children with disabilities. Programs to support siblings are now widely initiated (Edmundson, 1985) and networking systems for siblings are quickly being established (Powell & Gallagher, 1993). Parallel to these movements are increasing research efforts to study the effect of a child's disability on sibling relationships.

However, as demonstrated by other reviews in this volume and elsewhere, sibling research has been concentrated on clearly visible disabilities such as severe mental retardation, physical and sensory impairments (e.g., Dyson, 1989; Dyson & Fewell, 1989; Gamble, 1985; Gath, 1972; Gath & Gumley, 1987; Lobato, Barbour, Hall, & Miller, 1987), and chronic illness (Ferrari, 1984, 1987). Siblings of children with learning disabilities, a less visible condition, have been largely ignored.

About 4.5% of school-age children in the United States (Kirk & Gallagher, 1989) and Canada (Canada, Council of Ministers of Education, 1983) are identified as having learning disabilities. Individuals with learning disabilities make up one of the largest groups among the population of persons with disabilities (Mercer, 1986). Canadian statistics suggest that learning disability is the most prevalent disability among school-age children in that country (Canada, Council of Ministers of Education, 1983). It is probable, therefore, that the developmental consequences of learning disabilities are felt by a large number of siblings. This chapter addresses the effects of a learning disability on the child and his or her family, with a particular focus on ramifications for siblings. Major issues, such as learning disability as a developmental problem, are discussed; literature reviews are summarized; and directions for future research are suggested.

LEARNING DISABILITIES AS DEVELOPMENTAL PROBLEMS

The main characteristic of learning disability is significant difficulty in some area of listening, speaking, reading, writing, reasoning, or mathematical operation (Hamill, Leigh, McNutt, & Larsen, 1981). These conditions typically result in underachievement in academic work (Winzer, 1990) with secondary problems in social and emotional development (Mercer, 1986). Academic underachievement is often compounded by excessive motor activity or attention deficits (Mercer, 1986; Santrock & Yussen, 1990). Perhaps what most distinguishes learning disabilities from other disabilities is their invisible and seemingly benign character. A learning disability is present in a normally developing child with a normal range of intelligence (Reid, 1988). The disability is not readily discernible and has come to be viewed as a "hidden handicap" (Faerstein, 1981; O'Hara & Levy, 1984; Pfeiffer, Gerber, & Reiff, 1985). Moreover, as a primarily academic problem, learning disabilities are often not manifested until the school years.

A learning disability results in the need for special education and services, and is among the conditions being served under PL 94-142 in the United States. The special conditions inherent in learning disabilities also generate special problems for the child and his or her family, including siblings.

Effects on the Child

Learning disabilities involve a host of problems, among them a delay in diagnosis (Faerstein, 1981; O'Hara & Levy, 1984; Pfeiffer et al., 1985). It is estimated that an average lapse of 3.5 years occurs between the time of suspicion and diagnosis of the learning disability (Faerstein, 1986). Such delay in diagnosis results in delayed professional assistance. A hidden disability may also lead to normal social expectations for behavior and performance that are beyond the child's ability. Yet social tolerance and acceptance accorded to children with more visible disabilities may not be forthcoming for children with a learning disability (O'Hara & Levy, 1988). "Not looking handicapped has some pitfalls for these children in terms of other people's expectancies and frequently unrealistic demands" (Berman, 1979, p. 245). Research on chronic illness has shown that poorer child and family outcomes occurred when a child with a disability appeared to be typical (Jessup & Stein, 1985).

A large body of research has documented the consequences of learning disabilities for the child, including major problems in the areas of self-concept, social competence, and academic achievement.

Self-Concept Self-concept refers to "the description a person attaches to himself or herself" (Beane & Lipka, 1986, p. 5). Self-concept is an important determinant of behavior (Harvey & Greenway, 1984) and a primary organizer of personality (Coopersmith, 1967). Many factors can contribute to the development of a negative self-concept in children with learning disabilities, including academic failure and the resulting negative feedback at school; labeling, and the self-fulfilling prophecies that may result; and enrollment in a special education program, which deepens the child's sense of being different from others (Grolnick & Ryan, 1990). A negative self-concept could also derive from a child's realization that he or she is less capable than peers (Carroll, Friedrich, & Hund, 1984). Despite some conflicting findings, an overwhelmingly large body of research has found a lower self-concept in children with learning disabilities than in normally achieving peers (Carroll et al., 1984; Chapman, 1988; DeFrancesco & Taylor, 1985; Grolnick & Ryan, 1990; Hiebert, Wong, & Hunter, 1982; Margalit, Raviv, & Pahn-Steinmetz, 1988; Margalit & Zak, 1984; Rogers & Saklofske, 1985). Self-concept was found to be especially negative in the areas of cognitive competence (Heibert et al., 1982) and academic self-regulation (Grolnick & Ryan, 1990).

Social Competence and Behavior Adjustment Learning disability is often accompanied by hyperactivity, behavior problems, and emotional complications (Winzer, 1990). These characteristics may affect interactions with peers and result in social rejection (Margalit & Zak, 1984). Studies have also shown that children with learning disabilities manifest higher levels of anxiety (Margalit & Raviv, 1984); this was found to be especially true of children enrolled in part-time special education programs (Stein & Hoover, 1989). One alarming report stated that 35.8% of children ages 8–11 with learning disabilities had displayed symptoms of childhood depression (Wright-Strawderman & Watson, 1992). Although there are conflicting reports, children with learning disabilities have also been found to display not only more acting-out behavior problems, but also more shy-anxious behaviors than normally achieving students (Grolnick & Ryan, 1990). Teachers rated children with learning disabilities as being less socially competent (Grolnick & Ryan, 1990). These children may also be lacking in certain social-cognitive areas (Pearl, 1987).

Lack of social competence may result in less satisfactory social relations (Pearl, 1987) and may place children at risk for poor interpersonal relationships (Carlson, 1987). A large number of studies have found children with learning disabilities to have a lower social rating than normally achieving peers (Bryan, 1974; Gresham & Reschly, 1986; Priel & Leshem, 1990; Stone & La Greca, 1990). These children were commonly found to be less accepted though not more rejected, by peers. Stone and La Greca (1990), however, found these children over-represented in the rejected and neglected sociometric groups and under-represented in the popular and average groups. It must be noted, however, that not all children with learning disabilities have a low social status or are rejected by peers (Dudley-Marling & Edmiaston, 1985). Nonetheless, no studies have found children with learning disabilities to be more socially accepted than their normally achieving peers (La Greca & Stone, 1990).

Academic Underachievement Learning disabilities are also characterized by problems in cognitive areas; academic underachievement is the main distinguishing feature of children with these types of disabilities (La Greca & Stone, 1990; Winzer, 1990). When first- and second-grade children with learning disabilities were compared with normally achieving peers, significant differences were found, with children with learning disabilities scoring lower in reading comprehension and mathematics (Priel & Leshem, 1990). Third- through sixth-grade children with learning disabilities were rated by their teachers as having more learning problems than even their low-achieving normally developing peers (Grolnick & Ryan, 1990). Academic difficulties lead to frustration for the children and may generalize into a negative view of their own overall academic ability (Hiebert et al., 1982). Compounding the problem is the fact that parents and teachers have been found to hold lower academic expectations for adolescents with learning disabilities (Hiebert et al., 1982), which may have further negative effects on the academic achievement of these children (Priel & Leshem, 1990).

Effects on the Family

Specific stresses caused by a learning disability will affect the parents and permeate the family (Kaslow & Cooper, 1978; Pfeiffer et al., 1985). Parental stresses and adverse reactions to the child are posited to arise mainly from the invisibility of the disability and its sequelae. Ambiguous and conflicting diagnoses are common (Abrams & Kaslow, 1976; Kaslow & Cooper, 1978). Because the child's appearance does not reflect the disability, parents may deny its existence (Faerstein, 1981; Kaslow & Cooper, 1978), continuing to hold unrealistic expectations for academic and behavioral performance (Berman, 1979). Likewise, the delay in diagnosis is accompanied by ambivalence and uncertainty about the child's difficulty (Kaslow & Cooper, 1978). Delays in obtaining professional support mean that parents must deal with the child's behavior or emotional problems alone (O'Hara & Levy, 1984).

Parents often react to the above dilemma with frustration, guilt, uneasiness, and anxiety (Pfeiffer et al., 1985). These parental reactions and psychological states may continue indefinitely resulting in "chronic disappointment" (Willner & Crane, 1979). Chronic sorrow, much like that experienced by parents of individuals with mental retardation, may also be experienced by the parents of children with learning disability (O'Hara & Levy, 1988). Parental strain (Waggoner & Wilgosh, 1990), marital discord, and maternal depression may ensue (Kaslow & Cooper, 1978). Learning disabilities, therefore, have a profound negative impact on family dynamics (Abrams & Kaslow, 1976; Waggoner & Wilgosh, 1990).

Although one study found that parents of children with learning disabilities were no more anxious than parents of normally achieving children (Hiebert et al., 1982), there is also evidence of parental stress in the homes of children with learning disabilities. Mothers of boys with learning disabilities were found to be more anxious than mothers of control children (Margalit & Heiman, 1986). The family environment for a child with a learning disability is also unique in other ways. For instance, as perceived by the parents, the family environments of children with learning disabilities were more rigid, controlled, and ordered, with greater emphasis on personal growth but less tolerance for free expression than those of normally achieving children (Margalit & Heiman, 1986). These parental stresses and family characteristics are similar to those found among families of children with more visible disabilities (Dyson, 1991; Wikler, Wasow, & Hatfield, 1981).

Families of children with learning disabilities were rated as being less emotionally stable than families of normally achieving children (Owen, Adams, Forrest, Stolz, & Fisher, 1971). This is an attribute not reported for families of children with more visible disabilities. The unique family dynamics of children with learning disabilities are particularly illuminated by the finding that, in contrast to these families, families of children with mental retardation had lower expectations for personal growth and achievement (Margalit & Raviv, 1983). Maladaptive coping behaviors have also been reported in families of children with a learning disability (Pfeiffer et al., 1985).

It is clear that learning disabilities generate problems and needs for a child that are different from those associated with normal development or with other kinds of disabilities. Learning disabilities thus can be expected to have an impact on the siblings that may not only be different from that of normal development but that may also be both similar to and dissimilar from more visible conditions such as mental retardation and physical disability. In the first extensive literature review of family adaptation to learning disability, O'Hara and Levy (1988) proposed that family coping with learning disabilities has much in common with coping with other disabilities. For example, both types of families may share disappointment at the initial diagnosis and with their child's inability to live up to age-appropriate expectations. Parents may also progress through similar stages of adjustment to their children's disabilities. Moreover, both groups may experience common stresses at various points in the lifecycles of the children. But certain consequences may also be unique to siblings of children with learning disabilities.

SPECIAL PROBLEMS FOR SIBLINGS OF CHILDREN WITH LEARNING DISABILITIES

Studies of the general sibling population (Dunn, 1983; 1988; Stocker, Dunn, & Plomin, 1989) and special groups of siblings of persons with disabilities

(Dyson, Edgar, & Crnic, 1989) suggest that sibling effects may derive from both indirect and direct sources. The primary indirect source is parental mediation and the direct source is the sibling relationship itself. A child's learning disability may also affect a sibling through other pathways.

Family Mediation

Sibling effect is rarely independent of other family factors (Dunn, 1988). In the presence of a learning disability, siblings may be particularly influenced through parental adjustment. The family systems model (Munichin, 1985) would predict that parental and family stresses would reciprocally influence the siblings.

What special problems may siblings experience, then? In the absence of data, sibling problems associated with learning disabilities need to be inferred from research on siblings of children with more severe disabilities. Literature on more visible disabilities has identified a cluster of special problems faced by the siblings, including reduced parental attention and family resources (McKeever, 1983), increased caregiving responsibilities (Schwirian, 1976), pressure to make up for the sibling's deficiency (O'Hara & Levy, 1984), and role tension (Farber, 1959). While there has been no research to confirm the presence of these problems in siblings of children with learning disability, they are consistent with practitioners' views that such siblings may experience various conditions usually associated with visible disabilities (O'Hara & Levy, 1984). Siblings of children with a learning disability may also become angry and resentful of the extra attention given to the child with a learning disability at their expense (Abram & Kaslow, 1976; Berman, 1979). Additionally, siblings may feel embarrassed by the brother or sister's learning disability (Abram & Kaslow, 1976).

The Sibling Relationship

Special sibling problems in the presence of a child's learning disability can also be directly generated through the sibling relationship. Because of the intimacy of their relationship, siblings can affect each other in many domains (Sutton-Smith & Rosenberg, 1970), including intelligence (Zojonc, 1976) and affective and attitudinal development (Dunn & Munn, 1986; Sutton-Smith & Rosenberg, 1970). Research has linked siblingship and family size to the presence of learning disabilities (Melekian, 1990). Strong correlations were also found between children with a learning disability and their siblings in certain areas of verbal intelligence such as comprehension and the ability to discover similarities (Owen et al., 1971). Furthermore, higher correlations between sibling pairs were found on the Performance IQ scores of the Wechsler Intelligence Scale for Children (Wechsler, 1949) for sibling pairs with one member with a learning disability than for typical pairs (Owen et al.,

1971). Such evidence suggests that similarities between siblings in the presence of a learning disability may be greater than in the absence of the disorder. Developmental characteristics that are prominent in children with a learning disability, such as deficiencies in self-concept, social competence, and cognitive skills, thus may also be shared by their siblings.

REVIEW OF LITERATURE

No empirical study has yet examined the effect of a child's learning disability on the social and cognitive development of his or her siblings. However, as suggested by other chapters in this volume (e.g., Boyce & Barnett, chap. 15; Gallo & Knafl, chap. 9; Gamble, chap. 13; Howe, chap. 8; Lobato, chap. 4) and in the past literature (e.g., Breslau, Weitzman, & Messenger, 1981; Ferrari, 1987; Gamble & McHale, 1989; Lavigne & Ryan, 1979; Lobato et al., 1987), most studies of siblings of children with more visible disabilities have confirmed the potentially adverse effects of sibling experience in the presence of a child's visible disability, although a full range of effects have been noted.

To date there have been only two research reports on siblings of children with a learning disability. Richey and Ysseldyke (1983) investigated teachers' attitudes toward siblings of children with a learning disability. One group of elementary school teachers rated the expected performance of students whose siblings were taught by them previously. Another group of teachers rated the *hypothetical* younger siblings of students with a learning disability whom they were currently teaching. The results showed that in both the real and hypothetical conditions, teachers consistently rated siblings of children with a learning disability as performing less well in general academic, memory, and visual-perceptual skills than siblings of normally achieving children. Teachers further expected that the siblings of children with a learning disability would not only make less progress during the school year, but would require more support services.

In their study of familial etiology of learning disability, Owen et al. (1971) found that children with a learning disability and their siblings were significantly poorer in school behavior and adjustment and more deficient in arithmetic, handwriting, and other cognitive skills than normally achieving sibling pairs.

No direct measure of siblings of children with a learning disability was made in the study by Richey and Ysseldyke (1983) and the research focus of Owen et al. (1971) was not the siblings' adjustment. However, the results from these reports have significant implications. They lend support to the inference from research on siblings of children with visible disabilities that siblings of children with a learning disability may be at risk for social, cognitive, and academic difficulty.

In summary, through indirect parental mediation and direct sibling relationship, a learning disability in a child generates special problems that may have a negative impact on the normally achieving siblings. Theoretical predictions and indirect evidence would lead to the hypothesis that children may experience problems similar to those of their brother or sister with a learning disability. The need for study of children in the presence of a sibling's learning disability is clear.

FUTURE RESEARCH DIRECTIONS

What research directions need to be taken in the future? There are several important considerations.

A Theoretical Framework

The importance of a theoretical framework to lead educational and psychological investigation needs no more justification. As Boyce and Barnett point out (chap. 7, this volume) the adoption of theoretical models from other fields has stimulated research designs for studying siblings of children with mental retardation. A variety of theoretical frameworks have served such functions, the most common being the social-ecological model (Bronfenbrenner, 1979), family systems theory (Munichin, 1985), and the model of family stress and coping (Crnic, Friedrich, & Greenberg, 1983; Gamble & McHale, 1989). Research on siblings of children with learning disability would also benefit from a sound theoretical perspective.

The family systems theory has been utilized for conceptualizing the stress of families that include a child with a learning disability and for providing family intervention (Abrams & Kaslow, 1976; Pfeiffer et al., 1985). This theory would have much to contribute to the understanding of sibling adjustment within the home setting. However, because of the significant role of academic performance in the adjustment of children with learning disabilities, the school environment may also influence a sibling's development. A broader theoretical model such as the ecological model would generate a more comprehensive perspective on the impact of learning disability on siblings. This model views child development as the result of the interaction between the child and the surrounding ecological systems, which include those outside the home. Such a theoretical perspective would allow researchers to examine the development of siblings of children with a learning disability not only in the home, but also in the school context. The two social environments may further interact to affect a sibling's development in the presence of a child's learning disability. Studies of siblings of children with learning disabilities need to begin with a sound theoretical model that takes into consideration the influence of both the home and the school environment, individually or in interaction.

Adjustment of the Siblings

No study has directly examined the adjustment of siblings of children with learning disabilities, although there are reasons to believe that siblings of children with a learning disability may be at risk for unsatisfactory development. It is, therefore, essential to determine the impact of learning disabilities on a sibling. Caution is required, however, because potentially harmful family conditions associated with the presence of a learning disability in a child might tempt a researcher to focus solely on the negative sibling effect of learning disability. Efforts must be made to also identify any positive consequences of learning disabilities on siblings.

Positive effects of living with a sibling with a learning disability are likely, in view of research findings on more visible disabilities. This body of research reports that children encountered specific problems but also benefited from the experience of growing up with a sibling with mental retardation (Grossman, 1972) and that siblings of children with more visible developmental disabilities fared as well in self-concept and social competence as did siblings of children without disabilities (Dyson, 1989). Identification of a range of reactions, negative as well as positive, to life with a sibling with a learning disability would facilitate understanding of the differential sibling reactions to learning disabilities. The possibility of personal gains for children in a family with a child with a learning disability is indicated by one mother's remark that, "The kids have gotten values in a lot of ways well beyond their years . . . " (Waggoner & Wilgosh, 1990, p. 98).

Mediating Factors

Studies involving more visible disabilities have not found uniform results of a sibling's condition (Dyson, 1989). A critical issue thus arises regarding factors contributing to the intra-group variability. On the basis of studies of children with a variety of developmental disabilities, a range of mediating factors for the adjustment of siblings have been proposed (Lobato, Faust, & Spirito, 1988; Simeonsson & McHale, 1981) and found (Dyson, 1989; Dyson et al., 1989). Such factors include both demographic and psychological characteristics of the child with a disability, the sibling, and the family. Similar personal and psychological attributes may also influence the effect of learning disabilities on a sibling's adjustment.

As reviewed by Boyce and Barnett (chap. 7, this volume) and elsewhere (Lobato, 1983; Lobato et al., 1987), common demographic factors that may influence children's adjustment in the presence of a sibling with a visible disability are age, gender, birth order, and family socioeconomic status (SES), and, most commonly, an interaction of these factors. Older sisters were most vulnerable (Breslau, 1982; Gath, 1973), especially in families of lower SES (Farber, 1959; Grossman, 1972). Equally at risk are younger brothers (Lavigne & Ryan, 1979). Preschool children, by the nature of their cognitive and social limitations, are also likely to experience adjustment difficulty (Lobato et al., 1987). As age, gender, and, perhaps, birth order (Zajonc, 1976) are also important developmental variables, these factors must be taken into account in the study of siblings of children with learning disabilities.

Even more clinically useful than demographic factors are psychological attributes that may influence the development of siblings of children with a learning disability. Drawn from the ecological model of human development (Bronfenbrenner, 1979), such psychological variables would exist in the child's microsystem, most intimately consisting of his or her immediate family and the school personnel. The psychosocial environment of the family and the school may be of utmost importance to a sibling's adjustment in the presence of a child's learning disability.

The importance of family context to a child's development is well recognized, and researchers have called for understanding child development within the family context (Belsky, 1984; Crnic & Greenberg, 1987). As reviewed earlier, the family context involving a child with a learning disability has been reported to be different from that of normally achieving children and of children with visible disabilities (Margalit & Raviv, 1983). While studies have not examined the effect on the siblings of the distinct family conditions associated with a child's learning disability, many researchers and clinicians have linked family communication and interaction to learning disability. (Green, 1990; Kaslow & Cooper, 1978). The family's psychological environment may well influence a sibling's reaction. Future research, therefore, must explore the mediating factors present in the family psychological domain. Specific family factors that may exert an effect on a sibling are parental stress and family social environment. These aspects of family life have been found to be related to the adjustment of siblings of children with more visible disabilities (Dyson et al., 1989). Another factor mediating a sibling's development may be the functioning of the child with a learning disability since it is likely that the relationship between siblings is reciprocal.

Still another factor influencing a sibling's adjustment is the time when the diagnosis of the learning disability was made, a factor that was thought to influence parental reactions (Faerstein, 1981; O'Hara & Levy, 1984). A study of chronic illness further found that earlier diagnosis was associated with fewer behavior problems and a higher self-concept in the siblings (Ferrari, 1984).

Lastly, the school environment may also have an impact on a child's response to a sibling's learning disability. In his conceptual model of the sibling's social ecology, Howe (chap. 8, this volume) includes teachers as elements of the linkages to the sibling's adjustment in the presence of a child's chronic illness. The psychological impact that may derive from the school's social environment is especially not to be neglected in view of the finding cited earlier that teachers held lower expectations for siblings of children with learning disabilities (Richey & Ysseldyke, 1983). The lower achievement expectation may well result in lowered school performance by the siblings because of their awareness of teachers' lower expectations and the associated negative connotations. An undesirable self-concept may result (Richey & Ysseldyke, 1983).

Stress and Coping

The mere presence and necessary care of a child with a disability causes stress for the siblings (Dyson, 1989; McKeever, 1983). Major studies, however, have failed to find uniformly negative sibling outcomes. While positive outcomes of sibling experience involving a disability may be attributable to external mediating factors, as discussed earlier, and as illustrated by Barnett (chap. 15, this volume), an internal, psychological variable such as coping with stress may also be a contributing factor. This possibility has been supported by a recent study of siblings of children with more visible disabilities (Gamble & McHale, 1989). This study found that in the presence of a child with disabilities, siblings did not experience greater daily hassles, but did react to them differently than siblings of normally achieving brothers or sisters. In coping with conflict with the brother or sister with a disability, siblings also utilized "others-directed cognitions" more frequently than their comparison peers. Examples of "others-directed" cognitions were such behavior as thinking one's brother "a creep" and "wondering why a sister has to act that way" (Gamble & McHale, 1989, p. 369). Of greater concern, the style of coping was related to aspects of the siblings' psychological development, such as anxiety and feelings of depression. Is the same process experienced by the siblings of children with learning disabilities? Research into this question would enhance understanding of the process of stress and coping for these children.

A Lifecycle View of Sibling Adjustment

A lifecycle perspective holds that an individual's development changes over various stages of life in response to concomitant biological and social change (Erikson, 1963). Along with the lifecycle development of individuals, the lifecycle of the family in the presence of a child's visible and severe disability has also been supposed to signal differential family needs and, hence, diverse family developmental features over the stages of the lifecycle of family members (Turnbull & Turnbull, 1990). O'Hara and Levy (1988) further proposed a lifecycle framework for understanding the adjustment of parents in the presence of a learning disability in a child. As each stage of the lifecycle involves distinct parental developmental patterns and needs, the siblings would be affected as well. Parallel to changes in parental development, there are special problems that confront siblings at various stages of the lifecycle (O'Hara & Levy, 1988). The lifecycle model appears to be a useful approach for detailing sibling needs and changes over the course of major developmental stages.

Problems in Research on Siblings of Children with Learning Disabilities

As an unexplored area, research on siblings of children with learning disabilities would entail special methodological problems. While the field would have much to draw on from the more advanced stages of research involving more visible disabilities, several problems remain that may present obstacles and would require special research consideration.

The first problem confronting researchers would be the diagnosis and identification of learning disabilities. This disorder is manifested in disparate attributes, resulting in a lack of professional consensus on the definition of learning disabilities (Mercer, 1986). This mere fact speaks to the complexity of identifying this disability. Although a level of consensus has been reached with what appears to be an acceptable definition being provided by the National Joint Committee for Learning Disabilities, the agreement does not necessarily prevail in practice (Oliver, Cole, & Hollingsworth, 1991). States also vary in their definition of learning disability (Sprinthall & Sprinthall, 1990). Compounding this problem is the trend toward classifying students with mild mental retardation as having a learning disability, for fear of due-process litigation (Sprinthall & Sprinthall, 1990). This last problem alone has resulted in a 141% increase in the number of children identified as learning disabled from 1976 to 1988 (Sprinthall & Sprinthall, 1990). It goes without saying that these practices result in the inclusion of children who do not fit the definition. The consequence for research on siblings of children with learning disabilities may be the cataloguing of effects associated with conditions other than learning disability.

Furthermore, any observed effect of a sibling relationship involving a learning disability may be confounded by the presence of learning disabilities in both siblings. A familial basis of learning disability is suspected (Melekian, 1990; Owen et al., 1971), especially where there is the presence of central nervous system dysfunction (Oliver et al., 1991) or great discrepancies in aspects of intellectual ability (Owen et al., 1971). Familial causes, however, may be both hereditary and environmental (Oliver et al., 1991). Environmental correlates of learning disabilities are found to include low SES, education level of parents (Melekian, 1990; Oliver et al., 1991) and low birth order (Melekian, 1990). The hereditary and environmental causes of learning disabilities may both contribute to the development of the siblings. This is especially of concern in view of the finding of concordance of sibling pairs in intelligence scores, as reviewed earlier. Thus, sibling developmental characteristics observed in research may not be the result of the effects of the learning disabilities on the sibling relationship. Rather, the characteristics may have been the results of both hereditary and environmental conditions that have also contributed to the learning disability itself.

The diagnostic and etiological problems mentioned above may pose major methodological problems when a study aims to evaluate the effect of sibling relationship. A careful research design, therefore, is needed—one that will rule out rival hypotheses associated with the effects of inherent familial factors. Such a design should begin with a clear definition of learning disabilities for the identification of children and their siblings for study. Equally important, the study would need to control for the possible influence of an adverse home environment, which may have contributed to unsatisfactory development of not only the child with a learning disability but the siblings as well. Selection of family conditions that exclude the effect of poverty would be needed. These cautions should be followed with careful interpretations of the results regarding the effect of learning disability on a sibling's development.

CONCLUDING COMMENTS

A family environment that includes a child with learning disabilities will be characterized by a special, and potentially negative, social climate. Such a family environment would likely create sibling needs that are not only different from those commonly experienced by children at large but also different from those felt by children with siblings with more visible disabilities. Some siblings of children with learning disabilities may indeed require intervention. A more compelling reason for understanding siblings is to aid in prevention (O'Hara & Levy, 1984). This is because a healthy sibling would not only be able to help the child with learning disabilities, but also may him- or herself be at risk for deviant development. While studies involving more apparent disabling conditions have shown that having a sibling with a disability does not necessarily lead to deviant child outcomes (Dyson, 1989), preventing a child from maladjustment in a home containing a sibling with learning disabilities calls for special efforts. Preventive measures, however, would not be effective and adequate without knowledge of the sibling relationships involving a learning disability.

Research on siblings of children with learning disabilities represents a largely untapped field with great challenges awaiting researchers. In view of the possibly large number of siblings who may be affected by the presence of a learning disability in their brother or sister, there is an urgent need to study these siblings. It is ever more critical to explore psychological factors that may protect children from the potentially negative consequence of learning disabilities present in their siblings. Researchers studying siblings with learning disabilities have much to gain from studies involving more visible disabilities. Careful consideration of various facets of research, from the conceptual framework to the process of coping with sibling-related stress, would generate a sound study. Likewise, caution is required in observing potential research pitfalls arising from the nature of learning disability.

REFERENCES

Abrams, J., & Kaslow, F.W. (1976). Learning disability and family dynamics: A mutual interaction. *Journal of Clinical Child Psychology, 5,* 35–39.
Beane, J.A., & Lipka, R.P. (1986). *Self-concept, self-esteem and the curriculum.* New York: Columbia University.
Belsky, J. (1984). The determinants of parenting: A process model. *Child Development, 55,* 83–96.
Berman, A. (1979). Parenting learning-disabled children. *Journal of Clinical Child Psychology,* Fall, 245–249.
Breslau, N. (1982). Siblings of disabled children: Birth order and age-spacing effects. *Journal of Abnormal Child Psychology, 10,* 85–96.
Breslau, N., Weitzman, M., & Messenger, K. (1981). Psychologic functioning of siblings of disabled children. *Pediatrics, 67,* 344–353.
Bronfenbrenner, U. (1979). *The ecology of human development: Experiments by nature and design.* Cambridge, MA: Harvard University Press.
Bryan, T.H. (1974). Peer popularity of learning disabled children. *Journal of Learning Disability, 7,* 621–625.
Canada, Council of Ministers of Education. (1983). *Survey of special education in Canada, 1982–83.* Winnipeg: Canada Research and Council of Ministers of Education, Canada.
Carlson, C.I. (1987). Social interaction goals and strategies of children with learning disabilities. *Journal of Learning Disabilities, 20,* 305–311.
Carroll, J.L., Friedrich, D., & Hund, J. (1984). Academic self-concept and teachers' perceptions of normal, mentally retarded, and learning disabled elementary students. *Psychology in the Schools, 21,* 343–348.
Chapman, J.W. (1988). Cognitive-motivational characteristics and academic achievement of learning disabled children: A longitudinal study. *Journal of Educational Psychology, 80*(3), 357–365.
Coopersmith, S. (1967). *The antecedents of self-esteem.* San Francisco: N.H. Freeman.
Crnic, K.A., Friedrich, W.N., & Greenberg, M.T. (1983). Adaptation of families with mentally retarded children: A model of stress, coping, and family ecology. *American Journal of Mental Deficiency, 88*(2), 125–138.
Crnic, K.A., & Greenberg, M.T. (1987). Transactional relationships between perceived family style, risk status, and mother–child interactions in two-year-olds. *Journal of Pediatric Psychology, 12*(3), 343–362.
DeFrancesco, J.J., & Taylor, J. (1985). Dimensions of self-concept in primary and middle school learning disabled and nondisabled students. *Child Study Journal, 15,* 99–105.
Dudley-Marling, C.C., & Edmiaston, R. (1985). Social status of learning disabled children and adolescents: A review. *Learning Disability Quarterly, 8,* 189–204.
Dunn, J. (1983). Sibling relationships in early childhood. *Child Development, 54,* 787–811.
Dunn, J. (1988). Sibling influences on childhood development. *Journal of Child Psychology & Psychiatry, 29*(2), 119–127.
Dunn, J., & Munn, P. (1986). Siblings and the development of prosocial behavior. *International Journal of Behavioral Development, 9,* 265–284.
Dyson, L. (1989). Adjustment of siblings of handicapped children: A comparison. *Journal of Pediatric Psychology, 14*(2), 215–229.

Dyson, L. (1991). Families of young children with handicaps: Parental stress and family functioning. *American Journal on Mental Retardation, 95*(6), 623–629.

Dyson, L., Edgar, E., & Crnic, K. (1989). Psychological predictors of adjustment by siblings of developmentally disabled children. *American Journal on Mental Retardation, 94*(3), 292–302.

Dyson, L., & Fewell, R.F. (1989). A comparison of the self-concept of siblings of handicapped and nonhandicapped children. *Journal of Early Intervention, 13*(3), 230–238.

Edmundson, K. (1985). The "discovery" of siblings. *Mental Retardation, 23,* 49–51.

Erikson, E. (1963). *Childhood and society.* New York: Norton.

Faerstein, L.M. (1981). Stress and coping in families of learning disabled children: A literature review. *Journal of Learning Disabilities, 14,* 420–423.

Faerstein, L.M. (1986). Coping and defence mechanisms of mothers of learning disabled children. *Journal of Learning Disabilities, 19,* 8–11.

Farber, B. (1959). Effects of a severely retarded child on family integration. *Monographs of the Society for Research in Child Development, 24*(2, Serial No. 71).

Ferrari, M. (1984). Chronic illness: Psychological effects on siblings—I. Chronically ill boys. *Journal of Child Psychology and Psychiatry, 25,* 459–476.

Ferrari, M. (1987). The diabetic child and well sibling: Risks to well child's self-concept. *Children's Health Care, 15*(3), 141–147.

Gamble, W.C. (1985). *The experiences and coping strategies of children with handicapped and nonhandicapped siblings.* Unpublished doctoral dissertation, The Pennsylvania State University, University Park.

Gamble, W.C., & McHale, S.M. (1989). Coping with stress in sibling relationships: a comparison of children with disabled and nondisabled siblings. *Journal of Applied Developmental Psychology, 10,* 353–373.

Gath, A. (1973). Sibling reactions to mental handicap: A comparison of the brothers and sisters of mongol children. *Journal of Child Psychology and Psychiatry, 15,* 187–198.

Gath, A., & Gumley, D. (1987). Retarded children and their siblings. *Journal of Child Psychology and Psychiatry, 28*(5), 715–730.

Green, R. (1990). Family communication and children's learning disabilities: Evidence for Cole's theory of interactivity. *Journal of Learning Disabilities, 23*(3), 145–148.

Gresham, F., & Reschly, D. (1986). Social skill deficits and low peer acceptance of mainstreamed learning disabled children. *Learning Disability Quarterly, 9,* 23–32.

Grolnick, W.S., & Ryan, R.M. (1990). Self-perceptions, motivation, and adjustment in children with learning disabilities: A multiple group comparison study. *Journal of Learning Disabilities, 23*(3), 177–184.

Grossman, F.K. (1972). *Brothers and sisters of retarded children: An exploratory study.* Syracuse, NY: Syracuse University Press.

Hamill, D.D., Leigh, J.E., McNutt, G., & Larson, S.C. (1981). A new definition of learning disabilities. *Learning Disability Quarterly, 4,* 336–342.

Harvey, D.H., & Greenway, A.P. (1984). The self-concept of physically handicapped children and their non-handicapped siblings: An empirical investigation. *Journal of Child Psychology and Psychiatry, 25*(2), 273–284.

Hiebert, B., Wong, B., & Hunter, M. (1982). Affective influences on learning disabled adolescents. *Learning Disability Quarterly, 5,* 334–343.

Jessup, D., & Stein, R. (1985). Uncertainty and its relation to the psychological and social correlates of chronic illness in children. *Social Science and Medicine, 20,* 993–999.

Kaslow, F.W., & Cooper, B. (1978, January). Family therapy with the learning disabled child and his/her family. *Journal of Marriage and Family Counselling,* 41–49.

Kirk, S.A., & Gallagher, J.J. (1989). *Educating exceptional children* (6th ed.). Boston: Houghton Mifflin.

La Greca, A.M., & Stone, W.L. (1990). LD status and achievement: Confounding variables in the study of children's social status, self-esteem, and behavioral functioning. *Journal of Learning Disabilities, 23*(8), 483–490.

Lavigne, J., & Ryan, M. (1979). Psychologic adjustment of siblings of children with chronic illness. *Pediatrics, 63,* 616–626.

Lobato, D. (1983). Siblings of handicapped children: A review. *Journal of Autism and Developmental Disorders, 13*(4), 347–364.

Lobato, D., Barbour, L., Hall, L.J., & Miller, C.T. (1987). Psychosocial characteristics of preschool siblings of handicapped and nonhandicapped children. *Journal of Abnormal Child Psychology, 15*(3), 329–338.

Lobato, D., Faust, D., & Spirito, A. (1988). Examining the effects of chronic disease and disability on children's sibling relationships. *Journal of Pediatric Psychology, 13*(3), 389–407.

Margalit, M., & Heiman, T. (1986). Family climate and anxiety in families with learning disabled boys. *Journal of the American Academy of Child Psychiatry, 25*(6), 841–846.

Margalit, M., & Raviv, A. (1983). Mothers' perceptions of the family climate in families with a retarded child. *The Exceptional Child, 30*(2), 163–169.

Margalit, M., Raviv, A., & Pahn-Steinmetz, N. (1988). Social competence of learning disabled children: Cognitive and emotional aspects. *The Exceptional Child, 35*(3), 179–187.

Margalit, M., & Zak, I. (1984). Anxiety and self-concept of learning disabled children. *Journal of Learning Disabilities, 17,* 537–539.

McKeever, P. (1983). Siblings of chronically ill children: A literature review with implications for research and practice. *American Journal of Orthopsychiatry, 53,* 209–218.

Melekian, B. (1990). Family characteristics of children with dyslexia. *Journal of Learning Disabilities, 23*(6), 386–391.

Mercer, C.D. (1986). Learning disabilities. In N.G. Haring, & L. McCormick, (Eds.), *Exceptional children and youth* (4th ed.). Columbus: Charles E. Merrill.

Munichin, P. (1985). Families and individual development: Provocations from the field of family therapy. *Child Development, 56,* 289–302.

O'Hara, D.M., & Levy, J.M. (1984). Family adaptation to learning disability: A framework for understanding and treatment. *Learning Disabilities, 3*(6), 63–77.

O'Hara, D.M., & Levy, J.M. (1988). Family intervention. In K. Kavale, S. Forness, & M. Bender (Eds.), *Handbook of learning disabilities: Vol. 2. Methods and interventions.* Boston: College-Hill.

Oliver, J.M., Cole, N.H., & Hollingsworth, H. (1991). Learning disabilities as functions of familial learning problems and developmental problems. *Exceptional Children, 57*(5), 427–440.

Owen, F.W., Adams, P.A., Forrest, T., Stolz, L.M., & Fisher, S. (1971). Learning disorders in children: Sibling studies. *Monographs of the Society for Research in Child Development, 36*(4, Serial No. 144).

Pearl, R. (1987). Social cognitive factors in learning disabled children's social problems. In S.J. Ceci (Ed.), *Handbook of cognitive, social, and neuropsychological aspects of learning disabilities* (Vol. 2, pp. 273–294). Hillsdale, NJ: Lawrence Erlbaum Associates.

Pfeiffer, S.I., Gerber, P.J., & Reiff, H.B. (1985). Family-oriented intervention with the learning disabled child. *Journal of Reading, Writing, and Learning Disabilities International, 1*(4), 63–69.

Powell, T.H., & Gallagher, P.A. (1993). *Brothers and sisters: A special part of exceptional families* (2nd ed.). Baltimore: Paul H. Brookes Publishing Co.

Priel, B., & Leshem, T. (1990). Self-perceptions of first- and second-grade children with learning disabilities. *Journal of Learning Disabilities, 23*(10), 637–642.

Reid, D.K. (1988). *Teaching the learning disabled*. Needham Heights, MA: Allyn & Bacon.

Richey, L.S., & Ysseldyke, J.E. (1983). Teachers' expectations for the younger siblings of learning disabled students. *Journal of Learning Disabilities, 16*(10), 610–615.

Rogers, H., & Saklofske, D.H. (1985). Self-concepts, locus of control and performance expectations of learning disabled children. *Journal of Learning Disabilities, 18*(5), 273–278.

San Martino, M., & Newman, M.B. (1974). Siblings of the retarded: A population at risk. *Child Psychiatry and Human Development, 4*, 168–177.

Santrock, J.W., & Yussen, S.R. (1990). *Child development: An introduction* (4th ed.). Dubuque, Iowa: WCB.

Schwirian, P.M. (1976). Effects of the presence of a hearing impaired preschool child in the family on behavior patterns of older "normal" siblings. *American Annals of the Deaf, 121*, 373–380.

Simeonsson, R.J., & McHale, S.M. (1981). Reviews: Research on handicapped children: Sibling relationships. *Child Care, Health and Development, 7*, 153–171.

Sprinthall, N.A., & Sprinthall, R.C. (1990). *Educational psychology: A developmental approach* (5th ed.). New York: McGraw-Hill.

Stein, P.A., & Hoover, J.H. (1989). Manifest anxiety in children with learning disabilities. *Journal of Learning Disabilities, 22*(1), 66–71.

Stocker, C., Dunn, J., & Plomin, R. (1989). Sibling relationships: Links with child temperament, maternal behavior, and family structure. *Child Development, 60*, 715–727.

Stone, W.L., & La Greca, A.M. (1990). The social status of children with learning disabilities: A reexamination. *Journal of Learning Disabilities, 23*(1), 32–37.

Sutton-Smith, B., & Rosenberg, B.C. (1970). *The siblings*. New York: Holt, Rinehart & Winston.

Tew, B., & Laurence, K.M. (1973). Mothers, brothers, and sisters of patients with spina bifida. *Developmental Medicine and Child Neurology, 15*(Suppl. 6), 69–76.

Turnbull, A.P., & Turnbull, H.R., III. (1990). *Families, professionals, and exceptionality: A special partnership* (2nd ed.). Columbus OH: Charles E. Merrill.

Waggoner, K., & Wilgosh, L. (1990). Concerns of families of children with learning disabilities. *Journal of Learning Disabilities, 23*(2), 97–98, 113.

Wechsler, D. (1949). *Wechsler Intelligence Scale for Children: Manual*. New York: Psychological Corp.

Wikler, L., Wasow, M., & Hatfield, E. (1981). Chronic sorrow revisited: Parents vs. professional depiction of the adjustment of parents of mentally retarded children. *American Journal of Orthopsychiatry, 5*(1), 63–70.

Willner, S.K., & Crane, R. (1979). A parental dilemma: The child with a marginal handicap. *Social Casework, 60*, 30–35.

Winzer, M. (1990). *Children with exceptionalities: A Canadian perspective* (2nd ed.). Scarborough, Ontario: Prentice Hall Canada Inc.

Wright-Strawderman, C., & Watson, B.L. (1992). The prevalence of depressive symptoms in children with learning disabilities. *Journal of Learning Disabilities, 25*(4), 258–264.

Zajonc, R.B. (1976). Family configuration and intelligence. *Science, 192,* 227–236.

CHAPTER 11

Siblings of Children with Dual Diagnosis

Keith A. Crnic and Janice Lyons

Recently, there has been growing interest in dual diagnosis of children with mental retardation. Dual diagnosis is the presence of both mental retardation and psychopathology in the affected child. Although psychopathology has sometimes been considered to be a part of the constellation of problems inherent in retardation, more recent conceptualizations suggest that retardation does not necessarily include diagnosable behavioral and emotional disturbance, nor is it a sufficient condition to, by itself, cause psychopathology to occur (Matson & Frame, 1985).

As the chapters in this volume note, the sibling relationship is one of several critical relationships within the family, and as such may contribute in its own right to dual diagnosis for the child with mental retardation. The processes that may underlie sibling effects on dual diagnosis within the context of the family are the focus of this chapter. Before discussing these processes, it may be helpful to first examine the prevalence of psychopathology in children with mental retardation.

PSYCHOPATHOLOGY IN CHILDREN WITH MENTAL RETARDATION

Although retardation and psychopathology are functionally independent, there is clear evidence that children with mental retardation are at significantly greater risk for psychopathology than are children in the general population (Feinstein, Kaminer, Barrett, & Tylende, 1988; Jacobson, 1982; Matson, Barrett, & Helsel, 1988; Reiss, 1988). Reports of the prevalence of dual diagnosis vary greatly across studies and cohorts, but range from estimates of as low as 10% (Jacobson, 1982; Reiss, 1988) to as high as 100% (Webster,

1970). More typical estimates are between 20% and 40% of the population of children with mental retardation, depending on the criteria used to define psychiatric impairment and the relationship to the child of the reporters of behavioral and affective problems. Interestingly, Reiss (1988) reports that estimates of dual diagnosis are greater when more involved and knowledgeable caregivers (e.g., family members) are the source of information about psychopathology.

Children with mental retardation appear to display a range of psychopathologies when dual diagnosis is present. Jacobson (1982) reported epidemiological data from a survey of children in New York State that indicated that as many as 40% to 55% of children with mental retardation display behavior problems, with greater amounts of disturbance in children traditionally labeled as moderately or severely retarded. Minor behavior problems were most frequent, but severe cognitive, affective, and behavioral disturbances were prevalent as well.

Richardson, Koller, and Katz (1985), in a report from the classic Aberdeen studies, reported that about 60% of children with retardation showed behavior disturbance. The types of disorders found varied as a function of the severity of the retardation and the gender of the child. Hyperactive behavior was frequent among children with lower IQs, and aggressive conduct disorders were also more prevalent in children with IQs below 50. Antisocial behavior was more typical of children labeled as mildly mentally retarded. As with typically developing children, female children displayed more frequent emotional or internalizing problems than males.

Although it seems apparent that children with retardation are at greater risk for the development of significant psychiatric disturbances, the factors that cause such conditions in these children are less clear. The presence of retardation, classically defined as impaired intellectual functioning with concomitant deficits in adaptive skills, is not in itself sufficient to ensure the development of a psychopathological disorder. The likely multiple conditions under which dual diagnosis occurs are yet to be even minimally established.

FAMILY PROCESSES AND DEVELOPMENTAL PSYCHOPATHOLOGY

Despite the lack of knowledge about the conditions under which dual diagnosis occurs, and about the actual mechanisms that underlie its development, there is suggestive evidence that implicates family processes as one contributory source. For example, Richardson et al. (1985) reported that childrearing practices were related to behavior disturbances that occurred later in the lives of children with mental retardation, and that, in particular, instability in parental childrearing practices was more frequent in the sample of families with a member with mental retardation. Interestingly, when this instability was controlled, children with retardation showed no more behavior problems than did typical children. Instability in childrearing practices as a risk factor has important implications for dual diagnosis, as will be detailed later in the discussion on sibling relationships.

A number of investigators have recently suggested that families of children with mental retardation play a critical role in their children's general developmental trajectories (Blacher, Nihira, & Meyers, 1987; Crnic, Friedrich, & Greenberg, 1983; Kazak & Marvin, 1984). Certainly, there appear to be some important differences between families with children with retardation and those with typical children. Earlier studies suggested that families with children with retardation were subject to more marital problems, psychopathology in the parents, general psychosocial difficulties, and greater sibling distress, to mention just a few of the more frequently reported difficulties (Crnic et al., 1983). Often, these differences were attributed to the stresses associated with the presence of a child with mental retardation in the household (e.g., Beckman, 1983; Crnic et al., 1983) as well as the important ecological and psychosocial changes that families face as a result of having such a child. In essence, these notions tend to reflect the traditional stress-diathesis model of predicting pathological outcomes.

It is important to note from the outset that the authors do not view families as passive victims of circumstance. Quite the contrary, families with children with retardation are equally likely to function well as to function poorly, depending upon a myriad of contextual and individual factors (Crnic et al., 1983; Kazak & Marvin, 1984). There is a recent trend in the literature of focusing on the strengths and functional attributes of families with children with retardation, and this is a welcome change from the pathological emphasis of previous years. Nevertheless, it is important not to overcompensate to the degree that the "risk" status of families with children with retardation is lost amid the rush to normalize (or even glamorize) the presence of a child with retardation in the family.

Richardson et al.'s (1985) study, as well as more general reviews of family adaptations (Crnic et al., 1983; Kazak & Marvin, 1984) suggest that families may well play a critical role in the development of behavioral disturbances in children with retardation. Less clear, however, is the function of one specific family subsystem: the sibling relationship.

The focus on family processes, and sibling relationships in particular, in the prediction of psychopathology in children with retardation ignores other factors that may also contribute to the dual-diagnosis status. Biological, organic, or genetic considerations cannot be disregarded, and certainly contribute their share of the variance to psychopathological outcome. Nevertheless, there are strong suggestions from the growing empirical base on developmental psychopathology that families, and the complex interpersonal relationships that they involve, play a critical role in the development of psychopathological conditions during childhood. In the general population, family processes deeply affect the development of psychopathology during childhood. This is not to suggest that families, or any of the subsystems within families, are the sole cause of behavioral disturbances in children. Rather, there is a wealth of evidence that implicates various family contexts and processes as contributors among the complex processes involved (Martin, 1987). Sibling relationships are one critical subsystem of the family and are the focus of the present concern. It may, however, be useful to first briefly review family considerations relevant to the development of psychopathology during childhood.

The emergence of developmental psychopathology as a field (Cicchetti, 1984) has helped to focus attention on the interface between normal and atypical developmental processes. In regard to the role of families, Martin (1987) has suggested that a developmental perspective on family theory stresses the multiple and mutual influences that occur across time and result in the individual or interactional behaviors that are labeled as "symptoms." While such a conceptualization is attractive, Martin (1987) further notes that it is extremely difficult to translate into research that does justice to the concept. Nevertheless, a review of basic research on families and the development of psychopathology during childhood suggests that families in general, and sibling relationships in particular, contribute to the emergence of psychopathological conditions.

Marital Functioning

Marital functioning is one central family process that has been associated with the development of psychopathology in children (Emery, 1982). Marital discord has been associated with the development of behavior problems, especially problems involving lack of behavioral control. Cummings and his colleagues (Cummings, 1987; Cummings, Zahn-Waxler, & Radke-Yarrow, 1984) have likewise studied children's reactions to marital hostility. Not surprisingly, children often experience emotional distress following exposure to various forms of anger between their parents, and children exposed to repeated episodes of anger are the most likely to suffer negative outcomes. Boys appear more likely to respond with aggression, whereas girls may become more withdrawn or anxious. Gender is also salient in that boys seem to be more vulnerable overall to the negative effects of a discordant home.

Of particular interest, marital hostility has been found to be strongly related to agonistic behavior in both younger and older siblings (Brody, Stoneman, & Burke, 1987a). Although the mechanism underlying this relation is not yet clear, it has been hypothesized that marital discord may be indirectly associated with sibling agonistic behavior as a function of its influence on individual child functioning. As the individual child becomes distressed by the marital conflict, this distress subsequently affects his or her interactions with siblings. Conversely, marital discord might provide each child with models of conflictual problemsolving styles (Brody et al., 1987a) if conflicts are effectively resolved. Regardless, it is apparent that marital conflict is an important aspect of the family context affecting the nature of sibling relationships.

Parent–Child Interaction

Certainly, marital discord can affect parents' ability to focus their attention on parenting processes. Yet, individual characteristics of parents, such as depression or a nonaccepting attitude, can also influence parenting quality. Similarly, child characteristics, such as temperament, have an impact on the parent–child relationship. By their very nature, characteristics of both the parent and the child contribute to the future pattern of interactions.

Both positive and negative interchanges between parents and children become reciprocal (Martin, 1987). Parents who treat their children warmly are more likely to be treated warmly by their children. In addition, the friendly or unfriendly nature of parent–child interactions may generalize to sibling relationships within the family. Social learning and attachment theories provide possible explanations of the process by which relationship styles begin to characterize whole families.

Social learning theories suggest that children learn behaviors in their relationship with their parents and that these behaviors are then generalized to their interactions with others (Parke, MacDonald, Beitel, & Bhavnagri, 1988). Patterson (1982) suggests that reinforcement processes play an important role in conditioning family members to exchange aversive behaviors. His coercion theory suggests that family members train each other, through negative reinforcement processes, to increase the rates and intensity of their aversive behavior. Family members are reinforced for escalating the intensity of their attacks when the other member ceases the aversive behavior. Families that typically engage in coercive exchanges are likely to have a child who is socially aggressive (Patterson, 1982). Interestingly, in families that include a socially aggressive child, siblings reciprocate with equivalent levels of aggressive behavior toward the identified problem child (Patterson, 1984).

Attachment theory suggests that, through their early interactions with their caregivers, children develop internal working models of relationships, which become the basis for subsequent relationships (Bowlby, 1973). Children's relationships with their caregivers may determine whether they have positive or negative expectations for their relationships with their siblings and whether they are receptive to forming a relationship with a newborn sibling. It seems likely that securely attached children may be less threatened than insecurely attached children by the loss of attention following the introduction of the newborn. While various theories suggest that sibling relationships are affected by more general family patterns, specific research on parental behaviors is also informative. Parenting styles, such as Baumrind's (1967) authoritative, authoritarian, and permissive styles, are related to psychological health in children and can also influence the nature of sibling relationships. Authoritative parenting, considered the optimal parenting style for psychological health, is characterized by firm, consistent parental control in a warm, responsive context. Furman (chap. 2, this volume) has reported that mother–child relationship qualities are closely associated with sibling relationship qualities. He reports that warmth, personal closeness, and disciplinary warmth in parent–child relationships are related to warmth between siblings.

In summary, it seems apparent that general family factors are important in their own right to the development of psychopathological conditions during childhood. These family factors, however, also exert both direct and indirect influences on the nature of sibling relationships that may in turn make a further substantive contribution to problematic development.

Sibling Configurations

There has not been a wealth of research on specific sibling factors that contribute to the development of psychopathology in children. Siblings, however, are an important part of the family system, and the contribution sibling relationships may make to the development of psychopathology merits attention. Most of the research on the subject has focused on the global characteristic of birth order, with a lesser emphasis on age spacing and gender. Sibling birth-order position has not been a strong predictor of psychopathology. However, when birth order is combined with factors such as sibling spacing and gender of sibling there is some association with psychological disorders (Martin, 1987).

There is some evidence to suggest that firstborn males are more likely to have adjustment difficulties to a new sibling than are laterborn males (Fishbein, 1981; Lahey, Hammer, Crumrine, & Forehand, 1980). This relation is strengthened when the age spacing between the firstborn and the secondborn is less than 1 or more than 5 years (Kidwell, 1981). This may be explained by the child's resentment of a loss of unshared attention. It is possible that for age spacing of less than 1 year, the child essentially has always had to share parental attention, and that for periods longer than 5 years, the child has had a long period of unshared attention (Kidwell, 1981). It is unclear why males, but not females, are likely to be adversely affected by their firstborn status. Perhaps, as the literature on sex roles suggests, mothers put greater maturing demands on firstborn males than on firstborn females (Cushna, 1966).

The negative impact of birth order on middleborns has also been studied. There is some evidence to suggest that middleborns may be at greater risk of lower self-esteem if there is less than 2 years between the child and their next closest sibling (Kidwell, 1982). Middleborn children may have difficulty achieving individual recognition and a separate status within their families (Martin, 1987).

Although the bulk of the literature discusses the ways in which family processes affect sibling relationships, it is also the case that siblings and their interactions can affect parenting and family processes. Minor parenting hassles and the everyday frustrations and annoyances of childrearing are a source of stress in many parent–child relationships (Crnic & Greenberg, 1990). Problems caused by siblings and the sometimes conflictual relationships between siblings can be a particular stressor for parents. Certain family characteristics appear to increase the likelihood that parents will experience hassles as stressful. Among those relevant to sibling considerations are the number and gender of the children. Parents with more than one child tend to report more problems than do parents of only children. And parents of boys report more problems than do parents of girls. A clear relationship has been discovered between parent's report of hassles and children's behavior problems, such that parents with more childrearing problems raise children with more behavior problems (Crnic & Greenberg, 1990). These findings suggest that sibling relationships may contribute in some degree to a family context conducive to problematic development.

While there appear to be direct and indirect processes operating within sibling relationships that may facilitate behavioral difficulties, their influence is mediated by qualitative aspects of parental and family functioning. Dunn and her colleagues (Dunn, 1987, 1988; Dunn & Kendrick, 1982; Dunn & Munn, 1985) have studied parent–child relationship factors and sibling relationship outcomes longitudinally. Their findings indicated that mothers who discussed the new baby's desires and feelings with their firstborn child had children who shared a particularly friendly sibling relationship 1 year later. However, in families in which there was a sharp decline in mother–child communication following the birth of a secondborn child, and in which the older child reacted with withdrawal, the firstborn child was markedly hostile to the secondborn 1 year later (Dunn & Kendrick, 1982). Other, more perplexing findings, were also reported by Dunn & Kendrick (1982). When mothers and firstborn daughters had a high frequency of joint play both before and after the birth of the secondborn, the siblings were more likely to have a hostile relationship 14 months later. In contrast, when the mother–firstborn daughter relationship was confrontational or the mother became tired and depressed following the birth of the second child, the siblings shared a particularly friendly relationship 14 months later. Clearly, the nature of parental influences on sibling relationships is complex, and will require further study to explain these seemingly counterintuitive findings.

There appear to be multiple ways in which family processes can, both directly and indirectly, affect children and their relationship with siblings. Direct processes include ways in which parents interact with both of their children. Efforts that the parents make to reinforce their children for playing together might constitute a direct influence on the sibling relationship. Sibling relationships are also affected by a myriad of other factors that influence the family system. Parents who are depressed or are stressed by negative life events or by childrearing problems may be less responsive to their children's caregiving demands and need for nurturance. This family stress may, in turn, adversely affect the quality of the sibling relationship.

NORMAL SIBLING RELATIONSHIPS AND ADJUSTMENT

Although parents may aim to treat their children equally, research suggests that children are usually correct when they perceive differential treatment. Differences between children in age, temperament, birth order, and gender all result in parents treating children in dissimilar ways. Differential behavior may be due in part to natural variations in childcare as a result of developmental, temperamental, and gender differences among children. However, to the extent that children perceive these differences as inequities, differential treatment may constitute a threat to positive sibling relationships. Both maternal and paternal differential behaviors are associated with variations in sibling relationships (Brody, Stoneman, & McCoy, in press).

Mothers are frequently partial to the younger sibling (Dunn & Munn, 1985). Among toddlers, mothers were observed to be more affectionate with younger than with older siblings, and responded to the same behavior from older and younger siblings in different ways (Dunn & Munn, 1985). Although both siblings were equally likely to tease, start fights, and be physically aggressive, mothers tended to discipline the older sibling, but simply distract the younger sibling.

In middle childhood, the research findings on differential treatment and sibling behavioral outcomes vary. In one study, differential maternal behavior was associated with lower rates of all sibling behavior, both positive and negative (Brody, Stoneman, & Burke, 1987b). Thus, it seems that siblings may choose to avoid interaction with one another after several years of being treated differently by their mother. However, another study found differential maternal control, responsiveness, and attention to be related to competitive and conflictual sibling interactions in school-age children (Stocker, Dunn, & Plomin, 1989). Bryant and Crockenberg (1980) similarly reported that in families in which the mother was more responsive to one daughter than to the other, both sisters directed more negative behavior toward each other.

The above findings provide evidence that children are quite sensitive to inequities in their mother's behavior toward them and their sibling, and in fact seem to monitor their mother's interactions with their sibling with vigilance (Dunn, 1983). Although parents report their children's family and peer experiences to be essentially similar, the children themselves perceive that each sibling's experiences are very different (Daniels, Dunn, Furstenberg, & Plomin, 1985). Adolescents also report that their parents treat them and their siblings differently in areas such as maternal closeness and amount of say in family decisionmaking (Daniels et al., 1985; Furman & Buhrmester, 1985).

Adolescents' perception of differences in parental treatment have consistently been related to greater rivalry, conflict, and feelings of antagonism between siblings (Daniels et al., 1985; Furman & Buhrmester, 1985). Perceptions of differential treatment were also related to child adjustment. In the Daniels et al. (1985) study, the between-siblings correlation for emotional adjustment was .15. This low-magnitude relation implies that similarity between siblings may be primarily a result of genetic factors. Family environment factors appear to operate to make children different from, not similar to, one another (Daniels et al., 1985). Children who report being closer to their mother, having more say in family decisionmaking, more parental chore expectations, and a more friendly sibling relationship tend to be better-adjusted. Children who perceive their parents as treating them less favorably than their sibling have higher rates of adjustment problems (Daniels et al., 1985).

Differential behavior by parents may be related to differences between children as a function of age, temperament, birth order, or gender. As conflict develops, the conflict itself may intensify parents' struggle to treat the children differently, yet equally (Furman & Buhrmester, 1985). For example, parents may have higher expectations for the older sibling and therefore react more severely to the same conflictual behavior. These studies of normal sibling relationships within the family context provide a template for understanding more atypical contexts and the developmental processes that influence eventual competence.

SIBLINGS OF CHILDREN WITH MENTAL RETARDATION

The relationship between siblings when one child is mentally retarded has not been studied as extensively as many other facets of the lives of children with retardation. Nevertheless, there is a growing empirical base upon which a number of basic assumptions about these relationships can be made. An extensive review of this work will not be provided in this chapter, as there are several other chapters in this volume that describe these relationships in great detail (Stoneman & Brody, chap. 12, this volume). There are, however, a number of important issues to raise that bear directly on processes relevent to the development of psychopathology in children with retardation.

Direction of Effect

One important issue in sibling research on populations of persons with retardation involves the notion of "direction of effect." The majority of work to date has attempted to identify the effects of the child with retardation on the normal sibling. This basic paradigm suggests a unidirectional model of effect, and one that often assumes some negative outcome. That is, the field has been most interested in determining whether or not a child with retardation has a deleterious effect on his or her typically developing siblings. Certainly, this is an important question, yet it neglects the notion of reciprocity in relationships, as well as the likelihood that the typical sibling can influence the developmental trajectories of the child with retardation. Furthermore, the assumption of a pathological effect unfairly ignores the possible range of positive influences that may occur. It is the authors' contention that any understanding of the sibling relations between children with and without retardation must address bidirectionality of effects, assessing the full range of mutual influences that siblings have on one another.

Bidirectionality within the sibling relationship may be particularly important in regard to the development of psychopathology in children with retardation. In this respect, transactional models of developmental processes (Sameroff & Chandler, 1975) may prove enlightening. Transactional theories suggest that development is a function of an individual's biological and psychological characteristics in dynamic interaction with contextual or environmental influences over time. Furthermore, each interaction influences the nature of subsequent interactions between individuals within any context. Given that families are the primary developmental context (Bronfenbrenner, 1979), the nature of sibling interactions within families would seem to be one important transactional process influencing individual adjustment. Studies of sibling relationships in which one child has retardation indicate that these sibling pairs interact about as often as pairs of typical siblings (Stoneman, Brody, Davis, & Crapps, 1987), and the ongoing nature of these interactions is likely to influence the developmental trajectories of each.

Effects of Sibling Relations

With these considerations in mind, a number of studies suggest the possibility that sibling relationships may contribute to the development of behavioral and emotional problems in children with retardation. There is a wealth of evidence to suggest that these sibling interactions are more conflictual than are sibling interactions between typically developing children (Stoneman et al., 1987; Stoneman, Brody, Davis, & Crapps, 1988). In many cases, the greater conflict is related to various "marker" variables, or individual characteristics, such as sibling birth order, gender, or adaptive skill. For example, Stoneman et al. (1987) showed that children with retardation who had greater adaptive ability had much more positive and competent relationships with their typically developing siblings, while the opposite was true for those children with retardation who had a lower level of adaptive ability.

Interestingly, Stoneman, Brody, and their colleagues have also demonstrated that relations between children with retardation and their typical peers are characterized by greater managerial roles by the typically developing child and less compliance by the child with retardation. Stoneman et al. (1987) note that this interactive style mirrors that of parent interactions with children with retardation. In this case, direction of effect is difficult to tease apart. It may be that less-compliant children with retardation encourage greater managerial behavior by their siblings and parents. However, the possibility that more directive behavior by siblings results in less compliant behavior by children with retardation is equally plausible.

Differential treatment is likely to be an issue within these sibling relationships as well, although direct studies of such processes in families of children with retardation are not as plentiful as they are for families with only typically developing children. There is, however, evidence to suggest that parents treat their children with retardation differently than they do their other children. The parent–child-interaction literature suggests that parents are more directive and controlling with their children with retardation, as well as less affective and sensitive (Crnic et al., 1983; Stoneman et al., 1987). These differences in parental behavior toward children with and without retardation are found consistently across studies using varying methodologies, suggesting that the findings are accurate.

The effects of parental differential treatment within families in which one child has retardation are not clearly understood. Nevertheless, data from studies of normal sibling relationships clearly suggest that differential treatment is associated with greater conflict in sibling relationships and poorer behavioral and social adjustment in children (Daniels et al., 1985). Considering the evidence of differential treatment, as well as of greater sibling conflict, in sibling pairs with one member with retardation, the implications for the development of psychopathological conditions are apparent.

Perhaps it is obvious at this point that sibling relationships are best understood within the broader context of the family and its functional attributes. How well the family adjusts to daily demands and operates to resolve conflicts or problems influences the nature of sibling relationships. Conversely, sibling relationships also influence family functioning, contributing to the transactional nature of developmental processes within families. There is no direct evidence at this time to demonstrate how relationships between children with and without retardation affect the family, but a study by Stoneman, Brody, Davis, and Crapps (1989) provides some provocative suggestions. In their study of typical sibling relationships, Stoneman and her colleagues demonstrated that differences between the siblings, as indexed by differing temperamental qualities, was associated with greater marital and family stress. Furthermore, Martin's (1987) review of the relations between family functioning and child psychopathology indicates that greater marital and family stress are associated with the presence of psychopathology in children. Given that the presence of mental retardation in one child of a sibling pair provides an obvious "differentness," this condition may well contribute in some proportion to family functioning and subsequent adjustment problems for the child with retardation.

Shared and Nonshared Environments and Psychopathology

In the attempt to understand sibling relationships and their influence on individual adjustment, behavioral genetic research can provide some insights. This research has consistently indicated that siblings are much more dissimilar than similar along multiple dimensions, including personality and psychopathology (Daniels et al., 1985). As noted previously, the similarity between siblings is primarily a function of genetics, and not their shared family environment. It is common, however, to find only low-order correlations (.20) between individual personality characteristics of biological siblings (Buss & Plomin, 1984). Martin (1987) has likewise concluded that there is little evidence to suggest that siblings share conditions of psychopathology.

Schachter (1982) has proposed that *deidentification* explains some of the differences between siblings; that is, siblings may behave differently from each other as a defense against sibling rivalry. Although not in conflict with deidentification theory, proponents of behavioral genetics suggest that multiple environmental factors also operate within families, resulting in differences between siblings. These within-family influences involve nonshared experiences, although behavioral genetic studies do not typically delineate the specific nature of the nonshared experience. The focus of this research model is to delineate the variance that may be attributed to genetic and environmental components, while subdividing environmental influences into their shared and nonshared components.

Given the presence of retardation in one child within a family, it is likely that nonshared influences on siblings increase. There is ample evidence to suggest that parents behave differently toward their children with retardation, and perhaps these children are provided fewer opportunities for varied experiences because parents are overprotective (Crnic et al., 1983). Whether such experiential differences between siblings are related to developmental outcomes is yet to be fully determined, although the findings from Daniels et al. (1985) study of normal siblings suggest that such will be the case. The primary predictors of adjustment found by Daniels and her colleagues were differential maternal closeness, differential peer friendliness, and differential sibling friendliness. Each of these predictors can be considered a risk factor for children with retardation, given the empirical evidence (Crnic et al., 1983; Kazak & Marvin, 1984).

To date, there have been no published studies on sibling relationships in which one member is dually diagnosed. Thus, it is difficult to differentiate the influence of genetic, intrafamilial, and extrafamilial factors on the development of psychopathology in the child with retardation. Mash and Johnston (1983), however, reported on a study of sibling relationships and parental well-being in families that included children with diagnosed hyperactivity. These investigators found that interactions between hyperactive children and their siblings were characterized by higher conflict, regardless of the gender or birth order of siblings. The fact that gender and birth order did not mediate the conflict is meaningful, as these are the factors most often investigated in sibling research from a behavioral genetic perspective. Further, Stoneman et al. (1987) found that gender and birth order are critical factors influencing conflict in sibling relations when one member has retardation, although not dually diagnosed. The presence of psychopathology may change the nature of these relations.

Mash and Johnston (1983) further reported that maternal stress was related to greater negative behavior in the hyperactive sibling pairs. It's not possible, however, to disentangle the causative relations between these events. It is possible that having a more stressed mother may promote negative sibling behavior, and equally possible that more negative sibling interactions contribute to mothers' perceptions of stress. The degree to which material behavior and attitudes in general, and maternal differential treatment in particular, contribute to shared and nonshared experience for siblings remains to be determined. Nevertheless, this seems a critical area in which to further explore the nature of sibling relationships.

SIBLING RELATIONSHIPS AND DUAL DIAGNOSIS

So far, this chapter has addressed the nature of sibling relationships and dual diagnosis in, at best, an indirect fashion. In this section, the authors attempt to present a model that more clearly describes the processes and mechanisms that they suggest underlie the association between sibling relationships and the presence of psychopathology in children with retardation.

The Sibling Role

It should be noted from the outset that the authors are not attempting to implicate sibling relationships as the primary cause of the development of psychopathological conditions in children with retardation. There are clearly a myriad of factors that contribute to such conditions. Rather, it is the authors' contention that, as a significant relationship within the family context, the broad nature of sibling interactions and relations contribute in some degree to the development and maintenance of psychopathological conditions in children with retardation. Although the authors would not predict that substantial amounts of variance in such outcomes can be attributed to siblings, it is important to consider and delineate the degree to which such processes are, in fact, operative.

If the sibling relationship contributes to the development of psychopathology in children with retardation, how might it do so? The mechanisms that the authors believe may underlie such processes are presented in Figure 1. Notably, this model suggests a direction of effect different from that which characterizes much of the previous research on sibling relationships. It is also focused entirely on the prediction of psychopathology in children with retardation. This model does not attempt to incorporate elements of the sibling relationship that may serve to predict more positive attributes, even though these surely exist as well, and merit future consideration.

The Family Context

As stated previously, sibling relationships can only be fully understood within the context of the family. As such, notions of stress, family functioning, and parent–child transactions are central to providing a context from which sibling relationships can contribute to dual diagnosis. Stress plays a primary role in defining a base condition to which families must respond. It is reasonably well established that families with children with retardation experience more stress that do families with only typical children (Beckman, 1983; Crnic et al., 1983; Kazak & Marvin, 1984). This stress, however, appears to be predominantly related to the presence of a child with retardation and the

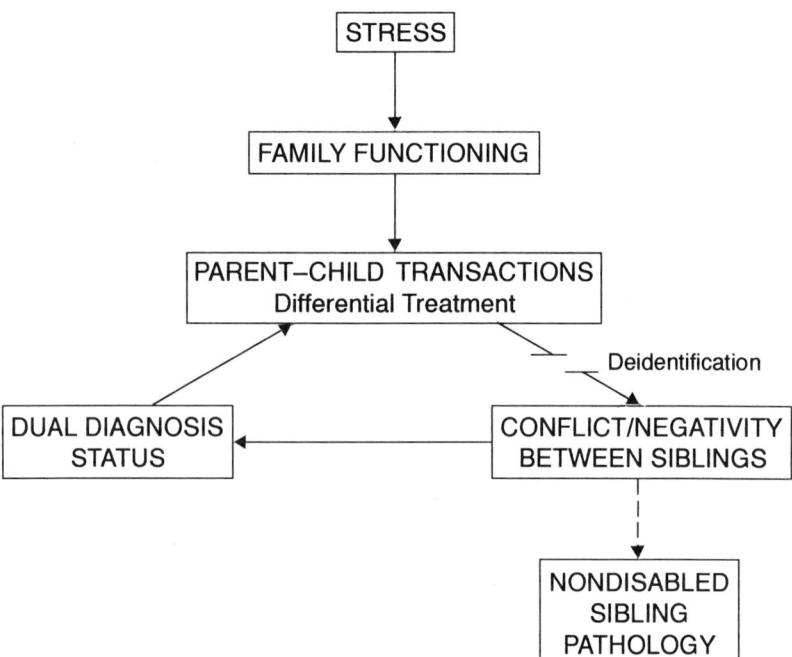

Figure 1. A model for family and sibling contribution to psychopathology in children with mental retardation.

demands that this situation places on a family. The primary measure used to assess stress has been the Questionnaire on Resources and Stress (Holroyd, 1974) and its various short forms (e.g., Friedrich, Greenberg, & Crnic, 1983), an instrument specific to families with children with disabilities. It is less clear how these families experience more general life stress or daily hassles (Crnic, 1991).

Regardless of the specific sources of family stress, research has also well established the diffuse adverse effects that stress has on numerous aspects of parent, child, and family functioning (Garmezy & Rutter, 1983). Stressful circumstances are associated with greater marital distress, parental psychological distress, and less positive parent–child interactions (Martin, 1987). As stress affects the nature of parent–child relationships over time (Patterson, 1983), it may also promote or exacerbate the differential treatment of siblings. At this point, this is both a theoretical and empirical question. However, given that parents do tend to treat children with retardation differently from typically developing children, and that families of children with retardation report more stress as a function of the retardation, it seems likely that differential treatment might be greater for sibling pairs of children with and without retardation.

Differential treatment is more an index of family functioning, but it does have explicit effects on the sibling relationship. In nearly every study on the process, parental differential treatment of siblings is associated with greater conflict and negativity between siblings. In turn, the research evidence to date suggests that conflict and negativity in the sibling relationship influences adjustment and competence, although marker variables such as birth order and gender mediate such effects.

Differential treatment, however, need not always lead to sibling conflict. There are likely a number of factors beyond age and gender that account for variability in this association. Coping strategies of the children may well prove important, but deidentification (Schachter, 1982) may be one specific coping mechanism that is pertinent to sibling relationships. In this sense, as siblings both perceive themselves differently and behave differently from one another (i.e., as they deidentify), less conflict is likely to emerge over differential treatment, and the greater the deidentification, the less conflict or negativity is likely to emerge. It may well be easier for siblings of children with retardation to deidentify from their sibling because the differences between them are often more apparent. Nevertheless, conflict between siblings is not likely to be entirely dissipated.

Under conditions in which families are stressed and less functional and sibling relationships are characterized by greater conflict in response to the family distress, it seems likely that these conflictual sibling relationships add to the conditions under which children with retardation may develop psychopathology. In this sense, the authors' model is additive. Sibling conflict and negativity increase the likelihood of dual diagnosis, but do so only within the context of distressed families in which differential treatment is common. It is unlikely that sibling conflict, even in sibling pairs that include a child with retardation, is sufficient in itself to lead to psychopathology, independent of family and parental functioning.

Finally, Figure 1 portrays a situation in which dual diagnosis contributes back to parent-child transactions and differential treatment. This suggests a cyclical loop in which the dual diagnosis condition further contributes to the occurrence of differential treatment. As greater differences in the children emerge, it may lead to more differential treatment by parents, which continues the cycle of subsequent conflict and negativity in sibling relationships that contributes to the development of psychopathology. Minimally, this would serve to maintain this condition over time, and might result in increased behavioral and emotional problems in one or both children.

At this point, the model is only hypothetical. It remains for investigators of family processes to test such processes. Nevertheless, there are strong suggestions in the extant research that such mechanisms may be operative in the development of psychopathology in children with retardation. As Brody and Stoneman (chap. 12, this vol.) suggest, investigators need to incorporate siblings into their family-research paradigms, paying particular attention to factors germane to sibling relationship quality and those family processes related to sibling relationships.

CONCLUDING COMMENTS

Several important caveats should be emphasized here. First, sibling relationships are a subsystem of the family unit, and cannot be fully understood without assessing the direct and indirect effects that the family has on them. Second, sibling relationships are reciprocal, and each sibling is affected by the other across multiple developmental domains. Sibling influences must be considered bidirectional. Finally, and perhaps most importantly, siblings of children with retardation have a range of influences on their brother or sister. Such influences may only contribute to psychopathology under rather specific circumstances. When such circumstances exist, it is likely that the unique contribution of sibling relationships to this process is relatively small, albeit of importance in developing a greater understanding of how children with retardation develop significant emotional and behavioral problems.

REFERENCES

Baumrind, D. (1967). Child care practices anteceding three patterns of preschool behavior. *Genetic Psychology Monographs, 75*, 43–83.

Beckman, P.J. (1983). The influence of selected child characteristics on stress in families of handicapped infants. *American Journal of Mental Deficiency, 88*, 150–156.

Blacher, J., Nihira, K., & Meyers, C.E. (1987). Characteristics of home environment of families with mentally retarded children: Comparisons across levels of retardation. *American Journal of Mental Deficiency, 91,* 313–320.

Bowlby, J. (1973). *Separation.* New York: Basic Books.

Brody, G.H., Stoneman, Z., & Burke, M. (1987a). Family system and individual child correlates of sibling behavior. *American Journal of Orthopsychiatry, 57*(4), 561–569.

Brody, G.H., Stoneman, Z., & Burke, M. (1987b). Child temperaments, maternal differential behavior, and sibling relationships. *Developmental Psychology, 23,* 354–362.

Brody, G.H., Stoneman, Z., & McCoy, J.K. (in press). Associations of maternal and paternal direct and differential behavior with sibling relationships: Contemporaneous and longitudinal analyses. *Child Development.*

Bronfenbrenner, U. (1979). *The ecology of human development: Experiments by nature and design.* Cambridge: Harvard University Press.

Bryant, B., & Crockenberg, S.B. (1980). Correlations and dimensions of prosocial behavior: A study of female siblings and their mothers. *Child Development, 51,* 529–544.

Buss, A., & Plomin, R. (1984). *Temperament: Early developing personality traits.* Hillsdale, NJ: Lawrence Erlbaum Associates.

Cicchetti, D. (1984). The emergence of developmental psychopathology. *Child Development, 55,* 1–7.

Crnic, K.A. (1991, May). *Social support predictions to family functioning one year following initial diagnosis.* Paper presented at the 24th Annual Gatlinburg Conference on Research and Theory in Mental Retardation and Developmental Disabilities, Miami.

Crnic, K.A., Friedrich, W.N., & Greenberg, M.T. (1983). Adaptation of families with mentally retarded children: A model of stress, coping, and family ecology. *American Journal of Mental Deficiency, 88,* 125–138.

Crnic, K.A., & Greenberg, M.T. (1990). Minor parenting stresses with young children. *Child Development, 61,* 1628–1637.

Cummings, E.M. (1987). Coping with background anger in early childhood. *Child Development, 58,* 976–984.

Cummings, E.M., Zahn-Waxler, C., & Radke-Yarrow, M. (1984). Developmental changes in children's responses to anger in the home. *Journal of Child Psychology and Psychiatry, 25,* 63–74.

Cushna, B. (1966, August). *Agency and birth order differences in very early childhood.* Paper presented at the meeting of the American Psychological Association, New York.

Daniels, D., Dunn, J., Furstenberg, F.F., & Plomin, R. (1985). Environmental differences within the family and adjustment differences within pairs of adolescent siblings. *Child Development, 56,* 764–774.

Dunn, J. (1983). Sibling relationships in early childhood. *Child Development, 54,* 787–811.

Dunn, J. (1987). Connections between relationships: Implications of research on mothers and siblings. In R. Hinde & J. Stevenson-Hinde (Eds.), *Relations between relationships.* Oxford: Oxford University Press.

Dunn, J. (1988). Relations among relationships. In S. Duck (Ed.), *Handbook of personal relationships.* New York: John Wiley & Sons.

Dunn, J., & Kendrick, C. (1982). *Siblings: Love, envy, and understanding.* Cambridge, MA: Harvard University Press.

Dunn, J., & Munn, P. (1985). Siblings and the development of prosocial behavior. *Child Development, 56,* 480–492.

Emery, R.E. (1982). Interparental conflict and the children of discord and divorce. *Psychological Bulletin, 92,* 310–330.

Feinstein, C., Kaminer, Y., Barrett, R.P., & Tylende, B. (1988). The assessment of mood and affect in developmentally disabled children and adolescents: The Emotion Disorders Rating Scale. *Research in Developmental Disabilities, 9,* 109–122.

Fishbein, H.D. (1981). Sibling set configuration and family dysfunction. *Family Process, 20,* 311–318.

Friedrich, W.N., Greenberg, M.T., & Crnic, K.A. (1983). A short form of the Questionnaire on Resources and Stress. *American Journal of Mental Deficiency, 88,* 41–48.

Furman, W., & Buhrmester, D. (1985). Children's perceptions of the quality of sibling relationships. *Child Development, 56,* 448–461.

Garmezy, N., & Rutter, M. (1983). *Stress, coping, and development in children.* New York: McGraw Hill.

Holroyd, J. (1974). The Questionnaire on Resources and Stress: An instrument to measure family response to a handicapped family member. *Journal of Community Psychology, 2,* 92–94.

Jacobson, J.W. (1982). Problem behavior and psychiatric impairment within a developmentally disabled population I: Behavior frequency. *Applied Research in Mental Retardation, 3,* 121–140.

Kazak, A.E., & Marvin, R.S. (1984). Differences, difficulties, and adaptation: Stress and social networks in families with a handicapped child. *Family Relations, 33,* 67–77.

Kidwell, J.S. (1981). Number of siblings, sibling spacing, sex, and birth order: Their effects on perceived parent–adolescent relationships. *Journal of Marriage and the Family, 43,* 315–332.

Kidwell, J.S. (1982). The neglected birth order: Middleborns. *Journal of Marriage and the Family, 44,* 225–235.

Lahey, D.B., Hammer, D., Crumrine, P.L., & Forehand, R.L. (1980). Birth order × sex interactions in child behavior problems. *Developmental Psychology, 6,* 608–615.

Martin, B. (1987). Developmental perspectives on family theory. In T. Jacob (Ed.), *Family interaction and psychopathology* (pp. 163–202). New York: Plenum.

Mash, E.J., & Johnston, C. (1983). Sibling interactions of hyperactive and normal children and their relationships to reports of maternal stress and self-esteem. *Journal of Clinical Child Psychology, 12,* 91–99.

Matson, J.L., Barrett, R.P., & Helsel, W.J. (1988). Depression in mentally retarded children. *Research in Developmental Disabilities, 9,* 39–46.

Matson, J., & Frame, C. (1985). *Psychopathology among mentally retarded children and adolescents.* Beverly Hills: Sage Publications.

Parke, R.D., MacDonald, K.D., Beitel, A., & Bhavnagri, N. (1988). The role of the family in the development of peer relationships. In R. DeV. Peters & R.J. McMahon (Eds.), *Social learning and systems approaches to marriage and the family* (pp. 17–44). New York: Bruner/Mazel.

Patterson, G.R. (1982). *Coercive family process.* Eugene, OR: Castalia.

Patterson, G. (1983). Stress: A change agent for family process. In N. Garmezy & M. Rutter (Eds.), *Stress, coping, and development in children* (pp. 235–264). New York: McGraw-Hill.

Patterson, G.R. (1984). Siblings: Fellow travelers in coercive family processes. *Advances in the Study of Aggression, 1,* 173–214.

Reiss, S. (1988). Dual diagnosis in the United States. *Australian and New Zealand Journal of Developmental Disabilities, 14,* 43–48.

Richardson, S.A., Koller, H., & Katz, M. (1985). Relationship of upbringing to later behavior disturbance of mildly mentally retarded young people. *American Journal of Mental Deficiency, 90,* 1–8.

Sameroff, A.J., & Chandler, M.J. (1975). Reproductive risk and the continuum of caretaking casualty. In F. Horowitz (Ed.), *Review of child development research* (Vol. 4, pp. 187–244), Chicago: University of Chicago Press.

Schachter, F. (1982). Sibling deidentification and split parent identification: A family tetrad. In M. Lamb & B. Sutton-Smith (Eds.), *Sibling relationships: Their nature and significance across the lifespan.* (pp. 123–151). Hillsdale, NJ: Lawrence Erlbaum Associates.

Stocker, C., Dunn, J., & Plomin, R. (1989). Sibling relationships: Links with child temperament, maternal behavior, and family structure. *Child Development, 60,* 715–717.

Stoneman, Z., Brody, J.H., Davis, C.H., & Crapps, J.M. (1987). Mentally retarded children and their same sex siblings: Naturalistic in-home observations. *American Journal of Mental Retardation, 92,* 290–298.

Stoneman, Z., Brody, G.H., Davis, C.H., & Crapps, J.M. (1988). Childcare responsibilities, peer relations, and sibling conflict: Older siblings of mentally retarded children. *American Journal of Mental Retardation, 93,* 174–183.

Stoneman, Z., Brody, G.H., Davis, C.H., & Crapps, J.M. (1989). Role relations between mentally retarded children and their older siblings: Observations in three in-home contexts. *Research in Developmental Disabilities, 10,* 61–76.

Webster, T.G. (1970). Unique aspects of emotional development in mentally retarded children. In F. Menolascino (Ed.), *Psychiatric approaches to mental retardation* (pp. 3–54). New York: Basic Books.

SECTION III

METHODOLOGICAL ISSUES FOR FUTURE CONSIDERATION

CHAPTER 12

Parameters for Inclusion in Studies on Sibling Relationships
Some Heuristic Suggestions

Gene H. Brody and Zolinda Stoneman

Since the 1970s, many researchers interested in child development have shifted their attention from the maturing individual to the larger interpersonal context in which he or she functions. This approach is reflected in the current focus on the family as the most influential interpersonal context and the most common functional unit of study. Most family investigators specifically suggest that certain definable family patterns and processes are crucial to understanding the development of competence, and that the identification of those patterns eventually may lead to more effective methods for the treatment and prevention of adjustment problems.

Although much information has been amassed about those patterns of parent–child relationships and interactions that forecast competence for individual youths, relatively little research has been devoted to investigating the quality of the sibling relationship and its contribution to the individual child's development. Information concerning sibling relationships that involve a child with a mental or physical disability or a chronic illness is particularly sparse. It is surprising that researchers have generally neglected to study these relationships, because by 1 year of age children spend as much time in interaction with their siblings as they do with their mothers, and far more than they do with their fathers (Lawson & Ingleby, 1974). Furthermore, for many people, siblings serve as important sources of emotional support throughout the lifespan. Such enduringly supportive ties appear to be at least partially rooted in the quality of the relationship during childhood. Data describe the persistence into adulthood of rivalrous feelings that originated in childhood, and their effect on the closeness of adult sibling relationships (Ross, Dalton, & Milgram, 1981; Ross & Milgram, 1982).

In this chapter the authors present heuristic information for researchers to consider when designing studies of sibling relationships that involve a child with a disability or chronic illness. The authors' suggestions arise from their research programs, which include both nondisabled sibling pairs and dyads in which one sibling has mental retardation. The initial focus is on broad assessment issues that investigators should consider in studying sibling relationships in general, then the authors turn to some specific points that their research indicates should be considered by those interested in studying dyads that include a sibling with a disability.

CONSIDERATIONS IN THE ASSESSMENT OF SIBLING RELATIONSHIPS

The authors begin with the premise that, in studying sibling relationships, researchers must acknowledge the interconnected and interlocking subsystems that families comprise. The boundaries between the sibling, parent–child, spousal, and extended family systems are permeable, so that events that transpire within one subsystem often have implications for relationships in the others. The study of sibling relationships, therefore, often necessitates the assessment of functioning in other family systems as well.

Recent assessments of sibling relationships have run the gamut of methods, ranging from global questionnaires (Brody & Stoneman, 1990) to complex observational systems that require a cadre of trained coders to observe several hours of family interaction (Patterson, Ray, Shaw, & Cobb, 1969). Olson (1977) has suggested a two-dimensional paradigm by which assessment methods are classified in terms of the reporter's frame of reference (insider versus outsider) and the type of data obtained (subjective high-inference versus objective low-inference). The frame-of-reference dimension describes the proximity of the assessor to the family, ranging from family members themselves to trained third-party observers. The data-type dimension refers to the level of inference required during data collection. At one end of the continuum are simple behavior counts that require virtually no inference on the part of the observer, and at the other end are abstract theoretical concepts e.g., rivalry, jealousy, and deidentification that must somehow be quantified. This model thus delineates four basic approaches to research on sibling relationships: high-inference self-report methods (questionnaires, interviews, standardized tests); high-inference observer reports (global observational ratings); low-inference self-report methods (behavior checklists); and low-inference observational techniques (trained observers using behavioral coding systems).

The theoretical perspective from which the study of sibling relationships and family functioning is planned influences the assessment method that is chosen and the nature of the resulting data. One's theoretical orientation will determine the dimensions of behavior (e.g., parental favoritism or marital conflict) that are considered relevant to the study, the ways in which variables are sampled and operationalized (e.g., through observations or self-reports), the family members whose behaviors are assessed (siblings, parents and children, the entire nuclear family), and the context (e.g., observation in a laboratory or in the home) that is best suited to the assessment of family processes. The authors consider data gathered from all types of assessment to be important, because each provides a unique perspective on the family. For example, information such as the perceived closeness of the sibling relationship can only be obtained from the siblings themselves, from the insider-subjective position. Although obtaining valid and reliable data from this domain is psychometrically difficult, the information thus obtained is a rich source of insight into aspects of family life that cannot be readily observed.

The problem of unreliable insider reports on family functioning in general, and sibling relations in particular, can be solved by creating more discriminating measures and training subjects to give accurate reports. It is important to determine the kinds of information that child and adult family members can most reliably provide, as well as the best ways of gathering this information through more sophisticated family-process measures. By training family members to provide accurate information on those features of their relationships that may be difficult to report, the authors acknowledge the fact that both researchers and subjects need training in order to observe behavior—others' or their own—accurately.

Context

The laboratory or clinic setting has been criticized for eliciting responses that do not accurately represent behavior in the natural setting. Gottman (1979) asked a sample of nonclinic families to audiotape problemsolving sessions, either at home or at a clinic. Analyses showed that the couples who interacted at home were more unilaterally and reciprocally negative, and engaged in less validation or contracting and more cross-complaining, than did a matched group who interacted in the laboratory. In addition, distressed and nondistressed couples could more easily be distinguished through home interactions than through those that took place in the clinic. Baum, Forehand, and Zegoib (1979) reported that 83% of their parent–child observations, in which awareness-unawareness manipulations were employed, showed evidence of reactivity effects; mothers tended to be more positive and active in structuring their children's behavior when they were aware that they were being observed. These studies indicate that behaviors observed in a laboratory may not be representative of behavior in the home setting.

Laboratory assessments of family interactions have also been criticized because the tasks in which family members are asked to participate are often unrelated to their day-to-day interactions (Gilbert & Christensen, 1985). In support of this position, Steinglass (1979) reports that most naturalistically gathered data portray families engaged in "maintenance," rather than problemsolving, behavior. Those interactive processes that typically have been assessed in research investigations, such as problemsolving and decisionmaking, thus constitute low–base-rate behaviors in the natural setting. Gilbert and Christensen (1985), however, point out that this lack of daily relevance does not automatically mitigate the theoretical and clinical utility of these tasks. Assessments of low–base-rate behaviors are valid if it can be demonstrated that the processes under investigation occur in the natural environments of at least some families, have an impact on the siblings, and can be assessed in ways that accurately represent those infrequent occasions on which families engage in them.

The issue of representative sampling extends to the recruitment of subjects as well; study participants must be similar to the members of the population to whom the research findings are to be applied. Both researchers and practitioners must consider the applicability of theoretical propositions based on sex, age, race, family lifecycle stage, religious beliefs, and socioeconomic status, acknowledging the dangers of extending research conclusions from one family type to another (Schumm, 1982). Unfortunately, very little empirical information is available to guide practitioners who work with siblings from several different types of families. As a result, most researchers who study minority families have used essays and qualitative analysis as their main research tools (cf. Staples & Mirande, 1980). When empirical information does not support traditional assumptions, researchers who consider culturally normal minority family patterns to be pathological tend to resist the findings. Normative data on different social groups and family types should be made available to practitioners and researchers in order to challenge such invalid views.

Sibling Gender

Child gender should be considered when examining measures of sibling interactions, relationship quality, and individual child outcomes, because a number of studies suggest that gender is significantly associated with differences in sibling relationships and interactions (see Brody & Stoneman, 1990). Furthermore, the child's gender may interact with disabled or chronically ill status to generate complex associations; failure to examine data separately for male and female children can result in the confounding of disability or chronic illness with child gender, so that interpretation of any results obtained becomes extremely problematic. Three of the authors' studies illustrate the importance of child gender to sibling relationships: one focused on self-selected interactional contexts and role relationships among same-sex and cross-sex school-age siblings, the second examined role relations between children with mental retardation and their older siblings, and the third assessed childcare responsibilities assumed by older siblings of children with mental retardation.

The first study (Stoneman, Brody, & MacKinnon, 1986) involved naturalistic, in-home observations of 40 sibling dyads for 50 minutes while they engaged in activities that they had selected themselves. The results implied that sibling-gender combination created interactional contexts that may have both direct and indirect effects on sibling interaction. For example, the ecology of younger male siblings' rooms varied according to the sex of the older sibling: Boys with older brothers had more traditionally masculine items and decorations in their rooms than did boys with older sisters. Similarly, boys with older brothers engaged in a greater proportion of male sex-typed activities, and proportionally fewer cross-sex activities, when playing with their siblings than did boys with older sisters. This pattern of activity choice also carried over into those times when the younger brothers played alone. Girls with older brothers engaged in more opposite-sex–typed activities than did girls with older sisters, both during times when the siblings played together and when they played alone. Thus, older siblings' gender not only influenced the activities in which the younger boys and girls engaged while playing with them, but also carried over into times when the younger sibling was playing alone.

Three behavioral measures—playmate, interactor, and solitary activity—were used to quantify roles assumed simultaneously by both members of the dyad. The playmate role was defined as joint play with a sibling; the interactor role as conversation, physical contact, or eye contact between siblings who were not engaged in joint play; and the solitary role as separate play with no verbal or nonverbal interaction taking place between siblings. Significant older gender—younger gender interactions emerged for all three of the roles. The data indicate that male sibling dyads spent less time as playmates and engaged in more solitary activity than did siblings in any other group. Older sister–younger brother pairs assumed the interactor role with each other less often than did siblings in other combinations.

Female pairs engaged in more teaching and managing of one another than did siblings in any of the other groups, which is in accordance with a consistent tendency reported in the sibling literature for girls to assume teacher and manager roles with their younger siblings (Brody, Stoneman, & Mac-

Kinnon, 1982; Cicirelli, 1973; Minnett, Vandell, & Santrock, 1983; Stoneman, Brody, & MacKinnon, 1984). Older girls with younger brothers emitted the most positive verbals, whereas siblings in same-sex pairs emitted the fewest. These results are consistent with both Schachter's (1982) and Tesser's (1980) theories, which predict increased friction between siblings who are more similar.

Children with mental retardation and their older, nondisabled siblings were observed during two, 1-hour home visits, as were a comparison group of siblings. Household and childcare responsibilities, peer contacts, and out-of-home activities among the older nondisabled children were also examined (Stoneman, Brody, Davis, & Crapps, 1987, 1988, 1989). Older sisters in both groups were more likely to assume management/guidance and teacher/helper roles than were older brothers. Older sisters of girls with mental retardation were almost four times as likely as older comparison sisters to assume teacher/helper roles. The only significant findings for participation in household tasks were related to gender and followed traditional sex-role patterns, with older sisters in both sibling groups assuming more responsibility for personal and adaptive tasks and meal preparation, and older brothers given greater responsibility for yard work and other outdoor tasks.

The authors found that older sisters babysat their younger siblings more often than did older brothers, a pattern that interacted with group membership. The older sisters of girls with mental retardation babysat the most often, while the older brothers of boys with mental retardation babysat as often as did older sisters in the comparison group. The older brothers in the comparison group babysat the least. In addition, the older sisters of girls with mental retardation had greater responsibility for the physical care of their younger siblings than did children in any other group.

The older brothers of children with mental retardation invited friends to their homes more frequently, and entertained more different friends in a 2-week period, than did siblings in any other group. Boys whose younger brothers had mental retardation visited the homes of more different friends than did older brothers in the comparison group or older sisters in either group.

The authors detected few gender differences when, in a recent study, they compared the interactional roles and parent-mediated childcare responsibilities of older children with mental retardation and their nondisabled younger siblings with those of a matched group of comparison siblings (Brody, Stoneman, Davis, & Crapps, 1991; Stoneman, Brody, Davis, Crapps, & Malone, 1991). This suggests that the presence of an older sibling with mental retardation is a powerful caregiving stimulus that influences the behavior of younger brothers and sisters equally. This exception notwithstanding, the research indicates that child gender exerts significant influence on interaction patterns and childcare responsibilities. By summing across child gender, researchers at least increase error variance, and may mask or confound results.

Individual Differences

The authors' research on the correlates of variation in the quality of sibling relationships has revealed the importance of considering individual differences in the personalities and competence levels of the children who are involved in the relationship. Although siblings share approximately 50% of their genetic makeup, their personalities can differ greatly (Plomin, 1986). In the authors' research with nondisabled siblings, they have sought to document the contribution of individual children's temperaments to variability in their sibling relationships. Below is a description of the ways in which the inclusion of this individual-difference dimension has enabled the authors to refine their understanding of sibling interaction.

In a series of studies on child temperament (Brody, Stoneman, & Burke, 1987; Stoneman & Brody, in press), mothers provided ratings of each of their children's levels of activity, emotional intensity, and persistence. The siblings themselves were observed in their homes while playing with a board game and a construction toy. High activity, high emotional intensity, and low persistence levels are associated with increased levels of agonistic behavior between sisters (Brody et al., 1987). A different pattern emerged, however, for the relation between temperament and behavior for male siblings. Their behavior was predicted most reliably by the younger brother's activity and persistence levels: High activity and low persistence were associated with more agonistic behavior from both siblings and more prosocial behavior from the younger sibling.

In a subsequent study (Stoneman & Brody, in press), the authors examined various combinations of sibling temperaments to ascertain whether temperament differences have an additive effect on conflicted sibling relationships, and whether the detrimental effects of a difficult temperament in one sibling are buffered by a less difficult temperament in the other sibling. The buffering process apparently operated among dyads in which the older sibling was low in activity level and the younger sibling was highly active. Such pairs displayed less-conflicted behavior than did those in which both the older and younger siblings were assessed as being highly active. When the younger sibling was less active than the older, the buffering process did not operate. This underscores the importance of considering such individual characteristics when examining variations in the quality of sibling relationships.

In summary, all children who are part of sibling and other family relationships are, first and foremost, individuals. To the extent that researchers can assess their individuality and make refined, theoretically based predictions from assessments, they will increase their ability to forecast the qualities of the sibling relationship.

Maternal and Paternal Direct and Differential Behavior

Much of the authors' research is designed according to a systems perspective (P. Minuchin, 1985; S. Minuchin, 1974), which emphasizes the interdependencies among social systems within the family (e.g., parent–child and sibling) as well as the ways in which each subsystem is affected by events that occur in the others. The authors have given particular attention to investigating the links between parent behavior and sibling relationships, using two approaches. First, they have examined the associations between behavior that parents enact directly with their individual children and that which the children enact with their brothers and sisters, because several theoretical orientations predict that these variables will be related. Social learning theorists suggest that children learn particular behaviors in their relationships with their parents, and that these behaviors generalize to their interactions with others (Parke, MacDonald, Beitel, & Bhavnagri, 1988). Attachment theorists propose that children's interactions are guided by internal working models of relationships that are derived from experiences with primary caregivers (Sroufe & Fleeson, 1986). Second, the authors have investigated differences between the behaviors that parents direct to individual children, a construct termed *differential treatment*. This concept has been described in theories of social learning (Bandura, 1977), psychoanalysis (Freud, 1916/1949), self-esteem maintenance (Tesser, 1980), and equity (Adams, 1965; Walster, Bercheid, & Walster, 1973).

The results of these studies indicate that the direct and differential behaviors that both mothers and fathers enact contribute unique variance to the quality of sibling relationships. Prior to these studies the literature had focused solely on associations between sibling relationships and maternal behavior. The authors' findings, presented below, suggest that future efforts to examine links between parental behavior and sibling relationships should include considerable effort to obtain data from both mothers and fathers.

The first study (Brody, Stoneman, & McCoy, 1992) involved in-home observations of 109 families, in which mothers and fathers were observed separately in triadic interactions with their 2 children and the sibling dyad was observed on a separate occasion. In addition, the older siblings reported their perceptions of their sibling relationships. These assessments were repeated 1 year after the initial evaluation. Hierarchical multiple-regression analyses were executed for both the concurrent and longitudinal assessments. In each hierarchical analysis the maternal predictors were added after the paternal predictors; the order of entry was then reversed in order to determine the unique variance that each parent's behavior contributed to the prediction of the sibling relationship variables.

The results revealed that 10 paternal and 2 maternal predictors accounted for unique variance in the concurrent analyses; for the longitudinal analyses, 6 paternal and 4 maternal predictors accounted for unique variance. These results are remarkable because descriptive analyses revealed mothers and fathers to be similar in the rates of differential behavior they direct to their children, and to differ on only one of the four direct behaviors examined. Although the rates of maternal and paternal direct and differential behavior are similar, fathers' behavior appears to have special significance both for individual children and for their sibling relationships. The authors propose that this salience of paternal behavior may arise from the relative scarcity of fathers' attention, compared to that of mothers, in everyday settings.

In a second study (Brody, Stoneman, & McCoy, 1992) the authors further examined mothers' and fathers' contributions to variations in the quality of sibling relationships to determine whether the ways in which families solve problems are associated with the degree of conflict in sibling interactions. Accordingly, the authors videotaped mothers, fathers, and siblings attempting to resolve conflicts that each sibling had presented for discussion. On separate occasions the siblings were observed in play activities. The most robust predictor of both contemporaneous and longitudinally observed sibling conflict was paternal favoritism during the family problemsolving process. Again, unequal treatment by fathers may be particularly salient, inducing particularly angry or rivalrous emotions that are actualized during sibling interactions.

Indirect Influences

Indirect influences operate through circumstances that arise from the presence in the family of the child with a disability or illness; relationships both inside and outside the family can be affected. For the nondisabled sibling, such influences can include the limitation of social activities due to the inability of the sibling with a disability to participate, or to peers' reactions to the child with a disability. Within the family, the stress and fatigue of caring for the child with a disability can influence the parents' childrearing practices and interactional style with their other children. In addition, family interactions can be influenced by the siblings' need to either help the parents care for a child with mental retardation, or to assume household responsibilities that the parents must bypass in order to care for the child with a disability. Studies of these influences on the siblings' development have so far been limited to the examination of certain mental health variables; further research is necessary to yield a more complete understanding of the effects on other aspects of child development.

Research is particularly lacking concerning the influence on the sibling relationship of the sibling's assumption of a quasi-parental role with the sibling with a disability. The authors' own research has yielded some preliminary findings on this subject and indicated the need for further study. Specifically, increased conflict and decreased positivity were associated with higher levels of caregiving responsibility among the older siblings of children with mental retardation, but not among siblings in the comparison group (Stoneman et al., 1988). In another study (Stoneman et al., 1991), in which the authors examined the same variables with children who had mental retardation and their nondisabled younger siblings, the opposite result unexpectedly emerged: those younger siblings who had more caregiving responsibilities experienced less-conflicted sibling relationships ($r_{(16)} = .60, p < .01$). Selection effects may have operated here. The authors found that parents were not likely to give younger siblings responsibility for babysitting the child with a disability if the sibling relationship was conflictual; it is possible that parents used such discretion in other areas of caregiving as well, such that the younger sibling was less likely to have caregiving responsibilities if conflict was the expected result.

CONCLUDING COMMENTS

The data presented in this chapter suggest that sibling gender, differences in individual children, children's relationships with both their mothers and fathers, and the indirect effects of having a sibling with a disability are important correlates of sibling-relationship quality. The authors believe that the literature on typical sibling relationships can offer important clues to the effects of various methodological strategies, and that their own studies of siblings of children with mental retardation have contributed to the refinement of their own research. Sibling pairs that include an atypical child are, first and foremost, pairs of brothers and sisters; they should be expected to be more similar to than different from typical sibling pairs. Sibling research in the disabilities field should therefore be seen as a natural extension of the research on typical siblings, rather than a new area of study.

If the field is to progress in determining the associations between family processes and sibling relationship quality in those families that include a child with a disability or chronic illness, every effort must be made to include constructs and procedures in the research that will yield optimally precise estimates of important parameters. The authors hope that consideration of the parameters presented in this chapter will help achieve this goal.

REFERENCES

Adams, J.S. (1965). Inequity in social exchange. In L. Berkowitz (Ed.), *Advances in experimental social psychology* (Vol.2, pp. 149–175). New York: Academic Press.

Bandura, A. (1977). *Social learning theory.* Englewood Cliffs, NJ: Prentice Hall.

Baum, C., Forehand, R., & Zegoib, L.E. (1979). A review of observer reactivity in adult–child interactions. *Journal of Behavioral Assessment, 1,* 167–178.

Brody, G.H., Stoneman, Z., & Burke, M. (1987). Child temperaments, maternal differential behavior, and sibling relations. *Developmental Psychology, 23,* 354–362.

Brody, G.H., & Stoneman, Z. (1990). Sibling relationships. In I.E. Sigel & G.H. Brody (Eds.), *Methods of family research: Biographies of research projects: Vol. 1. Normal families* (pp. 189–212). Hillsdale, NJ: Lawrence Erlbaum Associates.

Brody, G.H., Stoneman, Z., & MacKinnon, C. (1982). Role asymmetries in interactions between school-aged children, their younger siblings, and their friends. *Child Development, 53,* 1364–1370.

Brody, G.H., Stoneman, Z., & McCoy, J.K. (1992). Associations of maternal and paternal direct and differential behavior with sibling relationships: Contemporaneous and longitudinal analyses. *Child Development, 63,* 82–92.

Brody, G.H., Stoneman, Z., Davis, C.H., & Crapps, J.M. (1991). Observations of the role relations and behavior between older children with mental retardation and their younger siblings. *American Journal on Mental Retardation, 95,* 527–536.

Cicirelli, V.G. (1973). Effects of sibling structure and interaction on children's categorization style. *Developmental Psychology, 9,* 132–139.

Freud, S. (1949). *An outline of psychoanalysis.* New York: Norton. (Original work published 1916)

Gilbert, R., & Christensen, A. (1985). Observational assessment of marital and family interactions: Methodological considerations. In L. L'Abate (Ed.), *Handbook of family psychology and therapy* (pp. 413–438). Homewood, IL: Dow Jones.

Gottman, J.M. (1979). *Marital interaction: Experimental investigations.* New York: Academic Press.

Lawson, A., & Ingleby, J.D. (1974). Daily routines of preschool children: Effects of age, birth order, sex, social class, and developmental correlates. *Psychological Medicine, 4,* 399–415.

Minnett, A.M., Vandell, D.L., & Santrock, J.W. (1983). The effects of sibling status on sibling interaction: Influence of birth order, age spacing, sex of child, and sex of sibling. *Child Development, 54,* 1064–1072.

Minuchin, P. (1985). Families and individual development: Provocations from the field of family therapy. *Child Development, 56,* 289–302.

Minuchin, S. (1974). *Families and family therapy.* Cambridge, MA: Harvard University Press.

Olson, D.H. (1977). Insiders and outsiders views of relationships: Research studies. In G. Levinger & H. Rausch (Eds.), *Close relationships* (pp. 317–337). Amherst: University of Massachusetts Press.

Parke, R.D., MacDonald, K.D., Beitel, A., & Bhavnagri, N. (1988). The role of the family in the development of peer relationships. In R.D. Peters & R.J. McMahon (Eds.). *Social learning and systems approaches to marriage and the family* (pp. 17–44). New York: Bruner-Mazel.

Patterson, G.R., Ray, R.S., Shaw, D.A., & Cobb, J.A. (1969). *Manual for coding family interaction* (See NAPS Document #02134 for 33 pages of material; available from ASIS/NAPS, % Microfiche Publications, 440 South Park Avenue, New York, NY 10016)

Plomin, R. (1986). *Development, genetics, and psychology.* Hillsdale, NJ: Lawrence Erlbaum Associates.

Ross, H.C., Dalton, M.J., & Milgram, J. (1981). *Older adults' perceptions of closeness in sibling relationships.* Cincinnati, OH: University of Cincinnati. (ERIC/CAPS Document Reproduction Service No. ED 201 903)

Ross, H.G., & Milgram, J. (1982). Important variables in adult sibling relationships: A qualitative study. In M.E. Lamb & B. Sutton-Smith (Eds.), *Sibling relationships: Their nature and significance over the lifespan* (pp. 225–247). Hillsdale, NJ: Lawrence Erlbaum Associates.

Schachter, F.F. (1982). Sibling deidentification and split-parent identification. In M.E. Lamb & B. Sutton-Smith (Eds.), *Sibling relationships: Their nature and significance across the lifespan* (pp. 123–151). Hillsdale, NJ: Lawrence Erlbaum Associates.

Schumm, W.R. (1982). Integrating theory, management, and data analysis in family studies survey research. *Journal of Marriage and the Family, 44*, 983–998.

Sroufe, L.A., & Fleeson, J. (1986). Attachment and the construction of relationships. In W. Hartup & Z. Rubin (Eds.), *Relationships and development* (pp. 51–71). New York: Cambridge University Press.

Staples, R., & Mirande, A. (1980). Racial and cultural variations among American families: A decennial review of the literature on minority families. *Journal of Marriage and the Family, 442*, 887–903.

Steinglass, P. (1979). The home observation assessment method (HOAM): Real time naturalistic observation of families in their homes. *Family Process, 18*, 337–354.

Stoneman, Z., & Brody, G.H. (in press). Sibling temperaments, conflict, warmth, and role asymmetry. *Child Development*.

Stoneman, Z., Brody, G.H., Davis, C.H., & Crapps, J.M. (1987). Mentally retarded children and their older sibling relations. *Developmental Psychology, 23*, 354–362.

Stoneman, Z., Brody, G.H., Davis, C.H., & Crapps, J.M. (1988). Childcare responsibilities, peer relationships, and sibling conflict: Older siblings of mentally retarded children. *American Journal on Mental Retardation, 93*(2), 166–173.

Stoneman, Z., Brody, G.H., Davis, C.H., & Crapps, J.M. (1989). Role relations between mentally retarded children and their older siblings: Observations in three in-home contexts. *Research in Developmental Disabilities, 10*, 61–76.

Stoneman, Z., Brody, G.H., Davis, C.H., Crapps, J.M., & Malone, D.M. (1991). Ascribed role relations between children with mental retardation and their younger siblings. *American Journal on Mental Retardation, 95*, 527–536.

Stoneman, Z., Brody, G.H., & MacKinnon, C. (1984). Naturalistic observations of children's activities and roles while playing with their siblings and friends. *Child Development, 55*, 617–627.

Stoneman, Z., Brody, G.H., & MacKinnon, C.E. (1986). Same-sex and cross-sex siblings: Activity choices, roles, behavior and gender stereotypes. *Sex Roles, 15*, 495–511.

Tesser, A. (1980). Self-esteem maintenance in family dynamics. *Journal of Personality and Social Psychology, 39*, 77–91.

Walster, E., Bercheid, E., & Walster, G.W. (1973). New directions in equity research. *Journal of Personality and Social Psychology, 25*, 151–176.

CHAPTER 13

Measurement Considerations in the Identification and Assessment of Stressors and Coping Strategies

*Wendy C. Gamble
and E. Jeanne Woulbroun*

When considering sibling relationships, *stress* is not the first descriptive term to come to mind. A review of key topics in the literature describing the developmental significance of sibling relationships suggests that this may be an oversight. *Rivalry, competition, individuation,* and *caregiving* are terms often used to describe sibling relationships; terms that convey a sense of unpleasantness, work, or stress. These descriptions are typically used by adults. But stress is also a dominant theme in characterizations of sibling interactions from a child's perspective. Children will describe a sibling who "borrows" a favorite piece of clothing and returns it stained or stretched out. Others may describe a sibling who cruelly ridicules a best friend's appearance or behaviors. Most siblings describe jealousy and major conflicts, battles that they remember distinctly even as adults. Whether from an adult's or a child's perspective, there are qualities of all sibling relationships that can be described as stressful.

Although the term *stressful* has not been used to describe most sibling relationships, it has been used to describe the experiences of children growing up in homes where there is a child with a mental or physical disability or chronic illness. It is the authors' opinion, however, that the term stress, in reference to these children's experiences, is used in divergent and nonspecific ways. Furthermore, much of what is known about these children and the stressors they experience is drawn from informal clinical observations or parental reports and is marred by a variety of measurement problems. Thus, while it cannot be argued that nothing is known about the effects of a sibling with special needs on the other children, neither can it be said that researchers have obtained data of sufficient quantity or quality to fully understand these children's experiences. The authors will argue that investigators should take a closer look at stressors in these children's lives, a closer look at how best to conceptualize stress, as well as how best to determine its presence, absence, and magnitude.

In this chapter the authors begin with a brief discussion of what they know about siblings of children with disabilities or chronic health problems, and about the factors that mediate the impact on siblings of having such a child in the family. This discussion will be brief; more detailed and complete information can be found in other chapters in this volume. Existing information about the adjustment of siblings and the variables mediating adjustment, it will be argued, presents a static picture of the processes by which some do poorly while others thrive and benefit from their experiences. The most significant limitation of extant research is the failure to identify and evaluate specific events engendering stress and personal coping strategies. The authors will argue that a better understanding of the nature of the stressors experienced by children may help to unravel some of the mystery of observed variability in the nondisabled siblings' functioning. Three approaches to examining stressful experiences will be reviewed generally. Next, all three orientations will be described again, focusing on how they can inform the study of siblings of children with disabilities or chronic illness. Because the authors believe the third perspective, a transactional orientation in the study of stress and coping, to be the most beneficial for investigators, most of the discussion will elaborate on this perspective. Included in this latter section will be a discussion on conceptualizing and assessing children's and adolescents' coping strategies.

In the discussion to follow, the authors often refer to siblings of children with disabilities and of children with chronic illness as a single group. Only occasionally is a distinction made. By no means do the authors believe, however, that the experiences of these two groups are interchangeable, or even similar. Instead, the authors would argue that making predictions about the developmental consequences of growing up with a child with special needs on the basis of the particular disability or type of illness would prove far less productive than evaluating a variety of other factors to be identified. The authors hope readers will accept the rationale that the effects of specific disability types or illnesses are only part of a larger equation for understanding the adjustment of nondisabled or healthy children.

EFFECTS OF GROWING UP WITH AN EXCEPTIONAL SIBLING

The evidence regarding the effects of an exceptional sibling on other children in the family is mixed. Some studies characterize siblings of exceptional children as being "at risk" for a variety of psychological and even somatic complaints. The effects observed for siblings of children with mental disabilities include delinquency, immaturity, aggression, cruelty, depression, social isolation, learning problems, greater anxiety, lower self-esteem, and general maladjustment (Breslau & Prabucki, 1987; Cowen et al., 1986; Farber & Jenne, 1963; Grossman, 1972; Harvey & Greenway, 1984; McAndrew, 1976; Tew & Laurence, 1973; Tropauer, Franz, & Dilgard, 1970). There are similar findings for siblings of children with chronic illness who have been characterized as experiencing unspecified behavioral problems, psychosomatic disorders, allergies, and concerns about failure (Aply, Barbour, & Westmacott, 1967; Binger, Albin, & Feuerstein, 1969; Cairns, Clark, Smith, & Lansky, 1979; Tew & Laurence, 1973). Still other investigators argue that children with exceptional siblings are not any more likely to experience problems than are children in the general population, and that, in fact, some of these children appear to benefit from their experiences (Caldwell & Guze, 1960; Carr, 1988; Ferrari, 1984; Gayton, Friedman, Tavormina, & Tucker, 1977; Lloyd-Bostock, 1976; Lonsdale, 1978).

The consequences of growing up in a home with an exceptional sibling are varied. As Gallagher and Powell (1989) have noted, it may be helpful to envision these effects as forming a continuum with positive outcomes on one end and negative outcomes on the other. Furthermore, an individual child's position on the continuum is not static; at different points in time a child may either be doing well or be experiencing problems. Several factors have been identified as being capable of influencing where a child is functioning on the continuum. Demographic or family-structure variables are often seen as being capable of affecting adjustment; yet, considered individually, none of these variables is useful in identifying processes of influence. Variables typically invoked as mediating the effects of growing up with an exceptional sibling include age, gender, age spacing, birth order, family size, family socioeconomic status, and the type or severity of disability or illness (Breslau, 1982; Burton, 1975; Farber, 1959; Gath, 1974; Lauterbach, 1974; Lavigne & Ryan, 1979). These variables can only hint at what is actually going on in these homes to produce stress or subsequent adjustment problems. Because of the static nature of these variables there are considerable gaps in the field's understanding of this issue.

The conclusion that some children do well and others do poorly resonates as the major theme in discussions of vulnerable versus resilient children (Garmezy, 1981; Werner & Smith, 1982), and of more general stress and coping in childhood (Garmezy & Rutter, 1983). These mixed results may be interpreted as reflecting the reality of the children's experiences—some cope and adapt while others are apparently overwhelmed, succumbing to stress in ways that negatively affect their adjustment. The resilience-versus-vulnerability literature implies that there should be mixed results, or variability in functioning. Variability should be expected because these children are exposed to a different number of stressors, different kinds of stress, and stress of varying intensities. Furthermore, these children will have different kinds of personal and environmental resources available to buffer or protect them. To date, however, this conceptual approach has not been extensively drawn on to explore the processes whereby individual children cope and adjust in families where there is a member with a disability or chronic illness.

In contrast, the research literature is replete with studies of families' (as opposed to individual children's) efforts to adapt to an exceptional child. For example, Hill's (1949) ABCX model of Family Stress, or McCubbin and Patterson's (1983) revised Double ABCX models have been explicitly adopted by several investigators to examine stress in families with members who are disabled or chronically ill (Donovan, 1988; Kazak, 1987; McCubbin & Patterson, 1983; Wikler, 1986). These models assume that not every stressor will cause family crises. Instead, whether a particular stressful event (A) will result in a family crisis (X) depends on characteristics of the stressful event itself in interaction with family resources (B) and the family's subjective view of the stressor (C). McCubbin and Patterson (1983) have extended Hill's model by integrating a coping variable into the equation and conceptualizing adaptation to stress as a process occurring over a period of time.

Though not explicitly referencing either of these models, several other investigators argue for the need to evaluate direct and indirect influences of similar variables as a means of understanding familial adaptation to stressors associated with raising or growing up with a child with disabilities or chronic illness. In some instances, alternative models are proposed, such as Crnic, Friedrich and Greenberg's (1983) Adaptational Model, or Bubolz and Whiren's (1984) Family Ecological System Model. Otherwise, investigators assume that family life is profoundly affected by the presence of an exceptional child and that family adaptation will depend on some combination of the following variables: 1) characteristics of the child with disabilities or chronic illness, 2) parental adjustment, 3) qualities of the marital relationship, 4) presence and use of social support, 5) family perceptions of the illness or disabling conditions, 6) specific family coping strategies, and 7) family characteristics such as cohesiveness or adaptability (Burt, Cohen, & Bjorck, 1988; Gallagher, Beckman-Bell, & Cross, 1983; Hauser, Jacobson, Wertlieb, Brink, &

Wentworth, 1985; Kazak & Marvin, 1984; Longo & Bond, 1984; McAllister, Butler, & Lei, 1973; Mink, Nihira, & Meyers, 1983; Tavormina, Boll, Dunn, Luscomb, & Taylor, 1981; Wikler, 1986).

Despite the scope and depth of these investigations, there remain significant questions surrounding familial response and adaptation. One of these questions has to do with the experiences of other children in the family. The unit of analyses in the research articles cited above is typically either the family, the marital dyad, or a parent. Only rarely have stress and coping models been used to explore sibling adjustment specifically (Walker, 1988). The authors would argue that in conjunction with family models, adopting an evaluation of the individual experiences of children in these families may also be beneficial. To understand how these approaches compare, the authors, below review conceptualizations of stress as experienced by individuals.

CONCEPTUALIZATIONS OF STRESS

When describing how they use the term *stress,* investigators usually begin with a qualification, a qualification marked by an ambivalent tone. This qualification bemoans the fact that other stress researchers fail to operate from a conceptual or theoretical base, that stress is imprecisely defined, leading to a lack of precise measuring instruments, and that definitions are overly inclusive in identifying stimuli that cause stress. Disagreements on how to conceptualize stress are common, but the concept is typically used in one of three ways (Johnson, 1986; Lazarus & Folkman, 1984). Research on stress can be differentiated according to whether the primary focus is on the stressor as a stimuli, on the organism's response, or on the transaction between the organism and the environment.

Life-Events Perspective

For many, stress is defined by whether or not the organism has experienced a certain kind of stimuli or event. Investigators subscribing to this perspective focus mainly on a class of stressful stimuli or situations to which everyone may be exposed in their lives. These stimuli, frequently referred to as *life events,* include experiences ranging from catastrophes to common daily problems. Events may be further identified in terms of whether they are chronic or acute, whether the event is isolated or constitutes one in a sequence of problems, or whether events are intermittent (Elliott & Eisdorfer, 1982). Basic to this view is the assumption that there are many easily identifiable situations or events that, depending on their nature and number, may result in stress. Thus, stress can be assessed in terms of the number of life events experienced in a given period of time. A major limitation of this perspective, as noted below, is that it overlooks individual variability in the definition of what constitutes stress.

Response-Oriented Perspective

A second view of stress shifts the focus to the organism's biological or psychological response to situations; situations are identified as stressful depending on the nature of the response. This definition is prevalent in biology and medicine. Researchers infer stress when "the person is tense, anxious, depressed (indeed, stress is often treated as synonymous with these constructs), because he or she develops physical signs of arousal or activation, or because the individual shows certain biochemical changes (e.g., secretion of corticosteroids, and catecholamines)" (Johnson, 1986, p. 19). There are numerous methodological problems involved in establishing the causal links between stressors and identified responses, and some responses can be interpreted as indicating psychological stress when such is not the case. A second problem is that, as the next position argues, the links between stressors and responses may be due to a third set of variables, such as cognitive appraisals of the stimuli. Finally, responses from which stress is inferred include physical or psychological problems or dysfunction. A response-oriented view of stress does not leave room for the possibility that certain stressors may constitute a "challenge" that promotes positive growth or change.

Transactional Perspective

The third position, and probably the most popular, conceptualizes stress as a transaction between the person and the environment (Lazarus & Folkman, 1984). Central to understanding what causes psychological distress in different persons are two processes mediating the person–environment relationships: *cognitive appraisals* and *coping*. The stressfulness of a stimulus event depends on a person's view or appraisal of the situation. Appraisals are the evaluative processes through which a person determines why and how much disruption will ensue. Coping is the process by which the individual manages the demands of the environment that are appraised as being stressful. Conceptualizations of coping also frequently include efforts to manage emotions aroused by the stressor.

Several reasons can be given for adopting the transactional framework in assessing the adaptation of children with exceptional siblings. First, drawing distinctions among stressors, personal appraisals, specific coping responses, and adaptation imposes a structure on a research area that is otherwise imprecise. Such distinctions have not been recognized, and definitional ambiguities contribute to inconsistencies between reports. For example, it has been observed that other children are frequently expected to act as caregivers for a sibling with a disability (Farber, 1959; Gath, 1973, 1974). These caregiving responsibilities have alternatively been described as one aspect of the child's problem (caregiving creates stress), as part of the solution (involvement with the exceptional sibling constitutes an active coping response), or as an indication of the child's level of adaptation (greater involvement with the exceptional sibling may be evidence of adjustment). Different investigators use the terms *stress, coping,* and *consequences* to refer to distinctly different aspects of the adaptation process. This lack of clarity contributes to the difficulty of determining the overall effects on siblings of a brother or sister with a disability or chronic illness.

The transactional conceptualization may prove useful in delineating processes influencing the adjustment of siblings of children with special needs because it provides a relativistic view of stress and coping in two important respects. First, as Elliott and Eisdorfer (1982) have written, "stressors, reactions, and buffers or mediators are neither 'good' nor 'bad,' only consequences can be appropriately qualified as being desirable or undesirable" (p. 29). The proponents of a transactional model claim that much of the stress research explicitly seeks connections between stressful events and dysfunction or pathology (Holahan & Moos, 1990; Kobasa, 1982). As a result, coping responses such as avoidance or denial tend to be labelled as undesirable because they are frequently associated with negative outcomes. Recent investigations have illustrated the limitations of such an approach (Elliott & Eisdorfer, 1982). Researchers may not want to conclude, therefore, that children with exceptional siblings who resort to avoidance, denial, or even aggression as strategies for coping with the stresses in their lives are necessarily "at risk" for adjustment problems.

A second way in which this model is relativistic is that it assumes that there are individual differences in ways of adapting to stress. Such a view may be extended such that individual family members are assumed to differ in the ways that they adapt to the stress caused by a disease or disability. Differences will emerge because individual family members are exposed to different kinds of stressors in varying severity, and because they possess different resources (e.g., the number and ability of social network members) and evaluate events differently (e.g., the disabling condition is God's will, or is best explained scientifically). This conceptualization helps to explain variability in individuals' responses to stressors in general, and specifically to those within their own families.

MEASURING STRESS IN THE LIVES OF SIBLINGS OF EXCEPTIONAL CHILDREN

Accordingly, this review reveals three common ways in which stress has been conceptualized. All three orientations may be useful in exploring how children adapt to growing up with exceptional siblings, although the authors favor the third approach for the reasons just offered. Corresponding to each of these conceptualizations is a favored measurement approach with concomitant methodological advantages and problems. These measurement approaches are described generally, after which the authors turn their attention to a critique of each perspective and a discussion of its specific relevance to understanding the functioning of children with exceptional siblings.

Stimulus/Event-Oriented View

A number of instruments are available for assessing children's and adolescents' life events, including: 1) the Life Events Record (Coddington, 1972a; 1972b); 2) the Adolescent Perceived Events Scale (APES) (Compas, Davis, & Forsythe, 1985); 3) the Adolescent Family Inventory of Life Change (A-FILE) (McCubbin, Patterson, Bauman, & Harris, 1981); 4) Life Stress Inventory (Cohen-Sandler, Berman, & King, 1982); 5) Life Events and Coping Inventory (Dise-Lewis, 1988); and 6) several unnamed instruments (Burke & Weir, 1978; Gersten, Langer, Eisenberg, & Simcha-Fagen, 1977; Newcomb, Huba, & Bentler, 1981; Swearingen & Cohen, 1985; Tolor, Murphy, Wilson, & Clayton, 1983; Wright, 1985; Yamamoto & Felsenthal, 1982; Yeaworth, York, Hussey, Ingle, & Goodwin, 1980). The instruments identified vary in terms of scoring procedures, events listed, directions for completion, availability of psychometric information, and the ages of children or adolescents to whom each scale is designed to be administered.

These instruments make slightly different assumptions regarding life stressors and their impact on children and adolescents. Nevertheless, the developers of these scales share a basic interest in indexing the amount of change over a specified period of time, assuming that change scores will prove to be significantly associated with adjustment. Data from several different sources provide support for this relationship (Bedell, Giordani, Amour, Tavormina, & Boll, 1977; Dise-Lewis, 1988; Gad & Johnson, 1980; Johnson & McCutcheon, 1980; Siegel & Brown, 1988). These findings, however, indicate that life change may relate to adjustment problems for some, but not all, children. Assessing life change among children and adolescents with exceptional siblings should provide preliminary clues as to why some children are experiencing more adjustment problems than others. However, most investigators caution against focusing on direct linear relationships between life stress and adjustment-related outcomes.

If assessing life-event changes in the lives of siblings of children or adolescents with chronic illness or disabilities matches one's research questions, the instruments identified above may be useful, with certain qualifications. First, a majority of these scales were developed for use with older children and adolescents. With the exception of the Coddington scale (1972a, 1972b) for preschoolers and elementary school children, a scale that parents complete, tools specifically designed to assess younger children's experiences of recent life changes are not available. A second criticism of these instruments is that they may include stressful experiences for children and adolescents generally, but may not include a variety of events specific to the lives of children with exceptional siblings. For example, the following events are not included on the scales reviewed above, but the authors feel that they should be: renovation of the family home to accommodate a child with disabilities; changes in the child's physical appearance (e.g., hair loss, facial distortions, weight gain, or amputations); changes in the child's intellectual abilities; changes in the child's emotional state (e.g., child becomes depressed, angry, anxious, withdrawn, or talks frequently about dying); child's transfer into a mainstream program, or attendance at a special camp; institutionalization or hospitalization of the child; separation of the sibling from parents during the child's hospitalization, and adjustment to alternate caregivers during times of separation; or other changes for better or worse in the sibling's condition. As with any special group, an additional set of specific events may also need to be included to capture the uniqueness of some of these children's experiences (e.g., A Stress Scale for Children of Alcohol-Abusing Parents [Roosa, Sandler, Gehring, Beals, & Cappo, 1988]).

Response-Oriented View

One strategy for defining psychological stress assumes that certain conditions are necessarily stressful because they are correlated with particular dysfunctional outcomes. The experience of growing up as the sibling of an exceptional child is often assumed to be stressful because some children experience a greater incidence of emotional or behavioral disorders. This perspective corresponds to what was labelled earlier as a response-oriented view. One advantage of adopting this perspective is that it is, at first glance, methodologically straightforward. An investigator chooses outcome measures (e.g., depression, anxiety, indices of poor physical health) and, should a child score above or below a specified cutoff, he or she is declared as experiencing stress. Inferring stress in families with exceptional children based on evidence of adjustment problems in either parents or children continues to be a common practice (Cummings, 1976; Kazak & Marvin, 1984; Longo & Bond, 1984; Waisbren, 1980).

A majority of the investigations inferring stress from responses are based on self-, parent-, or teacher-reports of child functioning. Researchers with a broader conceptualization of stress frequently adopt a different level of analysis, inferring stressful experiences and coping responses from physiological or biochemical responses. The constellation of physiochemical changes associated with stress and coping may include increases in heart rate and cardiac output; increases in plasma catecholamines, cortisol, and endogenous opiates (Schneiderman & McCabe, 1985). Should an investigator generate a hypothesis that siblings of children with disabilities or chronic illness will have a different physiological reaction to stressors, then non–self-report laboratory assessments of responses may be an appropriate method for providing additional information about the ways in which these children are at risk. Evidence from studies on cortisol excretion as an index of coping effectiveness in childhood, however, is conflicting and sufficiently controversial to suggest a need for caution in gathering and interpreting data through these types of assessment procedures (Levine & Coe, 1985).

Stress as a Transaction Between Child and Environment

In response to the limitations of stimulus- and response-oriented views, many investigators have chosen to define stress as a transaction between the person and the environment. Most investigators promoting this conceptualization adopt the following definition of stress, or something similar to it: "Psychological stress is a particular relationship between the person and the environment that is appraised by the person as taxing or exceeding his or her resources and endangering his or her well-being" (Lazarus & Folkman, 1984, p. 19). This definition takes into account characteristics of the person on the one hand, and the nature of the environment and stressor event on the other. However, the judgment as to whether a particular person–environment relationship is stressful hinges on cognitive appraisals, or the individual's own evaluation of what is stressful. Thus, rather than asking whether or not a subject has experienced a set of predefined events during the previous six months, investigators working from this conceptualization use an open-ended interview format, asking respondents themselves to describe events that they find stressful. For example, one of the best known instruments, the Ways of Coping Checklist (Folkman & Lazarus, 1980), asks respondents to "take a few moments and think about the event or situation that has been *the most stressful for you during the last month*. By 'stressful' we mean a situation which was difficult or troubling to you, either because it made you feel bad or because it took effort to deal with it." This approach is in keeping with the assumption that it is appraised stress that will affect health or daily living.

A second distinction is that the transactional view posits a greater role for ordinary daily hassles in influencing health (DeLongis, Coyne, Dakof, Folkman, & Lazarus, 1982; Kanner, Coyne, Schaefer, & Lazarus, 1981). Daily hassles include familiar daily stressors, such as "unresolved conflicts, unfulfilled needs and personal inadequacy" (Lazarus & Folkman, 1984, p. 313). Most often these are problems that may seem minor, yet research findings suggest that, in comparison to life events, daily hassles are superior in predicting psychological and somatic adult symptoms (DeLongis et al., 1982; Kanner et al., 1981). This provocative work needs to be replicated with both adult and child samples.

Recent investigations of children's experiences of stressful events adopt a similar methodological approach in which children are instructed to identify "things that make kids your age feel bad, unhappy, or scared" (Band & Weisz, 1988, p. 248), or are asked to describe "what happened that made you feel bad, nervous, or worry?" (Lewis, Siegel, & Lewis, 1984, p. 117). Children are typically provided with more structure than adults; experimenters usually ask children if something stressful happened in a specific context, such as: 1) a separation from a friend, 2) a visit to the doctor's office, 3) a conflict with a parent or teacher, 4) a conflict with a friend, 5) a failure, or 6) a physical illness or accident (Band & Weisz, 1988; Gamble, 1991; Wertlieb, Weigel, & Feldstein, 1987).

This measurement approach to assessing stress allows that a particular event (whether major, or simply a daily hassle) constitutes a stress only after the child has appraised it and invested it with meaning, such that his or her perception or appraisal mediates the experience. This approach contrasts with one in which categories of events are specified a priori and assigned standardized weights as an index of disruptiveness, without regard for the psychological meaning of the events. If such a procedure were adopted, what kind of events would children with exceptional siblings name? For the time being it is possible to identify and characterize potential stressors for these children. In the following discussion the authors distinguish among a variety of events or conditions that have proven to be stressful for these children under some circumstances. Which of these events or conditions are stressful for a particular child at a particular time, however, will depend on the child's appraisal of the event and the individual and contextual supports available.

Although the transactional framework assumes that a broad array of events may create stress, this review will be more selective. Because the authors believe that the day-to-day difficulties arising in interpersonal relationships may be important in understanding the adjustment of siblings of children with disabilities or chronic illness, the examples chosen are stressors arising in sibling relationships, parent–child relationships, and the nondisabled child's relationships with peers and the wider community. The authors do not mean to suggest that all social interactions or other qualities of these relationships are inherently stressful. The goal, however, is to describe potential sources of difficulty in the lives of nondisabled siblings. In sum, the following sections detail what research suggests would constitute the major stressors or daily hassles from the perspective of siblings of children with disabilities or chronic illnesses.

STRESSORS IN THE SIBLING RELATIONSHIP

While studies of social processes in other areas of developmental psychology have increasingly adopted bidirectional models of influence, research on siblings of children with disabilities tends to investigate effects from a unidirectional perspective. This research, with few exceptions (McHale, Simeonsson, & Sloan, 1984; Miller & Cantwell, 1976; Stoneman, Brody, Davis, & Crapps, 1987, 1988), focuses on the effects of the child with disabilities on his or her brothers or sisters. The authors agree with those investigators who argue for and have pursued bidirectional and dyadic assessments of sibling relationships (Abramovitch, Corter, & Pepler, 1980; Brody, Stoneman, & Mackinnon, 1982; Dunn & Kendrick, 1982). Yet for the time being, the focus is on problems that nondisabled siblings might describe. Ideally, the exceptional siblings would be asked to describe problems as well, assuming they are mentally and physically competent to respond to this inquiry.

Speculating about potential problems associated with sibling interactions, the authors anticipate that the reports would fall into three broad categories, problems associated with: 1) meeting affectional needs, 2) providing direct services, and 3) developing an identity. The extent to which each of these functions is met depends on the characteristics of the individual child and his or her family.

Meeting Affectional Needs

"How can I deal with my mixed feelings?" Powell and Gallagher (1993, p. 75) identify this as a question frequently arising as a key concern of children with siblings with disabilities, regardless of the type of impairment. The affectional ties of disabled–nondisabled sibling dyads can be either positive or negative, and, in general, do not seem to differ from sibling relationships in which neither child has a disability or illness. There may be differences, however, in the ways in which feelings, both positive and negative, are expressed (Miller, 1974). Meeting affectional needs may prove to be stressful when certain emotions may not be expressed due to the fact that the sibling does not understand or cannot reciprocate the expression (e.g., by arguing or teasing back) or reciprocates inappropriately (e.g., hugs too hard). The emotional quality of these interactions is also influenced indirectly by parental expectations. Parents may prohibit overt expressions of hostility. For example, siblings of children who were oncology patients reported that the child was often free to hit or kick, while they were strictly prohibited from retaliating because the children bruised easily (Walker, 1988). The extent to which nondisabled siblings can find alternative means of expressing the emotions inherent in sibling relationships may contribute significantly to the degree of stress experienced.

The phrase "meeting affectional needs" brings to mind the attachment construct. There are several studies indicating that older children often act as subsidiary attachment figures for their younger siblings (Ainsworth, 1973; Dunn & Kendrick, 1982; Stewart, 1983). To the authors' knowledge, the development of attachments between children with disabilities or chronic illness and their siblings has not been explored. Formation of attachments between mothers and children with Down syndrome (Cicchetti & Sroufe, 1976; Emde & Brown, 1978; Serafica & Cicchetti, 1976), and between mothers and children with other disabilities (Fraiberg, 1974; Greenberg & Marvin, 1979; Nix, 1980), has been reported, leading the authors to believe that attachments formed between siblings when one has a disability or illness are highly probable; attachments may develop at a slower rate in some instances, but they develop nonetheless. If attachments exist, it would be expected that siblings would report stress when experiencing separations or when the relationship or attachment is threatened.

In sum, stressors associated with meeting affectional needs may include, but are not restricted to: 1) when a child with a disability or illness does not react to or reciprocate either positive or negative emotions directed at them; 2) when the child responds inappropriately to their own or to the sibling's emotions; 3) when, because of parental sanctions, emotions, especially anger, cannot be expressed toward the child; and 4) when separation threatens an attachment.

Provision of Direct Services

A second question frequently asked by siblings of children with disabilities is "what can I do to help Mom and Dad?" (Powell & Gallagher, 1993, p. 74). Both within the family and outside of it, siblings influence each others' development by taking care of or teaching each other, by serving as sources of information, playmates, confidantes, and companions. In those sibling dyads in which one child has a disability or illness, the degree to which one of the members can reciprocate may be limited, and there is a chance that the other child may find him- or herself assuming a large burden of care and responsibility. Investigators have noted that additional household responsibilities and demands for maturity beyond the age of these children may create stress, as well as restrict participation in other developmentally significant activities, such as extracurricular functions (Farber & Jenne, 1963). Alternatively, other investigators report that the responsibilities of childcare and household chores are not associated with negative effects on siblings (Stoneman & Brody, 1984). In fact, several authors recommend involving the nondisabled or healthy children in caregiving. For example, Kovacs and Feinberg (1982) suggest that integrating children into management routines so that they are expected to share responsibilities for care, such as assisting with a diabetic sibling's insulin shots and urine analysis, may provide these children with important instrumental ways of coping. Carrying medications to school is another example of involvement that is assumed to be beneficial (Klein, 1972).

Many factors contribute to the need for extra caregiving, or make childcare particularly demanding or unpleasant (e.g., the child's age or the nature of the disability). To date, neither parents' nor children's reports have been scrutinized in a way that would allow investigators to determine when caregiving and other responsibilities may qualify as stressors or create *role strain* (Goode, 1960) or *role tension* (Farber, 1959). At least two sources and types of role strain can be specified for exceptional sibling dyads. First, according to Goode, role strain does not arise simply as function of difficult or displeasing obligations. Roles are demanding because they are required at particular times and places, and frequently these demands are in conflict with fulfilling the obligations of other roles. For children with exceptional siblings, role strain may occur when the time spent babysitting limits the time available to complete homework assignments. Role strain may also arise because different roles are endowed with different meanings or expectations in relation to other individuals in the social environment. It may be important, therefore, to determine how children themselves perceive their roles, particularly in relation to how much control they have over their performance of the activities associated with the role. For instance, children's understandings of why they engage in particular activities with their siblings (e.g., "my parents expect me to" versus "I want to") may determine the degree to which these interactions are pleasant or unpleasant. Thus, a child's appraisals or evaluations of caregiving responsibilities along such dimensions as personal control or the meaning of a particular responsibility will determine the degree of stress. In sum, caregiving per se is not necessarily stressful. Instead the authors would argue that caregiving becomes stressful only under certain conditions, specifically when: 1) there are too many responsibilities, or they are too physically demanding; 2) the tasks are unpleasant or dirty; 3) the sibling is unresponsive, agonistic, or demanding; 4) caregiving responsibilities interfere with other desired activities; 5) efforts go unrecognized or unrewarded; and 6) sibling caregiving is not balanced by playful exchanges with the sibling, when the relationship is characterized by only one kind of interaction—childcare.

Influences on Developing Identities

In early studies Grossman (1972) and Schreiber and Feeley (1965) reported that the development of an identity separate from that of a child with disabilities seems to be of great importance to typical siblings. From her observations of adolescent sibling support groups, Grossman reported that "the issue of being similar to or different from the retarded sibling permeated many of the meetings (of siblings) and seemed to be a source of major concern for all group members. In fact, the experience with the group suggests that the main task of siblings of defective children is to avoid identifying with them" (p. 34). Wasserman (1983), however, observed that nondisabled siblings may actively identify with children with disabilities. Specifically, she hypothesized that siblings who feel that their brother or sister with retardation is the recipient of excessive parental attention, to their own relative neglect, may come to imitate certain behaviors in order to gain or regain parental affection. Wasserman also argued that siblings who experience guilt over a child's disability may attempt to alleviate some of their guilt through identification with the child.

Identification with a child with disabilities, however, can backfire, leading to confusion and anxiety. For example, some nondisabled siblings express concerns about their own health, body image, social competence, intelligence, and academic abilities, and experience problems in establishing a self-identity (see Grossman, 1972; Murphy, Pueschel, Duffy, & Brody, 1976; San Martino & Newman, 1974; Wasserman, 1983). When self-doubt arises, deidentification with the child with disabilities may be one means of reducing fears and anxieties about one's own competencies, as well as a way of strengthening one's sense of individuality and "normality." Deidentification can also backfire, however. If siblings invest large portions of their energy in defining themselves as different, this may be evidence of poor sibling relationships or a lack of cohesiveness in family relationships (siblings may deidentify with the family as a whole), or these efforts may be motivated by extreme anxiety.

In sum, nondisabled children may experience a unique set of stressors as a function of efforts to create an identity and recognize their own capabilities.

STRESSORS ASSOCIATED WITH THE PARENT–CHILD RELATIONSHIP

In this section, the parent–child relationship is the focus of discussion, or more specifically, those aspects of this relationship that may create stress for siblings of exceptional children. A review of the literature reveals at least four themes in parent–child relationships that are potentially linked to the occurrence of stress for nondisabled siblings, including: 1) a breakdown in communication channels; 2) discrepancies between the parent's and sibling's perceptions of the impact of the child's disability or illness; 3) hostile, punitive, overprotective, or rejecting parenting practices; and 4) the nature of the parent's adjustment to the stressors associated with the child's illness or disability.

Communication Patterns and the Need for Information

Grossman (1972) observed an intense curiosity about a brother's or sister's retardation among a group of teenage siblings undergoing counseling. There was frequently a startling lack of information, however, about the disabling condition, its manifestation, and its consequences. Similarly, adolescents in Schreiber and Feeley's (1965) discussion groups for siblings of children with disabilities expressed concern regarding the nature of mental retardation, the strengths and limitations to be expected of their brothers or sisters, and whether their siblings with retardation understood the nature of their own disability. Chinitz (1981) found that only one child in a group of nine siblings of children with disabilities was able to demonstrate any comprehension of the sibling's condition, yet even this child did not have a label for the diagnosis. Other children in the group could describe concrete, observable characteristics, but did not possess an understanding of the cause or consequences of the disabilities. Burton (1975) reports that 53% of her sample of mothers of children with cystic fibrosis had never discussed the disease with the siblings of the ill child. Explanations provided by the remaining 47% were simplistic and minimal. Apparently, siblings are often ill-informed about their brother's or sister's disabling condition or illness.

Despite their curiosity, however, typical children rarely ask questions related to a disability or its treatment (Burton, 1975; Gogan, Koocher, Foster, & O'Malley, 1977). Burton interpreted this trend as a reflection of the children's need to protect their parents—children fear that parents may lack the capacity to tolerate the disability or illness, and that questions may precipitate a breakdown or rejection of themselves. Thus, children avoid loss of contact and maintain the approval of their parents by keeping their thoughts and feelings to themselves. Meyerowitz and Kaplan (1967) found support for this notion, showing that children who were aware of their sibling's diagnosis of cystic fibrosis were a significant source of stress for their parents. It seems that family discourse about the disease may precipitate parental emotions such as sorrow, anger, or fear of losing control.

Murphy (1982) suggested that parents often lack the confidence and emotional strength to inform siblings about the diagnosis of a child with mental retardation, and they may actually try to keep them from learning about it. Carandang, Folkins, Hines, and Steward (1979) postulated that within the families of diabetic children, a natural flow of information about the illness is blocked by a coping pattern in mothers that is characterized by denial. Turk (1964) observed that this pattern of diminished communication spreads to other aspects of family life, producing a generalized "web of silence" (p. 69). Seligman (1983) writes, "although parents struggle with dark feelings of their own regarding their handicapped child, they seem to be able to find these more acceptable than similar thoughts held by the normal children" (p. 156). He adds that parents who try to protect or shield their other children from negative thoughts may be doing them a disservice. Parents may actually be blocking the child's need to express such thoughts.

The specific effects of inadequate information on the nondisabled or healthy children's coping efforts and adjustment are not yet known. There are, however, investigations that may bear upon this issue. First, some work shows that knowledgeable parents are better able to cope with their children's disability than are less-knowledgeable parents (Giannini & Goodman, 1963; Rapaport, 1962). In a study of college-age students, Grossman (1972) found that "the more open the discussions (about a mentally retarded child) the normal brother or sister remembered occurring in the family, and the more curiosity about it that they recalled expressing, the better their effectiveness in coping with the impact of the mentally retarded child's burden on their lives" (p. 138).

In addition to providing siblings with information about their brother or sister's disability or illness, training in intervention strategies may help them cope with various aspects of their relationship with the sibling. For example, Miller and Cantwell (1976) trained children with siblings with mental retardation to act as therapists. By providing the children with the training necessary to implement behavior modification procedures, these investigators expected to increase the frequency of positive interactions between children with retardation and their siblings. Miller and Cantwell considered their program to be effective inasmuch as children no longer complained about negative interactions between themselves and their siblings with mental retardation. The specific nature of training may vary from intervention program to intervention program (cf. Weinrott, 1974), yet the goal is to ensure that nondisabled children have the knowledge and ability to use the knowledge in a way that will reduce problems in their interactions with their exceptional siblings and with others in their communities.

In addition to needing information about a sibling's disability or illness and about effective strategies for handling those aspects of the relationship that are difficult, children also report that they need to know how and what to plan for the future (Grossman, 1972). Grossman described children's beliefs that they would be better able to adjust to their situations if they understood what the future would bring to them, their parents, and the child with a disability. Along these lines, Murphy et al. (1976) found that older adolescent siblings of children with Down syndrome were often aware of the genetic basis of this disorder and demonstrated concern and the need to know about their own chances of bearing a child with Down syndrome.

In short, as Wentworth (1974) reports, nondisabled children want parents to be honest with them. Interestingly, parents report a desire that professionals with whom they have contact also be honest (Seligman, 1983). Nevertheless, parents may fail to openly answer a sibling's inquiries about the child with a disability or about the sibling's own role in the child's life. Chinn, Winn, and Walters (1978) note that decisions about a child with a disability or illness are often made without prior discussion with, or explanation to, other children in the family who may be affected by them. These authors counsel that parents always communicate their plans to other children and explain the reasoning behind their decisions. Based on this review, the authors suspect that if asked about daily stressors in their lives, nondisabled children may mention the following situations involving parents: 1) when satisfactory answers to their questions are not forthcoming; 2) when information is lacking about how to respond in a particular situation, that is, when they lack the skills to manage the child with disabilities effectively or to respond to other people's reactions to the child; 3) when information is lacking about how a disability or disease affects their own health or future development; 4) when information is lacking about how the future will unfold and who will care for the sibling after he or she reaches adulthood; and 5) when opportunities to openly express or communicate negative feelings or concerns are not made available.

Discrepant Expectations and Perceptions

When siblings do possess information or have formed opinions about a disabling condition or illness, the result may be strain in their relationships with their parents when the information or opinion is different from a parent's own viewpoint. Crocker (1981) describes four such discrepancies capable of producing conflicts between parents and the nondisabled sibling. First, parents may expect the sibling to accept the child with a disability and emphasize the family's strengths and courage. In contrast, the nondisabled sibling may have a more negative view of the situation and a host of troubled feelings, including anxiety and jealousy. The sibling may possess a secret wish for a "normal" brother or sister, but may be reluctant to reveal his or her anxieties and wishes for fear of angering the parent. The parents themselves may be reluctant to recognize the sibling's unhappiness or hurt and may deny that problems exist.

The second discordant view that parents may hold is that any accomplishment is possible for the child with a disability, causing the parents to expect near-normal interactions and activities between the child and his or her typical siblings. But the siblings may lack this particular perspective because they are confronted with the limitations inherent in the atypical sibling relationship. This discrepancy between the parents' and the siblings' viewpoints could, in turn, lead to difficulties between them.

Crocker's third point is that siblings must cope with a double standard in the family for compliance with rules—the typical siblings may be expected to adhere to certain rules, whereas the child with special needs may have a less rigid set of standards. For example, Michaelis (1980) notes that siblings may resent that the child with a disability gets to "play," while they are expected to do homework. Eight- to thirteen-year-old children's comments in a support group for siblings of children with pediatric cancer reveal anger over different attitudes toward fighting and perceived unfairness. These children reported that children who were ill were often permitted to hit healthy siblings, who were never allowed to hit back (Bendor, 1990).

The fourth source of misunderstanding is when parents assume brothers and sisters are preoccupied with the needs and progress of the child with disabilities, when, in fact, they have, and need to have, a broad range of interests in other areas as well. For example, Bendor (1990) reports that children often come to resent having to share in caregiving, and, as a consequence, tension builds in the parent–child relationship. Tension may also result when parents and children have different views about how to spend family leisure time, when parents tend to choose only activities appropriate for the child with a disability or illness.

Crocker's (1981) analysis presents a useful overview of some of the kinds of problems that siblings of children with disabilities or chronic illness may face. When parents and children disagree or perceive situations differently, it is likely to create tension or problems in their relationships, resulting in conflict or lingering feelings of resentment, anger, rejection, vulnerability, or, in short, stress.

Parental Attitudes and Practices

Research on parenting attitudes and practices in families with exceptional children reveals that parenting is typically examined across dimensions, such as warmth–hostility and restrictiveness–permissiveness, and, as might be expected, results of these investigations are mixed. Parents of children with mental retardation have been characterized as rejecting, punitive, and overprotective (Cook, 1963; Cummings, Bayley, & Rie, 1966; Ricci, 1970; Waisbren, 1980). Parents of children with chronic illness have been characterized similarly as strict, overcontrolling, overprotective, and rejecting (Long & Moore, 1979; Markova, MacDonald, & Forbes, 1980; Walker, Ford, & Donald, 1987). In contrast, others have observed no differences between the attitudes expressed by parents of children with and without disabilities or chronic illness (Boll, Dimino, & Mattsson, 1978; Caldwell & Guze, 1960).

Substantiating the existence or absence of more hostile or negative childrearing attitudes and determining whether such attitudes apply to all children in the family or only to the child with a disability or illness seems critical. King (1981) investigated childrearing practices in families with chronically ill children and found no differences between the treatment of typical siblings and children with illness. This study suggests stability within families and was the only study of its kind that the authors were able to locate. There is insufficient evidence to reach conclusions about differences between families with and without exceptional children. However, the authors believe that if parents describe their parenting practices as strict or rejecting, this sets the stage for the experience of a variety of stressors by the nondisabled child.

Parental Personal Adjustment

Parents encounter certain stresses that continue over the lifetimes of children with disabilities or chronic illness. Some of the stressors are related to the characteristic hardships of having an exceptional child, such as the stigmatization, the prolonged burden of care, and concern over the child's and the family's welfare. Other stressors involve parents' emotional responses to the child's condition, such as parents' self-doubt or guilt, conflicts between parents' own needs and their child's needs, and parents' fear, confusion, and periodic grieving (Breslau, Staruch, & Mortimer, 1982; Farber, 1959;

Holroyd & McArthur, 1976; Tavormina et al., 1981; Tew & Laurence, 1973). Whereas parental reactions to having and caring for a child with disabilities are well documented, the impact of these emotional and behavioral responses on other family members is unknown. A vast literature documents the direct effects of the emotional climate of the home and parental discipline techniques on children's social, emotional, and cognitive development (Maccoby & Martin, 1984). Breslau and colleagues (Breslau & Prabucki, 1987; Breslau et al., 1982; Breslau, Weitzman, & Messenger, 1981) present data to suggest that the mother's psychological distress might be a mechanism linking chronic family stress with children's problems. The demands of daily care of a child with disabilities increase maternal distress, which in turn may have an adverse effect on the mother's parenting and on the other children.

As with parenting attitudes, the authors believe that parental personal adjustment will translate into stress for the nondisabled children when it is reflected in inconsistent, harsh, or neglectful parenting. It is possible to imagine parent–child relationships becoming excessively conflictual as a function of the parent's own adjustment problems. In contrast, emotional absence may occur; that is, the parent may be so distraught or depressed that he or she is unable to provide for the physical and psychological needs of other children. This experience may not be uncommon, as parents often say that they will have to attend to other children's needs "later," meaning either when a sick child dies or is cured (Cairns et al., 1979). Thus, when parents experience difficulties adjusting to diagnosis or treatment of a child's disability or illness, the authors believe that these conditions will create stress for other children, who will experience disruptions in parenting practices.

RELATIONSHIPS WITH PEERS AND INTERACTIONS WITH THE LARGER COMMUNITY

A final source of stress for siblings of exceptional children is their families' and their own interactions with the larger community, as these interactions may be affected by the special social circumstances that the disability causes. Both the quality and quantity of extra-familial communication may be affected by the presence of a child with disabilities. For instance, many families that include a child with a disability are relatively isolated (Birenbaum, 1971; Cairns et al., 1979; Falkman, 1977). The healthy children in these families may become aware of this isolation, perceive themselves as being different or stigmatized, and avoid social contacts. In addition, parents may strive to project an image of "normalcy" to others by carefully controlling communication about the disability (Birenbaum, 1971; Voysey, 1972). These parents may fear that "healthy children will give the game away" by revealing too much to teachers, relatives, neighbors, or peers (Voysey, 1972, p. 84). If parents are successful in convincing the healthy children not to share their experiences with others, they may be severely limiting the child's ability to form significant friendships and obtain support from others.

Powell and Gallagher (1993) identify at least four stressors specific to peer relationships. The special concerns that they identify include how to inform friends about a sibling with a disability, what to do when others tease the child, how to include a child with a disability in play with peers or create interactions whereby the friend will accept the child, and finally, how the sibling will influence dating relationships. With the passage and implementation of PL 94-192, children must also cope with the increased likelihood that the disabled sibling will attend the same school. If a sibling is in the same school environment, children are often expected to assume a "brother's keeper" role, travelling with the sibling to and from school, interpreting communications, and performing other caregiving tasks (Powell & Gallagher, 1985, p. 182). Children often feel compelled to guard their brother or sister with a disability or illness against discrimination. Siblings may explain, scold, fight, or remove the child with a disability or illness from threatening situations (Klein, 1972). A related problem is concern about how other children will respond to them personally, and fears of rejection once others find out about the child with a disability. Other stressors include stigmatization by teachers who associate a sibling with the child with a disability or illness in negative ways.

SUMMARY OF STRESSORS EXPERIENCED BY CHILDREN WITH SIBLINGS WITH DISABILITIES

In this section the authors have considered a variety of experiences that may prove to be stressful when growing up as a sibling of an exceptional child. The assumption guiding this discussion is that the stresses experienced are not related to the disabling condition or illness per se, but may be related to the exceptional child's direct and indirect impact on intra- and extra-familial personal relationships. It should be emphasized, however, that the stresses identified are not found in all families with exceptional children. Children may experience some, but not all of the circumstances outlined above. For instance, some siblings may find that the only stress that they must cope with is related to their friends' negative perceptions of people with disabilities. Other siblings may be required to care for a child with a disability because parents are too busy, too emotionally distraught, or unable to garner appropriate support from friends, relatives, or formal community services. In line with the arguments presented earlier, the number, type, and variety of potential stressors to which a child is exposed should be evaluated in terms of the consequences of those experiences for his or her adjustment.

In this discussion the authors do not describe stressful experiences from a developmental perspective. Whether or not children experience the stressors identified will depend on their age and relative cognitive and emotional maturity. Pre-kindergarten children are unlikely to recognize differences between their own and their parents' expectations. Younger siblings will perceive, and potentially be upset by isolated incidences of differences in their own treatment versus that received by the child with a disability. Reaching the conclusion that these incidences add up to a whole different set of standards of treatment would require more abstract thinking. This is not to imply that children of different ages would describe different types of events. Rather, the authors suspect that similar events would be named, but that perceptions of how stressful the event is would change with age and development. For example, a 7-year-old child may find it easier to introduce a friend to a sibling with a disability than the more self-conscious 12-year-old child. Likewise, because of the nature of the younger child's play activities, it may be easier for him or her to incorporate a sibling with a mental disability into activities than it would be for an older child.

In addition to developmental status, the authors suspect that gender may also be a factor in the identification of stressful events. For example, more often than not, in adolescence, a boy will pick up his date at her home. This ritual of dating allows adolescent males to more effectively hide the presence of a sibling if he feels embarrassed. Not so for adolescent girls, who are more likely to be found out. For males, it may be more stressful if they are discovered to be babysitting a sibling, or even worse, feeding or assisting the sibling in toileting. For girls, the same stigmas against caregiving may not apply. Finally, the nature of the stressors that arise for these children may also be a function of ethnicity and socioeconomic status.

The authors believe that age, gender, ethnic, and social-class variables are probably significant factors in children's ability to cope with the events that they experience as well. Since discussions of children's or adolescents' coping with stressor events are relatively new, there are only minimal data on the issue of age or gender differences in coping (Curry & Russ, 1985; Ebata & Moos, 1991; Elwood, 1987; Hamilton & Fagot, 1988). For the purposes of this discussion, the authors first need to establish what constitutes coping in childhood and adolescence, and then how current conceptualizations are applicable in assessing the coping efforts of siblings of children with disabilities or chronic illness.

COPING STRATEGIES

When a child experiences any of the interpersonal stressors identified above, he or she will attempt to cope in some way. Coping responses include children's attempts to change their perceptions of the situation and attempts to change the situation itself. That is, coping is a process, the function of which is to resolve a problem and regulate emotional distress (Lazarus & Folkman,

1984). The means of meeting these objectives may involve both cognitive processes and active manipulations of the environment. Results of recent investigations of children's and adolescents' coping strategies suggest that the responses employed may fit into several broad but distinct categories based on aggregates of specific responses. It is interesting that the same categories seem to emerge repeatedly from research projects conducted independently. Table 1 lists these coping categories, provides examples of the nature of the responses, and lists the investigators who have described such a category or included representative items on their coping scales.

The coping mechanisms of siblings of children who have special needs have been largely neglected as a focus of research. Researchers seem to have overlooked children's immediate reactions in favor of studying longer-term consequences for adjustment. The authors believe that the emergent categories of coping responses may be a missing link in understanding the effects of stressors associated directly or indirectly with a sibling with special needs. Children may choose to avoid dealing with parents when conflicts arise over discrepant expectations. Frustration associated with caregiving may lend itself to aggressive responses or crying and yelling. Social support seeking, whether for practical or emotional reasons, may be common when dealing with all kinds of problems, regardless of whom else is involved. A previous study has already established that some coping strategies, in this case strategies identified as self-cognitions (i.e., a category including responses such as avoiding the person responsible for the problem or telling yourself that everything will be okay), may be significantly correlated with adjustment measures and indices of the quality of the sibling relationship (Gamble & McHale, 1989). Since conducting that study, coping measures have been refined and improved, and the authors anticipate that coping-response variables should be even better predictors of adjustment.

The results of the studies cited in Table 1 show increasing convergence in conceptualizations and assessments of coping. Results also suggest that children as young as 6 years of age can adequately describe their own efforts to cope (Band & Weisz, 1988). Further, a majority of investigators examining children's and adolescent's responses to stress report that coping is not confined to extraordinary stressor events. Rather, evidence of coping with everyday stressors is plentiful (Band & Weisz, 1988; Elwood, 1987; Wertlieb et al., 1987). Finally, these coping studies reveal that not only do children identify a rich variety of responses, but that individual children will use several different forms of coping over time (Curry & Russ, 1985). Thus, there is support for Murphy's (1962) contention that children tend to take an active approach to the obstacles they face in their lives, bringing with them a variety of coping responses upon which to draw.

Several limitations of existing coping scales should be noted. Scale development has often proceeded with samples that are small and unrepresenta-

Table 1. Classification of coping strategies available to children and adolescents

Coping category	Example strategy	Examples in literature	
SUPPORT SEEKING (factors often emerge distinguishing between adult and peer support, but not always) (may include spiritual support seeking)	"I talked to a friend/parent about the problem."	Band and Weisz Curry and Russ Elwood Gamble Ryan Wertlieb, Weigel, and Feldstein Wills	(1988) (1985) (1987) (1991) (1988) (1987) (1985)
PHYSICAL AGGRESSION	Problem-focused: "I hit him to make him stop." Emotion-focused: "I kicked something, 'cause it helps me feel better."	Band and Weisz Dise-Lewis Gamble Lochman and Lampron Ryan Wills	(1988) (1988) (1991) (1986) (1988) (1985)
VERBAL AGGRESSION	Problem-focused: "I yelled at her to stop it." Emotion-focused: "I yelled to let the bad feelings out."	Band and Weisz Elwood Gamble Spirito, Stark and Williams	(1988) (1987) (1991) (1988)
DIRECT PROBLEM-SOLVING (includes information selection, direct behavioral actions, and cognitive efforts to solve problem)	"I tried to fix the problem or do something about it."	Band and Weisz Curry and Russ Elwood Gamble Kliewer Spirito, Stark, and Williams Wertlieb, Weigel, and Feldstein Wills	(1988) (1985) (1987) (1991) (1991) (1988) (1987) (1985)
AVOIDANCE/ DISTRACTION	"I stay away from him if I think we are going to fight." "I don't think about it."	Band and Weisz Curry and Russ Dise-Lewis Gamble Kliewer Ryan Spirito, Stark, and Williams	(1988) (1985) (1988) (1991) (1991) (1988) (1988)
DO NOTHING	"I give up." "I don't do anything."	Band and Weisz Elwood Gamble Kliewer Spirito, Stark, and Williams	(1988) (1987) (1991) (1991) (1988)
PHYSICAL EXERCISE		Kliewer Ryan Wills	(1991) (1988) (1985)
COGNITIVE RESTRUCTURING/ SELF-SOOTHING (may include use of fantasy and relaxation activities)	"I tried to see the good side or told myself things that would help me feel better."	Band and Weisz Curry and Russ Elwood Gamble Kliewer Ryan Spirito, Stark, and Williams Wills	(1988) (1985) (1987) (1991) (1991) (1988) (1988) (1985)

tive (e.g., children receiving dental treatment). Scale construction varies widely; some authors have simply rewritten items that originally appeared on instruments used with adults. Other authors have included items generated from interviews with children and adolescents. Some items are based on responses to hypothetical problems, while others reflect children's reports of efforts to cope with problems actually experienced. Often, items may only be relevant to specific situations ("I tried to concentrate on the muppet poster on the wall"). Further, much of the information resulting from these instruments is based on retrospective self-reports and may not represent a child's actual coping experiences, but rather their scripts of what they should or might do.

Despite these limitations, this emerging taxonomy of strategies should be relevant to understanding how siblings of children with disabilities or chronic illness adapt. Despite improvements made in recent years in conceptualizations and measures of coping, studies are needed to determine whether there are coping responses used by children with exceptional siblings that are not addressed on existing scales. The authors argue above that life-event scales could be modified by adding events representing these children's unique experiences. It would seem that a similar argument would apply to cases in which coping-response scales may need to be modified to reflect unique strategies, if any exist. Once it is certain that the appropriate strategies are being assessed for this group, it may be worthwhile to determine if children identified as being generally well-adjusted are employing different coping responses, as compared to children who are experiencing more adjustment problems. Are there strategies that appear to be more closely associated with adaptation for this group that may improve intervention efforts? Inferring a causal relationship between coping strategies and adjustment is problematic and suggests a need for more prospective studies. Furthermore, the authors suspect that the coping–adjustment link is complex, and that the role of a variety of individual, sibling, and family characteristics would need to be evaluated simultaneously in order to understand it properly. Nevertheless, the authors are confident that investigations of children's coping responses will eventually help to clarify the observed variability in adjustment.

CONCLUDING COMMENTS

Not everyone is sanguine about the value of adapting stress and coping research frameworks as a basis of investigation. The authors acknowledge a variety of limitations, yet, as argued, the nature and number of stressors experienced by children who have exceptional siblings, and their efforts to cope and adapt in response to these stressors, will play a central role in shaping their overall adjustment. Documenting what constitutes stress or coping for these children will have implications not only for the development of theoretical frameworks, but also for the design of effective prevention and intervention programs.

To encourage and assist other investigators to adopt such a perspective, the authors have attempted to identify measurement approaches for assessing stress and coping processes. One approach includes adopting a stress-as-stimuli perspective and employing life-event or life-change scales as indices of stress. An alternative approach would be to identify stress through an assessment of responses. Innovative developments in assessments of children's physiological responses to stress may result in information about inter- and intra-individual responses to stressors, as well as provide clues about coping effectiveness. Finally, stress may be conceptualized as a transaction between the child and his or her environment. The authors believe that the experiences of children with exceptional siblings may be usefully characterized through a documentation of children's reports of their day-to-day stressors, particularly for stress arising in interpersonal contexts. In conjunction with descriptions of stressful events, asking these children to report on or rate the type and/or frequency of their employing a variety of different coping strategies rounds out the information necessary to evaluate processes relevant to understanding variations in adjustment.

The literature on resilience/vulnerability and stress and coping in children and adolescents has much to teach about conceptual, methodological, and measurement strategies for evaluating the adjustment of siblings of children with disabilities and chronic illness. Therefore, just as some investigators have successfully adapted family stress and coping models for examining processes of adjustment to a disability or illness at the family level, other investigators may benefit from adopting existing frameworks in their efforts to better understand the specific problems that individual children in these families may face. Investigators may wish to adopt the perspectives and methods proposed in this chapter to learn more about siblings of children with disabilities or chronic illness.

REFERENCES

Abramovitch, R., Corter, C., & Pepler, D.J. (1980). Observations of mixed sex sibling dyads. *Child Development, 51,* 1268–1271.

Ainsworth, M.D.S. (1973). The development of infant–mother attachment. In B.M. Caldwell & H.N. Ricciuti (Eds.), *Review of child development research* (Vol. 3, pp. 1–94.). Chicago: The University of Chicago Press.

Aply, J., Barbour, R.F., & Westmacott, I. (1967). Impact of congenital heart disease on the family: Preliminary report. *British Medical Journal, 1,* 103–111.

Band, E.B., & Weisz, J.R. (1988). How to feel better when it feels bad: Children's perspectives on coping with everyday stress. *Developmental Psychology, 24*(2), 247–253.

Bedell, J.R., Giordani, B., Amour, J.C., Tavormina, J., & Boll, T. (1977). Life stress and the psychological and medical adjustment of chronically ill children. *Journal of Psychosomatic Research, 21,* 237–242.

Bendor, S.J. (1990). Anxiety and isolation in siblings of pediatric cancer patients: The need for prevention. *Social Work in Health Care, 14,* 17–35.
Binger, C.M., Albin, A.R., & Feuerstein, R. (1969). Childhood leukemia: Emotional impact on patient and family. *New England Journal of Medicine, 280,* 414–423.
Birenbaum, A. (1971). The mentally retarded child in the home and family cycle. *Journal of Health and Social Behavior, 12,* 55–65.
Boll, T., Dimino, E., & Mattsson, A. (1978). Parenting attitudes: The role of personality style and childhood long-term illness. *Journal of Psychosomatic Research, 22,* 209–213.
Breslau, N. (1982). Siblings of disabled children: Birth order and age-spacing effects. *Journal of Abnormal Child Psychology, 10,* 85–96.
Breslau, N., & Prabucki, K. (1987). Siblings of disabled children. *Archives of General Psychiatry, 44,* 1040–1046.
Breslau, N., Staruch, K., & Mortimer, E. (1982). Psychological distress in mothers of disabled children. *American Journal of Diseases of Childhood, 136,* 682–686.
Breslau, N., Weitzman, M., & Messenger, K. (1981). Psychological functioning of siblings of disabled children. *Pediatrics, 67,* 344–353.
Brody, G.H., Stoneman, Z., & Mackinnon, R. (1982). Role asymmetries in interactions among school-aged children, their younger siblings, and their best friends. *Child Development, 53,* 1364–1370.
Bubolz, M.M., & Whiren, A.P. (1984). The family of the handicapped: An ecological model for policy and practice. *Family Relations, 33,* 5–12.
Burke, R.J., & Weir, T. (1978). Sex differences in adolescent life stress, social support, and well-being. *Journal of Psychology, 98,* 277–288.
Burt, C., Cohen, L.H., & Bjorck, J. (1988). Perceived family environment as a moderator of young adolescents' life stress adjustment. *American Journal of Community Psychology, 16,* 101–122.
Burton, L. (1975). *The family life of sick children.* London: Routledge and Kegan Paul.
Cairns, N.U., Clark, G.M., Smith, S.D., & Lansky, S.B. (1979). Adaptation of siblings to childhood malignancy. *Journal of Pediatrics, 95,* 484–487.
Caldwell, B., & Guze, S. (1960). A study of the adjustment of parents and siblings of institutionalized and non-institutionalzed retarded children. *American Journal of Mental Deficiency, 64,* 845–855.
Carandang, M., Folkins, C.H., Hines, P.A., & Steward, M.S. (1979). The role of cognitive level and sibling illness in children's conceptualizations of illness. *American Journal of Orthopsychiatry, 49*(3), 474–481.
Carr, J. (1988). Six weeks to twenty-one years old: A longitudinal study of children with Down's Syndrome and their families. *Journal of Child Psychology and Psychiatry, 29,* 407–431.
Chinitz, S.P. (1981). A sibling group for brothers and sisters of handicapped children. *Children Today,* 21–23.
Chinn, P.D., Winn, J., & Walters, R.H. (1978). *Two-way talking with parents of special children.* St. Louis: C.V. Mosby.
Cicchetti, D., & Sroufe, L.A. (1976). The relationship between affective and cognitive development in Down's syndrome infants. *Child Development, 47,* 920–929.
Coddington, R.D. (1972a). The significance of life events as etiologic factors in the diseases of children: A survey of professional workers. *Journal of Psychosomatic Research, 16,* 7–18.
Coddington, R.D. (1972b). The significance of life events as etiologic factors in the diseases of children: A study of a normal population. *Journal of Psychosomatic Research, 16,* 205–213.

Cohen-Sandler, R., Berman, A.L., & King, R.A. (1982). Life stress and symptomatology: Determinants of suicidal behavior in children. *Journal of the American Academy of Child Psychiatry, 21,* 178–186.

Compas, B.E., Davis, G.E., & Forsythe, C.J. (1985). Characteristics of life events during adolescence. *American Journal of Community Psychology, 13,* 677–692.

Cook, J.J. (1963). Dimensional analyses of child-rearing attitudes of parents of handicapped children. *American Journal of Mental Deficiency, 68,* 354–361.

Cowen, L., Mok, J., Corey, M., MacMillan, H., Simmons, R., & Levison, H. (1986). Psychologic adjustment of the family with a member who has cystic fibrosis. *Pediatrics, 77,* 745–753.

Crnic, R.A., Friedrich, W.N., & Greenberg, M.T. (1983). Adaptation of families with mentally retarded children: A model of stress, coping and family ecology. *American Journal of Mental Deficiency, 88,* 125–138.

Crocker, A. (1981). The involvement of siblings of children with handicaps. In A. Milunsky (Ed.), *Coping with crisis and handicap* (pp. 239–252). New York: Plenum.

Cummings, S.T. (1976). The impact of the child's deficiency on the father: A study of mentally retarded and chronically ill children. *American Journal of Orthopsychiatry, 46,* 245–255.

Cummings, S., Bayley, H., & Rie, H. (1966). Effects of the child's deficiency on the mother. *American Journal of Orthopsychiatry, 36,* 595–608.

Curry, S.L., & Russ, S.W. (1985). Identifying coping strategies in children. *Journal of Clinical Child Psychology, 14,* 61–67.

DeLongis, A., Coyne, J.C., Dakof, G., Folkman, S., & Lazarus, R.S. (1982). Relationship of daily hassles, uplifts, and major life events to health status. *Health Psychology, 1,* 119–136.

Dise-Lewis, J.E. (1988). The Life Events and Coping Inventory: An Assessment of stress in children. *Psychosomatic Medicine, 50,* 484–499.

Donovan, A.M. (1988). Family stress and ways of coping with adolescents who have handicaps: Maternal perceptions. *American Journal on Mental Retardation, 92,* 502–509.

Dunn, J., & Kendrick, C. (1982). *Siblings: Love, envy, and understanding.* Cambridge, MA: Harvard University Press.

Ebata, A.T., & Moos, R.H. (1991). Coping and adjustment in distressed and healthy adolescents. *Journal of Applied Developmental Psychology, 12,* 33–54.

Elliott, G.R., & Eisdorfer, C. (Eds.). (1982). *Stress and human health: Analysis and implications of research.* New York: Springer-Verlag.

Elwood, S.W. (1987). Stressor and coping response inventories for children. *Psychological Reports, 60*(3), 931–947.

Emde, R.N., & Brown, C. (1978). Adaptation to the birth of a Down's syndrome infant: Grieving and maternal attachment. *Journal of Child Psychiatry, 17*(2), 299–323.

Falkman, C. (1977). Cystic fibrosis: A psychological study of 52 children and their families. *Acta Pediatrica Scandinavia* (Suppl. 290), 328–341.

Farber, B. (1959). Effects of a severely mentally retarded child on family integration. *Monographs of the Society for research in Child Development, 24*(2, Serial No. 71).

Farber, B., & Jenne, W.C. (1963). Family organization and parent–child communication: Parents and siblings of a retarded child. *Monographs of the Society for Research in Child Development, 28*(7, Serial No. 91).

Ferrari, M. (1984). Chronic illness: Psychosocial effects on siblings: Chronically ill boys. *Journal of Child Psychology and Psychiatry, 25,* 459–476.

Folkman, S., & Lazarus, R.S. (1980). An analysis of coping in a middle-aged community sample. *Journal of Health and Social Behavior, 21,* 219–239.

Fraiberg, S. (1974). Blind infants and their mothers: An examination of the sign system. In M. Lewis & L.A. Rosenblum (Eds), *The effect of the infant on its caregiver.* New York: John Wiley & Sons.

Gad, M.T., & Johnson, J.H. (1980). Correlates of adolescent life stress as related to race, sex, and levels of perceived social support. *Journal of Clinical Child Psychology, 9,* 13–16.

Gallagher, J.J., Beckman-Bell, P., & Cross, A. (1983). Families of handicapped children: Sources of stress and its amelioration. *Exceptional Children, 50,* 10–19.

Gallagher, P.A., & Powell, T.H. (1989). Brothers and sisters: Meeting special needs. *Topics in Early Childhood Education: Families in Special Education, 8*(4), 24–37.

Gamble, W. (1991). *Appraisals as multi-dimensional determinants of coping for youth and adolescence.* Unpublished manuscript, University of Arizona.

Gamble, W.C., & McHale, S.M. (1989). Coping with stress in sibling relationships: A comparison of children with disabled and nondisabled siblings. *Journal of Applied Developmental Psychology, 10,* 353–373.

Garmezy, N. (1981). Children under stress: Perspectives on antecedents and correlates of vulnerability and resistance to psychopathology. In A.I. Rabin, J. Aronoff, A.M. Barclay, & R.A. Zucker (Eds.), *Further explanations in personality* (pp. 196–267). New York: John Wiley & Sons.

Garmezy, N., & Rutter, M. (Eds.). (1983). *Stress, coping, and development in children.* New York: McGraw-Hill.

Gath, A. (1973). The school age siblings of mongol children. *British Journal of Psychiatry, 123,* 161–167.

Gath, A. (1974). Sibling reactions to mental handicap: A comparison of the brothers and sisters of mongol children. *Journal of Child Psychology and Psychiatry, 15,* 187–198.

Gayton, W., Friedman, S., Tavormina, J., & Tucker, F. (1977). Children with cystic fibrosis: I. Psychological test findings on patients, siblings, and parents. *Pediatrics, 59,* 888–894.

Gersten, J.C., Langer, T.S., Eisenberg, J.G., & Simcha-Fagan, O. (1977). An evaluation of the etiologic role of stressful life-change events in psychological disorders. *Journal of Health and Social Behavior, 18,* 228–244.

Giannini, M.J., & Goodman, L. (1963). Counseling families during the crisis reaction to mongolism. *American Journal of Mental Deficiency, 67*(5), 740–747.

Gogan, J., Koocher, G.P., Foster, D.J., & O'Malley, J.E. (1977). Impact of childhood cancer on siblings. *Health Social Work, 2*(1), 42–47.

Goode, W.J. (1960). A theory of role strain. *American Sociological Review, 25,* 483–496.

Greenberg, M.T., & Marvin, R.S. (1979). Patterns of attachment in profoundly deaf preschool children. *Merrill–Palmer Quarterly, 25,* 265–279.

Grossman, F.K. (1972). *Brothers and sisters of retarded children.* Syracuse, NY: Syracuse University Press.

Hamilton, S., & Fagot, B.I. (1988). Chronic stress and coping styles: A comparison of male and female undergraduates. *Journal of Personality & Social Psychology, 55,* 819–823.

Harvey, D.H.P., & Greenway, A.P. (1984). The self-concept of physically handicapped children and their non-handicapped siblings: An empirical investigation. *Journal of Psychology and Psychiatry, 25,* 273–284.

Hauser, S., Jacobson, A., Wertlieb, D., Brink, S., & Wentworth, S. (1985). The contribution of family environment to perceived competence and illness adjustment in diabetic and acutely ill adolescents. *Family Relations, 34,* 99–108.

Hill, R. (1949). *Families under stress.* New York: Harper & Row.

Holahan, C.J., & Moos, R.H. (1990). Life stressors, resistance factors, and improved psychological functioning: An extension of the stress resistance paradigm. *Journal of Personality and Social Psychology, 58,* 909–917.

Holroyd, J., & McArthur, D. (1976). Mental retardation and stress on the parents: A contrast between Down's syndrome and childhood autism. *American Journal of Mental Deficiency, 80,* 431–436.

Johnson, J.H. (1986). *Life events as stressors in childhood and adolescence.* Beverly Hills, CA: Sage Publications.

Johnson, J.H., & McCutcheon, S.M. (1980). Assessing life stress in older children and adolescents: Preliminary findings with the Life Events Checklist. In I.G. Sarason & C.D. Spielberger (Eds.), *Stress and anxiety* (Vol. 7, pp. 111–125). Washington, DC: Hemisphere.

Kanner, A.D., Coyne, J.C., Schaefer, C., & Lazarus, R.J. (1981). Comparison of two modes of stress measurement: Daily hassles and uplifts versus major life events. *Journal of Behavioral Medicine, 4,* 1–19.

Kazak, A.E. (1987). Families with disabled children: Stress and social networks in three samples. *Journal of Abnormal Child Psychology, 15,* 137–146.

Kazak, A., & Marvin, R. (1984). Differences, difficulties and adaptation: Stress and social networks in families with a handicapped child. *Family Relations, 33,* 67–78.

King, E. (1981). Child-rearing practices: Child with chronic illness and well sibling. *Issues in Comprehensive Pediatric Nursing, 5,* 185–194.

Klein, S.D. (1972). Brother to sister: Sister to brother. *The Exceptional Parent, 2,* 10–15.

Kliewer, W. (1991). Coping in middle childhood: Relations to competence, Type A behavior, monitoring, blunting, and locus of control. *Developmental Psychology, 27,* 689–697.

Kobasa, S.C. (1982). The hardy personality: Toward a social psychology of stress and health. In G.S. Sanders & J. Suls (Eds.), *Social psychology of health and illness* (pp. 3–32). Hillsdale, NJ: Lawrence Erlbaum Associates.

Kovacs, M., & Feinberg, T.L. (1982). Coping with juvenile onset diabetes mellitus. In A. Baum and J.C. Singer (Eds.), *Handbook of psychology and health: Vol. II. Issues in child health and adolescent health.* Hillsdale, NJ: Lawrence Erlbaum Associates.

Lauterbach, C.G. (1974). *Socio-behavioral adaptation of siblings of the mentally handicapped child.* Scranton, Pennsylvania: The Print Shop.

Lavigne, J.V., & Ryan, M. (1979). Psychologic adjustment of siblings of children with chronic illness. *Pediatrics, 63,* 616–627.

Lazarus, R.S., & Folkman, S. (1984). *Stress, appraisal, and coping.* New York: Springer-Verlag.

Levine, S., & Coe, C.L. (1985). The use and abuse of cortisol as a measure of stress. In T.M. Field, P.M. McCabe, & N. Schneiderman (Eds.), *Stress and coping.* Hillsdale, NJ: Lawrence Erlbaum Associates.

Lewis, C.E., Siegel, M.J., & Lewis, M.A. (1984). Feeling bad: Exploring sources of distress among pre-adolescent children. *American Journal of Health, 74,* 117–122.

Lloyd-Bostock, S. (1976). Parents' experiences of official help and guidance in caring for a mentally handicapped child. *Child: Care, Health and Development, 2,* 325–338.

Lochman, J.E., & Lampron, L.B. (1986). Situational social problem-solving skills and self-esteem of aggressive and nonaggressive boys. *Journal of Abnormal Child Psychology, 14,* 605–617.

Long, C., & Moore, J. (1979). Parental expectations for their epileptic children. *Journal of Child Psychology, 20,* 299–312.

Longo, D.C., & Bond, L. (1984). Families of the handicapped child: Research and practice. *Family Relations, 33,* 57–65.

Lonsdale, G. (1978). Family life with a handicapped child: The parents speak. *Child: Care, Health and Development, 4,* 99–120.

Maccoby, E.E., & Martin, J.A. (1984). Parent–child interaction. In E.M. Hetherington (Ed.), *Manual of child psychology: Vol. 4. Social development* (pp. 1–101). New York: John Wiley & Sons.

Markova, I., MacDonald, K., & Forbes, C. (1980). Impact of hemophilia on child-rearing practices and parental cooperation. *Journal of Child Psychology and Psychiatry, 21,* 153–162.

McAllister, R.J., Butler, E.W., & Lei, T. (1973). Patterns of social interaction among families of behaviorally retarded children. *Journal of Marriage and the Families,* 93–100.

McAndrew, I. (1976). Children with a handicap and their families. *Child: Care, Health and Development, 2,* 213–237.

McCubbin, H.I., & Patterson, J. (1983). The family stress process; The double ABCX model of adjustment and adaptation. In H.I. McCubbin, M.B. Sussman & J.M. Patterson (Eds.), *Social stress and the family: Advances and developments in family stress theory and research. Marriage and Family Review,* 6 (1, 2, pp. 7–38). New York: Haworth.

McCubbin, H.I., Patterson, J.M., Bauman, E., & Harris, L. (1981). *AFILE—Adolescent–Family Inventory of Life Events and Changes.* St. Paul: University of Minnesota, Family Social Science.

McHale, S.M., Simeonsson, R.J., & Sloan, J. (1984). Children with handicapped brothers and sisters. In E. Schopler & G. Mesibov (Eds.), *Issues in autism: Vol. 2. The effects of autism on the family* (pp. 327–342). New York: Plenum.

Meyerowitz, J.H., & Kaplan, H.B. (1967). Familial responses to stress. The case of cystic fibrosis. *Social Science & Medicine, 1,* 249–266.

Michaelis, C.T. (1980). *Home and school partnerships in exceptional children.* Rockville, MD: Aspen Publishers, Inc.

Miller, N., & Cantwell, D. (1976). Siblings as therapists: A behavioral approach. *American Journal of Psychiatry, 133,* 447–450.

Miller, S.C. (1974). An exploratory study of sibling relationships in families with retarded children. *Dissertation Abstracts International, 35*(2), 994B-2-995B.

Mink, I.T., Nihira, K., & Meyers, C.E. (1983). Taxonomy of family life styles: I. Homes with TMR children. *American Journal of Mental Deficiency, 87,* 484–497.

Murphy, A., Pueschel, S., Duffy, T., & Brody, E. (1976). Meeting with brothers and sisters of children with Down's Syndrome. *Children Today, 5,* 20–23.

Murphy, L.B. (1962). *The widening world of childhood: Paths toward mastery.* New York: Basic Books.

Murphy, M.A. (1982). The family with a handicapped child: A review of the literature. *Journal of Developmental and Behavioral Pediatrics, 3,* 73–82.

Newcomb, M.D., Huba, G.J., & Bentler, P.M. (1981). A multidimensional assessment of stressful life events among adolescents: Derivation and correlates. *Journal of Health and Social Behavior, 22,* 400–415.

Nix, K.S. (1980). Maternal attachment behaviors with defective versus normal infants. *Monographs: Mother–Infant Studies*. Denton, TX: College of Nursing, Texas Women's University.

Powell, T.H., & Gallagher, P.A. (1993). *Brothers and sisters—A special part of exceptional families* (2nd ed.). Baltimore: Paul H. Brookes Publishing Co.

Rapaport, L. (1962). The state of crises: Some theoretical considerations. *Social Services Review, 16*, 211–217.

Ricci, C.S. (1970). Analyses of child rearing attitudes of mothers of retarded, emotionally disturbed, and normal children. *American Journal of Mental Deficiency, 74*, 756–761.

Roosa, M.N., Sandler, I.N., Gehring, M., Beals, J., & Cappo, L. (1988). The children of alcoholics life-events schedule: A stress scale for children of alcohol abusing parents. *Journal of Studies on Alcoholism, 49*(5), 422–429.

Ryan, N.M. (1988). The stress-coping process in school-age children: Gaps in the knowledge needed for health promotion. *Advances in Nursing Science, 11*(1), 11–12.

San Martino, M., & Newman, M. (1974). Siblings of retarded children: A population at risk. *Child Psychiatry and Human Development, 4*, 168–177.

Schneiderman, N., & McCabe, P.M. (1985). Biobehavioral responses to stressors. In T.M. Field, P.M. McCabe, & N. Schneiderman (Eds.), *Stress and coping* (pp. 13–62). Hillsdale, NJ: Lawrence Erlbaum Associates.

Schreiber, M., & Feeley, M. (1965). Siblings of the retarded: A guided group experience. *Children, 12*, 221–225.

Seligman, M.S. (1983). Siblings of handicapped children. In M. Seligman (Ed.), *A family with a handicapped child: Understanding and treatment* (pp. 147–174). New York: Grune & Stratton.

Serafica, F.C., & Cicchetti, D. (1976). Down's syndrome children in a strange situation: Attachment and exploration behaviors. *Merrill-Palmer Quarterly, 22*(2), 137–150.

Siegel, J.M., & Brown, J.D. (1988). A prospective study of stressful circumstances, illness symptoms, and depressed moods among adolescents. *Developmental Psychology, 24*, 715–721.

Spirito, A., Stark, L.J., & Williams, C. (1988). Development of a brief coping checklist for use with pediatric populations. *Journal of Pediatric Psychology, 13*, 555–574.

Stewart, R.B. (1983). Sibling attachment relationships: Child-infant interactions in the strange situation. *Developmental Psychology, 17*(2), 192–199.

Stoneman, Z., & Brody, G.H. (1984). Research with families of severely handicapped children: Theoretical and methodological considerations. In J. Blacher (Ed.), *Severely handicapped young children and their families: Research in review* (pp. 179–214). New York: Academic Press.

Stoneman, Z., Brody, G.H., Davis, C.H., & Crapps, J.H. (1987). Mentally retarded children and their older same-sex siblings: Naturalistic in-home observations. *American Journal of Mental Retardation, 92*(3), 290–298.

Stoneman, Z., Brody, G.H., Davis, C.H., & Crapps, J.H. (1988). Childcare responsibilities, peer relations, and sibling conflict: Older siblings of mentally retarded children. *American Journal on Mental Retardation, 93*(2), 171–183.

Swearingen, E.M., & Cohen, L.H. (1985). Life events and psychological distress: A prospective study of young adolescents. *Developmental Psychology, 21*, 1045–1054.

Tavormina, J.B., Boll, T.J., Dunn, N.J., Luscomb, R.L., & Taylor, J.R. (1981). Psychosocial effects on parents of raising a physically handicapped child. *Journal of Abnormal Child Psychology, 9*(1), 121–131.

Tew, B., & Laurence, K.M. (1973). Mothers, brothers, and sisters of patients with spina bifida. *Developmental Medicine Child Neurology, 15*, 69–76.

Tolor, A., Murphy, V., Wilson, L.T., & Clayton, J. (1983). The high school readjustment scale: An attempt to quantify stressful events in young people. *Research Communication in Psychology, Psychiatry and Behavior, 8*, 85–111.

Tropauer, A., Franz, M., & Dilgard, V. (1970). Psychological aspects of the care of children with cystic fibrosis. *American Journal of Disabled Child, 119*, 424–432.

Turk, J. (1964). Impact of cystic fibrosis on family functioning. *Pediatrics, 34*, 67–71.

Voysey, M. (1972). Impression management by parents with disabled children. *Journal of Health and Social Behavior, 13*, 80–89.

Waisbren, S.E. (1980). Parents' reactions after the birth of a developmentally disabled child. *American Journal of Mental Deficiency, 84*, 345–351.

Walker, C.L. (1988). Stress and coping in siblings of childhood cancer patients. *Nursing Research, 37*, 208–212.

Walker, L.S., Ford, M.B., & Donald, W.D. (1987). Cystic fibrosis and family stress: Effects of age and severity of illness. *Pediatrics, 79*, 239–246.

Wasserman, R. (1983). Identifying the counseling needs of the siblings of mentally retarded children. *The Personnel and Guidance Journal*, 622–627.

Weinrott, M.R. (1974). A training program in behavior modification for siblings of the retarded. *American Journal of Orthopsychiatry, 44*, 362–375.

Wentworth, E.H. (1974). *Listen to your heart: A message to parents of handicapped children*. Boston: Houghton Mifflin.

Werner, E.E., & Smith, R.S. (1982). *Vulnerable but invincible: A longitudinal study of resilient children and youth*. New York: McGraw-Hill.

Wertlieb, D., Weigel, C., & Feldstein, M. (1987). Measuring children's coping. *American Journal of Orthopsychiatry, 57*, 548–560.

Wikler, L. (1986). Chronic stresses of families of mentally retarded children. *Family Relations, 30*, 281–288.

Wills, T.A. (1985). Stress, coping, and tobacco and alcohol use in early adolescence. In S. Schiffman & T. Wills (Eds.), *Coping and substance use* (pp. 67–94). New York: Academic Press.

Wright, L.S. (1985). Suicidal thoughts and their relationship to family stress and personal problems among high school seniors and college undergraduates. *Adolescence, 20*(79), 575–580.

Yamamoto, K., & Felsenthal, H.M. (1982). Stressful experiences of children: Professional judgements. *Psychological Reports, 50*, 1087–1095.

Yeaworth, R.C., York, J., Hussey, M.A., Ingle, M.E., & Goodwin, T. (1980). The development of an adolescent life change event scale. *Adolescence, 15*(57), 91–97.

CHAPTER 14

Lifetime Research on Siblings of Persons with Mental Retardation

Louis Rowitz

In order to address the complex issues involved in research on siblings of children with mental retardation, a number of conceptual and methodologic concerns need to be discussed. This is not a new concern, in that methodologic issues have been addressed by many family researchers in numerous contexts (Dyson, Edgar, & Crnic, 1989; Farber & Rowitz, 1986; Rowitz, 1992; Simeonsson & Bailey, 1986). A cursory review of the literature produced since the 1980s shows a concern with methodologic problems in many of the reported research studies (Ramey, Krauss, & Simeonsson, 1989). In addition, there is an increasing number of chapters, peer reviewed papers, and books dealing with the growing amount of instrumentation in family research that creates conceptual and methodologic problems (Grotevant & Carlson, 1989; Jacob & Tennenbaum, 1988; White, 1991). The late 1980s have also produced a number of literature review papers. For example, the book edited by Gallagher and Vietze (1986) has 17 chapters and reviews all aspects of the field's knowledge about the families of people with disabilities. There are two excellent chapters in the book, one by Simeonsson and Bailey and another by Brody and Stoneman, that review sibling research in particular. Singer and Irvin (1989) have edited a 22-chapter book that blends theory, research, and service issues of relevance to family members and their caregiving roles; several chapters of the book deal specifically with sibling issues in caregiving. And Crnic and Leconte (1986) have also studied siblings. There is an extensive review of the literature on siblings in a University of Connecticut doctoral dissertation in which Itzkowitz (1989) studies individuals who were part of the National Sibling Information Network at the University of Connecticut.

Searching for literature on methodologic concerns, the author found not only many articles related to methodological problems in family research (see the November, 1990 issue of the *Journal of Marriage and the Family*, which presents a review of family research during the 1980s) but also entire books devoted to examining the pros and cons of specific research designs (Miller, 1991). An excellent book by Magnusson and Bergman (1990) reviews data-quality issues in longitudinal research. Another book by Kelsey, Thompson, and Evans (1986) reviews new approaches to observational research for epidemiologists, and the techniques examined are important for all researchers of special populations. This chapter discusses a number of those issues that are raised by family researchers who work primarily in the field of social science research on typical families, as well as those who concentrate their research on families with a member with a disability.

THEORETICAL ISSUES

There are a large number of family researchers who do not tie their findings to any theory or even to other studies. In addition, a number of these studies do not build on family research in mainstream social science or on the extensive research literature in the maternal and child health field. An important exception to this criticism is the research that builds on the child development tradition, although the connection between typical development concerns and those related to the various developmental stages and milestones for children with disabilities is not always clear. There also appears to be an attempt to apply child development theory and methods to lifespan concerns, but this does not seem to be working. In addition, individual lifespan researchers appear to be working from different theoretical perspectives. Thus, it appears that what theory the field has is extremely muddied: specific studies do not tie their research to theoretical concerns; methods and theories do not seem to be coordinated; and theory and model building often seem to be the last priority on research agendas when they should actually be one of the first.

DESIGN ISSUES

Campbell (in press), in a chapter for the forthcoming *Encyclopedia of Sociology*, has reviewed problems related to research design, several of which are also outlined below. The first group of design issues includes concerns about consistency of sample over time. Attrition of the chosen sample over time is another significant problem for research designers. Campbell also notes that measurement protocols can create problems if the kinds of variables that can be studied over time are not documented.

Longitudinal Research Designs

The social and behavioral sciences literature is filled with discussions about the pros and cons of longitudinal and cross-sectional research designs. To this debate must be added the arguments about whether lifespan research studies need to be based on a longitudinal approach. The simple answer to this question is that it depends on the research questions to be addressed.

Campbell (in press) points out a number of common problems in longitudinal data analysis. First, there is the problem of interpreting measures and direction of change. Another problem is related to the lack of independence when there are two or more measures of an individual. Third, research studies that are complicated by multiple goals make it difficult to plan for observation and to analyze results. Other longitudinal study problems include the issues of construct validity, measurement error, natural changes in independent variables over time, and the increase in missing data over time. There is also a need to determine which time intervals are necessary for which variables. In fact, researchers often ignore the fact that all measures do not follow the same time interval; routinely recording all measures at each wave of the study may generate biases in interpretation if instruments are life-stage specific.

Ideally, a research design that allows for the benefit of longitudinal data with the added element of a new cross-sectional design sample during each wave offers the researcher the best of both worlds. The major limitation is always financial in nature.

Conflictual Lifestyles

Much family-based research is conducted from the perspective of the family of orientation. When siblings are young, the family of orientation is critical to their life adjustment. As they reach school-age and beyond, however, the educational system, peer group activities, the mass media, and many other influences break down the influence of the family of orientation on the siblings. With adulthood, many other groups and individuals further influence the siblings' lives. Despite these factors, many researchers continue to study the siblings from the perspective of the family of orientation, which leads to methodologic biases. The lifetime influence of the family of orientation is clearly an issue to be studied, as is shown by the following case study from the Rowitz and Farber follow-up study:

> Case No. 1372: I guess I have always had trouble accepting the fact that someone in my family was not perfect, and as a result I have spent my life trying to prove to the world that this in no way reflected on me, because I'm damn good if not perfect! It's been hard. (1988, p. 50)

Future research needs to examine all types of influences on the lives of siblings. The field has clearly ignored some of the complexities in research on older siblings. Although there are limits to cross-sectional research designs, these types of designs will provide much-needed information on lifespan concerns related to siblings within a specific time and space context. These issues are very important because of the fact that people change over time. Moreover, methodologic concerns may lead to new research opportunities to address questions that are creative and that build on methodologic flaws in earlier research studies.

Measurement Issues

Although measurement concerns are inherent in most of the sections of this chapter, several critical issues need to be addressed. First, there is a tendency in mental retardation research to rely on standardized instruments of various kinds that may or may not be appropriate to the questions addressed in sibling research studies. It appears that the instruments are almost more important than the research issues themselves. Instrument development needs to be undertaken if future research is to be relevant, reliable, and valid in the long run.

A second major concern is that of small sample size. Many sibling studies are based on extremely small samples, raising questions about the reliability and validity of the results. Samples should be larger if quantitative data analysis is to be meaningful. However, qualitative studies are possible with small samples because they allow for a depth of analysis that is often not possible with larger samples. The problem may boil down to an investigator's preference. Cost concerns might be similar for both qualitative and quantitative research. In addition, single case-study designs are also costly.

A third measurement issue relates to the problem of missing data. Siblings and other family members are often resistant to answering certain types of questions. These issues are also researchable in that an analysis of the question or question types that lead to missing data may help researchers to better understand stressful issues for families and to discover better ways to develop questions in the future.

A fourth measurement issue involves the important determination of which sibling in a family should be interviewed. The number of children in a family is an important consideration here. Gender and birth order relationships are also critical. In small families, all of the siblings may be interviewed. In large samples, other considerations may determine selection. Whatever the decision, methodologic concerns need to be addressed by the investigators.

In this section, problems related to the design of research studies on siblings of persons with mental retardation has been discussed; these problems need to be addressed and tied to theoretical and conceptual issues. Research gains its coherence from a blending of theory and design, from continually reconceptualizing theory in light of the researchers' analysis of the collected data, a process which is addressed in the remainder of this discussion.

BARRIERS TO OBTAINING DATA

There are many factors that affect the reliability and validity of the data collected on siblings and families. This section discusses some of the possible barriers in data collection, including problems with the sources of data on siblings, parents' unwillingness to allow access to siblings, the lack of information on siblings who become caregivers and on the spouses of siblings, and the growing concerns about the protection of privacy.

Sources of Sibling Data

A critical concern in a number of sibling studies is the fact that the information on siblings may not come from the siblings themselves, but rather from the siblings' parents. As the sibling gets older and is perhaps interviewed directly, it may be impossible to compare the siblings' own reports to the parents' past reports on them. An added concern is whether different instruments are used when the sibling is interviewed directly or reported on through interviews with the parents. Selective bias must also be considered, as the results of the sibling reports may differ with the choice of mother or father as respondent. Reports by parents may also differ according to the gender of the sibling. Some of these issues were addressed in the early work of Farber (1959). Finally, siblings may be less willing than their parents to engage in a research study, a factor that may increase the nonresponse rate significantly. The topic of sibling response may be an important issue for further research.

The Problem of Overprotective Parents

In 1986, the author and Farber followed up on the families that Farber had interviewed in 1959 (Farber, 1960). One of the interesting sidelights of the follow-up is the question as to whether the parent respondent would give the researchers the names and addresses of their adult children. A number of the parents said that they did not want to provide this information. Some of the explanations were that their other children never really knew their brother or sister with a disability because the child had been institutionalized at an early age. A number of parents did not want their other children bothered. Some parents shielded some of their children and not others. A recent, as yet unpublished cross-sectional study by Rowitz, Heller, Farber, and their colleagues involved 482 families with a member with mental retardation living in the Chicago area; in this study, parents were found to be selective about the siblings whom they were willing to let the research team contact. Preliminary impressions of this data seem to indicate that there were no significant differences based on ethnicity or race, but other researchers do not report this same finding. Researchers need to determine if other factors are involved, such as length of survey, intrusiveness of the questions, urban/rural residence, gender of siblings, and socioeconomic status (Spitze & Logan, 1991).

Lack of Data on Sibling Caregivers

Since parents typically die at some point during the lifespan of their children, it is often necessary for siblings of persons with disabilities to assume the role of caregiver. Since studies are generally oriented toward parents, investigators search for parents through the person with disabilities or through agencies or parent groups. Although there is an increase in the study of sibling caregivers whose aged parents have died, there is still a need to study sibling caregivers whose parents die earlier in life (Coward & Dwyer, 1990). Additional complications are caused by the fact that female siblings are probably the most likely to become a caregiver, although this may not be a clear-cut determination in that family size, birth order, gender of the other siblings, and numerous other factors may determine who will assume primary responsibility for the sibling with disabilities on the death of the parents (Spitze & Logan, 1991). In addition, another concern is the fact that female siblings are harder to find because of name changes. The issue of caregiving is an important one in that a sibling may find him- or herself a caregiver to both aging parents and a family member with mental retardation. Intergenerational caregiving is an important research issue with associated methodologic difficulties.

Lack of Information on the Spouses of Siblings

Since spousal influence may be a key factor in the tendency of the sibling to maintain contact with a brother or sister with disabilities, spouses of siblings should also be contacted. New research methodology protocols will need to be developed to achieve this. The question of why the spouses are cooperative or not needs to be investigated, and the gender of the spouse may also be a factor. In fact, the marital status and marital history of siblings should be investigated in order to determine if having a brother or sister with a disability affects the marital life of siblings. A methodologic bias may occur if spouses of siblings refuse to cooperate in a study of sibling families.

Another important issue is that of intergenerational factors. The study of grandparents of people with disabilities may provide information on the patterns of family adjustment that either become disrupted or carry through a family over more than one generation. In addition, the study of the children of siblings would also provide interesting data on the long-term effects of disability on the family constellation.

The Privacy Issue

People are becoming more and more protective of their privacy, and thus it is becoming more and more difficult to get people to participate in research studies. This is partly a regional issue; urbanites tend to be less willing to participate than people in rural areas. Members of minorities prefer to be interviewed by members of their own group. Women are less willing to be interviewed by men. All of these factors will affect research activities in the future. Who does the interview and how privacy is protected will clearly be factors that must be addressed in the research protocol.

Human subjects review committees are becoming more concerned with studies that used to be considered exempt from a major review. Consent forms are being reviewed carefully, and questionnaires are being examined for intrusiveness. More consistent university reviews are occurring at regular intervals. Honesty in the process of carrying out studies is being tested, and any intimation of fraud in the process of the study is being investigated. Another important issue may be the extent of the researchers' personal involvement with the families that they study. The sending of letters, or holiday or birthday cards, may create an unintentional bias in the research process. All of these issues will create methodologic concerns for the research investigator.

SOURCES OF SAMPLING BIAS

A final area of methodologic concern is the series of potential sources of sampling bias discussed below, including demographic confounds and the problems associated with intergenerational sampling and with using service facilities and parents' groups as data sources. These sources need to be taken into consideration in the interpretation of research findings and in any attempt to generalize the results. Sampling bias also offers an interesting data analysis opportunity in that the findings of a biased sample can give unique insights into the lives of special subgroups of the population.

Intergenerational Sampling Biases

As implicated in the above discussion, all present sibling samples are statistically biased. First, there must be a person with a disability before a sibling becomes eligible for selection in a study. If there is a bias toward the selection of people with disabilities, this bias affects other levels of the sampling process. For example, individuals with disabilities who are selected because they use a particular service program would automatically exclude people with disabilities who do not do so. At the parental level, it is possible that parents will not allow the inclusion of their family members in a research study. In addition, the parents themselves may not be interested in being involved in the study. If the parents do not allow their children without disabilities to be involved in the research, further sampling bias occurs, as discussed above. A sibling may also refuse to be involved in a study, as was also previously discussed. For these reasons, sibling research is very complex, and it is almost always difficult, if not impossible, to generalize the results.

Demographic Confounds

Demographic biases also affect the generalizability of research findings. For example, many past research studies on families and siblings were based on the study of one ethnic or racial group, and the group studied tended to be white. Some of this is now changing, but the field still has not gone far enough. In the now classic Farber studies (1959, 1960), there are almost no minority families included in the final study reports, although data was collected on some black families. Many of our sibling studies in the child-developmental field also lack cultural diversity. Cross-ethnic and -racial groups comparisons are necessary in a society as complex as that of the United States. In the recent study by Heller, Markwardt, Rowitz, and Farber, data show that Hispanic families with children with disabilities tend to include younger parents than white or black families, at least in the Chicago area. Thus, age may also be a confounding variable. And finally, studies across countries are also needed.

Many family studies focus on the urban family, although Brody, Stoneman, and their colleagues have looked at rural families (Brody, Stoneman, Davis, & Crapps, 1991; Stoneman, Brody, Davis, Crapps, & Malone, 1991). However, this research does not look at urban–rural factors in detail. All urban areas are not necessarily alike; there are important differences between Chicago, Los Angeles, New York, and Atlanta. Generalizations may be impossible without these comparisons.

The gender factor also needs to be considered. In his early studies, Farber (1959) pointed out that sisters often had direct caregiving responsibilities, in contrast to the brothers of children with disabilities. Lifespan studies should also look at the gender factor to see how the differences between sisters and brothers of individuals with disabilities change over time. Literature of the 1990s shows that the gender factor may be more complex than originally argued (Spitze & Logan, 1991). Gender issues may be tied to other family constellation factors such as age, family size, distance from parents in adulthood, socioeconomic standing, and racial or ethnic status.

Another type of demographic confound is related to the level and type of disability in a family member. Many studies assume a homogeneity in the sibling with a disability. Some researchers, like Farber, include only families of persons with severe disabilities in the sample (Farber, 1959). In their follow-up study, Rowitz and Farber (1988) found that diagnostic classifications change over time. Thus, people that fit into the sample at one point in time might not fit in at a later time because diagnostic criteria have changed. There is also enough literature to show that families with a family member with a mild disability have different problems than families of persons with severe disabilities (Farber, 1968). These methodologic issues will clearly affect the longitudinal design of studies.

The type of disability may also be a factor. Dyson et al. (1989) argue that sibling reactions may vary with the type of disability. We do not yet interface the research streams in the area of physical disability with the research in the area of mental retardation and mental illness (see Philp & Duckworth, 1982, and Howe, chap. 8, this volume). There is also extensive literature on children with chronic illness and their impact on family adjustment (see Gallo & Knafl, chap. 9, this volume).

The marital status of the parents also needs to be investigated thoroughly. Single parent families show different adjustment patterns than families that have both parents present. Many of the early studies in the field showed that the divorce rate tended to be low for parents with children with disabilities. As is the case with society as a whole, more recent studies show that divorce may be more common today. This sociological phenomenon needs to be addressed further, since many studies still assume an intact family situation. The marital status of the siblings is also a critical demographic variable. If the sibling chooses to remain single or not to have children if married, the reasons for these decisions need to be investigated. Sibling marital status may also be a factor in the willingness of the sibling to take responsibility for a sibling with a disability.

As pointed out above, the variable of socioeconomic status is also critical. Studies of people with mild forms of mental disability tend to be predominantly composed of families from lower socioeconomic classes, while studies of families with members with severe disabilities may include families from more varied socioeconomic classes (Farber, 1968). Adjustment patterns for families from different socioeconomic classes will probably differ. Many family studies ignore this factor.

The variable of birth order, which is often ignored in the research, also needs to be addressed. Siblings who were born before the child with disabilities could possibly have different issues in adjustment than siblings who were born after. A further methodologic concern would be how birth order affects sibling lifetime adjustment in the first place. Nature versus nurture issues would also need to be addressed. Finally, gender issues and birth order might also be interactive.

Problems with Samples Drawn from Service Facilities or Parents' Groups

Most researchers draw their samples from agencies that serve people with disabilities. This automatically creates a sampling bias that many researchers are willing to live with. When you are trying to find a sample for a condition with a fairly low incidence rate, door to door surveys tend to be quite expensive. Since people do not access the service delivery system the same way, a sample drawn from one service sector may create methodologic problems. If an agency loses touch with a person with a disability and his or her family, a case in a longitudinal study could become lost. As people with disabilities leave schools from age 18–21 and move into the community, they may not access services offered by agencies. This aging-out phenomenon could create problems. As siblings leave school, they may also age out or choose to no longer participate in a long-term study. Finally, families in service programs may be more willing to participate if there was some financial incentive than they would be if the purpose was research alone.

The author (Rowitz, 1973) studied individuals with mental retardation who were admitted to a specialized clinic over an 8-year period. He reported that the demographic characteristics of users of the clinic changed over time. The changes were due to such factors as the expansion of special education districts in suburban Chicago and changes in state regulations and admission policies. Thus, sampling-frame decisions must take into account agency-based factors that could seriously bias the selection of cases for a study.

Since people with mental retardation may need to use the various service delivery systems over time, the use of services is clearly an important factor in family dynamics and adjustment. The author (Rowitz, 1981) conducted a retrospective analysis of the services utilized by a sample of clinic users prior to the use of the clinic. This study documented that the use of services is a complicated process, and that new users of a clinic come with all sorts of different service histories. If the service history variable is not explored, a service history bias enters the picture relative to the sample to be studied in the new family study.

Samples drawn from parents' groups or organizations are also biased (Farber, 1959, 1960). Not all parents become members of advocacy groups. Involvement may also be strongly affected by such factors as socioeconomic status. And people who join organizations are simply different than people who do not join. An additional factor is the recent attempt to empower families (Dunst, Trivette, & Deal, 1988). The empowerment movement may change the configuration of members of parents' organizations, leading to new potential sampling biases, but it could also lead to a number of interesting research studies.

CONCLUDING COMMENTS

A major issue to be addressed in family studies in mental retardation is the difficulty of generalizing results to other populations. With the flaws that have been mentioned above, there are extreme difficulties in looking at the long-term effects of research. Consistent findings across studies are just beginning to be documented. Time and space issues complicate the process because changes in governmental regulation, admission policy issues, evolution of the service delivery system, a remedicalization of the mental retardation field, an expansion of the community integration philosophy, and many other societal changes affect the findings of research and are often, if not always, outside of researchers' design and control. Professionals in the field need to explore the issue of generalization and develop methods for determining how generalization is defined.

In this chapter, the author has opted to look at methodologic issues from a contextual perspective rather than a statistical one. There are clearly many issues involved in lifetime research on siblings. These issues involve theory, measurement concerns, sampling problems, cross-sectional and longitudinal issues, generalization problems, and so on. Investigators will need to explore these issues as research strategies continue to evolve.

REFERENCES

Booth, A. (Ed.). (1990). Family research in the 1980s: The decade in review [Special issue]. *Journal of Marriage and the Family, 52*(4), 807.

Brody, G.H., Stoneman, Z., Davis, C.H., & Crapps, J.M. (1991). Observations of the role relations and behavior between older children with mental retardation and their younger siblings. *American Journal on Mental Retardation, 95*(5), 527–536.

Campbell, R.T. (in press). Design and analysis in longitudinal research. In E.F. Borgatta (Ed.), *Encyclopedia of sociology.* New York: Macmillan.

Coward, R.T., & Dwyer, J.W. (1990). The association of gender, sibling network composition, and patterns of parent care by adult children. *Research on Aging, 12*(2), 158–181.

Crnic, K.A., & Leconte, J.M. (1986). Understanding sibling needs and influences. In R.R. Fewell & P.F. Vadasy, *Families of handicapped children* (pp. 75–95). Austin, TX: PRO-ED.

Dunst, C., Trivette, C., & Deal, A. (1988). *Enabling and empowering families: Principles and guidelines for practice.* Cambridge, MA: Brookline Books.

Dyson, L., Edgar, E., & Crnic, K. (1989). Psychological predictors of adjustment by siblings of developmentally disabled children. *American Journal on Mental Retardation, 94*(3), 292–302.

Farber, B. (1959). Effects of a severely mentally retarded child on family integration. *Monographs of the Society for Research in Child Development, 24*(2, Whole No. 71).

Farber, B. (1960). Family organization and crisis: Maintenance of integration in families with a severely mentally retarded child. *Monographs of the Society for Research in Child Development, 25*(1, Whole No. 75).

Farber, B. (1968). *Mental retardation: Its social context and social consequences.* Boston: Houghton Mifflin.

Farber, B., & Rowitz, L. (1986). Families with a mentally retarded child. In N.R. Ellis & N. W. Bray (Eds.), *International review of research in mental retardation* (Vol. 14). Orlando, FL: Academic Press.

Gallagher, J.J., & Vietze, P.M. (Eds.). (1986). *Families of handicapped persons: Research, programs, and policy issues.* Baltimore: Paul H. Brookes Publishing Co.

Grotevant, H.D., & Carlson, C.I. (1989). *Family assessment.* New York: Guilford Press.

Heller, T., Markwardt, R., Rowitz, L., & Farber, B. *Adaptation by Hispanic families to a member with mental retardation.* Unpublished manuscript.

Itzkowitz, J.S. (1989). *The needs and concerns of brothers and sisters of individuals with disabilities.* Unpublished doctoral dissertation, University of Connecticut, Storrs.

Jacob, T., & Tennenbaum, D.L. (1988). *Family assessment: Rationale, methods, and future direction.* New York: Plenum.

Kelsey, J.L., Thompson, W.D., & Evans, A.S. (1986). *Methods in observational epidemiology.* New York: Oxford University Press.

Magnusson, D., & Bergman, L.R. (Eds.). (1990). *Data quality in longitudinal research.* New York: Cambridge University Press.

Miller, D.C. (1991). *Handbook of research design and social measurement.* Beverly Hills: Sage Publications.

Philp, M., & Duckworth, D. (1982). *Children with disabilities and their families: A review of research.* Windsor, Berkshires: Nfer-Nelson Publishing Co.

Ramey, S.L., Krauss, M.W., & Simeonsson, R.J. (Eds.). (1989). Special issue on research on families. *American Journal on Mental Retardation, 94*(3).

Rowitz, L. (1973). Socioepidemiological analysis of admission to a state operated outpatient clinic for retarded children. *American Journal of Mental Deficiency, 78*(3), 300–307.

Rowitz, L. (1981). Service paths prior to clinic use by mentally retarded people. In R.H. Bruininks, C.E. Meyers, B.B. Sigford, & K.C. Lakin (Eds.), *Deinstitutionalization and community adjustment of mentally retarded people* (AAMD Monograph No. 4). Washington, DC: American Association on Mental Deficiency.

Rowitz, L. (1992). Family research in mental retardation: A historical overview. In R. Antonak & J. Mulick (Eds.), *Transitions in mental retardation* (Vol. 5). Norwood, NJ: Ablex Publishing Co.

Rowitz, L., & Farber, B. (1988). *Changing effects of community service in family adaptation to mentally retarded adults over time, final report* (Report No. 90DD0070101). Washington, DC: Administration on Developmental Disabilities.

Simeonsson, R.J., & Bailey, D.B. (1986). Siblings of handicapped children. In J.J. Gallagher & P.M. Vietze (Eds.), *Families of handicapped persons: Research, programs, and policy issues* (pp. 67–77). Baltimore: Paul H. Brookes Publishing Co.

Singer, G.H.S., & Irvin, L.K. (Eds.). (1989). *Support for caregiving families: Enabling positive adaptation to disability.* Baltimore: Paul H. Brookes Publishing Co.

Spitze, G., & Logan, J.R. (1991). Sibling structure and intergenerational relations. *Journal of Marriage and the Family, 53*(4), 871–884.

Stoneman, Z., Brody, G.H., Davis, C.H., Crapps, J.M., & Malone, D.M. (1991). Ascribed role relations between children with mental retardation and their younger siblings. *American Journal on Mental Retardation, 95*(5), 537–550.

White, J.M. (1991). *Dynamics of family development.* New York: Guilford Press.

CHAPTER 15

Toward a More General Model for Research on the Well-Being of Siblings of Persons with Disabilities

W. Steven Barnett

As others have noted, research on families of children with disabilities has been highly fragmented (Ramey, Krauss, & Simeonsson, 1989). Even studies ostensibly focused on the same topics vary tremendously in their theoretical frameworks, outcome variables, other variables for which data are collected, and measures used to operationalize variables. In part, this is because the field is a relatively young area of interdisciplinary inquiry. Even a casual review of the literature shows that the study of the effects of children with disabilities on their brothers and sisters should include more attention to specifying exactly what kinds of effects are being studied and how those effects arise.

In particular, it is the author's impression that most researchers who study siblings of children with disabilities view their work as focusing on the well-being of children. However, only very rarely is the relationship between well-being and what is actually studied made explicit. Sometimes it seems to be implicitly assumed that the focal outcome variables are measures of well-being, when deeper reflection might indicate that the two are only indirectly related. This chapter seeks to clarify the concept of well-being and its measurement and to suggest ways that a focus on well-being and its determinants

---

This research was supported in part by NICHD Grant No. RO1HD22999. The author is grateful for the extensive comments of this volume's editors and the comments of Amartya Sen and Urie Bronfenbrenner whose works provide the foundation for this chapter. As always, the chapter's shortcomings are the sole responsibility of the author.

might provide a common conceptual framework for producing and interpreting research on siblings of persons with disabilities.

The chapter is composed of three general sections. The first section reviews alternative theoretical models that have been used in research on general well-being. It is argued that most models are incomplete because of disciplinary limitations and, as a result, produce misleading results when employed in empirical research. The second section proposes a comprehensive conceptual model as a remedy to this problem. The model attempts to encompass a broad range of perspectives using Bronfenbrenner's ecological-systems model. General implications for research are outlined. The third section explores the specific implications of the model for research on siblings of children with disabilities generally and in conjunction with the economic theory of the family.

REVIEW OF THEORETICAL MODELS

The conceptualization and measurement of well-being are among the most fundamental theoretical problems in social science research, as well as in professions such as medicine, law, and education. As Juster, Courant, and Dow (1985) have noted, different groups of social scientists have taken different approaches to the study of well-being. Economists, for example, have conceptualized well-being as an individual's psychological happiness or satisfaction, but have largely eschewed efforts to directly assess well-being. Instead, they have relied on a theory of consumer choice in which each individual seeks to maximize psychological satisfaction derived from leisure, material goods, and services. This theory allows them to focus the study of well-being and its production and distribution, on the measurement and understanding of the stocks and flows of material goods, services, and leisure that are the sources of satisfaction.

Other social scientists have taken a broader view of well-being and employed a wide variety of social indicators or quality-of-life measures. These indicators include measures of mortality, disability, physical health, mental health, nutritional status, divorce, suicide, crime, pollution, educational attainment, literacy, stressful events, and family structure and function. The interpretation of these indicators and their relationship to well-being seem to have been considered obvious for the most part. Often, however, it is unclear whether these indicators were considered to be direct measures of well-being or were themselves variables that contribute to well-being. An exception is the work of social scientists who have asked people directly about their life satisfaction and happiness and interpreted the responses as self-perceptions of well-being.

The importance of self-perceptions of well-being varies, depending on the perspective of the researchers. For some researchers, satisfaction and happiness are the essence of well-being, although they may, like economists, be skeptical of the validity of self-reports. For others, satisfaction and happiness are the results of individual valuation and perception of well-being. In the latter case, well-being itself may be assessed by comparison with an independent standard of the good life—a conception of what is best for human beings to be, do, and experience. This standard might be derived through rational argument, divine inspiration, or other paths to knowledge.

Research on Self-Perceptions of Well-Being

Researchers who have focused on subjective well-being measures have done so by asking two general questions: "How satisfied are you?" and "How happy are you?" The two questions produce different responses, the most widely accepted explanation for this being that satisfaction is primarily a cognitive assessment, while happiness is primarily an emotional state (Campbell, Converse, & Rogers, 1976; Andrews & Withey, 1976). These questions are asked both with respect to one's life as a whole and with respect to specific aspects of one's life, with varying levels of detail. The global measures of satisfaction and happiness correlate in the range of 0.5–0.7 (Inglehart & Rabier, 1986).

There are a number of consistent findings with respect to subjective measures of well-being (Inglehart & Rabier, 1986; Juster & Courant, 1986). Self-reported life satisfaction and happiness vary greatly across nations, but are only weakly related to economic and demographic differences among nations, suggesting that cultural differences are important determinants of response. The relationship of personal characteristics to reported well-being is similar across western countries. Within countries, stable characteristics such as ethnicity, linguistic group, religious identification, and gender have relatively small influences on self-reported well-being. Other variables such as income, marital status, occupation, age, education, and religiosity are more strongly, but still only modestly, related to reported well-being. However, recent changes in economic or social variables have a relatively great impact on reported well-being. It appears that reported well-being is much more strongly related to how recent economic and social conditions compare to expectations and aspirations than to the absolute level of those conditions. Finally, much remains to be learned about the determinants of reported well-being, for despite their general stability, extreme changes have occurred for entire nations that researchers cannot adequately explain.

Psychological Models of Well-Being Psychologists have produced extensive literature relating psychological and social-psychological variables to well-being. Those studying quality-of-life measures have sought to relate these variables to both overall measures of well-being and separate measures for positive affective (enjoyment), negative affective (emotional upset), and cognitive dimensions. Abbey and Andrews (1986) estimated structural models linking measures of internal control, control by others, role ambiguity, negative life events, social conflict, perceived personal success, social support, stress, and depression to measures of well-being as a whole and to separate measures for positive affective, negative affective, and cognitive assessments of well-being. Depression was found to have an extremely strong negative relationship and stress a strong negative relationship to reported well-being. Moderate positive relationships with at least some aspects of reported well-being were found for perceived personal success, internal control, and social support.

Curiously, while Abbey and Andrews (1986) found that the positive and negative affective dimensions of well-being appeared to be distinct, this was not true for the cognitive dimension. The authors speculate that the absence of evidence of a distinct cognitive dimension might reflect shortcomings of the cognitive index used (though one might just as easily make the same conclusion about the positive affect measure with which it is apparently confounded). Another possibility is that the differences between cognitive and affective dimensions might be found in relationship to noncognitive variables that are not included in the model.

Another interesting finding is that positive concepts (e.g., internal control and social support) tended to be more strongly related to the positive dimension of well-being, while negative concepts (e.g., anxiety, stress, and depression) tended to be more strongly related to the negative dimension. One possible explanation for this is that it reflects the effects of personality characteristics on response or self-perception. Costa and McCrae (1980) found evidence that stable personality characteristics measured 10 years earlier influenced reported well-being. In their study extroversion was related to positive, but not negative, affect and neuroticism to negative, but not positive, affect.

Family Research Models of Well-Being Family researchers have also focused on psychological variables, but with an emphasis on stress and coping, and a somewhat different conception of well-being. For example, Lavee, McCubbin, and Olson (1987) estimated a structural model for family well-being that relates well-being to stressful events, normative lifecycle transitions, strain, marital adjustment, and sense of coherence (appraisal of the situation and ability to cope). As with the psychological studies, all variables were measured by self-report. Family well-being and marital adjustment were treated as latent variables measured by husbands' and wives' reports. The researchers found a very strong effect of marital adjustment (comparable to that of nationality or depression) and moderate effects of strain and sense of coherence.

The approach used by Lavee et al. raises questions about the use of measures of subjective well-being that do not arise in the more general psychological research on well-being. One is the question of what meaning is to be attached to family well-being as opposed to individual well-being. Does it make sense to conceptualize family well-being as something different from the well-being of the individuals who comprise the family? Interestingly, Lavee et al. did not ask wives and husbands about the well-being of the family. If family well-being is different from the well-being of the individuals, then it would seem to be appropriate to ask them to report on family well-being, rather than their own. Under this assumption, the structure hypothesized by Lavee et al., in which reports of one's own well-being are used to measure family well-being would seem to be logically inconsistent.

If, however, family well-being is no more than the well-being of individuals, then are there reasonable assumptions under which it makes sense to combine the individuals' measures? The problem is compounded by evidence that the structural models relating other variables to well-being are not the same for men and women (Bryant & Verloff, 1986; McLanahan & Adams, 1989; Silverberg & Steinberg, 1987). Perhaps most importantly, the conceptualization of family well-being as a function of the well-being of its members raises the question of the appropriateness of omitting measures of children's and other family members' well-being.

Another question raised by the model used by Lavee and colleagues is the extent to which the variables related to well-being measure determinants of well-being or are measures of well-being in specific domains. At least some aspects of the family-strain and marital-adjustment measures might be viewed as self-reported satisfaction or happiness with marriage and family. This seems to be particularly problematic for the marital-adjustment measure, which concerns satisfaction with a partner's behavior, comfort with and concerns about family processes, and role satisfaction. Thus, it may be that these two variables relate to family well-being primarily because they measure satisfaction with family life. Another concern is that responses about strain and marital adjustment could reflect personality differences that are, in turn, associated with differences in reported well-being.

Economic Models of Well-Being In economics, well-being has been conventionally defined as psychological well-being, or *utility*, and viewed as depending on the combination of available goods, services, and leisure that entered into an individual's utility function. In the last several decades this view has been modified by developments in household production theory (Becker, 1965; Lancaster, 1966). In this new view, utility-yielding *commodities* are produced from a combination of nonmarket (household) time, purchased goods and services, and aspects of the environment. An intertemporal perspective is taken in which household production includes consumption and investment activities, with investment requiring the sacrifice of current consumption (which influences current well-being) with the aim of increasing future consumption (which influences future well-being).

Although it is not a necessary part of this view, some economists (Michael & Becker, 1973; Muellbauer, 1974; Pollack & Wachter, 1975) have introduced a further set of assumptions under which household behavior can be modelled using the standard microeconomic theory of competitive markets and maximization. Under these assumptions, households respond to implicit prices in determining how much of each commodity to produce and how much time to devote to the labor market. Each household is assumed to maximize its utility given its income from property and potential income from labor.

Juster and colleagues (Juster & Courant, 1986; Juster, Courant, & Dow, 1985) have elaborated this model of well-being to allow household activities to contribute to utility directly (i.e., because some activities are valued in themselves) as well as instrumentally (i.e., because they produce commodities that are valued). The satisfaction that activities yield directly is referred to as "process benefits." This gives rise to the notion of process well-being, which is dependent on the activities currently being conducted. In Juster and Courant's model, well-being depends on both "states of being," such as being married and having children, and on activities such as playing with a child. Thus, activities can be valued as consumption activities (yielding process benefits and consumption of commodities), as investment activities (producing changes in states of being), or both.

From Juster and Courant's perspective, most of the research on subjective measures of global quality of life or well-being has addressed the question of well-being as associated with states of being. Thus, self-reported well-being, as measured in these studies, depends on past activities and the resulting state of being. Juster and Courant have proposed to add to this research by obtaining measures of process well-being, measures of well-being associated with the immediate consumption value of activities and not only with their investment value and resulting states of being.

In order to obtain data on process well-being, people (in national surveys) were asked about satisfaction derived from specific activities and time use. Further questions were asked about the reasons for satisfaction, and the responses indicated that for the most part people evaluated their satisfaction based on the intrinsic value (process value) of activities, rather than the extrinsic (income-producing or investment) value. These data produced some surprising results. Reported satisfaction from work was higher than satisfaction from most leisure activities. Reported satisfaction from activities with children was higher than satisfaction from any other type of activity. Perhaps more in line with expectations, reported satisfaction from housework was lower than from any other type of activity.

The high level of satisfaction reported from activities with children and the lack of differences between those with and without children in satisfaction gained from other activities stands in stark contrast to the findings of other researchers that families with children report lower overall life satisfaction and lower satisfaction with marriage and family. Juster and Courant (1986) argue that the finding of no differences associated with the presence of children or with other social and demographic variables is a result of the use of raw scores, which fail to acknowledge that each person has his or her own "anchor point" (p. 160) or baseline for reporting satisfaction. One person might center responses around 7.5 and another around 2.5, for reasons that don't necessarily reflect a difference in well-being.

To adjust for variations in anchor points, responses regarding satisfaction were recalculated for each person as the difference from his or her own mean for each activity. Juster and Courant argue that these mean-adjusted responses have greater empirical validity, as they are much more strongly related to actual time use for various activities and to the social, economic, and demographic characteristics of the respondents. An alternative interpretation of mean-adjustment not considered by Juster and Courant is that mean-differencing removes the effects of those psychological or context variables not included in their model that would raise or lower the satisfaction reported from all activities. If this were the case, it would not be surprising that a better fit to the other variables is obtained with the mean-adjusted well-being measure. The mean-adjusted variables show lower reported satisfaction with activities for women, married persons, younger persons, and those with children. This does not rid the study of all apparent anomalies, as most other studies find that married people report greater life satisfaction.

Juster and Courant argue that differences should appear between reports of process well-being and reports of state well-being, since process well-being represents transitory measures of satisfaction derived from activities that may be undertaken, in part, to produce improved states of being later. Lower process well-being for those who are married or have children can be explained in terms of a lifecycle model in which people sacrifice current process benefits for future improvements in states of being (or, it might be added, future process well-being). In addition, it seems reasonable to view some states that contribute greatly to overall satisfaction as constraining the activities that generate process benefits. As every parent knows, despite the satisfaction generated by children and by activities with them, they greatly constrain the other activities that can be pursued and the extent to which they can be enjoyed, such that it would not be surprising to see satisfaction from those activities fall.

Beyond Self-Perceptions of Well-Being

An alternative (though similar in some respects to the household production model) approach to the conceptualization and measurement of well-being in economics that is not tied to a psychological view of well-being has been developed by Sen (1987, 1985). Sen's rationale for this new approach, raises several criticisms of the utility model, criticisms that would apply equally well to other conceptions of well-being as a purely psychological state. The most important of these criticisms is that the psychological approach can lead to the neglecting of the actual physical conditions of life, and most researchers would find this objectionable. Sen (1985) poses the problem in this way:

> The destitute thrown into beggary, the landless laborer precariously surviving at the edge of subsistence, the overworked domestic servant working round the clock, the subdued and subjugated housewife reconciled to her role and her fate, all tend to come to terms with their respective predicaments. The deprivations are suppressed and muffled in the scale of utilities (reflected by desire-fulfillment and happiness) by the necessity of endurance in uneventful survival. (p. 21)

The question is whether researchers wish to rely entirely on a person's own evaluation of well-being, even though that evaluation is itself a product of the conditions of his or her life. Empirical studies seem to confirm that one's evaluation of well-being is relative to one's past, to the lives of others like oneself, and to one's expectations for the future. Moreover, a person's valuation depends on current and past states of being, including education and socialization. As philosophers have put it, the pig does not want to be Socrates, nor does the pig believe that it would be better off as Socrates.

What Sen offers as an approach to the measurement of well-being is a focus on functionings and capabilities. Sen (1985, p. 10) identifies quality of life with being and doing and defines a *functioning* as "an achievement of a person: what he or she manages to do or to be." Examples of functionings given by Sen are being well-nourished, well-clothed, mobile, and taking part in community life. Capabilities are the set of possibilities for functioning that a person can effectively choose. The distinction between capabilities and functioning and their roles with respect to well-being can be illustrated with an example. A child who never plays a musical instrument may not do so because she doesn't like to play, has no time to play because of responsibilities for the care of a sibling, has no musical training because the family cannot afford it, or is precluded from playing available instruments by a disability. The functioning is the same, but the capabilities differ, and it is argued that well-being differs in these cases because of the difference in capabilities. Sen's theoretical model of well-being is set out in Figure 1 for added clarity. Dotted lines denote the weakness of utility's links to the model and its possible exclusion.

It should be noted that in Sen's view, people do not always choose the functioning that yields the greatest well-being from among their capabilities. They might choose to reduce their well-being in order to increase someone else's or out of a sense of duty. In this approach, the definition of the good life does not appear to include sacrifice, or at least it need not include sacrifice. Indeed, the definition of the good life, of the ways in which functionings and capabilities are to be valued, is left an open question. One possibility is

Toward a More General Model for Research on Well-Being 341

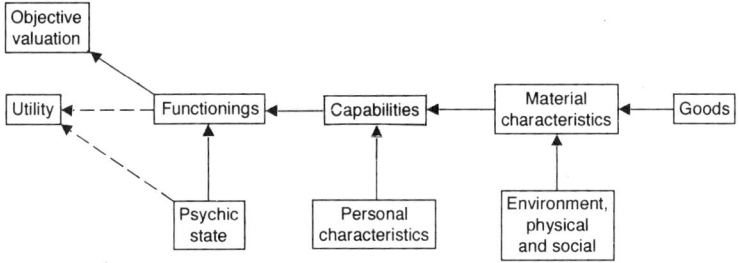

Figure 1. Psychological valuation, functionings, capabilities, and their sources. (From Muellbauer, J. [1987]. Professor Sen on the standard of living. In A. Sen et al., *The standard of living* [pp. 39–58]. Cambridge: Cambridge University Press; reprinted by permission.)

subjective evaluation, perhaps by each individual, of their own functioning and capabilities relative to others. Another is objective valuation, and the problems here are even more difficult with respect to children and to persons with mental disabilities. Whatever theoretical or practical resolution is made, Sen points out that complete (unambiguous) rankings of all the functionings and capabilities may not be possible.

What Sen does provide is a clear argument that the elements to be valued in determining well-being are functionings and capabilities, and that it is these that should be the focus of data collection in assessing well-being. Functioning and capabilities can be directly measured through observation and interviews regarding states of being, nonmarket and market activities, and substantive choices that have been made and those that could be made in the future. In some cases, questions about happiness and satisfaction might provide useful information (happiness might be considered one important functioning) and purchases of market goods might provide indirect information about functionings (such as the ability to go to school without being ashamed of one's clothes). In general, the measures that this view suggests as the focus of studies of well-being differ from those suggested by two other approaches: the traditional economic view, which focuses on the measurement of purchased goods and services, and the more recent household production approach, which focuses on household production of commodities.

A MORE COMPREHENSIVE APPROACH

There are several reasons to consider the development of a comprehensive, but eclectic, approach to research on well-being, its elements, and its determinants. One is that researchers are unlikely to arrive at complete agreement on fundamental questions about the nature of well-being and its measurement. Even those who agree on a relatively well-developed conceptualization of well-being may leave some fundamental issues unresolved. Another is that the findings of the empirical studies conducted by researchers from different traditions suggest that a more accurate and complete understanding of well-being might be obtained through theoretical models and data collection that span the various disciplines.

It is readily apparent that even if a common definition of well-being were adopted, each discipline would continue to focus on a different set of variables that are believed to determine well-being. If each discipline has correctly identified part of the process, then work in each suffers from bias, due to the exclusion of variables and the improper specification of types of relationships better understood by other disciplines. The strength and importance of the relationships studied by researchers in each of the disciplines discussed above are such that this would seem to be more than a minor problem. It follows that a comprehensive, interdisciplinary theoretical framework could be extremely productive in primary research and in interpreting the results of discipline-limited research.

Bronfenbrenner's (1979, 1989) ecological systems model for research on human development provides one starting point for this broader interdisciplinary conceptual framework. As a broad, explicitly intertemporal (lifecourse) person–context–process model for research in which the family has a central role, it has much in common with recent economic, psychological, and family-relations models that define and explain well-being. In some ways, it may be viewed as a meta-theoretical framework within which more detailed theories originating in specific disciplines can be arrayed. Moreover, Bronfenbrenner's conceptualization of development has much in common with a conceptualization of well-being as the valuation of functionings and capacities. One might even define the ecology of well-being as:

> the scientific study of the progressive, mutual accommodation, *throughout the life course,* between an active growing human being, and the changing properties of the immediate settings in which the developing person lives as this process is affected by the relations between these settings, and by the larger contexts in which the settings are embedded. (Bronfenbrenner, 1989, p. 188)

Bronfenbrenner's most basic statement about development suggests that this framework adequately fits well-being:

> The characteristics [well-being, functionings, capabilities] of the person at a given time in his or her life are a joint function of the characteristics [well-being, functionings, capabilities] of the person and of the environment of the course of that person's life up to that time. (1989, p. 190)

If well-being is viewed as the value of functionings and capabilities that are, in turn, the outcomes of a set of processes or interactions with the environment, then functionings and capabilities are analogous to developmental outcomes. The processes producing functionings and capabilities are analogous to development, which is defined by Bronfenbrenner (1989, p. 191) as "the set of processes through which properties of the person and the environment interact to produce constancy and change in the characteristics of the person over the life course."

The author would like to suggest that the similarity between these sets of concepts is not merely a matter of analogy—functionings can be identified as developmental outcomes, and capabilities as potential outcomes, given the constraints imposed by the environmental elements that are beyond a person's control. From this perspective, developmental outcomes studied by human development researchers may be viewed as a subset of a broader class of developmental outcomes that are, for the most part, more obviously social (e.g., a person's marital development, parental development, and professional/vocational development). This identification of interests allows researchers from separate traditions to exchange significant insights with each other. A particularly interesting contribution from economic models of well-being may be that development can be seen as including important elements of choice.

Bronfenbrenner (1989) put forward a set of principles for theory and research design relating to human development. The author has modified and reorganized these into a set of tentative proposals for theory and research on well-being. In addition, these principles have been expanded to encompass a greater scope of well-being. The extent to which they are found to be reasonable and useful will provide one assessment of the validity of the links that the author has drawn between well-being and human development.

Proposal 1 Psychological well-being and material well-being as measured by functionings and capabilities are joint products of the individual and environment. They are inextricably embedded in particular environmental settings that include family, community, polity, and economy. Well-being depends on functionings and capabilities that can be adequately defined and understood only in terms of interactions between individuals and specific environments. These interactions may merely be perceptions. For example, fear that other people will react negatively to a sibling with a disability may reduce well-being, regardless of whether or not the fear is realistic or based on actual experiences. Thus, the accurate measurements of these interactions requires data on both actual activities and perceptions.

Proposal 2 Differences in subjective valuations, functionings, and capabilities between groups from different cultures or subcultures are, in part, a function of experience, in the course of growing up, with the types of valuations, functionings, and capabilities common in the culture or subculture at a particular period of its history. It follows that measures of functioning and capabilities should be contextually based and interpreted in light of the cultures or subcultures in which the person was raised and currently lives. Variations in subjective valuations among cultures or subcultures are critical in interpreting and understanding variations in the development of functionings and capabilities.

Proposal 3 An individual's functionings and capabilities vary across time and place as a function of the different contexts in which that person lives. A comprehensive description of well-being requires the measurement of functionings and capabilities in all of the significant contexts that a person experiences. Researchers should consider obtaining valuations and measurements of these functionings and capabilities from a variety of persons, including, most importantly, the subjects themselves.

Proposal 4 The attributes most likely to shape the development of a person's functionings and capabilities are modes of behavior or belief that reflect an active, selective, structuring orientation toward self and the environment or tend to provoke reactions from the environment. One implication is that research designs should provide for the possibility of differences in functionings and capabilities associated with gender, age, and socially defined group memberships (race, ethnicity, caste). Attempts should be made to capture the processes by which such differences are produced and to develop elaborated theoretical models that go beyond the social address or labels in explaining the differences in processes.

Proposal 5 Well-being derives from states of being defined in terms of functionings and capabilities and also from the exercise of functionings in various activities or processes. Well-being arising from the former may be called *state well-being,* and that provided by the latter, *process well-being.* Thus, activities are critical targets of research on well-being, both because they directly produce well-being and because they are instrumental in improving functionings and capabilities. From a lifecourse view of well-being, people are seen as trading well-being at one time for well-being at another. It might be argued that well-being derives *directly* from states of the world, as well. However, it is the author's view that purely psychological interaction with states of the world produces psychological functionings. For example, having a sibling with a disability does not by itself affect well-being. However, sympathy with a sibling (even one with whom there is no real interaction) can affect well-being.

Obviously, the approach presented here is not yet fully developed. A pictorial representation of the proposed theoretical framework that attempts to integrate the economic and human ecology models is presented in Figure 2. In this hybrid model, personal characteristics, the characteristics of goods and services to which the person is entitled, and the characteristics of environments such as the family, community, and state combine to define the individual's capability set. This capability set can be defined as all of the subsets of activities and results of those activities that are attainable by the individual. Based on the person's psychic state, broadly defined as his or her beliefs, attitudes, values, desires, and inclinations, the individual chooses a set of activities and the cumulative outcomes of those activities at a given time. Together, these are referred to as functionings. In turn, functionings influence

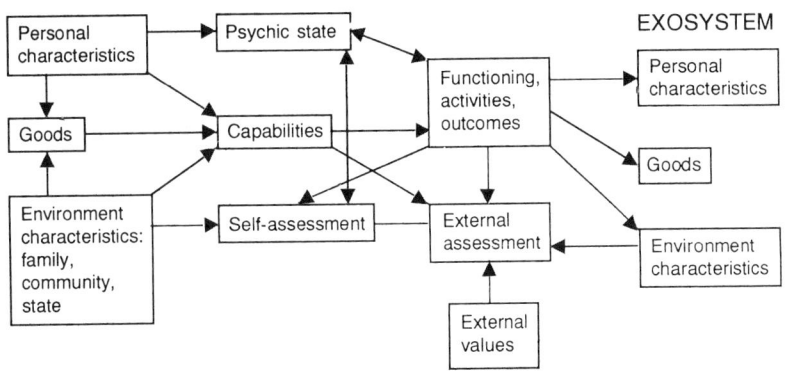

Figure 2. An interdisciplinary framework for research on well-being.

personal characteristics, the goods and services to which one is entitled, and the environments, though the individual effects of most persons on their environments will become much smaller when moving from limited environments, such as the family household, to very large environments, such as a nation-state or economic system. This loop back to the original elements of the model reflects the developmental nature of well-being, which is partially cumulative, evolves over time, and contributes to its own evolution.

The separate inclusion of valuative assessments as elements in the model reflects the view that well-being is determined by applying values to the factors that contribute to well-being, an issue that is frequently avoided in research on well-being. Two types of valuation of functionings and capabilities to assess well-being are included: self-assessments and external assessments. Self-assessments are affected by the psychic state, which includes the persons own values and preferences, and by functionings and capabilities. External assessments result from the application of external values to functionings, capabilities, and self-assessment of well-being, allowing for comparisons to others in the environment.

It is noteworthy that, with one exception, there are no direct lines in the model from personal characteristics, goods, and the environment to either assessment of well-being. The single exception is that the well-being of others in the environment may (but need not) enter into either self-assessed or externally assessed well-being. This reflects the view that these things do not directly contribute to well-being, though they may contribute to well-being through purely psychological means. For example, a person's well-being is not directly affected by the fact that seals are killed for their fur, though knowledge of this practice, even if inaccurate, may result in a person feeling less well-off. Whether this is purely a matter of empathy or sympathy is left open. Similarly, interpersonal comparisons of well-being might alter a person's self-assessment because of the feelings they engender, or because they provide a kind of standard for evaluating well-being.

The elements of the model described thus far are pictured as being enclosed in an exosystem, that is, a cultural or subcultural system that is infused throughout the model, influencing the elements of the model and shaping and constraining the relationships among the elements. Thus, variations in culture or subculture may not only alter the characteristics of the elements of the model (most obviously the psychic state, which might reflect the effects of religion, for example) but may also shape and constrain the relationships among elements. To some extent this is true of environments such as the family, as well. A family may not only contribute resources to activities, but may also constrain how family members combine their own time and goods in activities. The exosystem differs from other systems in that it is not limited to particular environments, but is lodged in many individuals and institutions or social environments. In addition, subcultures may be nested within cultures and several subcultures or cultures may co-exist, or even overlap, within individuals and institutions. It is important to note that self-assessment and external assessment are embedded in the exosystem such that valuative determinations of well-being are influenced by culture.

A significant difference between the hybrid model and the economic model pictured in Figure 1 is the explicit recognition of bidirectionality in some relationships. This is partly accomplished through the completion of the loop back to the initial model elements. For example, personal characteristics and family characteristics influence (through functionings) the amounts of goods to which a person is entitled. These functionings may be purely psychological: simply knowing that certain goods are in one's possession may alter the person and family, though probably not to the extent that the actual use of the goods would. One's psychic state is directly influenced by capabilities and functioning, and self-assessed well-being affects, and is affected by, psychic state. Of course, there is no presumption that effects are equally strong in both directions in any of the relationships.

IMPLICATIONS FOR RESEARCH ON SIBLINGS OF PERSONS WITH DISABILITIES

This chapter suggests that combining the view of well-being developed by Sen and others in the field of economics with the ecological framework for the study of development proposed by Bronfenbrenner produces a useful framework for interdisciplinary research on well-being. The section above set out the general implications of this framework; this section considers in detail some of the implications for research on siblings of children with disabilities.

One implication of the proposed theoretical framework is that the range of outcome variables studied in the field could be greatly expanded. As review chapters in this volume make clear (Boyce & Barnett, chap. 7, this volume; Stoneman & Brody, chap. 12, this volume; Gallo & Knafl, chap. 9, this vol.; Howell, chap. 8, this volume), most research has concentrated on mental health outcomes, such as depression, anxiety, maladjustment, emotional/ behavioral disorders, stress, and self-esteem). When other outcomes, such as sibling activities or relationships, have been examined, the tendency has been to view them as being important because they may affect mental health. It is suggested that functionings and capabilities measured in terms of activities and broadly defined developmental outcomes should in themselves be of interest, apart from their relationship to mental health.

There are a number of other implications of the proposed framework for improvements in sibling research that should be at least briefly noted. Given the evolutionary and cumulative nature of well-being and the potential for trade-offs over time, longitudinal studies would be highly desirable. Most studies have measured sibling effects at only one point in time, although there has been some effort to examine variations in effects with age. Most studies have not included children and adults together, so that it is not even possible to use cross-sectional data to try to trace effects from childhood into the adult years.

The model indicates that it is desirable to measure well-being and its determinants in multiple environments and from multiple perspectives. Researchers have done this to some extent. For example, researchers frequently examine effects on children at home and at school and use teacher, as well as parent, reports. However, researchers have less often sought to determine the extent to which there are actual differences in activities and outcomes across environments, as opposed to differences in how activities and outcomes are perceived. A major benefit of the use of the proposed framework might be an increase in the number of researchers who distinguish between perceptions of activities and outcomes and the activities and outcomes themselves. Research on siblings has relied heavily on self-reports regarding mental states, sibling relationships, and family functioning, but has not tended to explicitly characterize these as self-perceptions. This model would encourage the joint use of observation and multiple reports, including self-report.

Rather than proceed with a general discussion, it may be more useful to outline a specific research agenda derived from the proposed theoretical framework. As indicated earlier, the framework allows for the introduction of more detailed theory and provides a structure for the interaction of theories from multiple disciplines. Thus, it should be possible to demonstrate the use of the framework by drawing on the economic theory of the family. Other researchers may judge what insights might be derived from this and from the effects of introducing their disciplinary theories into the framework together with economic theory.

A useful way to begin investigating how a person with a disability might affect a sibling's well-being is to consider how siblings generally contribute to each other's well-being. In the economic theory of the family (Becker, 1981) there is relatively little emphasis on direct sibling benefits, although it is recognized that, as adults, siblings may be important sources of financial support for each other. Most of the emphasis has been on siblings as rivals for family resources. However, it is a relatively simple matter to explicitly consider a broader range of sibling effects within the general framework of the economic theory of the family.

As children in a family, siblings can affect each other's well-being through direct interaction, or indirectly through other persons in the family. Typically these are the parents, but it is recognized that societies differ in the importance and roles assigned to family members. In particular, extended families are much more important to children in some societies than in the typical western industrialized society. All of the ways in which effects might emerge are dependent on the economic, political, and cultural systems within which the family is embedded.

From an economic perspective, siblings can be regarded as contributing to consumption activities through companionship, and to investment activities through education that affects cognitive, socio-emotional, moral, and perhaps even physical development. Siblings with disabilities may not only be less able to contribute to childhood activities, but might actually detract from the enjoyability of some activities. However, overcoming the difficulties caused by a disability might increase the value attributed to some activities. Similarly, children with disabilities might contribute more or less to a sibling's development in various domains. Effects would be expected to differ with age, sex, birth order, and number of siblings.

Direct effects could also result from purely psychological responses to having a sibling with a disability (a state of the world). Children may feel better or worse about their own characteristics or experiences simply because of what they know about their sibling with a disability. A child may be saddened or distressed as a direct result of a sibling's condition and experiences. A child might experience guilt, depression, or other psychological problems for the same reason. Obviously, such concerns have motivated noneconomic research, though the causes of these effects may not often be thought of as the result of perceptions alone, but of daily interactions as well. In terms of the model proposed in this chapter these would be effects of perceptions on the psychic state or on the subjective valuation of a state of the world. In the first case, this could alter well-being as an effect on mental health and as an effect on the way the individual evaluates her or his well-being. In the second case, this could alter well-being because the person includes the well-being of the sibling with a disability in the set of circumstances that is evaluated in the subjective self-assessment of well-being.

As noted earlier, economists have devoted greater attention to the consideration of how siblings affect resource allocation within the family. Families allocate resources for both consumption and investment purposes, and investment has thus far received the greatest attention. There is no general agreement on how this allocation process should be modelled. However, all models are concerned with how the family allocates purchased goods and services, parental time (to activities and to specific children), and children's time (for activities, parents, and each other). This can be extended to a model that includes capabilities and functionings. Different allocations result in different levels and types of consumption and investment in children, and consumption and investment affect current and future well-being.

Generally, how would a sibling with a disability be expected to affect the allocation of resources and activities conducted with those resources? First, the disability could be expected to raise the costs of some consumption and investment activities more than others. The precise effects on the costs of activities would depend on the nature and severity of the disability, among other things. For example, the cost of going out to dinner is higher if the disability makes a child more difficult to get ready and transport, presents problems of physical access to restaurants, produces an appearance or behavior that is disconcerting to other restaurant patrons, or (in the most limiting case) requires that the child be left at home under care. Second, the returns from some investment activities will be altered. For example, the returns to investing in cognitive human capital may be changed by profound mental disability.

The consequences of these effects on costs and return from investment depend on the other determinants of parental behavior and on parental goals. What are the social norms for allocation of family resources to children? How strong are they, and to what extent are there exceptions or different norms if a child has a disability? Even from a perspective in which families make allocation decisions relatively free of external constraints, there are many uncertainties. Given the inevitable differences among children, which are especially great when a child has a serious disability, parents are faced with trade-offs between equity and efficiency. To what extent do parents decide how much to invest in each child with a view toward maximizing the total return? To what extent do parents provide compensatory investment to children who are less capable? Are parents constrained by concerns about fairness from venturing far from equality in the allocation of any resource? To what extent do parents judge the fairness of their allocation of resources based on the long-term consequences for each child's well-being, as opposed to the amounts given to each child? These questions can be answered only through empirical research.

The economic literature, with Becker's (1981) as the most well developed theoretical example, appears to have included two errors that are particularly relevant to families of children with disabilities. The first of these is the modelling of family behavior as if families were concerned with the impact of their investments in children on narrowly defined economic productivity rather than on general well-being. The second, and related, error is to assume that the marginal productivity of investment in children declines faster for less capable than it does for more capable children. Children who have severe disabilities may obtain very large marginal increases in well-being from investments well beyond the amounts of family resources invested in their siblings. For example, an extremely large investment in medical care might be required to preserve the life of a child. Also, it might be that a large investment in education for a child with a disability could make the difference between adult institutionalization and independent living, and this contribution to well-being might be much more effective than the contribution of resources for the special education of an intellectually gifted sibling.

One insight from economics that may be especially useful in research on families of children with disabilities is that families are likely to respond by changing the mix of resources devoted to consumption and investment, the pattern of resource allocation over time, and the types of consumption and investment activities in which they engage. These changes would result from the effects of the disability on the costs and returns of various activities. Thus, they would differ with the nature, severity, time of onset, expected effects on lifespan, and other characteristics of the disability. For example, parents of a child with a disability that severely limited the return of investment in cognitive capabilities who would survive them by many years might respond by allocating resources so as to create a much larger financial bequest for their child with a disability, while allocating more than most families to the development of their other children's productive capabilities in order to increase the long-term financial capability of the other children to provide for their disabled sibling. Thus, investments in other children motivated by a concern for the child with a disability would depend on how strong an interest parents expected adult siblings to take in the welfare of the child with a disability. An important factor in determining the kinds of trade-offs made between consumption and investment will be the economic situation of the family, especially the amount of financial wealth that can be allocated to children in the form of bequests.

While the focus has usually been on the effects of a child with a disability on the allocation of resources among siblings, reallocation of a fixed amount of resources among children is not the only option families have. Families could reallocate resources from parents to children, or, taking a broader view, from grandparents, grandchildren, and other family members to children. Parents could also reallocate resources from their current consumption activities or from investment in resources for their future, such as retirement income. Parents might provide more time to their children by reducing time devoted to the generation of income from employment (and thus reducing the purchase of goods and services or savings), time spent on leisure activities, or time for self-care and sleep. Parents might devote more purchased goods and services to children by reducing their own consumption or saving or by increasing time spent working for pay. As with all of these family allocation decisions, the choices might vary over time depending on the implications of the disability for costs and returns at various points over the lifespan.

All of these resource-allocation decisions can have a variety of effects on the sibling of a child with a disability. They can be expected to affect the amount of time and purchased goods and services received from the parents and the types of activities engaged in with the parents, alone, or with peers. These allocation decisions affect a child's well-being at any given point in time through immediate effects on capabilities and functioning and long-term development. In order to understand the effects, they must be viewed from a lifespan perspective. In addition to these direct effects on the child, there will be indirect effects related to the child's assessment of the well-being of the parents similar to those of the perceived well-being of the sibling with a disability.

With adult siblings of persons with disabilities the family of concern shifts to, or is altered to include, the family formed by each adult sibling. Adults continue to be psychologically influenced by the perceived characteristics and well-being of the sibling with a disability. A disability might or might not affect the value of the companionship and psychological–emotional support that a sibling could provide (either directly or by altering the development of the sibling relationship). The effects of the disability on interactions might make positive, as well as negative, contributions to a person's well-being. In so far as the sibling is affected, consequences might be felt by the sibling's spouse and children, as well.

Adult siblings may be affected directly by the material well-being and needs of their sister or brother with a disability through continuing interactions with other siblings and members of the family of origin. For example, direct effects might result from expenditures for the care of a sibling with a disability, or because the sibling's reduced income and wealth precludes depending on them as a financial resource in hard times. Direct effects can result from time spent in a variety of activities with the sibling, including direct care. Obviously, these may not only alter the quality of the emotional relationship between the adult sibling and his or her spouse and children, but they may alter activities with family members and the allocation of resources to them. In concrete terms, if more time and money are spent on an adult sibling with a disability, there will be less to allocate to a spouse or children. And if demands, or expectation of future demands, on an adult's resources are great enough, it might affect decisions about marriage and children.

Another type of effect on adults results from the way those in the larger social environment perceive and respond to siblings. Indirect effects might include an impact on the marriageability of an adult sibling because of perceived financial or time liabilities due to the demand for future care of a brother or sister with a disability, a reduction in family wealth or income, or a reduction in social opportunities due to the limited capabilities of a sibling, or because the characteristics of a person with disabilities are taken as a signal of the capabilities of the nondisabled sibling. For similar reasons there might be negative effects on the nondisabled sibling's employability, attainment of social position, and general social status. Obviously, these indirect effects vary to a great extent with the culture.

The impact of culture, which pervades institutions and the minds of the persons who inhabit them, and of the social and economic structure of society must not be underestimated. These effects are the most important reasons that researchers and others, such as policy makers, for instance, must be extremely careful in making generalizations across time, place, and culture of origin, though the potential for effects from differences in the relative prices and return of various activities should not be neglected. Similarly, researchers should expect variations in effects due to gender, ethnicity, and class as a result of cultural perceptions about these characteristics of persons. These cultural impacts may be a matter of perceptions about people, about relationships among people, or both. Barnett (1982) has provided extensive evidence of cross-cultural variations in the implications of mental retardation, for example.

Examples of societal perceptions that have varied over time are the views, widely held early in this century in the United States, that mental retardation is related to moral degeneracy in the individual and family, that siblings of a child with mental retardation are likely to have some related, if less obvious, limitation, and that siblings are likely to have children with mental retardation or other undesirable characteristics. Despite the inaccuracy of these perceptions, they had a powerful impact on family activities with a child with mental retardation and on the direct and indirect effects on siblings. Even if the family of a child with mental retardation rejected such beliefs based on their own experiences, they were influenced by the knowledge that others retained those beliefs. It is hardly surprising that in such circumstances some families made efforts to hide children with mental retardation or did not introduce them into public life. The immediate and long-term well-being of all the children could have been damaged in ways that are largely inconceivable today. In this light, one of the most important aspects of the normalization movement for disabled persons may be that costs to families are reduced by including a child with disabilities in public activities, thus altering the perceptions of society at large.

An example of the effects of social and economic structure of a society is provided by societies where kinship relationships largely determine entitlement to resources. If one's material well-being depends on the productivity of one's brother-in-law because entitlement to resources are primarily determined by this kinship, a sibling's disability may have a very different impact on marriageability than it would in a society where entitlement to resources depends primarily on the market earnings of a person and his or her spouse. If a family's entitlement to resources depends on the mother's brother's ability to produce goods and services, then a brother's disability may greatly reduce his sister's marriageability. However, if a family's entitlement to resources depends on the mother's brother's inherited rights to property and production, then a brother's disability may have no impact on marriageability. Similarly, the expected resource demands on a sibling, and the consequences for family formation and childbearing, might be quite different depending on whether a society provided adequate income to all persons with disabilities through government programs.

CONCLUDING COMMENTS

This paper has begun to develop an interdisciplinary theoretical framework to clarify, broaden, and unify research on the well-being of siblings of persons with mental retardation. It is called a framework because it provides only a general structure that must be filled in with more specific theory. This framework was partially elaborated with economic theory to demonstrate its usefulness and the limitations of previous research. The disciplines that have been most active in this field have tended to define well-being in terms of mental health and to focus on psychological reactions and relationships as the basis for understanding how a person is affected by a sibling with a disability. This is found to be a quite limited perspective. However, a traditional economic perspective would have been limited to the material and financial aspects of life. It is hoped that the development and exploration of this framework will suggest how much has been left untouched by previous research and how much could be gained by research employing this broad framework and drawing on multiple disciplines.

REFERENCES

Abbey, A., & Andrews, F.M. (1986). Modeling the psychological determinants of life quality. In F.M. Andrews (Ed.), *Research on the quality of life* (pp. 85–116). Ann Arbor: Institute for Social Research, University of Michigan.

Andrews, F.M., & Withey, S.B. (1976). *Social indicators of well-being in America.* New York: Plenum.

Barnett, W.S. (1982). *Economics and mental retardation.* Unpublished doctoral dissertation, University of Michigan, Ann Arbor.

Becker, G.S. (1965). A theory of the allocation of time. *Economic Journal, 75,* 493–517.

Becker, G.S. (1981). *A treatise on the family.* Cambridge: Harvard University Press.

Bronfenbrenner, U. (1979). *The ecology of human development: Experiments by nature and design*. Cambridge, MA: Harvard University Press.

Bronfenbrenner, U. (1989). Ecological systems theory. *Annals of Child Development, 6,* 187–249.

Bryant, F.B., & Verloff, J. (1986). Dimensions of subjective mental health in American men and women. In F.M. Andrews (Ed.), *Research on the quality of life* (117–46). Ann Arbor: Institute for Social Research, University of Michigan.

Campbell, A., Converse, P., & Rodgers, W. (1976). *The quality of American life*. New York: Russell Sage.

Costa, P.T., & McCrae, R.R. (1980). Influence of extroversion and neuroticism on subjective well-being: Happy and unhappy people. *Journal of Personality and Social Psychology, 38,* 668–678.

Inglehart, R., & Rabier, J.R. (1986). Aspirations adapt to situations—But why are the Belgians so much happier than the French. In F.M. Andrews (Ed.), *Research on the quality of life* (pp. 1–56). Ann Arbor: Institute for Social Research, University of Michigan.

Juster, F.T., & Courant, P.N. (1986). Integrating stocks and flows in quality of life research. In F.M. Andrews (Ed.), *Research on the quality of life* (147–170). Ann Arbor: Institute for Social Research, University of Michigan.

Juster, F.T., Courant, P.M., & Dow, G.K. (1985). A conceptual framework for the analysis of time allocation data. In F.T. Juster & F.P. Stafford (Eds.), *Time, goods, and well-being*. Ann Arbor: Institute for Social Research, University of Michigan.

Lancaster, K. (1966). A new approach to consumer theory. *Journal of Political Economy, 74,* 132–157.

Lavee, Y., McCubbin, H.I., & Olson, D.H. (1987). The effect of stressful life events and transitions on family functioning and well-being. *Journal of Marriage and the Family, 49,* 857–873.

McLanahan, S., & Adams, J. (1989). The effects of children on adults' psychological well-being: 1957–1976. *Social Forces, 68*(1), 124–146.

Michael, R., & Becker, G.S. (1973). On the new theory of consumer behavior. *Swedish Journal of Economics, 75*(4), 378–396.

Muellbauer, J. (1974). Household production theory, quality and the 'hedonic technique'. *American Economic Review, 64*(6), 977–994.

Muellbauer, J. (1987). Professor Sen on the standard of living. In A. Sen et al., *The standard of living* (pp. 39–58). Cambridge: Cambridge University Press.

Pollack, R.A., & Wachter, M.L. (1975). The relevance of the household production function and its implications for the allocation of time. *Journal of Political Economy, 83,* 255–277.

Ramey, S.L., Krauss, M.W., & Simeonsson, R.J. (1989). Research on families: Current assessment and future opportunities. *American Journal of Mental Retardation, 94*(3), ii–vi.

Sen, A.K. (1985). *Commodities and capabilities*. New York: North-Holland.

Sen, A.K. (1987). The standard of living: Lecture I, Concepts and critiques, and Lecture II, Lives and capabilities. In A. Sen et al., *The standard of living* (pp. 1–38). Cambridge: Cambridge University Press.

Silverberg, S.B., & Steinberg, L. (1987). Adolescent autonomy, parent–adolescent conflict, and parental well-being. *Journal of youth and adolescence, 16*(3), 293–312.

Conclusion

Common Themes and Divergent Paths

Zolinda Stoneman

> Our confusion was not unusual . . . for we had been taught that siblings are, at best, minor actors on the stage of human development, that their influence is supposed to be fleeting, and that it is the parents who principally determine one's identity. (Bank & Kahn, 1982, p. 5)

The 1980s brought a resurgence of research interest in siblings, but the preceding decades were characterized by the general belief expressed in the statement above—that parents, particularly mothers, are the primary socializers of children, with sibling influences being relatively unimportant. The chapters in this volume provide strong affirmation that this view has changed. Brothers and sisters exert major, enduring influences on development. These influences begin even before the birth of a younger sibling and persist across the lifecourse. Parents may still be more powerful sources of social influence than are siblings, but it is increasingly being recognized that in several areas of development, especially in the development of social competence, siblings may have an equal or greater influence than do parents (Beckman & Lieber, 1992; Lamb, 1982; Watson-Gegeo & Gegeo, 1989). In addition to affecting social and developmental outcomes, researchers now realize that a strong, loving relationship between siblings can have a lifelong impact on happiness and quality of life.

As was the case with research on the families of individuals with disabilities, research on siblings within these families has historically focused on identifying pathology and dysfunction. This body of research had its roots in clinical practice. Confronted with families experiencing serious and disruptive problems, professionals became interested in determining the patterns of family dysfunction that resulted from the presence of a member with a disability. And, of course, it is true that what researchers find is largely determined by what they choose to measure. Researchers interested in documenting sibling dysfunction focused on assessing compromised mental health, problems in school, and maladaptive behavior.

The results were also determined by the designs of these studies. Siblings and families constituting study samples were generally drawn from clinic populations, skewing results toward families who were experiencing significant problems. Many early studies did not include comparison groups, or employed poorly matched comparison samples (Stoneman, 1989). In essence, siblings of children with disabilities or chronic illnesses were being compared to the researcher's vision of the "ideal" sibling relationship and "ideal" sibling outcomes. Any problems experienced by the siblings or deviations from the researcher's subjective ideal were attributed to the presence of disability or illness in one of the children in the family. Other possible causes of the identified difficulties were often ignored.

In direct reaction to this negative bias, a new perspective appeared in the literature, namely a focus on family strengths (i.e., Stoneman & Brody, 1982; Summers, Behr, & Turnbull, 1989). Researchers noted that many families seemed to be coping very well with the presence of a child with a disability. Typical siblings in these families were mentally and emotionally healthy and were succeeding in school and in other important environments. A new research emphasis was launched, the effort to identify and measure the strengths of families, including siblings, of individuals with disabilities.

The chapters in this volume lead to the conclusion that both of these approaches, the pessimistic search for sibling pathology and the optimistic effort to document sibling strengths, may allow a strongly held bias about anticipated outcomes to overshadow what is perhaps the most important research question: namely, why do some siblings cope well with their family situation while others do not? It is the heterogeneity among siblings that promises to yield important information about family and individual processes that facilitate coping and adaptation in some siblings and impede these positive outcomes in others. To this end, our knowledge will be advanced by utilizing a balanced, theory-driven research approach, sensitive to both the strengths of siblings and their families and the difficulties that they experience.

The reawakening of research interest in siblings has not been accompanied by a comparable growth in theory. This is unfortunate. Models are needed to explain the impact of siblings on development and to allow insight into those factors that affect the quality of the sibling relationship. Bank and Kahn (1982) noted that developmental theory is "strangely silent" (p. 5) concerning siblings. The absence of theory has been especially evident in the fields of mental retardation and disability, in which family models incorporating sibling influences and specific aspects of disability have been markedly absent. Family theory and theory related to mental retardation and disability have each developed in isolation, with little cross-fertilization between them

(Stoneman, 1990). The contributors to this volume provide family models specific to disability and chronic illness that promise to move the field forward.

COMMON THEMES

Several common trends are evident in the chapters in this volume. Perhaps the most salient is the strong interest in the impact of sibling caregiving on the caregiver, as well as on the receiver of care, and on the family in general. The increased frequency of caregiving, particularly among older sisters, emerges as a consistent finding across studies and samples. The effect of this increased level of caregiving on individual siblings, however, is less clear. Findings from studies examining effects on typical siblings have been inconsistent (Boyce & Barnett, chap. 7, this volume) and studies have generally not examined the effect of sibling caregiving on siblings with disabilities or chronic illnesses. Seltzer and Krauss describe the role of "family vice president," in which one adult sibling is designated as having primary responsibility for a sibling with mental retardation, second only to the caregiving responsibility assumed by parents. Evidence of intergenerational caregiving further reinforces the importance of understanding the effects of sibling caregiving across the lifespan and the predictors of these effects.

A second theme that runs across the chapters in this volume is the importance of understanding siblings in the context of the families in which they live, which include parents, other siblings, and members of the extended family. Families are comprised of complex systems of relationships that mutually influence one another. The sibling relationships of children with mental retardation, disability, or illness can only be understood by studying these relationships in the context of the children's family. Family factors are probably more predictive of sibling outcomes than are individual characteristics of the child with a disability.

In the introduction to his and Sutton-Smith's edited book on sibling relationships, Lamb (1982) noted that the focus of sibling research is moving "from effects to processes" (p. 1). This move from the examination of sibling status effects (e.g., birth order, gender, disability) to process-oriented research is evident in the work presented in this volume. Studies comparing groups of siblings to each other, including those comparing families with and those without a child with a disability, can reveal little about formative processes; they can tell us that sibling groups differ from each other, but they cannot tell us why. Integration of process and group-difference research approaches, both within and across studies, will be maximally effective in advancing our understanding. This combined approach will reveal group differences and will also allow us to gain insight into the family and sibling processes that underlie those differences.

Third, researchers voice strong agreement on the importance of studying the sibling relationship across the lifespan, as it is frequently noted that it is, for many individuals, the longest-lasting human relationship. Neither parent–child relationships nor marriages have as long a duration. In addition, the average lifespan of persons with disabilities is increasing. Because many individuals with mental retardation, disabilities, and illnesses remain dependent on their families into adulthood, understanding the sibling relationship across the lifespan is increasingly more important.

Another theme evident throughout the conference from which this volume arose, and across these chapters, is the frustration at the meager array of instruments available to measure important constructs surrounding families and disability. Important constructs such as stress, coping, and family adaptation lack universally-accepted measurement instruments. Some measures, such as the Questionnaire on Resources and Stress (Holroyd, 1974), have been developed specifically for families with a member who has a disability. These measures, however, are inappropriate for the general population and, thus, do not allow comparisons between families with and without a member with a disability. Furthermore, instruments developed for the general population do not speak to the experiences of families with a member with a disability or illness, and thus fail to capture constructs of particular importance for understanding these families.

A fifth area of agreement concerns the need to develop instruments that reliably obtain family and sibling information from siblings with disabilities, especially siblings with mental retardation. The viewpoint of the sibling with a disability or chronic illness is an important perspective missing from the research presented in this volume. Mothers, fathers, teachers, typical siblings, outside observers, clinicians, and peers all provide their perspectives, but information from persons with disabilities is conspicuously absent.

DIVERGENT PATHS

In addition to revealing common themes, the chapters in this volume also indicate that researchers are taking quite different approaches to the study of siblings of individuals with mental retardation, disabilities, and chronic illnesses. Some researchers are primarily interested in understanding individual sibling outcomes, particularly for the typical sibling; others focus their efforts on understanding the relationship between siblings. The general sibling literature has evolved from focusing almost exclusively on birth-order effects on individual development to focusing on factors that enhance or compromise the sibling relationship itself. Researchers interested in disability, however, tend to be most interested in learning more about how siblings without disabilities are affected. It might be argued that those factors that facilitate healthy outcomes in typical siblings would be the same as the factors that positively affect relationships between siblings. The validity of this assumption, however, is uncertain.

Another difference among the scientists contributing to this volume concerns their focus on specific types of disability or illness or on more global approaches that focus on processes that generalize across different disabilities or illnesses. Issues concerning categorical and noncategorical approaches are discussed by Gallo and Knafl (chap. 9). Researchers taking a disability-specific view hold that characteristics of different disabilities or illnesses vary greatly and should not be expected to similarly affect siblings or the sibling relationship. Other researchers are interested in general processes that operate across different disabilities or illnesses. An alternative approach, focusing on functional classification, addresses the impact of functional aspects of disability (e.g., caregiving demands placed on the family, degree of physical mobility) that span different illnesses and disabilities, rather than focusing on traditionally defined diagnostic categories. By combining information obtained from these different approaches, it will be possible to discover effects on siblings and on the sibling relationship that can be attributed to general phenomena that span disability and illness categories, effects that are specific to one disability or chronic illness, and effects that are related to specific functional aspects of disability, such as increased sibling caregiving.

In addition, researchers contributing to this volume come from diverse disciplinary backgrounds; many work in entirely separate professional worlds. Although sharing a common interest in siblings, they attend different professional conferences, publish in different journals, and collaborate with different colleagues. Several of the participating researchers had never met before the NICHD conference that sponsored these chapters.

Disciplinary differences among participating researchers can be as basic as a lack of agreement about the use of terms such as "chronic illness" or "physical disability;" as topics for the conference papers were being solidified, divergent views on the definitions of these terms emerged. For example, is a child with cerebral palsy chronically ill? Persons from a health/medical background and those studying chronic illness tend to answer "yes;" those from non-medical disciplines and those interested in disability are more likely to say "no." These distinctions are important because they directly affect the selection of study samples, the assignment of families to disability or illness groups, and the interpretation of study findings. Researchers using the same terms are not always referring to the same families; researchers using different terms may, in fact, be studying the same samples.

These issues go well beyond the definition of study samples. As pointed out by Barnett, disciplinary bias in research can lead to inconsistent conceptualization of important processes and constructs, and to the exclusion of important variables. Like persons touching various parts of the proverbial elephant, researchers use different sources of information to learn about siblings. Each source provides useful information, but a full understanding can only arise from the amalgamation of many bits of information from diverse sources into one complex composite picture. There is a strong need for researchers from different disciplinary perspectives to develop more effective means of communication, to disseminate information to each other, and to collaborate. Furman's analogy of "dressing the fish" (chap. 2, this volume), in which areas of specialization overlap each other like scales, aptly characterizes this ideal.

FUTURE DIRECTIONS

Although the work in this volume represents great progress in understanding siblings of individuals with mental retardation, disabilities, and chronic illnesses, much remains to be done. Sibling researchers have primarily concentrated their efforts on understanding siblings of individuals with mental retardation and chronic illnesses, and the literature on these siblings is substantial and growing. But this is not the case with siblings of individuals with physical and sensory disabilities. These siblings have generally been overlooked by sibling researchers, and few efforts targeting these siblings are currently underway. In reviewing existing literature for this conference, participating scientists noticed an absence of research focusing on siblings of individuals with dual diagnoses or learning disabilities; these are important voids to be filled by future studies.

To date, researchers have preferred to study siblings living in white, middle class families. Siblings living in poverty and siblings who are members of minority groups have seldom been studied. Changes in the demographic composition of this country, combined with the disproportionate representation of disabilities in minority groups and in families who live in poverty, suggest a clear need for researchers to focus attention on these siblings.

Haggerty, Roughman, and Pless (1975) used the term "new morbidity" to refer to a group of negative child outcomes that are more likely to occur among families living in poverty. More recently, Baumeister and colleagues (Baumeister & Kupstas, 1987; Baumeister, Dokecki, & Kupstas, 1988) suggest that new morbidity outcomes result from a transaction of behavioral, environmental, and biological factors that act in concert, producing effects that are cumulative, long-lasting, and intergenerational.

Baumeister and Kupstas (1987) concluded that children living in poverty are one-and-a-half to two times more likely to have a disability than are children living in more affluent homes. Associations between mental retardation and poverty are even stronger. Their analyses suggest that even severe forms of mental retardation, long thought to be evenly distributed across social classes, are also more concentrated among poor families. Recently, childhood AIDS and infants prenatally exposed to drugs and alcohol have become additional factors in the new morbidity. Among children with mental retardation, 70%–75% live in a context of poverty and environmental deprivation (Zigler & Hodapp, 1986). This group is all but invisible in the research on families of children with mental retardation (Stoneman, 1990) and is similarly ignored in research focusing on siblings. Many of these children come from multiproblem homes in which parents face numerous challenges coping with daily life. In many of these families, more than one child has mental retardation or some other disability. Understanding of these siblings is not well served by the uni-directional models that now dominate research. Researchers cannot attempt to understand siblings living in these families without addressing the wider social system or without crossing interdisciplinary boundaries.

In his chapter, Weisner (chap. 3, this volume) argues that the cultural place in which children live is the single most important factor in understanding their lives, and that information gained from studying one group of siblings cannot automatically be generalized to other siblings who do not share a common culture or ethnic background. Because of the strong research bias toward studying white families, we know little about the very large groups of siblings of African American, Hispanic, Asian, and Native American heritage. According to Barnett (chap. 15, this volume), not only are individual and family well-being culturally influenced, but relationships between processes and outcomes may also vary depending on the cultural-group membership of the family. In addition, measurement strategies that produce valid assessments for one cultural group may have a different meaning, or be entirely invalid, for another. In a multicultural society, scientists can ill afford to concentrate exclusively on one ethnic group. Ethnocentrism has been common in the past, but this must change as researchers confront the future.

Researchers must also focus on the changing family context in which siblings live. Societal changes have resulted in an increased number of single-parent homes, reconstituted families, children experiencing divorce, dual-career families, and children living with grandparents and other extended-family members. The two-parent home in which the mother is a full-time caregiver is becoming less common. Taking its place are a wide variety of family forms in which today's children are raised, and some of these families include children with mental retardation, disability, or chronic illness. It is important to understand the impact of various family structures on siblings in these families. Most research to date has focused on one child per family; with the study of siblings, this expands to two children. Larger family groups, however, have as yet received little research attention. The important role of grandparents and other extended-family members has also often been ignored.

Theories in the general sibling literature have potential benefits for guiding research on siblings of individuals with mental retardation, disability, and chronic illness. These include models of deidentification, in which siblings minimize rivalry by becoming different from each other (Schachter, 1982), sibling attachment (Crnic & Lyons, chap. 11, this volume; Gamble & Woulbroun, chap. 13, this volume; Seltzer & Krauss, chap. 5, this volume; and Stewart, 1983), and self-esteem maintenance, in which sibling similarity and comparison processes are believed to influence sibling friction and distancing (Tesser, 1980). Other theories, such as those derived from the literature on family stress and coping (Gamble & Woulbroun, chap. 13, this volume), lifespan development (Rowitz, chap. 14, this volume; and Seltzer & Krauss, chap. 5, this volume), role theory (Stoneman & Brody, chap. 1, this volume), exchange theory (Seltzer & Krauss, chap. 5, this volume), social learning theory (Crnic & Lyons, chap. 11, this volume), and economic theories of well-being (Barnett, chap. 15, this volume) will also be useful in guiding research on siblings. Research on siblings during times of family or individual transition, on the impact of social support on siblings, the interface between siblings and service systems, and on the association between religiosity and the sibling relationship are all fertile areas for future study.

Other important areas for future research are derived from the work of behavioral geneticists, who have demonstrated that siblings evince greater differences than similarities in major developmental areas and that the ways that environments are experienced by siblings living in the same home can differ as much as those of two unrelated children living in different families (Plomin, 1989; Rowe & Plomin, 1981). It has been argued that the most developmentally relevant variations in family environments occur within, rather than between, families, acting as nonshared intrafamily variations that serve to make siblings different from each other (Plomin, 1987). Researchers have only recently begun to investigate nonshared environments in families in which one child has a chronic illness or disability.

Most studies of family environments have focused on differential treatment by parents. The first research question in this vein concerns the degree to which parents treat siblings differently, the second, more important question concerns the meaning that this differential treatment has for the siblings. The final question asks what impact differential treatment has on the sibling relationship and on individual sibling outcomes. When one sibling has a disability or chronic illness, does differential treatment hold different meanings for the children? Is it the meaning that children attach to differential treatment that determines whether it will have a deleterious effect? It would seem plausible that a family could display greater absolute levels of differential treatment and yet have siblings that perceive less favoritism, depending on their interpretation of events. Two typical children in the same family may experience the family situation quite differently, yielding different individual and relationship outcomes. These questions and others surrounding differential treatment are addressed in numerous chapters in this volume, including in-depth discussions by Furman, chap. 2; Crnic and Lyons, chap. 11; Brody and Stoneman, chap.

12; and Weisner, chap. 3. This is an exciting new area of research that promises to lead to important insights.

Research on siblings of individuals with mental retardation, disabilities, and chronic illnesses is difficult, time-consuming, and expensive. Low-incidence samples are hard to locate, measurement issues are complex, and a large number of extraneous variables must be controlled in order for findings to be meaningful. To study siblings of children with illness or disability, eight sibling gender combinations must be considered (e.g., two sisters, older sibling has disability; two sisters, younger sibling has disability), as well as age spacing, sibling age, family size, and relative birth order compared to other children in the family. Other family factors, such as single- versus two-parent homes, ethnicity, severity and type of disability, and age of onset of disability further increase the complexity. The difficulty of the task has resulted in seasoned sibling researchers turning their attention to other, easier-to-study issues. When researchers in the areas covered by this NICHD conference were called and invited to participate, several well-published researchers declined, explaining that they were no longer actively engaged in sibling research related to mental retardation, disabilities, or chronic illnesses. The reasons given pointed to the difficulty of sustaining programmatic research on siblings, particularly in the identification and recruitment of study samples. These difficulties can also discourage new researchers from entering the field of sibling research. It is hoped that conferences such as that sponsored by NICHD will assist in retaining active scientists in this field, as well as in supporting the entry of new researchers into this area of study.

There is a perverse law that operates in many research fields: the importance of any research question is inversely proportional to the ease of designing and implementing research to address that question. Partial proof of this law can be found in the large number of studies conducted with university undergraduates. The scarcity of studies focusing on siblings of individuals with mental retardation, disabilities, and chronic illnesses provides additional evidence. As noted by Rowitz, (chap. 14, this volume), studies tend to use heterogeneous groups of children living in extremely diverse family contexts. These problems are compounded by small sample sizes.

Despite these challenges, the chapters in this volume clearly demonstrate that research on siblings of individuals with mental retardation, disabilities, and chronic illnesses is very much alive. The importance of studying siblings outweighs the difficulty of the task. The level of excitement and promise expressed by the contributors to this volume bodes well for the future. Multifaceted support will be needed, however, to sustain this enthusiastic effort over time. Scientists struggling with pragmatic difficulties in conducting sibling research must support each other. Professional isolation demoralizes researchers and decreases the likelihood of sustained effort. Funding agencies must recognize the importance of sibling research, as well as understand the level of resources needed to conduct theoretically and empirically sound research in this complex area. This includes a commitment to fund longitudinal sibling studies. Finally, researchers must form partnerships with service providers and families (including siblings themselves), so that these most important participants in the research process perceive that they have a stake in the outcome of the studies being conducted that is sufficiently important to warrant their active participation in the research effort.

REFERENCES

Bank, S.P., & Kahn, M.D. (1982). *The sibling bond.* New York: Basic Books.

Baumeister, A.A., Dokecki, P.R., & Kupstas, F.D. (1988). *Preventing the new morbidity: A guide for state planning for the prevention of mental retardation and related disabilities associated with socioeconomic conditions.* Nashville: Vanderbilt University.

Baumeister, A.A., & Kupstas, F. (1987). *The new morbidity: Implications for prevention and amelioration.* Paper presented at the meeting of the Royal Society of Medicine on social and environmental factors in the prevention and amelioration of mental handicap.

Beckman, P.J., & Lieber, J. (1992). Parent–child social relationships and peer social competence of preschool children with disabilities. In S.L. Odom, S.R. McConnell, & M.A. McEvoy (Eds.), *Social competence of young children with disabilities: Issues and strategies for intervention* (pp. 65–92). Baltimore, MD: Paul H. Brookes Publishing Co.

Haggerty, R.J., Roughman, K.J., & Pless, I.V. (1975). *Child health and the community.* New York: John Wiley and Sons.

Holroyd, J. (1974). The Questionnaire on Resources and Stress: An instrument to measure family response to a handicapped family member. *Journal of Community Psychology, 2,* 92–94.

Lamb, M.E. (1982). Sibling relationships across the lifespan: An overview and introduction. In M.E. Lamb & B. Sutton-Smith (Eds.), *Sibling relationships: Their nature and significance across the lifespan* (pp. 1–11). Hillsdale, NJ: Academic Press.

Plomin, R. (1989). Environment and genes. *American Psychologist, 44,* 105–111.

Plomin, R. (1987). Behavioral genetics and intervention. In J.J. Gallagher & C.T. Ramey (Eds.), *The malleability of children* (pp. 15–24). Baltimore: Paul H. Brookes Publishing Co.

Rowe, D.C., & Plomin, R. (1981). The importance of nonshared environmental influences in behavioral development. *Developmental Psychology, 17,* 517–531.

Schachter, F.F. (1982). Sibling deidentification and split-parent identification: A family tetrad. In M.E. Lamb & B. Sutton-Smith (Eds.), *Sibling relationships: Their nature and significance across the lifespan* (pp. 123–152). Hillsdale, NJ: Academic Press.

Stewart, R.B. (1983). Sibling attachment relationships: Child–infant interactions in the strange situation. *Developmental Psychology, 19,* 192–199.

Stoneman, Z. (1989). Comparison groups in research in families with mentally retarded members: A methodological and conceptual review. *American Journal on Mental Retardation, 94,* 195–215.

Stoneman, Z. (1990). Conceptual relationships between family research and mental retardation. In N.W. Bray (Ed.), *International review of research in mental retardation* (pp. 161–201). San Diego, CA: Academic Press.

Stoneman, Z., & Brody, G.H. (1982). Strengths inherent in sibling interactions involving a retarded child: A functional role theory approach. In N. Stinnett, J. DeFrain, K. King, H. Lingren, G. Rowe, S. VanZandt, & R. Williams (Eds.), *Family strengths: Positive support systems*. Lincoln, Nebraska: University of Nebraska Press.

Summers, J.A., Behr, S.K., & Turnbull, A.P. (1989). Positive adaptation and coping strengths of families who have children with disabilities. In G.H.S. Singer & L.K. Irvin (Eds.), *Support for caregiving families: Enabling positive adaptation to disability* (pp. 27–40). Baltimore: Paul H. Brookes Publishing Co.

Tesser, A. (1980). Self-esteem maintenance in family dynamics. *Journal of Personality and Social Psychology, 39*, 77–91.

Watson-Gegeo, R.A., & Gegeo, D.W. (1989). The role of sibling interaction in child socialization. In P.G. Zukow (Ed.), *Sibling interaction across cultures: Theoretical and methodological issues* (pp. 54–76). New York: Springer-Verlag.

Zigler, E., & Hodapp, R.M. (1986). *Understanding mental retardation*. Cambridge: Cambridge University Press.

INDEX

Academic underachievement, learning disability and, 238
Acquired immunodeficiency syndrome (AIDS), see HIV infection
Action, norms for, in ecocultural niche, 54
Activities
  of siblings of persons with mental retardation, 163–169
  social engagement in, 8
  see also specific type
Adaptive competence, 13–15
Adjustment
  normal sibling relationships and, 260–261
  out-of-home placement and, 122
  in childhood, 127–128
  parental, 305–306
  of siblings of children with learning disabilities, 243, 244
  see also Learning disabilities
  of siblings of children with mental retardation, 148
  early research on, 149, 160
  recent research on, 160–161
  of siblings of children with physical disability or chronic illness, 203–204
  noncategorical characteristics related to, 230–231
Adolescence
  out-of-home placement in, 128–130
  psychological well-being in, siblings with mental retardation and, 149, 160
Adult sibling relationships, of persons with mental retardation, 99–113
  antecedents and consequences of, 99–100

availability of siblings and, 107–108
care for aging parents and, 120
effect on maternal well-being, 111
family environment and, 109–110
future research on, 111–113
out-of-home placement and, 130–131
research findings on, 106–111
review of literature on, 103–106
studies of dyads and, 171–172
support provided by siblings and, 108–109
theoretical perspectives on, 100–103
Affectional needs, stress and, 298–299
Affective support, adult siblings and, 108–109
Affective tone, of sibling relationship, 8–9
Africa, sibling relationships in, 55–58
Age
  as mediating variable, in research on siblings of persons with mental retardation, 175, 176
  see also Adolescence; Adult sibling relationships; Childhood; Older siblings; Young siblings; Younger siblings
Aggression, 16
  parental response to, 17–18
Aging parents, nondisabled sibling caring for, burden of care for sibling as well as, 120
AIDS, see HIV infection
Anticipatory management, by parents, relationship between nondisabled siblings and, 40
Anxiety, in siblings of children with mental retardation, 161
Assessment instruments, life events and, 294

Attachment theory, adult sibling relationships of persons with mental retardation and, 102
Attention, parental, differential, see Differential parenting
Attitudes
of nondisabled siblings, toward out-of-home placement, 131
of parents, as stressor, 305
Automatic parenting, 19–20

Balanced reciprocity, 102
Behavior problems
learning disability and, 237–238
marital problems related to, 22–23
mental retardation and, 254
see also Dual diagnosis
Bias, in lifetime research on siblings of persons with mental retardation, 327–330
Bidirectionality, in social ecology, 206
Birth order
as mediating variable, in research on siblings of persons with mental retardation, 175–176
see also Older siblings; Sibling configurations; Younger siblings
Boundary conditions, risk-factor studies and, 202–204
Brothers, see Gender
Burden of care, shifting across lifespan, out-of-home placement and, 120

Capabilities, in measurement of well-being, 340–341, 343–344
Care demands, 10–12
adaptive competency and, 14
cultural beliefs and, 72–73, 75
shifting burden of care across lifespan and, out-of-home placement and, 120
sibling caregivers and, lack of data on, 326
on siblings of children with mental retardation, 163–167
activities and, 168–169
as stressor in sibling relationship, 299–300

Categorical approach, to research on siblings of children with chronic illness, 216–218
Causal-process research, on siblings of children with physical disability or chronic illness, 186–187, 204–209
social ecology principles and, 205–206
studies using, 206–209
Childcare, see Care demands
Childhood
out-of-home placement in, 127–128
sibling dyads in, studies of, 170–171
Childrearing strategies, 24
see also Parenting
Chores, see Household chores
Chronic health problems
characteristics of, as moderators of influence on sibling adjustment, 203–204
research on siblings of children with, 185–210, 215–232
agenda for, 232–233
categorical approach to, 216–218
causal-process research, 186–187, 204–209
dimensions of, 221, 222–227
disease course in, 219
effects of illness on siblings in, 229–230
functional factors in, 219–220
methodology of, 221, 228–229
noncategorical approach to, 216, 219–220, 230–233
onset of illness and, 220
risk-factor research, 185–204
strategies for literature review of, 220–221
visibility of illness and, 220
risks related to, 185–204
influences on sibling relationship, 12
see also Risk-factor research
see also Disabilities
Chronic sorrow
effect on parenting, 20
learning disability and, 238
see also Depression
Cognitive characteristics, of young siblings, 86–88

Index   369

Cognitive competence, 13
  learning disability and, 238
  younger siblings and, role asymmetry and, 7
Cognitive dimensions of well-being, 336
Communication patterns, in parent–child relationship, stress and, 301–304
Community interactions, stress and, 306–307
Community residence, permanent care versus, sibling involvement and, 119–120
Comparative research, ethnography and, 63–64
Competence
  adaptive, 13–15
  cognitive, 13
    learning disability and, 238
    role asymmetry and, 7
  language, 13
  of sibling with disability, as mediating variable in sibling relationships, 176
  social, 13–15
    learning disability and, 237–238
Computers, in research, 146
Conceptual issues
  adult sibling relationships, 99–113
    see also Adult sibling relationships
  ethnographic and ecocultural perspectives, 51–78
    see also Ecocultural niche; Ethnographic research
  issues and interventions for young siblings, 85–95
    see also Young siblings (infancy to 7 years)
  out-of-home placement, 117–135
    see also Out-of-home placement
  sibling relations in family context, 3–26
    see also Family-context model
  sibling relations of nondisabled children, 31–48
    see also Nondisabled children, sibling relationships of
Conflict
  increase in, with increased care demands, 11
  spousal
    effects of, 21–23
    see also Marital relationship
Conflictual lifestyles, siblings of children with mental retardation and, 323–324
Consistency of parenting, see Parenting, consistency of
Context, as parameter for inclusion in studies, 277–278
Contrived research, naturalistic research versus, ethnography and, 63
Control procedures, measurement method and, in risk-factor research, 192–196
Coping
  strategies for, 308–311
  stress and
    measurement considerations, 287–312
    in siblings of persons with learning disability, 245
    in siblings of persons with mental retardation, 172–173
Correlational research designs, experimental designs versus, ethnography and, 63
Cross-cultural research, universals and diversity in, 58–60
Cued-recall procedure, in time-use research, 166
Culture
  defined, 53
  ethnicity versus, 53
  mental retardation and, impact of child with, 134–135
  see also Ecocultural niche

Death, sibling's response to
  out-of-home placement and, 135
  at young age, 88
Demographics
  adult sibling relationships and, 103–104
  siblings of children with learning disabilities and, 243–244
  as source of sampling bias, in lifetime research on siblings of persons with mental retardation, 327–329

Depression
  parental, effect on parenting, 19–20
  in siblings of children with mental retardation, 161
Development, lifespan, 100–102
Developmental delay, families with children with, ecocultural niche and, 64–78
Developmental psychopathology, family processes and, 254–260
Developmental status
  relationship between nondisabled siblings and, 46–47
  relationship of nondisabled sibling and sibling with disabilities and, 171, 175
Differential parenting, 24, 25
  as parameter for inclusion in studies, 282–283
  relationship between nondisabled siblings and, 38–39
  adjustment and, 260–261
  see also Equality of treatment
Disabilities
  young children's understanding of, 86–88
  see also Chronic health problems; *specific type*
Discipline, strategies of, relationship between nondisabled siblings and, 39–40
Discrepancies, in expectations and perceptions, parent–child relationship and, 304–305
Distractible behavior, parental response to, 17
Domestic tasks, *see* Household chores; Task allocation
Down syndrome
  siblings of children with, psychological well-being of, 149, 160
  see also Mental retardation
Dual diagnosis, 253–268
  family processes and, developmental psychopathology and, 254–260
  prevalence of, 253–254
  sibling relationships and, 265–268
    family context of, 266–268
  type of psychopathology in, 254

Eastern Africa, sibling relationships in, 55–58
Ecocultural niche, 51–53
  cross-cultural research and, universals and diversity in, 58–60
  families with developmentally delayed children and, 64–78
    data on, 65–70
    ecocultural influences in, 70–71
    equality and, 71–72
    parental concerns and reports from, 74, 75–78
    task allocation and, 71, 72–73, 75
    variations in siblings' lives based on, 55–58
  see also Ecological perspectives; Ethnographic research
Ecological perspectives
  out-of-home placement and, 119, 124–127
  see also Ecocultural niche; Social ecology
Economic models of well-being, 337–339, 348–351
Education for All Handicapped Children Act (PL 94-142)
  learning disabilities and, 236
  out-of-home placement and, 130
  nondisabled siblings and, 120–122
Egocentricity, of young siblings, 86
Embeddedness, in social ecology, 205
Emotional characteristics, vulnerabilities and, of young siblings, 86–88
Environment, *see* Ecocultural niche; Family environment; School environment
  child and, stress as transaction between, *see* Transactional perspective, stress and
Equality of treatment
  cultural beliefs and, 71–72
  see also Differential parenting
Ethnicity, 23
  culture versus, 54
  see also Culture
  siblings of persons with mental retardation and, 180
Ethnographic research, 51–53
  epistemological status of, 61–64
  methods in, 60–61
  see also Ecocultural niche

Event-oriented view, *see* Life-event perspective
Exchange theory, adult sibling relationships of persons with mental retardation and, 102–103
Expectation, discrepant, parent–child relationship and, 304–305
Expected impairment, 145
Experimental research designs, correlational designs versus, ethnography and, 63
Externalizing patterns, sibling of child with physical disability or chronic illness and, 198–200

Family, learning disability effects on, 238–239
  sibling problems and, 240
Family behavior, young sibling's interpretations of, 87
Family constellation, risk-factor studies and, boundary conditions in, 202–203
Family-context model, 3–26
  characteristics of individual siblings in, 9–17
  see also Individual siblings
  parenting in
    family characteristics affecting, 21–23
    individual parent characteristics affecting, 19–20
    individual sibling characteristics affecting, 17–19
    variables influencing sibling relationships through, 23–25
  sibling relationship and, 5–9
    family characteristics affecting, 21–23
    parenting variables affecting, 23–25
    siblings of children with dual diagnosis and, 266–268
    siblings of children with learning disabilities and, 244
Family environment
  effect on adult sibling relationships, 109–110
  psychopathology and, 264–265
  see also Ecocultural niche

Family interactions, social influences on, direct and indirect, 5
Family processes, developmental psychopathology and, 254–260
Family research models of well-being, 336–337
Family size, adult sibling relationships and, 103–104
Family social-process variables, in research on siblings of persons with mental retardation, 176–177
Family systems theory, siblings of children with learning disabilities and, 240, 242
Favoritism, *see* Differential parenting
Frequency rating scales, in time-use studies, 165–166
Functionings, in measurement of well-being, 340–341, 343–344

Gender
  adult sibling relationships and, 104
  care demands and, 163–164
  household tasks and, 166
  as mediating variable, in research on siblings of persons with mental retardation, 173, 175, 176
  as parameter for inclusion in studies, 278–281
Generalized reciprocity, 102
Geographic mobility, adult sibling relationships and, 103, 104
Groups, for young siblings, 91–92

Health risks, 12, 185–204
  see also Chronic health problems
  see also Risk-factor research
Heuristic information, for consideration in research design, 275–284
HIV infection, young siblings of child with, 92–95
  national survey on, 93–94
  parent interviews on, 94–95
Holistic methods, particularistic methods versus, ethnographic research and, 62–63
Hospitalization, young siblings' responses to, 87–88
  visitation and, 88–91

Household chores, 14
  time use and, siblings of children with mental retardation and, 163–167
  see also Task allocation
Human immunodeficiency virus, *see* HIV infection
Hyperactivity
  environment and, 265
  see also Behavior problems

Identities, developing, sibling relationship and, 300–301
Illness
  chronic, *see* Chronic health problems
  see also Disabilities
Impairment, expected, 145
Inconsistent parenting, *see* Parenting, consistency of
Individual differences
  as parameter for inclusion in studies, 281–282
  siblings of persons with mental retardation and, 179
Individual siblings
  aggression of, 16
  care demands of, 10–12
  characteristics of, 9–17
  effects on parenting, 17–19
  effects on relationship between nondisabled siblings, 45–47
  competence of
    cognitive and language, 13
    social and adaptive, 13–15
  health risks to, 12
  noncompliance of, 16
  physical disability of, 15
  sensory disability of, 15–16
Infants, *see* Young siblings (infancy to 7 years)
Infection, newborn nurseries and, sibling visitation of, 89, 90
Information
  need for, parent–child relationship and, 301–304
  for young siblings
    about HIV infection, 93–95
    misconceptions and, 86–87
    support groups and, 91–92

Institutionalization
  community residence versus, sibling involvement and, 119–120
  before PL 94-142 enactment, 121–122
Intensive care, newborn, sibling visitation and, 88–91
Intergenerational sampling biases, in lifetime research on siblings of persons with mental retardation, 327
Internalizing, sibling of child with physical disability or chronic illness and, 197–198
Isolation, of young siblings, 87–88

Knowledge, representational, in ecocultural niche, 53–54

Language competence, 13
Learning disabilities, 235–247
  as developmental problems, 236–239
  diagnosis of, 236
    research problems involving, 246
  effects on family, 238–239
  familial etiology of, 241
  incidence of, 235
  in more than one sibling, 246
  problems in child with, 236–238
  siblings of children with
    adjustment of, 243, 245, 424
    family mediation of effects on, 240
    future research on, 242–247
    lifecycle view of adjustment of, 245
    literature review on, 241–242
    mediating factors in, 243–245
    positive effects on, 243
    research problems involving, 246–247
    sibling relationship and, 240–241
    special problems for, 239–241
    stress and coping in, 245
    theoretical framework for study of, 242
Life-event perspective, stress and, 291
  measurement of, 294–295
Life expectancy, mental retardation and, 100

Lifecycle perspective, sibling adjustment to learning disability and, 245
Lifespan development theory
  adult sibling relationships of persons with mental retardation and, 100–102
  attachment and, 102
  out-of-home placement and, 127–131
    in adolescence, 128–130
    in adulthood, 130–131
    in childhood, 127–128
    impact on nondisabled siblings of, 132–133
  shifting burden of care and, 120
Lifestyles, conflictual, siblings of children with mental retardation and, 323–324
Lifetime research, on siblings of persons with mental retardation, 321–331
  barriers to data in, 325–327
  design issues in, 322–324
  sampling bias in, 327–330
  theoretical issues in, 322
Longitudinal research designs, siblings of children with mental retardation and, 323

Marital relationship
  developmental psychopathology and, 256–257
  effects of, 21–23
    on relationship between nondisabled siblings, 41
  of siblings, lack of information on, 326
Meanings, in ecocultural niche, 54
Measurement issues
  in lifetime studies of siblings of persons with mental retardation, 324
  in studies of stress, 287–312
    response-oriented view and, 295–296
    stimulus/event-oriented view and, 294–295
    as transaction between child and environment, 296–297

Mental retardation
  adaptive competency and, 13–14
  adult sibling relationships of persons with, 99–113
    see also Adult sibling relationships, of persons with mental retardation
  behavior of children with, affecting parenting, 18
  care demands and, 11
  cognitive competency and, 13
  impact of child with, cultural variations in, 134–135
  life expectancy and, 100
  noncompliance and, 16
  out-of-home placement and, see Out-of-home placement
  psychopathology and, see Dual diagnosis
  research on siblings of persons with, 145–180, 261–265
    activities and time use in, 163–169, 178
    direction of effect in, 261–262
    effects of sibling relations in, 262–264
    future directions for, 179–180
    lifetime, 321–331
    mediating variables in, 173–177, 178–179
    psychological distress/well-being in, 148–149, 160–161, 178
    recent studies in, 152–159
    reviews of, 150–151
    sample studied in, 147–148
    self-concept in, 161–163
    sibling relationships in, 169–172, 177–178
    stress and coping in, 172–173
  role asymmetry and, 7
  social engagement and, 8
  societal changes in attitudes and practices regarding, 146–147
Methodology
  lifetime research, 321–331
    see also Lifetime research
  measurement considerations, stressors and coping strategies and, 287–312

374   Index

Methodology—*continued*
  parameters for inclusion in studies, 275–284
    context, 277–278
    gender, 278–281
    general considerations, 276–277
    indirect influences, 283–284
    individual differences, 281–282
    parental direct and differential behavior, 282–283
  in research on siblings of children with chronic illness, 221, 228–229
  in research on siblings of children with learning disabilities, problems in, 246–247
  for research on well-being, 333–353
    see also Well-being, general model for research on
  in time use studies, 165–167
Mood, parental, effect on parenting, 19–20
Mother(s), well-being of, adult sibling relationships' effect on, 111
Multiple perspectives, on sibling relationships of nondisabled children, 34–37

Naturalistic research, contrived research versus, ethnography and, 63
Negative reciprocity, 102
Newborn nurseries, young siblings' visitation of, 88–91
Nominal measurement, quantitative measurement versus, ethnographic research and, 62
Noncategorical approach, to research on siblings of children with chronic illness, 219–220
Noncompliance, 16
  parental response to, 17
Nondisabled children
  sibling relationships of, 31–48
    in adulthood, 103–105
    individual characteristics affecting, 45–47
    multiple perspectives on, 34–37
    parents and, 37–45
    qualitative features of, 31–34
    see also Nondisabled siblings

Nondisabled siblings
  adult, of persons with mental retardation, *see* Adult sibling relationships, of persons with mental retardation
  out-of-home placement and, *see* Out-of-home placement
  parents' relationship with, mental retardation of sibling and, 18
  relationships between, *see* Nondisabled children, sibling relationships of
  see also Older siblings; Younger siblings
Norms, for action, in ecocultural niche, 54
Nurseries, newborn, young siblings' visitation of, 88–91

Old age, sibling relationships in, 101, 103–106
Older siblings
  care demands and, 11, 165
  competency differences and, 13
  stress in, coping and, 172–173
  see also Birth order
Out-of-home activities, of siblings of children with mental retardation, 167
Out-of-home placement, 117–135
  attitudes of nondisabled siblings toward, 131
  ecological perspective on, 119, 124–127
  effects on siblings of, 132
  lifespan considerations of, 127–131, 132–133
  research on
    context for, 124–131
    proposed agenda for, 131–135
    sibling involvement after, 133–134
    sibling perspective and, rationale for focused study of, 118–124
Overprotectiveness, of parents, as barrier to obtaining data, 325

Parent(s)
  aging, caring for sibling as well as, 120

of children with HIV infection, views
  on needs of young siblings,
  94–95
concerns of, ecocultural niche and,
  74, 75–78
decision for out-of-home placement
  of child, nondisabled siblings'
  influence on, 128
depression in, effect on parenting,
  19–20
direct behavior of, 23–24
disagreement of, 21, 22
marital relationship of, *see* Marital
  relationship
overprotective, as barrier to obtaining
  data, 325
personal adjustment of, 305–306
personality of, 20
relationship with child, *see* Parent–
  child relationship
response of, to learning disability,
  238–239
role assignment by, 6
role in sibling relationships
  empirical study of, 41–45
  of nondisabled children, 37–45
temperament of, 20
see also Family *entries*; Mother(s)
Parent–child relationship
  developmental psychopathology and,
    257–258
  effects on relationship of nondisabled
    siblings, 38
  with nondisabled sibling of child with
    disability, *see* Parent–
    nondisabled child relationship
  stressors associated with, 301–306
  see also Parenting
Parent–Child Relationship Questionnaire (PCRQ), 41
Parent–nondisabled child relationship
  mental retardation of sibling and,
    18
  see also Parent–child relationship
Parental Management Inventory (PMI),
  41, 42
Parenting
  anticipatory management in, 40
  attitudes and practices in, as
    stressors, 305
  automatic, 19–20

consistency of, 24
marital difficulties and, 21, 22
differential, *see* Differential parenting
discipline in, *see* Discipline
family characteristics affecting,
  21–23
individual parent characteristics affecting, 19–20
individual sibling characteristics affecting, 17–19
as parameter for inclusion in studies,
  282–283
sibling socialization and, *see* Sibling
  socialization
Particularistic methods, qualitative/holistic methods versus, ethnographic research and, 62–63
PCRQ, *see* Parent–Child Relationship
  Questionnaire
Peer interactions
  care demands versus, 11–12
  stress and, 306–307
Perceptions, discrepant, parent–child relationship and, 304–305
Permanent care, community residence
  versus, sibling involvement and,
  119–120
Personality, parental, 20
Physical aggression, 16
  see also Aggression
Physical disabilities, 15
  research on siblings of children with,
    185–210
  see also Chronic health problems
PL 94-142, *see* Education for All Handicapped Children Act
Placement, out-of-home, *see* Out-of-home placement
Play, inhibition of, health risks and, 12
PMI, *see* Parental Management Inventory
Policy issues
  adult sibling relationships and, 112
  out-of-home placement and, 126
Preschoolers, *see* Young siblings (infancy to 7 years)
Privacy issue, as barrier to obtaining
  data, 326–327
Project CHILD sample, ecocultural data
  from, 65–70
  see also Ecocultural niche

Psychological adjustment, *see* Adjustment
Psychological models of well-being, 335–336
Psychopathology
  developmental, family processes and, 254–260
  mental retardation and, *see* Dual diagnosis
  shared and nonshared environments and, 264–265
Psychosocial characteristics
  siblings of children with learning disabilities and, 244
  of young siblings, 88
Public Law 94–142, *see* Education for All Handicapped Children Act

Qualitative methods, particularistic methods versus, ethnographic research and, 62–63
Quantitative measurement, nominal measurement versus, ethnographic research and, 62

Reciprocity, adult sibling relationships of persons with mental retardation and, 102–103
Relative birth order, *see* Birth order
Representational knowledge, in ecocultural niche, 53–54
Research
  conceptual issues in, *see* Conceptual issues; *specific issues*
  ethnographic, *see* Ethnographic research
  on siblings of children with dual diagnosis, 253–268
    see also Dual diagnosis
  on siblings of children with learning disabilities, 235–247
    see also Learning disabilities
  on siblings of children with physical disabilities and chronic illness, 185–210
    see also Chronic health problems, research on siblings of children with

on siblings of persons with mental retardation, 145–180
  lifetime research, 321–331
  see also Mental retardation, research on siblings of persons with
Research methodology, *see* Methodology
Resource allocation, within family, sibling effects on, 348–351
Response-oriented perspective, stress and, 292
  measurement of, 295–296
Retardation, *see* Mental retardation
Risk-factor research, on siblings of children with physical disabilities or chronic illness, 185–204
  control procedures and measurement in, 192–196
  design issues in, 188–196
  findings on boundary conditions, 202–204
  findings on general levels of risk, 196–202
  sampling methods in, 188–192
Role asymmetry, 6–7
Role tension, 149
  caregiving and, 11, 163

Sampling bias, in lifetime research on siblings of persons with mental retardation, sources of, 327–330
Sampling methods, in risk-factor research, 188–192
  sample size effects and, 200
School environment, child's response to learning disability and, 244–245
Self-concept
  of child with learning disability, 236–237
  of sibling of child with disability, 161–163, 196–197
Self-perceptions, of well-being, research on, 335–339
Sensory disability, 15–16
Service delivery models, out-of-home placement and, sibling involvement and, 119–120
Sex, *see* Gender

Sibling configurations
  developmental psychopathology and, 258–260
  see also Birth order
Sibling data, sources of, 325
Sibling involvement
  benefits of, for placed individual, 123
  permanent care versus community residence and, 119–120
    see also Out-of-home placement
  postplacement, nature of, 133–134
Sibling relationship
  adult, see Adult sibling relationships
  in family-context model, 5–9
    see also Family-context model
  learning disability and, 240–241
  stressors in, 297–301
    see also Stress; Stressors
Sibling Relationship Questionnaire (SRQ), 35–36
Sibling socialization, 25
  goals of, 24
  practices of, 24
Siblings
  individual, see Individual siblings
  older than child with disability, see Older siblings
  young, see Young siblings (infancy to 7 years)
  younger than child with disability, see Younger siblings
Sisters, see Gender
Social competence, 13–15
  learning disability and, 237–238
Social ecology, principles of, 205–206
Social engagement, sibling, 7–8
Social influences, direct and indirect, on family interactions, 5, 282–284
Social-process, family, as variable in research on siblings of persons with mental retardation, 176–177
Socialization, sibling, see Sibling socialization
Societal changes
  child with mental retardation and, 146–147
  research influences of, 146

Socioeconomic class
  adult sibling relationships and, 104
  care demands and, 164
Sorrow, chronic, see Chronic sorrow; Depression
Spousal conflict, effects of, 21–23
Spouses, of siblings, lack of information on, 326
SRQ, see Sibling Relationship Questionnaire
Staff, out-of-home placement and, 126
Stimulus-oriented view, see Life-event perspective
Stress
  conceptualizations of, 291–293
  effects of growing up with exceptional sibling and, 289–291, 307–308
  peer and community relationships and, 306–307
  family, learning disability and, 238–239
  out-of-home placement and, in childhood, 127
  in siblings of persons with learning disability, 245
  in siblings of persons with mental retardation, 172–173
  see also Role tension
Stressors
  coping strategies and, measurement considerations of, 287–312
  in parent–child relationship, 301–306
  in sibling relationship, 297–301
Study, units of, in social ecology, 205
Support, provided by adult siblings, 108–109
Support groups, for young siblings, 91–92
Symptomatology, clinical levels of, in sibling of child with physical disability or chronic illness, 200–202
Symptoms
  externalization of, sibling of child with physical disability or chronic illness and, 198–200
  internalization of, sibling of child with physical disability or chronic illness and, 197–198

System boundaries, in social ecology, 205–206

Task allocation
  cultural beliefs and, 72–73, 75
  see also Care demands; Household chores
Temperament, parental, 20
Theoretical developments
  from other fields, use in research of, 146
  see also Research; *specific theories*
Time-diary methodology
  in activity research, 167–168
  in time-use research, 166–167
Time use, of siblings of persons with mental retardation, 163–169
Toddlers, *see* Young siblings (infancy to 7 years)
Transactional perspective, stress and, 292
  measurement of, 296–297

Well-being
  in adolescence, siblings with mental retardation and, 149, 160
  economic models of, 337–339, 348–351
  family research models of, 336–337
  general model for research on, 333–353
  comprehensive approach to, 341–346
  focus on functionings and capabilities and, 339–341
  implications for research on siblings of persons with disabilities, 346–353
  review of theoretical models and, 334–341
  self-perceptions of well-being and, 335–339
  maternal, adult sibling relationships' effect on, 111
  psychological models of, 335–336
  self-perceptions of
    alternative approach versus, 339–341
    research on, 335–339

Young siblings (infancy to 7 years), 85–95
  characteristics and vulnerabilities of, 86–88
  of child with HIV infection, 92–95
  practices and interventions with, 88–92
  psychosocial characteristics of, 88
Younger siblings
  in caregiving roles, 11, 165–166
  noncompliance with, 16
  role asymmetry and, 7
  see also Birth order

Stafford Library
Columbia College
1001 Rogers Street
Columbia, Missouri 65216